F.V.

WITHDRAWN

CONCEPTS AND ISSUES
IN SCHOOL CHOICE

Edited, with introductions by

Margaret D. Tannenbaum

Mellen Studies in Education
Volume 23

The Edwin Mellen Press
Lewiston/Queenston/Lampeter

Library of Congress Cataloging-in-Publication Data

Concepts and issues in school choice / edited, with introductions by
Margaret D. Tannenbaum.
      p.   cm. -- (Mellen studies in education ; v. 23)
    Includes bibliographical references.
    ISBN 0-7734-9129-5
    1. School choice--United States--History. 2. Educational
vouchers--United States. 3. Magnet schools--United States.
I. Tannenbaum, Margaret D. II. Series: Mellen studies
in education (Lewiston, N.Y.) ; v. 23.
LB1027.9.C64   1995
370'.01--dc20
                                  94-40515
                                  CIP

This is volume 23 in the continuing series
Mellen Studies in Education
Volume 23 ISBN 0-7734-9129-5
MSE Series ISBN 0-88946-935-0

A CIP catalog record for this book is available from the British Library.

The Edwin Mellen Press
Box 450
Lewiston, New York
USA 14092-0450

The Edwin Mellen Press
Box 67
Queenston, Ontario
CANADA L0S 1L0

The Edwin Mellen Press, Ltd.
Lampeter, Dyfed, Wales
UNITED KINGDOM SA48 7DY

Printed in the United States of America

CONCEPTS AND ISSUES
IN SCHOOL CHOICE

TABLE OF CONTENTS

ACKNOWLEDGEMENTS

Areen, Judith & Christopher Jencks. Education Vouchers: A Proposal for Diversity and Choice. *Teachers College Record,* February 1971. Reprinted with permission from *Teachers College Record.*

Butts, J. Freeman. Private Pursuit of the Public Purse. *Phi Delta Kappan,* September 1973. Reprinted with the permission of the *Phi Delta Kappan.*

Clewell, Beatriz C. & Myra F. Joy. *Choice in Montclair, New Jersey.* January 1990. Reprinted with permission from Beatriz C. Clewell and Myra F. Joy, a Policy Information Paper, Princeton, NJ: Policy Information Center, Educational Testing Service, January 1990.

Clinchy, Evans. Public School Choice: Absolutely Necessary But Not Wholly Sufficient. *Phi Delta Kappan,* June 1987. Reprinted with permission of the *Phi Delta Kappan.*

Cohen, David & Eleanor Farrar. Power to the Parents? The Story of Education Vouchers. *The Public Interest,* Summer 1977. Reprinted with permission of the authors from: The Public Interest ©1977 by National Affairs, Inc.

Coons, John. Of Family Choice and Public Education. *Phi Delta Kappan,* September 1973. Reprinted with permission of the *Phi Delta Kappan.*

Coons, John. Principle and Prudence in the Design of Choice. *Equity and Choice,* Fall 1992. Reprinted by permission of Corwin Press, Inc.

Doyle, Dennis. Here's Why School Choice Will Boost Student Motivation. *The American School Board Journal,* July 1989. Reprinted with permission, from *The American School Board Journal,* July. Copyright 1989, the National School Boards Association. All rights reserved.

Doyle, Dennis. Our One-Size-Fits-All Public Schools Derive From a 19th Century Concept That Needs Updating. *The American School Board Journal,* July 1989. Reprinted with permission, from *The American School Board Journal,* July. Copyright 1989, the National School Boards Association. All rights reserved.

Esposito, Frank. The New Improved Sorting Machine: A Recent Study. *Public School Choice National Trends and Initiatives.* New Jersey Department of Education, December 1988.

Fege, Arnole & Millie Waterman.Where PTA Stands on School Choice. *PTA Today,* February 1989. Reprinted with permission from the February 1989 PTA Today published by the National PTA, Chicago.

i

Finch, Lewis W. The Claims for School Choice and Snake Oil Have a Lot in Common. *The American School Board Journal,* July 1989.Reprinted with permission, from *The American School Board Journal,* July. Copyright 1989, the National School Boards Association. All rights reserved.

Foote, E. T. Toward Voluntary Desegregation: The Beginnings of theSt. Louis Plan. *Equity and Choice,* February 1988. Reprinted by permission of the author.

Friedman, Milton. The Voucher Idea: Selling Schools Like Groceries. *The New York Times,* September 23, 1973. Copyright © 1973 by *The New York Times* Company. Reprinted by permission.

Fund, John H.Champion of Choice. *Reason,* October 1990. Reprinted with permission from the October 1990 issue of *Reason* magazine. Copyright 1990 by the Reason Foundation, 3415 S. Sepulveda Blvd, Suite 40, Los Angeles, CA 90034.

Glenn, Charles. Controlled Choice in Massachusetts Public Schools. *The Public Interest,* Spring 1991. Reprinted with permission of the author from: The Public Interest ©1991 by National Affairs, Inc.

Glenn, Charles. Who Should Own the Schools? *Equity and Choice,* February 1988. Reprinted by permission of Corwin Press, Inc.

Heid, Camilla A. & Lawrence E. Leak. School Choice Plans and the Professionalization of Teaching. *Education and Urban Society,* February 1991.Reprinted by permission of Corwin Press, Inc.

Kolderie, Ted. The Essential Principles of Minnesota's School Improvement Strategy, *Equity and Choice,* Winter 1988. Reprinted by permission of the author.

LaPierre, Bruce. The St. Louis Plan: Substantial Achievements and Unfulfilled Promises. *Equity and Choice,* February, 1988. Reprinted by permission of the author.

Lee, Dwight R. The Uncertain Prospects for Education Vouchers. *Intercollegiate Review,* Volume 21, Number 3, Spring 1986. Reprinted with permission from Intercollegiate Studies Institute, Inc.

Manhattan Institute for Policy Research. *The Right To Choose: Public School Choice and the Future of American Education.* Reprinted with permission from the Manhattan Institute for Policy Research.

Meier, Deborah. Central Park East: An Alternative Story. *Phi Delta Kappan,* June 1987. Reprinted with permission of the *Phi Delta Kappan.*

Nathan, Joe. School Choice Works in Minnesota. *The Wall Street Journal.* April 22, 1993. Reprinted with permission of *The Wall Street Journal* ©1993 Dow Jones & Company, Inc. All rights reserved.

Paulu, Nancy. *Improving Schools and Empowering Parents: Choice in American Education. A Report Based on the White House Workshop on Choice in Education,* October 1989.

Raywid, Mary. Public Choice, Yes; Vouchers, No! *Phi Delta Kappan,* June 1988. Reprinted with permission of the *Phi Delta Kappan.*

Raywid, Mary Ann. Synthesis of Research on Schools of Choice. *Educational Leadership.* April 1984. Reprinted with permission of the Association for Supervision and Curriculum Development, Copyright 1984 by ASCD. All rights reserved.

Rossell, Christine H. The Carrot or the Stick for School Desegregation Policy? *Urban Affairs Quarterly,* March 1990. © 1990. Reprinted by permission of Sage Publications, Inc.

Sandler, Andrew B. & David E. Kapel. Are Vouchers A Viable Option for Urban Settings? *The Urban Review,* Winter 1988. Reprinted with permission from *The Urban review.*

Selden, David. A Critic Changes His Mind. June 1975. Reprinted with permission from Nations' Schools and Colleges, Capitol Publications, Inc., P.O. Box 1453, Alexandria, VA 22313-2053, (703)683-4100.

Selden, David. Vouchers – Solution or Sop? *Teachers College Record,* February 1971. Reprinted with permission from *Teachers College Record.*

Shanker, Albert. If Teachers Get Choices...Shouldn't Parents? *New York Times,* June 18, 1989. Reprinted with permission from the author.

Shanker, Albert. Let the Buyer Beware: With School Vouchers Come Hucksters. *New York Times,* July 20, 1980. Reprinted with permission from the author.

Tannenbaum, Margaret. Vouchers Are A Viable Option for Urban Settings. *The Urban Review,* March 1990. Reprinted with permission from *The Urban Review.*

Tannenbaum, M. D. & Tannenbaum, T. (1992). *Secondary school students' attitudes toward schools of choice and what choices they would make.* A paper presented to the American Educational Research Association, San Francisco. Reprinted with permission from the authors.

Trent, Stanly C. School Choice for African-American Children Who Live in Poverty. *Urban Education,* October 1992. Reprinted by permission of Corwin Press, Inc.

Tyack, David. Can We Build a System of Choice That Is Not a 'Sorting Machine' or a Market-Based 'Free For All'? *Equity and Choice,* Fall 1992. Reprinted with permission from the author.

iii

Winborne, D. G. Will School Choice Meet Students' Needs? *Education and Urban Society*, February 1991. Reprinted by permission of Corwin Press, Inc.

Wise, Arthur E. & Linda Darling Hammond. Educational Vouchers: Regulating Their Efficiency and Effectiveness. *Educational Researcher*, November 1983. Copyright 1983 by the American Educational Research Association. Reprinted by permission of the publisher.

CONCEPTS AND ISSUES IN SCHOOL CHOICE

INTRODUCTION

From the development of schools in colonial New England to the present time, not only has government steadily increased its control over the form, content, funding, and clients of schools, but that control has become increasingly centralized. Although there was little initial objection from parents to the biblically-based schooling of their children in the New England and Middle Atlantic colonies, by the time mandatory attendance and child labor laws were enacted in the nineteenth century, tension between the state and the family over the schooling of children was evident. Throughout the twentieth century, consolidation has consistently reduced the number of existing school districts and the state and federal levels of government have more frequently promulgated educational policy, thereby reducing local —and certainly, family— control over schools and schooling.

Since 1955, when economist Milton Friedman first detailed his voucher plan in *Free to Choose*, proposals to provide families with clear choices not only among programs (such as college prep or vocational) but among schools themselves have developed in three distinct stages: **vouchers** —during the 1960s and early 70s, **magnet schools** (in particular for desegregation)—during the 1970s, and public **schools of choice** —during the 1980s. Each of these proposals represents a somewhat varying constituency dealing with overlapping sets of social and educational problems, but what they all have in common is the underlying assumption that individuals should have the right to choose the schools their children attend.

The current proposals for public schools of choice cannot fully be understood from both an historical and conceptual perspective without an understanding of those forces that brought forward —and opposed— vouchers and magnets, and the extent to which they were successful or unsuccessful. This volume will present articles which best capture the voices of each of the three decades as they try to articulate their visions of what is the best balance between the parent and the state in the control of children's schooling. Although the chorus of defenders of parent-control-through-choice will be more resounding, an effort has been made to provide a contrapuntal view from those who have historically opposed this perceived attack on the venerated concept of public schools. One of the most interesting developments to follow in the course of the debate is the way in which powerful voices in the public school establishment —on both the collective and individual levels— have "changed their tune" in the last thirty or so years. Following the Alum Rock Voucher Experiment, David Selden, president of the AFT from 1968 to 1974, described in print how "A Critic Changes His Mind" (1975), after visiting Alum Rock. Moreover, the current AFT president, Albert Shanker, has gone from vigorous debunker (1980) to sometimes supporter (1989) of parent choice in schooling.

HISTORICAL BACKGROUND
The Colonial Period

The question of who will determine the form, content, conditions, and purposes of schooling for children has persisted since the passage of the 1647 Old Deluder Satan Act, which asserted the right of the church to the minds of youngsters. There was little resistance from the majority of citizens inasmuch as those who expressed any disagreement with the Puritan founders of the Massachusetts Bay Colony were quickly expelled from the community. One salient result of this intense homogeneity of beliefs was an educational system that went rapidly forward in meeting the educational goals and objectives that these religious beliefs required. This phenomenon can be viewed from at least two perspectives. On the one hand, it can be seen as an intensely localized form of school control which responded to the values of an identified community. On the other hand, there was no provision made for individual parents or groups of parents who disagreed with the prevailing philosophy to acquire schooling for their children at "public" expense.

Quite a different picture emerged in the Middle Colonies. Although the purpose of schooling was as deeply religious as that in Massachusetts Bay, there was such a variety of religions that a consensus could never have been reached and, thus, each denomination provided schooling that catechized students in its views. Thus, loosely speaking, there was a system of controlled choice provided for parents and, as time went on, many of these denominational schools received public funds –a system often referred to as multi-establishment.[1]

As the eighteenth century came to a close, so important did the federal government think education was to the welfare of the new nation that the passage of the Northwest Ordinances in 1787 mandated that each new territory in the Northwest must set aside a specific plot of land for the purpose of providing revenue for schooling. In addition, the Philosophical Society hosted a contest for proposals for a national system of schools as the major vehicle for integrating the various cultural, ethnic, and language groups that were present in the colonies. Although the Tenth Amendment actually left control over schooling as one of the "reserved powers" to the states , these activities made clear that it was not going to be optional in the new nation.

Nineteenth Century

As The Common School Movement, at least in the North, saw the fight for publicly supported and controlled schools being won, and as late nineteenth century compulsory attendance legislation and child labor laws were enacted, two major developments impacted on the ability of parents to choose from various forms of schooling for their children. First, the very essence of the Common School Movement was that all children would be exposed to a common experience —no more schooling that reflected individual religious differences. This was reinforced by Horace Mann's conception of a non-sectarian school structure, which meant that the King James version of the Bible would be read daily without comment (that

---

[1]One could argue that this is a contradiction of terms in that establishment has generally meant state support of a single denomination. Thus multi-establishment is not establishment.

was the non-sectarian part). Thus, everyone was exposed to the "common" religion —Protestant, Catholic, and Jew alike— and the right of a central state government to dictate the form schooling would take and tax the public to provide it was established. Secondly, as compulsory attendance legislation was passed, the state went even further and mandated that parents, if they were to have access to the taxes they paid for schooling, would have to send their children to those schools approved by this same state government. Thus, the parents' opportunity to choose what they perceived to be the best environment in which to school their children was severely circumscribed, as many could not pay taxes to support public schools and, at the same time, provide tuition to send their children to private schools.

Twentieth Century

By the time the last state passed its compulsory attendance laws in 1918, the clear hegemony of the government over the family in determining whether or not children would attend school was established. Meanwhile, first in 1892, then in 1918, the National Education Association convened committees to attempt to determine what would constitute approved curriculum for secondary schools. Thus, the process of standardization and centralization was begun. Not only would the state compel districts to provide schools through taxation and parents to send their children to school for a specified length of time each day for a stipulated number of years, but also the major professional organization began the process of trying to make sure that every child was exposed to a standard curriculum.

However, such an approach to schooling was not one arrived at overnight. Several developments throughout the twentieth century conspired to bring it about. Despite the recommendations of the 1918 *Seven Cardinal Principles of Secondary Education* emphasizing social growth, the secondary curriculum remained primarily college-preparatory. And, prior to the Depression, because so few young people continued their schooling long enough to graduate from (or, in many cases, even to begin) high school and the majority of students who remained were college bound, a standardized curriculum was a moot issue. It wasn't until the Depression, when those young people who earlier would have left school to work and help support families remained in school, that it began to become evident that the accepted college-preparatory curriculum would not meet their needs and there was any real effort to provide a varied curriculum.

By the post-World War II period, the most frequent pattern of the secondary curriculum was four tracks: College Prep, Business, General, and Vocational (with social prestige for students in the tracks accorded in that same rank order). During the 1960s competing forces emerged to begin to draw tight the tension between standardization and constraint, on one hand, and variety and choice, on the other. In 1965 the federal government passed legislation such as The *Elementary and Secondary Education Act* and *The Economic Opportunity Act* to provide compensatory education for disadvantaged children, allegedly to bring them on a par in their schooling with other children. At the same time, Revisionist scholars were launching a crusade to show that American schools were designed to protect the status and power of the ruling class, that the Common School image protected a class-segregated reality, and that schools as they existed would never provide minorities and the disadvantaged with the means to climb the social/economic ladder. As the pressure to integrate schools and provide back-to-basics curriculums for deprived (usually minority) elementary inner-city students mounted and as more and more of these same students completed high school and were admitted to college, SAT and other standardized test scores declined (the exact opposite of what was intended).

Two related developments during the 1970s, which sought to increase variety and individualization, actually advanced the drive to intensify academic "rigor" and "tighten" standards for all students: the open classroom movement at the elementary level and alternative schools at the secondary. The intent of both was to provide choices for students. They contributed, however, to the public perception that schools were failing to give students those basic academic skills that society would demand of them. There was a further perception that disadvantaged students, least socialized to direct their own educational activities, suffered the most. The explanation for the failure of these innovations is that teachers were never trained in the methods necessary to make them successful. Disadvantaged elementary students were unable on their own to complete work in open classrooms and failing secondary students were placed in alternative schools. Thus, these "alternative" ways of schooling achieved little more than fad status.

By 1983 *A Nation at Risk* could call for longer school days and years, more schooling for teachers, and higher academic achievement measured through more standardized tests. Superintendents, as in Philadelphia, would receive public (if not professional) approval by issuing the directives such as the one previously described.

We have reached the last decade of the twentieth century with an unprecedented level of sustained attention paid to education from the legislative, executive, and judicial branches of all levels of government for a longer period than ever before in history. The tension between who will control children's education has taken a slightly different twist, with many state legislatures attempting to place control in the hands of parents through choice legislation, but with teachers' and administrators' associations, large numbers of post-secondary educators, and the National Association for the Advancement of Colored People opposing such moves.

This volume will attempt to examine through a series of articles those voucher, magnet, and choice proposals that have emerged during this ongoing struggle in order to show from a historical perspective the development of the concept of 'choice.' This will include not only an examination of the changing social and political agendas that affected the views of those most involved in the choice debate, but an effort to understand the unique aspects of our society that makes this a major question. An attempt is made to include representative writings from the major "voices" in the discussion as well as articles that provide both a broad and intense look at choice programs and arguments for and against them.

Finally, given her pro-orientation to the choice concept, this author will propose the ways in which the advantages of a choice system can be maximized and dangers minimized. This will include, in the final chapter, a discussion of the accompanying restructuring necessary to fully realize the potential of American education for meeting the dual goals of equity and excellence, while maintaining a commitment to providing for the diverse needs of students.

SECTION I - VOUCHERS

INTRODUCTION

Education vouchers are certificates that would be issued by the government to parents to "purchase" schooling for their children. Parents would select schools —public or private— which would then collect the vouchers and turn them into the government to be redeemed for cash to run the schools. This would result in providing parents with a variety of schools from which to choose and would require schools to compete for students.

This is the basic voucher idea, which has existed since Adam Smith proposed in *The Wealth of Nations* (1776) that government give money directly to parents for the purchase of education. The original supporters of this idea focused on the concept of competition, which would supposedly improve educational offerings, and the mechanisms of the free market, which would destroy the government monopoly of schools. More recent proponents of vouchers have identified their potential for equalizing educational opportunity as their most important characteristic. Not only would funds for schooling be more equitably distributed but the possibility of choosing one's school, now limited to only those who can afford either tuition or expensive real estate, would be available to all.

The most outspoken opponents of vouchers have been teacher organizations and some academicians. They argue that vouchers would destroy American public schools as we know them, would violate the separation of church and state required by the First Amendment, would result in resegregation of inner city schools, and would not solve the most serious educational problems we face. Opponents insist that vouchers would dramatically increase the overall costs of education and question whether the majority of parents are capable of choosing the best education for their children. Further, they maintain, those who would be most negatively impacted by vouchers are those members of racial and social class groups already suffering from prejudice and inequity.

Historical Background and Specific Voucher Proposals

Unregulated Voucher Plan

The architect of this plan is Milton Friedman (1955), called by some the "guru" of education vouchers. The primary purpose of the unregulated voucher is to create free-market competition that will result in the "survival of the fittest" forms of schooling. It is unregulated in two senses: it may be used for any form of schooling—public or private— and parents may supplement it with their own dollars to send their children to schools that charge a tuition greater than the value of the voucher.

This form of voucher received an enormous amount of negative publicity when, subsequent to *Brown v. Topeka, Kansas* (1954), four southern states (Louisiana, Mississippi, Alabama, and Virginia) instituted unregulated voucher systems (sometimes called tuition grants) in order to avoid desegregating the public schools. They were subsequently ruled unconstitutional. Since then, any proposal to use vouchers to provide parents with choice has not been able to shake the negative image acquired in these states. In fact, the strongest opponents of vouchers have consistently argued that, if enacted, they would result in the reversal of whatever limited success we have had at integrating schools, especially those in the inner city.

The Regulated, Compensatory Model

This model was originally developed in 1970 by Judith Areen and Christopher Jencks working together at the Center for the Study of Public Policy in Cambridge. Although, according to its designers, the primary basis for it is the libertarian ideal of choice, it encompassed a number of egalitarian principles as well. It had the following features:

1. Parents would receive a voucher for each school-aged child roughly equivalent to the per-pupil cost of education in the local public schools.

2. Participating schools, public or private, would have to accept the voucher

as full payment for the child's education, charging no additional tuition.

3. Participating schools would have to accept all applicants, unless there were more applicants than places, in which case half of the student body would be chosen by lottery.

4. Schools which took children from poor or disadvantaged families would be given additional incentives, i.e., "compensatory payments."

5. A regulating agency would be established to provide consumer information and make certain that participating schools were abiding by the eligibility requirements.

Christopher Jencks, the Center for the Study of Public Policy, and Alum Rock

In 1971 what was then referred to as a voucher experiment was put in place in Alum Rock School District in San Jose County, California. The federal government (Office of Economic Opportunity —OEO) had turned to the Harvard-based Center for the Study of Public Policy, under the direction of Christopher Jencks, to have them develop a model for schooling that would address the needs of minority groups and respond to the growing pressure for decentralization of schools. Originally the plan put forward by Jencks (described above) was to include the non-public schools, but California initially failed to pass the enabling legislation necessary for their participation. When they finally did, only one non-religious school participated, and that for only a short time. Thus, although it has always been referred to as a voucher experiment, it was what we now describe as a system of public schools of choice.

The Alum Rock experiment was initially funded for the amount of $5 million for five years and some additional funds were subsequently provided to do follow-up and shut-down activities. Although the experiment was designed to last for five years, it was in essence over by the third year, as it became evident to participating teachers that the most basic components of a true voucher system were not in place. Of the eighteen elementary schools in the district, initially only six agreed to participate in the experiment. Because the similarity in curriculum and method of these six did not promise much in the way of competition and diversity, OEO and the district worked out a "mini-school" plan in which each participating school would develop at least three alternatives for parents to choose from. These mini-schools would be developed by teachers with similar interests and would differ from each other on the basis of curriculum or instructional method.

Early on, however, problems arose out of the initial need to protect the jobs and salaries of teachers. The vouchers were not distributed on the basis of the size of the student body attracted to particular mini-schools. Low cost mini-schools (whose younger, less experienced teachers had lower salaries) were required to return some of their voucher income to the district so that high-cost mini-schools could pay their high salaried teachers, thus eliminating most of the financial incentive for mini-schools to attract additional students and meet enrollment demands beyond their original limits. Thus, programs that may not have survived in a truly competitive situation did so with the overflow from more popular mini-schools.

Although this model was originally accepted by the OEO as transitional, it was evident, by the end of the second year of the demonstration, that a full-scale model would not be realized. Furthermore, this voucher experiment was vitiated in the respects that most voucher advocates consider vital to a satisfactory test. In the first place, because of the absence of nonpublic school participation, there was no external competition. Secondly, the fact that teachers who were unable to attract clients were assured of jobs for the duration of the experiment meant that there was no competition internal to the system either.

Integration, Busing, and Finance Reform

Although vouchers used to avoid desegregation orders were ruled unconstitutional during the 1960s, interest in a means of providing subsidies to families for private schooling was revived in the early 70s. Court decisions regarding mandatory busing and financing contributed to this revival.

In 1971 the U.S. Supreme Court ruled in *Swann* that mandatory busing to achieve integration was not unconstitutional. At about the same time federal courts in Detroit and Richmond indicated that cross busing throughout entire metropolitan areas might be necessary to remedy segregation that resulted from housing patterns. During the following decade the "white flight" of families from urban to suburban schools represented an abandonment of those increasingly racially conflicted schools with declining academic achievement to pursue what was perceived to be higher quality education in more property-rich districts in the suburbs.

At the same time, however, countervailing forces were operating. In the *Serrano* (California – 1971), *Rodriquez* (Texas – 1972), and *Robinson* (New Jersey – 1972) decisions, the state supreme courts ruled that it was unconstitutional for the quality of education a child received to be based on the wealth of the family or community and that the state must find some other means than local real estate taxes to fund schools in order to eliminate the fiscal inequities among school districts. In both California and New Jersey this resulted in a reallocation of the tax burden for schools to the point where, after approximately a decade, the state was shouldering approximately 50% of it, whereas previously the local government had carried up to 90%, most of that collected through real estate taxes. Although the financial —and resulting educational— edge experienced by suburban schools was somewhat eroded, wealthier districts were able to tax themselves at an ever higher rate than previously, thus preventing the equalization of expenditure at which *Robinson* was aiming, resulting in New Jersey's even placing spending caps on districts for a short period of time. But this was obviously not going to get suburban legislators re-elected, and the caps were removed. The net effect was that in reality, *Robinson* in New Jersey, as *Serrano* in California, was never truly implemented, equalization of *per capita* expenditure was never achieved. Out of all this, however, a substantial suburban public school population increasingly interested in private education, along with those urban parents who could not afford expensive suburban real estate but could find the money for tuition for private schools in the city, formed a natural constituency for vouchers.

California and the Initiative for Family Choice

In the mid 1970s John Coons and Stephen Sugarman put forward a proposal for family choice in schooling, which included a form of vouchers, which they hoped to get on the California ballot. This proposal allowed for three types of schools to be funded through public taxes: already existing public schools, those currently designated private schools, and a new entity called "family schools," which school boards would be required to provide if a hundred or more families got together requesting a particular type of school. Coons and Sugarman emphasized the importance of parental or family choice and coupled this with a plan to tax a family based on the combined factors of the tuition level of the school chosen and the family income level. Recognizing the political realities of getting such an initiative on the ballot, they proposed that the second two types of schools would be funded at 90% of the rate of currently existing public schools. However, this was not a strong enough incentive to overcome the enormous political forces working against such a radical proposal in the late 1970s and early 1980s, when the issue received nationwide attention. Not the least of these forces was the extremely powerful California teachers' association. Although Coons and Sugarman both continued to publish extensively, throughout the 1980s, on family choice in schooling, ultimately they were unable to get the proposal on the California ballot.

The Coons and Sugarman plan, like the Alum Rock experiment, was actually a broad-based school choice plan rather than a voucher proposal. However, chronologically it emerged during the period when the concept of school choice was carried primarily through the language of vouchers. In fact, their proposal provided the pivot point for the conceptual change from vouchers to choice as we moved into the 1980s.

Overview of Articles

Although all of the articles in this section discuss vouchers, many have actually crossed the conceptual line to a nearly full-blown discussion of public/private school choice An attempt is made to give general background information on the voucher concept, historical perspective, an overview of the Alum Rock voucher experiment, and some arguments for and against vouchers.

The section begins with the now classic article by Milton Friedman, "The Voucher Idea: Selling Schools Like Groceries," in which he invites us to imagine a scenario in which the government undertook to distribute food in the same way it does education. He considers several ramifications of this analogy and then proceeds to discuss and respond to the following problems with and objections to the voucher system: the church-state issue, financial cost, the possibility of fraud, the racial issue, the economic-class issue, doubt about new schools, and the impact on public schools. He concludes that the greatest obstacle to the implementation of free market competition in schooling is the perceived self-interest of the educational bureaucracy.

In "Education Vouchers: Proposal for Diversity and Choice," Judith Areen and Christopher Jencks propose a new vocabulary that redefines the traditional distinction between 'public' and 'private' based rather on <u>how</u> schools are run rather than <u>who</u> runs them. After outlining the six guidelines they propose for establishing a voucher system, they discuss how these guidelines would handle most of the problems and objections that have been raised about vouchers, concluding with the status of the plans (1971) for establishing a voucher demonstration.

In "Power to the Parents? The Story of Educational Vouchers," David Cohen and Eleanor Farrar address the question of whether the parents in Alum Rock actually acquired more power through the voucher experiment there. After a thorough analysis of the political and social forces that brought about Alum Rock, they go on to describe how many of those same forces worked to limit choice, restrict competition, and protect established roles and power within the system, thereby precluding parents from acquiring much power. Nonetheless, they point out, parents were happy with the program <u>just because</u> they had more choices. Furthermore, teachers —who initially resisted the whole experiment because of the fear that teachers would be subject to the whim of both administrators <u>and</u> parents— actually acquired <u>more</u> power and they, too, liked the idea of being able to choose the classrooms, curriculum, and students with which they would like to work.

In pro and con fashion R. Freeman Butts and John Coons exchange views of vouchers and the proposed California "Initiative for Family Choice." Butts argues that vouchers, in general, and the proposed California initiative, specifically, represent the private pursuit of the public purse in that they primarily address the self-interest of their major proponents rather than the overall good of the political community as a whole. He maintains that only a public school system under public control, as it is now defined, can achieve the historical ideals of a common civic community. Coons describes the California plan in great detail, making clear exactly how the mechanics of admissions and pupil protection, financing and tuition, and distribution of information about schools would work. He challenges

Butts' interpretation of the historical facts, accusing him of abusing the English language in his use of the terms 'public' and 'private,' maintaining that American public schools have always been an elitist and undemocratic system, paid for through public taxes.

A second pair of articles, both authored by David Selden, president of the AFT from 1968 to 1974, presents both sides of the issue, written before and after Selden's "conversion" as a result of visiting the Alum Rock voucher demonstration site. He describes how his major objections to vouchers had centered on concerns that they would introduce "hucksterism" into education and would violate the doctrine of separation of church and state, but he notes that neither had happened at Alum Rock. He suggests that the experiment's emphasis on teacher control, its diversity, and its encouragement of good community relations might bring about a new form of learning that would contribute to the humanizing of American education.

Between 1980 and 1989 Albert Shanker, president of the AFT since 1974, went from crying out "Let the Buyer Beware: With School Vouchers Come Hucksters" to asking "If Teachers Get New Choices, Shouldn't Parents?" His early opposition focused on the possibilities for fraud and deceit in an open school market, while the later article describes the way in which school personnel and parents could be advantaged through providing school choice.

Once again the meaning of the terms 'public' and 'private' are examined in "Educational Vouchers: Regulating Their Efficiency and Effectiveness" by Arthur E. Wise and Linda Darling Hammond. They suggest that there will be no less regulation and bureaucracy under vouchers than there is currently and question whether a voucher system could deliver education any more efficiently. After a review of some of the current voucher literature, the authors contend that the most serious issues arise because vouchers will bring about public funding of the private sector, thereby undermining the "public accountability that accompanies pluralistic decisionmaking" currently in education.

In another companion set of articles, authors debate the value of vouchers for urban settings. In "Educational Vouchers: A Viable Option for Urban Settings?" Andrew B. Sandler and David E. Kapel maintain that vouchers would not reduce inequity, would not increase choice, and would not improve the quality of education. They offer as an alternative, site-based management in which each school would have its own elected school board with broad decision-making authority. Margaret D. Tannenbaum, in "Vouchers Are a Viable Option for Urban Settings," responds to all of Sandler and Kapel's arguments, pointing out that site-based management is completely consistent with a voucher system.

Dwight R. Lee, picks up Milton Friedman's grocery metaphor and runs with it, asking us to "imagine a successful movement to have all local governments establish grocery stores for the purpose of providing, at no charge, a proper diet for everyone." He envisions all of the social, political, economic and bureaucratic ramifications of such a system and the responses to those fanatics who might suggest that choice of food and places to shop for it should be a private matter. He claims that the debate about vouchers can only be understood by realizing that public school lobby's defense against vouchers has nothing to do with the advantages or disadvantages of vouchers but is a facade protecting their own private interests, "using political influence to realize private gain at public expense."

The Voucher Idea: Selling Schools Like Groceries
Milton Friedman

A fable may dramatize the true source of the nation's present discontent with our public schools: Suppose that, 50 or 75 years ago, the U.S. had adopted the same institutional arrangements for the distribution of food as it did adopt for elementary and secondary schools. Suppose, that is, that retail provision of groceries had been nationalized, that food was paid for by taxes and distributed by Government-run stores. Each family would be assigned to a store, as it is now assigned to a school. on the basis of its location. It would be entitled to receive, without direct payment, a collection of foods, as its children are entitled to receive a collection of classes. It would be able to choose among foods, as its children choose among subjects. Presumably this would done by giving each family some number of ration points and assigning point prices to various foods. Private grocery stores would be permitted (just as private schools are), but persons shopping in them would be taxed for the support of the public stores just the same.

Can there be any doubt what retail food distribution would be like today if this system had been in effect? Would there be supermarkets and chain stores? Would the shelves be loaded with new and improved convenience products? Would stores be using every device of human ingenuity to attract and retain customers?

Suppose that under such a system you were unhappy with your local grocery. You could not simply go to a different store unless you were able and willing to pay twice for your groceries, once in taxes and again in cash. No, you would have to work through political channels to change the elected or appointed Grocery Board, or the Mayor, or the Governor, or the President. Obviously this would be a cumbrous, inefficient process. And suppose you had different ideas from your neighbors about the kind of service you wanted? What then? You would have to find a neighborhood of like-minded people to which you could move.

Of course the well-to-do would escape all this by patronizing the few luxury establishments that would arise to cater to them. they would willingly pay twice for their food, just as they now pay twice for the schooling of their children. (I do not blame them. It is right and proper that parents should deny themselves in order to purchase the best products they can for their children's bodies or minds. I blame only those well-meaning persons who, while sending their own children to private schools, self-righteously lecture the "lower classes' about their responsibility to put up with government-supplied pablum in the "public interest.")

Consider the producer rather than the consumer. The supermarket is a modern invention that has contributed enormously to the well-being of the masses. What would the inventor have done —if he had existed at all— in the hypothetical world of government grocery stores? In the actual world, all he had to do to try out his idea was to use his own capital, or persuade a few people to venture some capital, and set up shop. In the hypothetical world, he would have to launch a successful political campaign to persuade a local grocery board, an entrenched civil service and harried legislators that his idea was worth trying. Obviously, innovations would come primarily from the few private stores serving the well-to-do.

Ask yourself what activities in the U.S. have participated least in the technological revolution of the past century. Is there any doubt that schooling, mail service and legislative activity head the list? Grocery stores would be on the list, too, if they had been government-owned.

Schooling is not groceries. Yet the many and important differences do not invalidate the comparison. The delivery of mails is not the same as the delivery of schooling, yet both are inefficient and technologically progressive for the same reason: They are conducted mostly by private enterprises operating in a competitive market.

The same contrast applies to schooling itself. As Adam Smith wrote nearly 200 years ago, "Those parts of education, it is to be observed, for the teaching of which there are no public institutions, are generally the best taught." That is equally true today: Music or dance, secretarial skills, automobile driving, airplane piloting, technical skills-all are taught best when they are taught privately. Try talking French with someone who studied it in public school, then with a Berlitz graduate.

As the fable suggests, the way to achieve real reform in schooling is to give competition and free enterprise greater scope; to make available to children of low- and middle-income parents, particularly those living in slums, a range of choice in schooling comparable to that which the children of upper-income parents have long enjoyed. How can the market be used to organize schooling more effectively? The most radical answer is to put schooling precisely on a par with food: Eliminate compulsory schooling, government operation of schools and government financing of schools except for financial assistance to the indigent. The market would then have full rein.

A slightly less radical answer is to put schooling on a par with smallpox vaccination or getting a driver's license: Require every person to have at least a minimum level of schooling, as he is required to be vaccinated or to take a driving test before he is granted a license —but let the schooling be obtained privately and at the parents' expense. Again, except for the indigent.

These solutions have much to be said for them as ways to further both freedom and equal opportunity. However, they are clearly outside the range of political feasibility today. Accordingly, I shall discuss a more modest reform —one that would retain compulsory schooling, government financing and government operation, while preparing the way for the gradual replacement of public schools by private schools.

The City of New York spends about $1,500 per year for every child enrolled at public elementary and secondary schools. Parents who send their child to a private school therefore save the city about $1,500. But they get no benefit from doing so. The key reform would be for the city to give such parents a voucher for $1,500 to pay for schooling their child (and for no other purpose). This would not relieve them of the burden of taxes; it would simply give parents a choice of the form in which they take the schooling that the city has obligated itself to provide.

To widen still further the range of choice, parents could be permitted to use the vouchers not only in private schools but also in other public schools —and not only in schools in their own district, city or state, but in any school anywhere that is willing to accept their child. This would involve giving every parent a voucher and requiring or permitting public schools to finance themselves by charging tuition. The public schools would then have to compete both with one another and with private schools.

Today the only widely available alternative to a local public school is a parochial school. The reason is that only churches have been in a position to subsidize schooling on a large scale and only subsidized schooling can compete with "free" schooling. (Try selling a product that someone else is giving away!) The voucher plan would produce a much wider range of alternatives. In the first place, choice among public schools themselves would be enormously increased. The size of public school would be set by the number of customers it attracted, not by politically defined geographical boundaries. Parents who organized nonprofit schools, as a few pioneers have, would be assured of funds to pay the costs. Voluntary organizations —ranging from vegetarians to Boy Scouts to the Y.M.C.A.— could set up schools and try to attract customers. And, most important, new sorts of private schools would arise to tap the vast new market-perhaps Mom-and-Pop schools like Mom-and-Pop grocery stores, perhaps also highly capitalized chain schools, like supermarkets.

But why require parents to spend the voucher in a single school? Why not divisible vouchers? Let part be spent for the core school, and the rest for mathematics lessons, music lessons, or vocational training purchased from another source. One does not buy all one's groceries at a single store. Why should one by all of a child's schooling at a single school?

Let us examine in detail some problems with the voucher plan and some objectives that have been raised to it:

(1) The *church-state issue* . Parents could use their vouchers to pay tuition at parochial schools. Would this violate the First Amendment? Whether it does or not, is it desirable to adopt a policy that might strengthen the role of religious institutions in schooling?

On June 25, the Supreme Court struck down by a 6-to-3 majority laws in New York and Pennsylvania that provided for reimbursing parents for part of the tuition paid to nonpublic elementary and secondary schools. The majority held that the laws "have the impermissible effect of advancing religion." The minority (in three separate dissents) urged that "government aid to individuals generally stands on an entirely different footing from direct aid to religious institutions" (Chief Justice Burger); that "preserving the secular functions of these schools is the overriding consequence of these laws" (Justice White) and that the Court failed to "distinguish between a new exercise of power within constitutional limits and an exercise of legislative power which transgresses those limits" (Justice Rehnquist).

To this nonlawyer, the tuition-reimbursement plans appear to be at least kissing cousins of the voucher plan that I have outlined. However, as I read the decisions, two differences might lead the Court to rule favorably on a full-fledged voucher plan: The voucher plan would apply to all parents, not simply those with children in nonpublic schools; and it would grant the same sum to all parents not, as in the particular tuition-reimbursement plans struck down, a sum much smaller than the per pupil cost (a point that Justice Powell referred to explicitly in the majority decision).

Whatever the fate of a full-fledged voucher plan, it seems clear that the Court would accept a plan that excluded church-connected schools but applied to all other private and public schools. Such a restricted plan would be far superior to the present system, and might not be much inferior to a wholly unrestricted plan. Schools now connected with churches could qualify by subsidizing themselves into two parts: a secular part reorganized as an independent school eligible for vouchers, and a religious part reorganized as an after-school or Sunday activity paid for directly by parents or church funds.

The constitutional issue will have to be settled by the courts. But it is worth emphasizing Justice Burger's point the vouchers would go to *parents not to schools*. Under the G.I. Bill, veterans are free to attend Catholic or other religious colleges, and, so far as I know, no First-Amendment issue has ever been raised. Recipients of Social Security and welfare payments are free to contribute to churches from their Government subsidies, with no First-Amendment question being asked.

Indeed, I believe that the penalty now imposed on parents who do not send their children to public schools produces a *real* violation of the spirit of the First Amendment, whatever lawyers and judges may decide about the letter. The penalty abridges the religious freedom of parents who do not accept the liberal, humanistic religion of the public schools, yet, because of the penalty, are impelled to send their children to public schools.

In practice, the voucher plan might well reduce the role of parochial schools by eliminating their privileged position as the only effective alternative to public schools for most people. In the first instance, parochial schools would benefit, but soon they would encounter far greater competition than they do today. However, I hasten to add that my advocacy of the plan in no way hinges on whether this conjecture is correct.

(2) *Financial cost.* A second objection to the voucher plan is that it would raise

the total cost of schooling —because of the cost of paying for children who now go to parochial and other private schools. This is a "problem" only if one neglects the present discrimination against parents who send their children to nonpublic school; universal vouchers would end the inequity of using tax funds to schools some children but not others. And current laws impose the responsibility on the state to school *all* children, not just children now in public schools. Moreover, there are two offsetting considerations: First, growing financial difficulties are forcing many nonpublic schools to close, which also raises governmental costs. Second, under a voucher plan, parents who now send their children to nonpublic schools might be more favorable to higher public expenditures for schooling.

There would, however, be a real problem of finding enough money to begin with. One way to meet it is to make the amount of the voucher less than current expenditures per public-school child. Take present total expenditures on schooling, divide by the number of eligible children and let the resulting sum —or some amount between that sum and present expenditures per public-school child— be the amount of the voucher If $1,500 is now spent per public-school child in New York, $1,300 spent in a competitive school would provide a far higher quality of schooling. Witness the drastically lower cost per child in parochial schools. (The fact that elite, luxury schools charge high tuitions is no counter argument, any more than the $7.25 charged at the "21" Club for its Twenty-one Burger means that McDonald's cannot sell a hamburger profitably for 25 cents.)

The net effect of a compromise plan, making the voucher somewhat less than the current average cost, would be: (a) to require public schools to economize somewhat; (b) to give parents of children who now attend a public school the alternatives of keeping them there or transferring them to any other school, public or private, at no financial cost if the school's tuition is $1,300 or less, or a cost equal to the excess of the school's tuition over $1,300; (c) to enable parents of children who now attend a parochial school to keep them there if they wish, relieved of the tuition they have been paying (almost invariably less than $1,300), or to take advantage of any of the other advantages available to parents of public-school children; (d) to relieve parents of children now attending elite private schools of $1,300 of the annual cost of schooling their children, as a partial offset to the school-tax payments they will continue to have to make.

(3) *The possibility of fraud.* How can one assume that the voucher is spent for schooling, not diverted to beer for papa and clothes for mama? The answer is that the voucher would have to be spent in an *approved* school or teaching establishment. True, this does mean some government regulation of the schools, but of course private schools are regulated to some extent now, to assure that attendance at them satisfies compulsory schooling requirements. Compared to current regulation of public schools, the government requirements in a voucher plan would be a mere trifle.

A more subtle problem is the *kind* of schooling for which the vouchers may be used. The major justification for both compulsory schooling and government financing of schooling is the so-called "neighborhood effect" —i.e., the assertion that schooling benefits not only the children and their parents but also the rest of us by promoting a stable and democratic society. But do all kinds of schooling contribute to responsible citizenship? Where should the line be drawn?

The voucher plan does not create this problem. It simply makes it more visible. Much that is taught today in public schools cannot readily be justified as conferring benefits on the community at large. I regard it as a virtue of the voucher plan that forces us to face this issue rather than evade it.

(4) *The racial issue.* Voucher plans were adopted for a time by a number of Southern states as a device to avoid integration. They were ruled unconstitutional. Discrimination under such a plan can be easily prevented by permitting vouchers to be used only in schools that do not discriminate. However, a more difficult problem has troubled some students of vouchers. This is the possibility that a voucher plan might increase racial and class separation in schools, exacerbate racial conflict and foster an increasingly segregated and hierarchal society.

I believe that it would have precisely the opposite effect —that nothing could do more to moderate racial conflict and to promote a society in which black and white cooperate in joint objectives, while respecting each other's separate rights and interests. Much objection to forced integration reflects not racism but more or less well-founded fear about the physical well-being of children and the quality of their schooling. Integration has been most successful when it has been a matter of choice not coercion.

Violence of the kind that has been rising apace in public schools is possible only because the victims are compelled to attend the schools that they do. Give them effective freedom to choose and students —black and white, poor and rich, North and South— will desert in droves any school that cannot maintain order. Let schools specialize, as private schools would, and the pull of common interest will overcome the pull of color, leading, I believe, to far more rapid integration than is now in process —in fact, not on paper.

The voucher scheme would completely eliminate the busing issue. Busing would occur, and might indeed be increased, but it would be wholly voluntary--just as the busing of children to music and dance classes is today.

I have long been puzzled that black leaders have not been the most vigorous proponents of the voucher plan. Their constituents would benefit from it most; it would give them power over the schooling of their children, eliminate the domination of both the citywide politicians and, even more important, of the entrenched bureaucracy. Black leaders themselves frequently send their children to private schools. Why do they not help others to do the same? My tentative answer is that vouchers would also free the black man on the street from domination by his leaders, who correctly see that control over local schooling is a powerful political lever.[1]

(5) *The economic-class issue.* The question that has perhaps divided students of vouchers more than any other is their likely effect on social and economic class structure. Some have argued that the great value of the public school has been as a melting pot in which rich and poor, native and foreign-born, black and white have learned to live together. This image had much validity for small communities and still does. But it has almost none for large cities and their suburbs. In them, the public school has fostered residential stratification, by tying the kind and the cost of schooling to residential location. Most of the country's outstanding public schools are in high-income enclaves —Scarsdale or Lake Forest or Beverly Hills. Such schools are better regarded as private tax shelters than as public schools. If they were, in the strict sense, private, their cost would not be deductible

---

1 Some black educators have supported the voucher plan. In his recent remarkable book "Black Education. Myths and Tragedies," Thomas Sowell concludes: "Voucher systems are no panacea. All that can be claimed for them is that they offer important benefits not obtainable under the existing institutional structure, without making the other problems any worse. In the world as it is, that is a very large advantage.

in computing Federal income tax. But the cost is deductible as local taxes because the high-cost and high-quality school is nominally public.

Elementary schools would probably still be largely local under a voucher plan. But even they might be less homogeneous than they are now, because of the indirect effect of the voucher plan in making residential areas more heterogenous. and secondary schools would almost surely be less stratified. Schools defined by common interests —one stressing, say the arts; another, the sciences; another, foreign languages— would perforce attract socially and economically more heterogenous clienteles from a wide variety of residential areas.

One feature of the voucher plan that has aroused particular concern is the provision that parents may "add on" to the voucher; that is, if the voucher is for, say, $1,300, a parent could add another $500 to it and send his child to a school charging $1,800 tuition. Some fear that the result might be even wider differences in school expenditures per child than now exist, because low-income parents would not add to the amount of the voucher while middle-income and upper-income parents would supplement it extensively.

This possibility has particularly worried Christopher Jencks and his associates at the Center for the Study of Public Policy in Cambridge, Mass., who conducted an O.E.O-financed study of vouchers. In their 1970 report, "Education Vouchers," they assert. on the basis of the most casual empiricism, that "an unregulated market would redistribute resources away from the poor and toward the rich." Being confirmed egalitarians, they respond by proposing first that the voucher be larger for children from low-income families than for others; second, that voucher schools be required (among other things) to "(a) accept a voucher as full payment of tuition: (b) accept any applicant so long as it had vacant places: (c) if it had more applicants than places, fill at least half of these places by picking applicants randomly."

I have great sympathy for the proposed "compensatory" voucher. For a variety of reason, cost of schooling are greater in slum areas than elsewhere, so that vouchers of equal dollar amount would not purchase equal schooling. In addition, I share the motives of those who believe that taxpayers should be willing to help the children of the poor. Moreover, with few exceptions, governmental expenditures benefit disproportionately middle- and upper income groups, so compensatory voucher would only help to redress the balance. As a realist, however, I believe that it is a mistake to recommend a compensatory voucher. In the first place, the political facts that account for the present bias in government spending will also prevent compensatory vouchers. In the second place, equal per child vouchers, while failing short of the ideal, would be a great improvement over what now exists.

The proposed restrictions on voucher school are not justified in the principle from the point of view even of confirmed egalitarians like Jencks, let alone of persons like my self who regard freedom as the primary social goal, though welcoming as a desirable by-product, the tendency for a free society to foster equality of both opportunity and outcome. Equality surely should refer to the whole of the income or wealth of families. Can the egalitarian say, it is all right for the well-to- do to spend any income that the tax collector leaves them on riotous living, but they must be penalized (by being denied a voucher) if they try to spend more than the publicity specified sum on schooling their children?

The very poor would benefit the most from the voucher plan. For the first time, poor parents would have a real opportunity to do something about their children's schooling. Social reformers, and educational reformers in particular, often self righteously take for granted that the poor have no interest in their children or no competence to choose for them. This, I believe, is a gratuitous insult. The poor have had limited opportunity to choose. But U.S. history has amply demonstrated that given the opportunity, they will often sacrifice greatly, disinterestedly and wisely for their children's welfare. Even the poorest are capable of scraping up a few extra dollars to improve the quality of their children's schooling, although they could not replace the whole of the present cost of public schooling.

In the middle classes, there is now much private expenditure on schooling, but most of it goes for music, dancing, golf and similar skills that supplement the public school. The voucher plan would enable people to spend their own money as well as the voucher on what they regard as most valuable.

The net effect, I believe, would be a larger total sum spent on schooling, with that sum, if anything, more evenly divided. But this, too, like Jencks's opposite conclusion, is a judgement, not a documented finding. Fortunately, we do not need to rely on casual empiricism in the Alum Rock School district in San Jose, Calif., goes even further than Jencks by restricting the use of the vouchers to public schools. A proposed experiment in New Hampshire is designed to go in the other direction, toward an unrestricted voucher —though unfortunately the recent Supreme Court decisions have induced New Hampshire to exclude parochial schools.The results of these experiments may provide some solid evidence by which to judge the likely outcome of unrestricted vouchers.[2]

(6) *Doubt about new schools*. Is this not all a pipe dream? Private schools now are almost all either parochial schools or elite academies. Will the effect of the voucher plan not simply be to subsidize these, while leaving the bulk of the slum dwellers in inferior public schools? What reason is there to suppose that alternative will really arise?

My grocery fable perhaps suggests the answer. The absence of alternatives when there is no market does not mean that none would arise when there *is* one. Today, cities, states and the Federal Government spend about $50 billion a year on elementary and secondary schools. That sum is about a third larger than the total their proposed spent annually in restaurants and bars for food and liquor. The smaller sum surely provides an ample variety of restaurants and bars for people in every class and place. The larger sum, or even a minor fraction of it, would equally provide an ample variety of schools. It would offer a vast market that would attract a host of entrants, both from the public schools and from other occupations. In the course of giving occasional talks on the voucher plan, I have been enormously impressed by the number of persons who have come to me afterward and said something like; "I have always wanted to teach [or run a school] but I couldn't stand the educational bureaucracy, red tape and general ossification of the public schools. Under your plan, I'd love to try my hand at starting a school."

(7)*The impact on public schools*. It is essential to separate the rhetoric of the professional public-school bureaucracy from the real problems that would be raised. The National Education Association and the American Federation of

---

2 One feature of the Jacobs report that is both surprising and depressing is that although the study was designed to develop voucher experiments the authors were content to accept their own casual empirical judgement about the effect of unrestricted vouchers on equality and to foreclose any test of it in their proposed experimental design. If, as they believe, the effect of vouchers on the dispersion of amounts spent on schooling is so crucial, ought not experiments be designed to furnish tested evidence on this point?

Teachers claim that vouchers would "destroy the public-school system" which has been the foundation and cornerstone of our democracy. Claims like this are never accompanied by any evidence that the public-school system is in fact, under current conditions, achieving the great results claimed for it —whatever may have been true in earlier times. Nor is ever made clear why, if the public-school system is performing so magnificently, it need fear competition from nonpublic, competitive schools.

The real problem arises from the defects, not the virtues, of the public schools. In small, closely knit communities where public schools, particularly elementary schools, are now reasonably or highly satisfactory, I doubt that even the most comprehensive voucher plan would have much effect. The public schools would remain dominant, perhaps improved by the threat of potential competition. But elsewhere, and particularly in the urban ghettos where the public schools are failing so dramatically, most parents would doubtless try to send their children to other schools.

Difficulties would arise from a possible exodus of quality pupils from some public schools. The parents who are most concerned about their children's education are likely to be promptest in transferring them, and even if their children are no smarter than those who remain, they will be highly motivated to learn and will have favorable home backgrounds. Such a sorting-out process goes on now, but, it can be argued, the voucher plan will greatly accelerate it, so that many public schools will be left with "the dregs," society's rejects, and will become, by virtue of the well-documented effect of the students on a school, even poorer in quality than now.

As the private market took over, the quality of all schooling would rise so much that even the worst, while it might be *relatively* lower in the scale, would be better in *absolute* quality. And many of today's rejects are rejects only because the schools are so poor. As store-front academies and similar institutions have demonstrated, many "rejects" perform admirably in a school that evokes their enthusiasm instead of their antipathy.

Nonetheless, it is possible that, at least for at a time, some children who remain in public schools will get even poorer schooling than they do now. This raises the moral dilemma that we are all familiar with: Are we justified in imposing poorer quality schooling on some children to leaven the schooling of others? It is easy to answer "yes" for other people's children , almost impossible to be so saintly or so diabolical —I do not know which— as to say "yes" for one's own children.

I am comforted in my own negative answer by three considerations. First, the possibility is purely hypothetical; it has neither been demonstrated by experiment nor rendered probable by any persuasive indirect factual evidence. Second, I am convinced that at worst the phenomenon would be temporary. Third, the children who would be benefitted most are form the very same social and economic groups as those who, it is feared, would be harmed.

There is no doubt what the key obstacle is to the introduction of market competition into schooling: the perceived self-interest of the educational bureaucracy. The role of this interest group is nothing new, as demonstrated by a fascinating study by British economist Edward West on the development of compulsory and government financed schooling in New York State (Journal of Law and Economics, October, 1967). West demonstrated that teachers and public officials who wanted higher pay and more job-security spearheaded the pressure that led to full assumption of financing by the government, which came with the Free School Act of 1867, and compulsory schooling, which came later. On the present situation, let me quote an eloquent, if bitter, judgement by Kenneth B. Clark:

"It does not seem likely that the changes necessary for increased efficiency of our urban public schools will come about because they should.... What is most important in understanding the ability of the educational establishment to resist change is fact that public school systems are protected public monopolies with only minimal competition from private and parochial schools. Few critics of the American urban public schools —even severe ones such as myself— dare to question the givens of the present organizations of public education . . . Nor dare the critics question the relevance of the criteria and standards for selecting superintendents, principals and teachers, or the relevance of all of these to the objectives of public education —providing a literate and informed public to carry on the business of democracy— and to the goal of providing human beings with social sensitivity and dignity and creativity and a respect for the humanity of others.

"A monopoly need not genuinely concern itself with these matters. As long as local school systems can be assured of state aid and increasing Federal aid without the accountability which inevitably comes with aggressive competition, it would be sentimental, wishful thinking to expect any significant increase in the efficiency of our public schools. If there are no alternatives to the present system - short of present private and parochial schools, which are approaching their limit of expansion - then the possibilities of improvement in public education are limited."

Let me give the last word to my great master. Before there was a United States of America, Adam Smith wrote:

"When there no public institutions of education, no system, no science would be taught for which there was not some demand; or which the circumstances of the times did not render it either necessary or at least fashionable to learn . . . Were there no public institutions for education, a gentleman . . . could not come into the world completely ignorant of everything which is the common subject of conversation among gentlemen and men of the world . . . .

"The public can facilitate [the] acquisition [of the most essential parts of education] by establishing in every parish or district a little school, where children may be taught for a reward so moderate, that even a common laborer may afford it; the master being partly, but not wholly paid by the public; because, if he was wholly, or even principally paid by it, he would soon learn to neglect his business."

Educational Vouchers: A Proposal for Diversity and Choice

Judith Areen

Christopher Jencks

Ever since Adam Smith first proposed that the government finance education by giving parents money to hire teachers, the idea has enjoyed recurrent popularity. Smith's ideal of consumer sovereignty is built into a number of government programs for financing higher education, notably the G.I. Bill and the various state scholarship programs. Similarly a number of foreign countries have recognized the principle that parents who are dissatisfied with their local public school should be given money to establish alternatives.[1] In America, however, public financing for elementary and secondary education has been largely confined to publicly managed schools. Parents who preferred a private alternative have had to pay the full cost out of their own pockets. As a result, we have almost no evidence on which to judge the merit of Smith's basic principle, namely, that if all parents are given the chance, they will look after their children's interests more effectively than will the state.

During the late 1960s, a series of developments in both public and nonpublic education led to a revival of interest in this approach to financing education. In December, 1969, the United States Office of Economic Opportunity made a grant to the Center for the Study of Public Policy to support a detailed study of "education vouchers." This article will summarize the major findings of that report and outline briefly the voucher plan proposed by the Center.[2]

The Case for Choice. Conservatives, liberals, and radicals all have complained at one time or another that the political mechanisms which supposedly make public

---

[1] Estelle Fuchs, "The Free Schools of Denmark," *Saturday Review*, August 16, 1969.

[2] For a complete description of the Center proposal, *see Education Vouchers: A report on Financing Education by Payments to Parents*. Prepared by the Center for the Study of Public Policy, Cambridge, Massachusetts, December, 1970.

schools accountable to their clients work clumsily and ineffectively.[3] Parents who think their children are getting inferior schooling can, it is true, take their grievances to the local school board or state legislature. If legislators and school boards are unresponsive to the complaints of enough citizens, they may eventually be unseated. But mounting an effective campaign to change local public schools takes an enormous investment of time, energy, and money. Dissatisfied though they may be, few parents have the political skill or commitment to solve their problems this way. As a result, effective control over the character of the public schools is largely vested in legislators, school boards, and educators--not parents.[4]

If parents are to take genuine responsibility for their children's education, they cannot rely exclusively on political processes. They must also be able to take individual action on behalf of their own children. At present, only relatively affluent parents retain any effective control over the education of their children. Only they are free to move to areas with "good" public schools, where housing is usually expensive (and often unavailable to black families at any price). Only they can afford nonsectarian, private schooling. The average parent has no alternative to

---

[3] For other discussions of the need to encourage alternatives to the present public schools, see Kenneth Clark, "Alternative Public School Systems," *Equal Educational Opportunity*. Cambridge: Harvard University Press, 1969; James S. Coleman, Toward Open Schools," *The Public Interest*, Fall, 1967; Anthony Downs, "Competition and Community Schools," written for a Brookings Institution Conference on the Community School held in Washington, D.C., December 12-13, 1968, Chicago, Illinois, revised version, January, 1969; Milton Friedman, "The Role of Government in Education," *Capitalism and Freedom*. Chicago: University of Chicago Press, 1962; Christopher Jencks, "Is the Public School Obsolete?" *The Public Interest*, Winter, 1966; Robert Krughoff, "Private Schools for the Public," *Education and Urban Society* , Vol. II, November, 1969; Henry M. Levin, "The Failure of the Public Schools and the Free Market," *The Urban Review*, June 6, 1968; Theodore Sizer and Phillip Whitten, "A Proposal for a Poor Children's Bill of Rights," *Psychology Today*, August, 1968; E.G. West. *Education and the State*. London: Institute of Economic Affairs, 1965.

[4] School management has been increasingly concentrated in the hands of fewer educators and school boards. The number of school districts, for example, declined from 127,531 in 1930, to less than 20,440 in 1968. The number of public elementary schools dropped from 238,000 to less than 73,000 in the same period. The concentration is particularly striking in urban areas. The New York City School Board alone is responsible for the education of more students than are found in the majority of individual states. Los Angeles has as many students as the state of South Carolina; Chicago as many as Kansas; Detroit as many as Maine. Nearly half of all the students in public schools are under the control of less than 4 percent of the school board. *See*, U.S. Department of Health, Education, and Welfare, Digest of Education Statistics (1969).

his local public school unless he happens to belong to one of the few denominations that maintain low-tuition schools.

Not only does today's public school have a captive clientele, but it in turn has become the captive of a political process designed to protect the interests of its clientele. Because attendance at a local public school is nearly compulsory, its activities have been subjected to extremely close political control. The state, the local board, and the school administration have established regulations to ensure that no school will do anything to offend anyone of political consequence. Virtually everything of consequence is either forbidden or compulsory. By trying to please everyone, however, the schools have often ended up pleasing no one.

A voucher system seeks to free schools from the restrictions which inevitably accompany their present monopolistic privileges. The idea of the system is relatively simple. A publicly accountable agency would issue a voucher to parents. The parents could take this voucher to any school which agreed to abide by the rules of the voucher system. Each school would turn its vouchers in for cash. Thus parents would no longer be forced to send their children to the school around the corner simply because it was around the corner.

Even if no new schools were established under a voucher system, the responsiveness of existing public schools would probably increase. We believe that one of the most important advantages of a voucher system is that it would encourage diversity and choice *within the public system.*. Indeed, if the public system were to begin matching students and schools on the basis of interest, rather than residence, one of the major objectives of a voucher system would be met without even involving the private sector. Popular public schools would get more applicants, and they would also have incentives to accommodate them, since extra students would bring extra funds. Unpopular schools would have few students, and would either have to change their ways or close up and re-open under new management.

At this last possibility suggests, however, there are great advantages to involving the private sector in a voucher system if it is properly regulated. Only in this way is the overall system likely to make room for fundamentally new initiatives that come from the bottom instead of the top. And only if private initiative is possible will the public sector feel real pressure to make room for kinds of education that are politically awkward but have a substantial constituency. If the private sector is involved, for example, parents can get together to create schools reflecting their special perspectives or their children's special needs. This should mean that the public schools will be more willing to do the same thing--or old ideas that are now out of fashion in the public schools--would also be able to set up their own schools. Entrepreneurs who thought they could teach children better and more inexpensively than the public schools would have an opportunity to do so. None of this ensures that every child would get the education he needs, but it would make such a result somewhat more likely than at present.

Beyond this, however, differences of opinion begin. Who would be eligible for vouchers? How would their value be determined? Would parents be allowed to supplement the vouchers from their own funds? What requirements would schools have to meet before cashing vouchers? What arrangements would be made for the children whom no school want to educate? Would church schools be eligible? Would schools promoting unorthodox political views be eligible? Once the advocates of couchers begin to answer such questions, it becomes clear that the catch phrase around which they have united stands not for a single panacea, but for a multitude of controversial programs, many of which have little in common.

Revised Vocabulary . To understand the voucher plan recommended by the Center, it is useful to begin by reconsidering traditional notions about "public" and private education. Since the nineteenth century, we have classified schools as "public" if they were owned and operated by a governmental body. We go right on calling colleges "public" even when they charge tuition that many people cannot afford. We also call academically exclusive high schools "public," even if they have admissions requirements that only a handful of students can meet. We call neighborhood schools "public" despite the fact that nobody outside the neighborhood can attend them, and nobody can move into the neighborhood unless he has white skin and a down payment on a $30,000 home. And we call whole school systems "public," even though they refuse to give anyone information about what they are doing, how well they are doing it, and whether children are getting what their parents want. Conversely, we have always called schools "private" if they were owned and operated by private organizations. We have gone on calling these schools "private," even when, as sometimes happens, they are open to every applicant on a nondiscriminatory basis, charge no tuition, and make whatever information they have about themselves available to anyone who asks.

Definitions of this kind conceal as much as they reveal, for they classify schools entirely in terms of *who* runs them, not *how* they are run. If we want to describe what is really going on in education, there is much to be said for reversing this emphasis. We would then call a school "public" if it were open to everyone on a nondiscriminatory basis, if it charged no tuition, and if it provided full information about itself to anyone interested. Conversely, we would call any school "private" if it excluded applicants in a discriminatory way, charged tuition, or withheld information about itself. Admittedly, the question of who governs a school cannot be ignored entirely when categorizing the school, but it seems considerably less important than the question of how the school is governed.

Adopting this revised vocabulary, we propose a regulatory system with two underlying principles:

- No public money should be used to support "private" schools.

- Any group that operates a "public" school should be eligible for public subsidies.

The Proposal. Specifically, the Center has proposed an education voucher system (for *elementary* education) which would work in the following manner:

1. An Educational Voucher Agency (EVA) would be established to administer the voucher. Its governing board might be elected or appointed, but in either case it should be structured so as to represent minority as well as majority interests. The EVA might be an existing local board of education, or it might be an agency with a larger or smaller geographic jurisdiction. The EVA would receive all federal, state, and local education funds for which children in this area were eligible. It would pay this money to schools only in return for vouchers. (In addition, it would pay parents for children's transportation costs to the school of their choice.)

2. The EVA would issue a voucher to every family in its district with children of elementary school age. The value of the basic voucher would initially equal

the per pupil expenditure of the public schools in the area. Schools which took children from families with below-average incomes would receive additional incentive payments. These "compensatory payments" might, for example, make the maximum payment for the poorest child worth double the basic voucher.

3. To become an "approved voucher school," eligible to cash vouchers, a school would have to:

a. Accept each voucher as full payment for a child's education, charging no additional tuition.

b. Accept any applicant so long as it had vacant places.

c. If it had more applicants than places, fill at least half these places by picking applicants randomly and fill the other half in such a way as not to discriminate against ethnic minorities.

d. Accept uniform standards established by the EVA regarding suspension and expulsion of students.

e. Agree to make a wide variety of information about its facilities, teachers, program, and students available to the EVA and to the public.

f. Maintain accounts of money received and disbursed in a form that would allow both parents and the EVA to determine where the money was going. Thus a school operated by the local board of education (a "public" school) would have to show how much of the money to which it was entitled on the basis of its vouchers was actually spent in that school. A school operated by a profit-making corporation would have to show how much of its income was going to the stockholders.

g. Meet existing state requirements for private schools regarding curriculum, staffing, and the like. Control over policy in an approved voucher school might be vested in an existing local school board, a PTA, or any private group. Hopefully, no government restrictions would be placed on curriculum, staffing, and the like, except those already established for all private schools in a state.

4. Just as at present, the local board of education (which might or might not be the EVA) would be responsible for ensuring that there were enough places in publicly managed schools to accommodate every elementary school age child

who did not want to attend a privately managed school. If a shortage of places developed for some reason, the board of education would have to open new schools or create more places in existing schools. (Alternatively, it might find ways to encourage privately managed schools to expand, presumably by getting the EVA to raise the value of the voucher.)

5. Every spring each family would submit to the EVA the name of the school to which it wanted to send each of its elementary school age children next fall. Any children already enrolled in a voucher school would be guaranteed a place, as would any sibling of a child enrolled in a voucher school. So long as it had room, a voucher school would be required to admit all students who listed it as a first choice. If it did not have room for all applicants, a school could fill half its places in whatever way it wanted, choosing among those who listed it as a first choice. It could not, however, select these applicants in such a way as to discriminate against racial minorities. It would then have to fill its remaining places by a lottery among the remaining applicants. All schools with unfilled places would report these to the EVA. All families whose children had not been admitted to their first-choice school would then chose an alternative school which still had vacancies. Vacancies would then be filled in the same manner as in the first round. This procedure would continue until every child had been admitted to a school.

6. Having enrolled their children in a school, parents would give their vouchers to the school. The school would send the vouchers to the EVA and would receive a check in return.

Some Caveats. The voucher system outlined above is quite different from other systems now being advocated; it contains far more safeguards for the interests of disadvantaged children. A voucher system which does not include these or equally effective safeguards would be worse than no voucher system at all. Indeed, an unregulated voucher system could be the most serious setback for the education of disadvantaged children in the history of the United States. A properly regulated system, on the other hand, may have the potential to inaugurate a new era of innovative and reform in American schools.

One common objection to a voucher system of this kind is that many parents are too ignorant to make intelligent choices among schools. Giving parents a choice will, according to this argument, simply set in motion an educational equivalent of Gresham's Law, in which hucksterism and mediocre schooling drive out high quality institutions. This argument seems especially plausible to those who envisage the entry of large numbers of profit-oriented firms into the educational marketplace. The argument is not, however, supported by much evidence. Existing private schools are sometimes mere diploma mills, but on the average their claims about themselves seem no more misleading, and the quality of the services they offer no lower, than in the public schools. And while some private schools are run by hucksters interested only in profit, this is the exception rather than the rule. There is no obvious reason to suppose that vouchers could change all this.

A second common objection to vouchers is that they would "destroy the public schools." Again, this seems far fetched. If you look at the educational choices made by wealthy parents who can already afford whatever schooling they want for their children, you find that most still prefer their local public schools if these are at all adequate. Furthermore, most of those who now leave the public system do so in order to attend high-cost, exclusive private schools. While some wealthy parents would doubtless continue to patronize such schools, they would receive no subsidy under the proposed system.

Nonetheless, if you are willing to call every school "public" that is ultimately responsible to a public board of education, then there is little doubt that a voucher system would result in some shrinkage of the "public sector and some growth of the "private" sector. If, on the other hand, you confine the label "public" to schools which are equally open to everyone within commuting distance, you discover that the so-called public sector includes relatively few public schools. Instead, racially exclusive suburbs and economically exclusive neighborhoods serve to ration access to good "public" schools in precisely the same way that admissions committees and tuition charges ration access to good "private" schools. If you begin to look at the distinction between public and private schooling in these terms, emphasizing accessibility rather than control, you are likely to conclude that a voucher system, far from destroying the public sector, would greatly expand it, since it would force large numbers of schools, public and private, to open their doors to outsiders.

A third objection to vouchers is that they would be available to children attending Catholic schools. This is not, of course, a necessary feature of a voucher system. The courts, a state legislature, or a local EVA could easily restrict participation to nonsectarian schools. Indeed, some state constitutions clearly require that this be done. The federal Constitution may also require such a restriction, but neither the language of the First Amendment nor the legal precedent is clear on this issue. The First Amendment's prohibition against an "establishment of religion" can be construed as barring payments to church schools, but the "free exercise of religion" clause can also be construed as requiring the state to treat church schools in precisely the same way as other private schools. The Supreme Court has never ruled on a case of this type (e.g., G.I. Bill payments to Catholic colleges or Medicare payments to Catholic hospitals). Until it does, the issue ought to be resolved on policy grounds. And since the available evidence indicates that Catholic schools have served their children no worse than public schools,[5] and perhaps slightly better, there seems no compelling reason to deny them the same financial support given other schools.

The most worrisome objection to a voucher system is that its success would depend on the EVA's willingness to regulate the marketplace vigorously. If vouchers were used on a large scale, state and local regulatory efforts might be uneven or even nonexistent. The regulations designed to prevent racial and economic discrimination seem especially likely to get watered down at the state and local level, or else to remain unenforced. This argument applies, however, to *any* educational reform, and it also applies to the existing system. If you assume any given EVA will be controlled by overt or covert segregationists, you must also assume that this will be true of the local board of education. A board of education that wants to keep racist parents happy hardly needs vouchers to do so. It only needs to maintain the neighborhood school system. White parents who want their children to attend white schools will then find it quite simple to move to a white neighborhood where their children will be suitably segregated. Except perhaps in the South, neither the federal government, nor the judiciary is likely to prevent this

---

[5] Andrew Greeley and Peter Rossi. *The Education of Catholic Americans.* Chicago: Aldine, 1966.

traditional practice.

If, on the other hand, you assume a board which is anxious to eliminate segregation, either for legal, financial, or political reasons, you must also assume that the EVA would be subject to the same pressures. And if an EVA is anxious to eliminate segregation, it will have no difficulty devising regulations to achieve this end. Furthermore, the legal precedents to date suggest that the federal courts will be more stringent in applying the Fourteenth Amendment to voucher systems than to neighborhood school systems. The courts have repeatedly thrown out voucher systems designed to maintain segregation, whereas they have shown no such general willingness to ban the neighborhood school. Outside the South, then, those who believe in integration may actually have an easier time achieving this goal with voucher systems than they will with the existing public school system. Certainly, the average black parent's access to integrated schools would be increased under a voucher system of the kind proposed by the Center. Black parents could apply to any school in the system, and the proportion of blacks admitted would have to be at least equal to the proportion who applied. This gives the average black parent a far better chance of having their children attend an integrated school than at present. There is, of course, no way to compel black parents to take advantage of this opportunity by actually applying to schools that enroll whites. But the opportunity would be there for all.

The Proposed Demonstration. The voucher plan described above could in theory be adopted by any local or state jurisdiction interested in increasing diversity in schools and parental choice in selection of schools. In the long run it is not much more expensive than the present system. But the Center has recommended to OEO that a demonstration project be financed first, carefully monitored to test the effects of dispensing public education funds in the form of vouchers. The Center has recommended that at least 10,000 elementary school students be included in the demonstration site, and that the demonstration city (or part of a city) should contain a population which is racially and economically heterogeneous. Ideally some alternative schools should already exist in the selected area, and the prospects for beginning other new schools should be reasonable.

In March, 1970, staff and consultants of the Center embarked on an extensive investigation of the feasibility of conducting a demonstration project. Superintendents of schools in all cities with a population in excess of 150,000 in the 1960 census, which were not under court or administrative order to desegregate their school systems, were contacted by mail. Expressions of interest were followed up. Meetings were held in interested cities around the country. Local and state school administrators were contacted, as were interested school officials, teachers' groups, parents' organizations, and nonpublic schools.

As of November 1, 1970, five communities had decided to apply for preliminary planning funds. If one or more of these cities decides to conduct a demonstration of the voucher program, we may have a chance at last to test what contributions a voucher program could make to improving the quality of education available to children in this country. If, on the other hand, the National Education Association and the American Federation of Teachers have their way, we shall have no test at all.

Power to the Parents?—
the Story of Education Vouchers

David K. Cohen
Eleanor Farrar

Education vouchers were the *enfant terrible* of recent school reforms. Yet the idea seemed appealingly innocent: Instead of giving money to public schools and thus requiring either mandatory attendance or additional outlays for private schools, vouchers would directly aid families so that they could enroll their children in schools of their own choice. The idea of vouchers gained the attention of many reformers in the 1960's because it promised to solve so many educational problems. Christopher Jencks and other radical critics thought vouchers would improve ghetto education by offering parents and teachers alternatives to the failing public schools. The country's impatient youth liked the idea because it would enable more people to afford their "free" schools. Some Catholics thought vouchers might boost enrollments in parochial schools, which were sagging under the pressure of rising costs and shifting values. And Milton Friedman, searching everywhere for some vestige of capitalism in mid-century America, discerned a market mechanism in parent choice and promptly pronounced vouchers the only hope for educational efficiency.

The idea was attractive partly because it seemed to address such disparate hopes. But everyone agreed that vouchers would promote "competition," which would loosen up public school systems grown rigid with age, size, and professional power. The fear of losing students and revenues would move schools to improve curricula and increase responsiveness.

One might think that a notion with such diverse appeal would take the country by storm. Instead, it stirred up a hornets' nest of opposition. Teacher organization viewed competition among schools as an invitation to union-busting —a fear that Professor Friedman's endorsement did nothing to relieve. Administrators were afraid of losing control over budgets and appointments. Civil libertarians were apprehensive that the flow of public monies to sectarian schools would represent a breach of the constitutional separation between church and state —a concern that was not alleviated by Catholic support for vouchers. Civil-rights advocates were in favor of allowing urban blacks to choose their own schools, but balked at the prospect of granting whites the same freedom of choice —which, they held, would be a disaster for desegregation. Finally, many thought that vouchers would eviscerate one of the nation's few egalitarian institutions by paying for private education at the tax-payers' expense: public schools would then become the alternative of last resort, reserved for those without the wit to go elsewhere.

Whereas most federal educational programs are launched with Congressional hoopla and Presidential panegyrics, vouchers were thus introduced in an angry political atmosphere. The idea excited visions of change in the minds of both radical and conservative theorists, but it produced only nightmares for the moderate masses known despairingly as "liberals" six or eight years ago. Given their fears, the wonder is that the idea of vouchers was not stillborn.

It wasn't partly because it was conceived in something of a political vacuum. The idea had caught the fancy of the few left-wing bureaucrats still remaining at the Office of Economic Opportunity (OEO) while the Johnson Administration was coming unstrung over Viet Nam. Partly as a result of their help, Jencks and several of his Cambridge colleague were awarded a grant to study the feasibility of vouchers. The result was a thick report that —like many studies— solemnly announced that the ideas of its authors were indeed feasible. In fact, there was even a plan describing how vouchers would work (*Education Vouchers: A Report on Financing Elementary Education by Grants to Parents,* Center for the Study of Public Policy, 1970), which was duly dispatched to Washington.

By that time the Nixon Administration had begun reshaping OEO: Tired old liberal ideas and big give-away programs were out; modest experiments were in. The new OEO staff knew the difference between Milton Friedman and Christopher Jencks, but they read the report, and after some exploration —and a bit of urging from the authors and their friends in the Administration— decided to give vouchers a try.

Support for vouchers by the Nixon OEO did not exactly assuage the fears and suspicions of liberals, who responded with a barrage of criticism delivered through the mails, the media, lobbyists, and Members of Congress, and in some often nasty confrontations euphemistically known as "briefings." The new OEO staff were somewhat taken aback by the ferocity of this response, but stuck to their commitment to social-science experiments: All they sought, they said, was a dispassionate test of the idea. They didn't favor vouchers —just new alternatives. If vouchers were half as bad as everyone said, then they would deservedly sink without a trace; if not, then who knows —perhaps they merited consideration. A curious collection of conservative theorists, radical reformers, Republican politicians, and social experimenters thus managed to persevere under the banner of science. In 1969 a federal effort was launched to test education vouchers. It was a frail craft, but it did float.

Eight years later, it still does. In the meantime a good deal of evidence has been accumulated —some of it from a single school district in Alum Rock, California, which has operated a trial program for several years; some of it concerning the extensive efforts to get other areas to try vouchers. One wonders what might be learned from all this evidence. It would be a mistake to anticipate a definitive verdict, for the experience has been limited. Anyway, no decision could be conclusive about something as interesting and problematic as education vouchers. But the experience so far does illuminate several points of interest. Does the diagnosis of school problems still make sense now that the prescription has been administered and the patient observed? And what has become of reforms? We will address these questions on the premise that something may be learned —both about "what is wrong with schools" and about federal efforts to "set things right."

Implementing a Test

Education vouchers seemed an appealing way to correct the balance of power in education, to reduce the sway of professionals and increase the influence of parents. It was hoped that if parents could exercise free choice, schools would compete by undertaking new educational ventures, which would presumably succeed only if they truly reflected the wishes of the parents. The mere existence of competitors, it was reasoned, would weaken the monopoly in education by encourage in schools to be responsive to the public.

This idea made sense to both radical and conservative reformers because it placed responsibility for school problems squarely on the public education monopoly —a large, clumsy, and perverse creature that had become by 1968 a popular political scapegoat. Professionalized bureaucracies, it was held, had become calcified, unresponsive, insensitive to cultural variations, and capable only of doing the same dreary things, year after year.

This was a trendy diagnosis of school problems, but hardly a promising prognosis for a voucher test. After all, the educational bureaucracy presumably was in charge everywhere, from Albuquerque to Xenia. Why should the established authorities tolerate an idea designed to diminish their power and make their lives much more uncomfortably competitive? The federal sponsors of the voucher test program never had a clear answer to this question, but they began with efforts to organize local parents and citizens. The notion was to pressure the local monopolists from below: It was hoped that if enough grassroots support could be mustered, school boards and professionals would have to cooperate with a test.

But this approach didn't square with the reformers' diagnosis of school problems: Local authorities could be expected to resist such a challenge, and Nixon's OEO was in no position to agitate against them. At that time, OEO was slathering itself in social science; and besides, there was Daniel P. Moynihan, then the President's counselor, who had just published a book about how OEO had made social problems worse by stirring up local communities. So organizing communities to force a voucher test seemed uncomfortable in principle.

Worse yet, it did not work. The insurgent forces were never powerful enough to produce a voucher experiment, and as a result federal reformers began again at the top. Enlisting administrators and board members seemed more appropriate, but it did not help much either. Aside from the fact that educators sympathetic to vouchers were hard to find, turning to them did not solve the political problems, for in almost every case, local administrators lacked the power to mount a test. After all, they had boards, teachers, principals, and parents to worry about, none of whom was ecstatic about vouchers. So the same difficulty kept turning up a different forms. The federally organized local forces were too weak to succeed without support from within the school power structure, and administrators within the bureaucracy were impotent because they lacked outside support. The ensuing story illuminates a problem that has plagued so many federal agencies and faddish foundations: how to produce political reform in somebody else's town with only bright ideas, some outside consultants, and a little free cash.

Growing up at the grass roots

The voucher plan drawn up by Jencks and his associates at the Center for the Study of Public Policy (CSPP) was cautious and carefully hedged. It favored individual choice, but in harmony with several competing values. The plan sought to shield minority and poor students from discrimination, to ensure maximum protection for consumers against the claims or indifference of schools, and to prevent public schools from becoming the alternative of last resort. The resulting idea for a "regulated compensatory voucher" was thus a complex and cumbersome creation —an effort to promote freedom of choice, equality, and due process all at once, while radically revising public schools.

The voucher plan was thus something of a Rube Goldberg contraption. It supplied fiscal incentives for schools to enroll poor children and to prevent economic discrimination. It provided detailed admission policies permitting applicants their choice of schools, schools their choice of applicants, and applicant lotteries —all at once— to protect the families' desires to select schools, the schools desires to select their students, and the authors' desires to prevent discriminatory admissions. And the scheme included an elaborate plan for an Education Voucher Agency, independent of the participating schools, to administer voucher distribution and accounting, oversee school quality, and provide consumers with information to make informed choices.

CSPP, then, did not propose a simple idea. Milton Friedman had argued for simplicity, favoring a laissez-faire approach on the view that regulation would interfere with operations. But the authors of the CSPP plan demurred: They argued that vouchers could take many forms, but nearly all would be an absolute "disaster" for education. Besides, they were not convinced that operations would get underway unless the plan included safeguards to mollify angry opponents. Avoiding trouble, they said, would require dispensing with the simplicities of Friedman's free market, and faithfully following their plan. but as a result, the CSPP voucher project embraced the worst of both worlds. On the one hand, although the plan strained to protect equality and avoid discrimination, these efforts neither appeased the liberals nor reduced their opposition. On the other hand, making what had been a simple idea infinitely complex impeded easy discussion, quick comprehension, and local adaption.

OEO hired CSPP to stimulate the local discussion and adoption process, but there were two problems. First, the CSPP staff was a rather implausible group for such work: Its members were bright, but few had been in a school since they were students (several had been schooled at such places as Andover and Choate). They were inclined to believe that the people who ran the public schools were either dim or nasty —or both. Second, although CSPP staffers tended to be partisans of "community organization," they rather liked living in Cambridge. This posed a few difficulties when it came to inciting the masses in Peoria.

The situation in Washington did not help. Vouchers were new and controversial, and lacked a real constituency within the government. By contrast, the other big OEO experiment, the negative income tax, had taken years to percolate through the higher civil service in the 1960's; much of the bureaucracy remained intact and supportive after the Republicans took over. In addition, there was Mr. Moynihan, an articulate and powerful negative-income-tax advocate close to a President who wanted to make something like the tax experiment into law. Vouchers, however, had no such support. Moynihan more or less liked the idea, and he liked the people at Cambridge who liked it. But few others in Washington did, and many did not. Vouchers were thus something of a political albatross for OEO.

As a result of all these difficulties, voucher projects did not take fire in local communities.[1] The chief reason was that no stable or cohesive support for the plans ever developed in any of the cities. One possible source of support was the Catholics, but they preferred other approaches to parochial-school aid. Worse yet, most of the other local participants who favored vouchers did not favor Catholics. The CSPP report was uneasy about the Supreme Court decision permitting vouchers in church school: the CSPP organizing staff was reluctant to see its pet

---

[1]Interestingly, the written analyses of the efforts to organize and promote vouchers are not available. OEO and the National Institute of Education (NIE) funded such histories, but so far they remain unavailable to anyone but NIE and the authors. This article is thus based on interviews with participants in many of the prospective sites, on the CSPP and NIE files, and on interviews with NIE, OEO, and CSPP staffers.

project tainted by parochial affiliation. So even when Catholics were supportive, they were encouraged to be discreet.

CSPP and OEO expected the poor and minorities to be another natural interest group. Their children, after all, were being so badly served by the schools; surely these parents would welcome alternatives. But the poor were mostly unorganized; any effort to turn them into an active interest groups would have required vastly more time, energy, and personnel than CSPP had. Its part-time and episodic contact with local communities meant that CSPP could deal only with organized groups, or coalitions of such groups, or leaders who seemed likely to invent or recruit groups for themselves.

Blacks were organized, but their ideas about school reform had been shaped by decades of civil-rights struggle over education. In seeking to desegregate schools they had learned to distrust any scheme that either placed the burden on minority choice or allowed whites not to choose minority schools. So when a group of white academics proclaimed vouchers to be a new solution to black school problems, established black organizations were either hesitant or hostile. Local organizing on behalf of vouchers quickly became entangled with local political conflicts over race and education. In Seattle and Rochester, for example, integrationists saw vouchers as a way out for whites; consequently they opposed a test, which they regarded as either a racist trick or sabotage. CSPP pleaded that its plan would protect integration, but local civil-rights advocates---given their experience with "freedom of choice" and their knowledge that vouchers were sponsored by the same Nixon Administration that opposed busing and favored neighborhood schools---were either hostile or skeptical. Worse yet, although the pledges of CSPP failed to placate the integrationists, they were sure to offend potential voucher supporters who opposed integration. Either way, the organizers lost.

Another reason for the lack of local enthusiasm was the fragmentation of political power in the cities. The voucher-project staff labored under a delusion widespread among recent school reformers: that political power in urban education is centralized and monolithic, and that organized grassroots power is needed to overcome resistance.[2] But although there was often little change in city schools, this resulted more often from decentralized and fragmented local power structures. The voucher field staff found the power of urban superintendents seriously hampered by politically divided boards, by the autonomy of principals and district administrators, by the power of organized interest inside and outside the schools, and by bureaucracies with powers and minds of their own. While it was possible to keep school systems running through complicated treaties among these groups, it was difficult to change the rules in any important way without throwing the agreements into doubt---and the parties into a mild panic.

Vouchers, of course, were not just any change: They would have required the renegotiation of all treaties binding a city school system together. The idea thus raised anxieties all around; when vouchers appeared in cities like Seattle, San Francisco, and Rochester, many principals were opposed, teacher organizations were skeptical or hostile, most central administrators were dubious or completely negative, and school boards were divided. The problem was less monolithic resistance than decentralized uneasiness.

Working from within

Since there was little indigenous support for education vouchers. OEO and CSPP were gradually moved to try a different tack---organizing a test by gaining the support of local boards and superintendents. Several sites with interested administrators or board members were duly found. These school districts were much smaller and, for the most part, much more homogeneous than the cities in which earlier work had been done.

But support from the top, even in such relatively manageable places, was no more effective politically than pressure from below had been elsewhere. Once again, a major problem was the fragmentation of political power. The superintendent in East Hartford, Connecticut, for example, was personally quite committed to vouchers, but many teachers and principals were opposed. Given the explosiveness of the voucher idea, the superintendent then grew cautious. The chairman of the New Hampshire state board of education, a devotee of Friedman's

---

[2]Christopher Jencks. "Is the Public School Obsolete?" The Public Interest, No. 2 (Winter 1996). pp.18-27.

economics, was also a strong supported of vouchers. With a clear majority of the board, he got a state planning grant for a "free market" voucher test from an unwilling OEO (the Nixon White House helped), but then had problems lining up local districts. Only after securing extra federal money and promising local districts the chance either to influence decisions or to bail out, did he manage to persuade five districts in the southern part of the state to allow preliminary planning. As time went on, of course, even these districts became aware of the practical implications of vouchers; finally, they dug in their heels, and would not buy a test.

The other major reason that efforts to work down from the top failed was that state and local leaders were committed to vouchers because they liked the idea---not because there were real local problems that vouchers might solve. It was easy to favor competition and choice, and to oppose the bureaucracy, but in practice choice and competition turned out to have hard and nasty meanings: Parents could choose some local schools and not others; some schools would be forced either to expand to meet demand, or to turn away interested parents; other local schools could shrink or close, costing the jobs of teachers and principals. All this meant there would be some very angry teachers and principals---and that meant trouble.

None of these possibilities was entirely clear at the outset. But as planning progressed, local administrators gradually realized that they were being asked to sacrifice a fairly comfortable situation in favor of a much more prickly and unsettled one. In New Hampshire, the local administrators responded by trying to remove the sting from vouchers by redefining the plan, removing most of the choice and competition with an engaging Yankee directness. The superintendent in East Hartford also tried this, and avoided decisions whenever possible. In both cases, local administrators grew ever more unwilling to meet the bare minimums of a local voucher test: They became increasingly allergic to encouraging choice, supporting new alternatives, allowing unchosen schools to fail, or permitting a strong and independent voucher agency. Equivocation and compromise took over. The more local leaders learned about this dream of reform, the more nightmarish it seemed.

As a consequence, efforts to secure test sites were often makeshift operations. Almost nothing ever happened on time; almost nothing was done well. Indeed, it often seemed that almost nothing would have happened at all had not CSPP and

NIE kept up a constant stream of bureaucratic and technical support. CSPP wrote the local proposals to get the NIE money. In both New Hampshire and East Hartford, CSPP helped to draw up schedules and then harassed the locals into heeding them. CSPP designed training programs for teachers, put together community information campaigns, wrote letters for the administrators, and in many other ways did the work for the locals. Without such "technical assistance" the local efforts would have fizzled out early on. As things turned out, all that help only postponed the inevitable. By 1976 all the potential test sites had failed.

Working from within thus proved as unsuccessful as groping at the grass roots. Insiders and intellectuals saw vouchers as a solution to vague and abstract problems, such as monopoly power in education---not as the solution to the day-to-day problems of running a school system. But contrary to the received doctrine of contemporary school reformers, local communities were not primarily concerned with power, choice, and participation. As a result, they did not work themselves into a sweat of enthusiasm for vouchers, and there was thus no real pressure for change---even when the opportunity fell into their laps.

The Alum Rock experience

But in Alum Rock, California, by contrast, administrators at least fancied there were real local problems that vouchers would help to solve, which helped generate political and administrative support for a test. The schools in Alum Rock were in poor financial shape in 1971, and Superintendent William Jefferds thought they had other shortcomings as well.[3] They had long been run tightly from the top: there had been little flexibility within the system for some time; and the same old jobs were being done in the same old way. Jefferds felt that the system was in danger of stagnating and that education for the numerous black and Chicano students needed

---

[3]This section of the article is based on several sources: the published reports of the Rand Corporation, the evaluator of the Alum Rock efforts; interviews with staff at NIE and Alum Rock; and interviews with Rand researchers. The Rand publications most useful are E. Levinson, with S. Abramowitz, W. Furry, and D. Joseph. "The Politics and Implementation of the Alum Rock Multiple Option System: The Second Year, 1973-74." Analysis of the Education Voucher Demonstration. A working Note (May 1975): Stephen S. Weiner and Konrad Kellen. "The Politics and Administration of the Voucher Demonstration in Alum Rock: the First Year, 1972-73." Analysis of the Education Voucher Demonstration. A Working Note (August 1974); Daniel Weiler, A Public School Voucher Demonstration: The First Year at Alum Rock (June 1974).

to be improved.

The superintendent of this small school district thus wanted a voucher test because he wanted to decentralize the Alum Rock schools and because he needed money. But if decentralizing the schools struck top administrators as the right course, no one knew how to pay for it. At the same time, OEO was fresh from several stunning defeats in other cities, and feared that without a working demonstration the whole voucher project might soon sink. At first, Alum Rock excited no one: It was a smallish district near San Jose composed largely of minority and poor families, with little promise of diversity in its schools or interest in its community. But in the early discussions, Jefferds quickly learned that OEO and CSPP needed him more than he needed them, and OEO and CSPP found an avid enthusiast for parental involvement and innovation at the school level.

The ensuing negotiations were not easy. One reason was that some Washington and Cambridge staffers still felt that Alum Rock was a silly place to try anything. Another was that Jefferds nearly lost to the local opponents of vouchers on one occasion, and barely avoided defeat by postponing everything for several months. A third reason was the failure of the California legislature to pass quickly a bill permitting public monies to flow to private schools, something everyone regarded as necessary for a voucher demonstration,

The most important problem in the negotiations, however, involved differences between the priorities of OEO and Alum Rock, OEO wanted a test of consumer sovereignty, while Alum Rock wanted OEO support for its decentralization plan: OEO had the money, and Alum Rock provided a potential test site. OEO didn't like the idea of such an "impure" test, but OEO had to take what it could get. Jefferds' superior bargaining position became obvious when he got OEO to produce some money for his decentralization program even before Alum Rock agreed to the voucher test. As is so often the case with professional reforms, the only way to get anything done is to let the locals do what they like---as long as they say they are doing what the reformers like. The reformers are really at the mercy of those they are reforming.

Cooking up the voucher test thus began with one small and dusty California school district, poor and discontented. To this were added two rather different recipes for political reform, a dollop of federal dollars, and intermittent doses of outside advice. With such ingredients and so many contending cooks, it is no surprise that the result was eventually something of a stew. But if Alum Rock did not test a single clear plan, its experience does throw some light on how vouchers worked in practice---if not how they might have worked in principle.

What happened when Alum Rock tried to reform its schools? Did more diverse educational offerings result? Did schools become much more responsive to parents? Did the power of professionals wane while that of parents waxed? Were families more satisfied? Was schooling improved?

The central theme in our answer to these questions is that the Alum Rock voucher test confounded almost all expectations---from the cautious hopes of Christopher Jencks to the dire warning of Albert Shanker. There was indeed more consumer choice, but not consumer sovereignty. Parents had more freedom to choose among more varied educational offerings, but as far as anyone can tell, they gained little power. Only the school-level professionals gained in that respect. Not only did teachers and principals inherit power from the central office as a result of decentralization, but they also acquired influence from the greater flexibility, uncertainty, and fiscal leeway that followed from parent choice.

Limiting choice and restricting competition

One point of the reforms in Alum Rock was to offer families more options for their children and to give professionals more latitude in defining school programs. But these choices created uncertainty, and unsettled parents and professionals. In a meeting to discuss proposals called by the district in the spring of 1971, parent representatives worried that children might not be able to attend their neighborhood schools. They sought and obtained a "squatter rights" agreement whereby children already enrolled could attend neighborhood schools if they liked. Parent representatives also saw to it that every voucher school would offer at least two alternative programs. to prevent children from being forced out of a local school by distaste for the program offered. (OEO sought a compromise after the first year of the demonstration, guaranteeing everyone his first-choice school for the following September---if he signed up before May.) Thus rather than seizing the initiative to expand choice or to enhance power, parents tried to make sure that neighborhood attendance was secure and that neighborhood schools would not be overly innovative.

It was expected that once parents were given the wherewithal to choose among schools, educators would vie to expand their enrollments and incomes. School professionals, however, were concerned with protecting their jobs, It was thus agreed that teachers who left a voucher school for reasons associated with the demonstration would be given priority in assignments to other schools, or that OEO would cover their salaries while they were assigned to headquarters. No one was to be put out on the street by consumer preferences.

This eased things for teachers who did not succeed, and at the outset no one worried about those who did. As it turned out, however, even success was no bed of roses. Teachers in schools that recruited more students were not rewarded with higher salaries: Although their school would receive more in tuitions, the money was to be spent for more teachers or materials. As a result, competitive success only produced more of the problems teachers struggled with every day: more children, more planning, more meetings, more colleagues, more noise at recess, more disruptions at lunchtime, and so on. Success brought more bother than benefit.

This nicely illuminated the great discrepancy between the ways teachers and voucher advocates thought of school problems. Teachers wanted better working conditions: room to breathe, to prepare, to teach, perhaps even to invent. Voucher advocates wanted better market conditions: to improve educational performance by turning up the competitive heat. Although teachers were hungry for more of the things professionals habitually crave —autonomy, more resources, and less pressure—reformers thought they already had a surfeit.

It is hard to imagine more of a mismatch. Had anyone noticed it, he might have suspected that competition would fail, or would have crazy consequences. But the reformers scored low on both sociology and school experience. The real surprise is that they scored so high on economic mythology. It is quite a testament to the continuing power of capitalism in American culture that liberal reformers not only failed to notice the obvious in education, but so thoroughly ignored the evidence concerning the effects of economic competition that littered the social landscape.

In any event, Alum Rock professionals were under no such illusions. Before the demonstration was half over they changed the market aspects of the voucher scheme to suit their purposes. The first step was to restrict demand by making it impossible for schools to expand indefinitely to meet enrollment pressures. After a year's trial with such expansion, teachers and administrators insisted that each school be given enrollment limits. From that point on, schools only needed to maintain enrollments at capacity levels, which assured the usual income without producing more than the usual strain. And since such limits meant that the less appealing schools would get the overflow from the more appealing schools, the chances for "success"---measured by enrollment---increased vastly all around.

However, the mere fact that public schools agreed to ease competition among themselves did not mean that nonpublic schools could not seek a share of the market. OEO had expected nonpublic school participation, but at first the California legislature would not permit it. OEO and Alum Rock therefore agreed to begin the demonstration as a "public-school-only" effort. Initial work focused on creating diversity within the public sector by encouraging differentiation and competition among "mini-schools" within existing buildings.

In the fall of 1973, the legislature finally enabled nonpublic schools to enter the demonstration. But partly because of the efforts of such public-spirited groups as the California Teachers Association, the legislation was quite restrictive. It permitted public monies to flow only to schools under the "exclusive control" of the local authorities, and it provided that the local certified employee councils (the professionals' bargaining agent) could formally review all policies in each voucher demonstration. In addition, it required that all participating schools be subject to district rules concerning teacher certification, curriculum standards, and student discipline, as well as other general rules and regulations.

Since Alum Rock was a poor district, it had no established private schools, and there were thus no disappointed private educational entrepreneurs. But a few months before the enabling legislation was passed, a group of four young teachers interested in "free schools" set out to organize an alternative school within the demonstration. The prospective school called "Gro-Kids" got a small planning grant in the spring of 1973, and operated an afterschool program the following fall.

The omens were not auspicious for Gro-Kids, however; the district leadership was ambivalent, and the teachers' organization was hostile. As a result, the certified employee council took the view that private schools could enter only if they met most of the operating standards of the public schools. This meant that Gro-Kids would be obliged to hire certified teachers and provide roughly the same staff/student ratios, salaries, and fringe benefits.

These conditions meant that private voucher schools in Alum Rock could differ from public voucher schools only in the ways public schools differ from one another. This left room for important differences, but they would be pedagogical and philosophical. The voucher idea had once again been radically revised. Although the organizers of Gro-Kids persisted and the school board voted to admit the new school in the winter of 1974, momentum had been lost. When parent choices for the following school year were made, no one selected Gro-Kids. It promptly vanished.

Alum Rock professionals thus sharply reduced the scope of economic competition, making life hard for private schools, eliminating school expansion, and protecting individual teachers from competitive failure. The voucher plan was drastically modified because schools are presently governed more by political than market forces; in Alum Rock, economic competition had no effective advocates. Such competition might have had a chance if it offered something to at least some of the participants, but it didn't.

Protecting roles and power

The failure to promote economic competition among Alum Rock schools still left plenty of room for other kinds of competition. But there was less than might have been expected, largely because of the effects of the district decentralization program. Some time before the voucher demonstration, decentralization had begun in six schools whose principals had expressed a desire for more authority. Superintendent Jefferds had procured OEO funds to prepare the six principals for more power through team-building and sensitivity training. The principals went into the training with a common interest in more authority, but they came out of it with a strong sense of group identity and an even stronger desire to get more power from the central office.

It was in precisely these six schools that the voucher experiment began. Conflicts between the goals of vouchers and decentralization---between parent power and principal power---developed almost instantly. The principals were extremely sensitive to anything that might tend to divide them, and competition among schools was exactly such a policy. They could accept programmatic differences, but they resisted such competitive devices as advertising, comparative evaluations, and the like, which would draw attention to the differences and encourage parents to act on them. Thus, the commitment by the district to increase the power of the principals through decentralization was in conflict with the commitment by OEO to encourage parent power by extending choice.

The Sequoia Institute was one focus of this conflict. Sequoia was directed by a former CSPP staffer, and the rest of its top staff were either Chicano or black. It was a bastard child of the Education Voucher Agency proposed by CSPP, an independent non-profit organization under contract to the school district, which Jefferds and OEO agreed would help set voucher policy and manage certain aspects of the demonstration. From Jefferds' point of view, Sequoia would legally be part of the district and under his control, even though it was an autonomous organization. But OEO hoped it would be more independent, effectively acting as an advocate for vouchers and parents: to provide parents with counseling and information, to speak for parents at all levels of the demonstration, to evaluate the performance of schools and students and disseminate the information so that parents could make informed choices, and to help monitor the project and insure that vouchers were not abused or misused.

Sequoia and the principals were incompatible from the start. The principals began by opposing the mere existence of the institute on the grounds that any addition to the bureaucracy would erode decentralization. They also objected to its view of parent advocacy and evaluation, and vigorously resisted publishing comparative information that might encourage competition among schools.

When Sequoia tried to press ahead with evaluations in the first year, the principals blocked the effort. During the second year, the Sequoia staff counterattacked and won permission to proceed, but by then it was so late that the information could only be used in the third year. and even then the principals made sure that parents were only provided information on the mini-schools attended by their own children. Information on other mini-schools---necessary to make comparisons---would have to be requested by each parent.

A similar struggle took place over the effort by Sequoia to provide counselors to help parents make choices and deal with school staff. The principals argued that if parents wanted information or help they should come to the schools' professional staff members, not some outside group. For the first year the Sequoia counselors thus lived in limbo: then they were assigned to individual schools, as principals had demanded. Their advocacy role was redefined by changing the job description, the place of work, and the chain of command.

In fact, this was the pattern throughout the history of Sequoia: New roles were redefined and transformed into old ones. Sequoia's assistant director for evaluation became the district's director of evaluation. Sequoia's director became a district administrator: the parent counselors became school registrars (some said clerks): and Sequoia became part of the district administration. In each case, the role that had initially been conceived as a reform was progressively redefined until it was hardly distinguishable from long established and accepted practice. Not surprisingly, Sequoia did not work as OEO hoped. The reform that Alum Rock administrators wanted proved more durable than the reform they were paid to adopt.

Parent power

A similar story can be told about parent power. Parent advocacy groups were established for each mini-school and an overall Education Voucher Advisory Committee (EVAC) was created at the district level. These groups were purely advisory, having neither resources nor any formal role in decision-making. By contrast, EVAC had not only legitimacy but visibility, its own budget, defined powers, and potential for affecting the conduct of the experiment. Still, its parent members were neither aggressive nor particularly effective. They took an active role only on matters that directly and obviously affected them, such as neighborhood attendance, and even then they were far from consistent. The parent members generally tended to be absent, poorly informed, and deferential to the professionals holding EVAC seats. Parents simply did not take advantage of the opportunities for gaining power. Like the district professionals, they accepted existing roles.

This might be explained by the fact that parents were at a real disadvantage in EVAC; expecting them to act effectively in such circumstances may be foolish. Evidence of how parents used the voucher scheme to become more powerful might better be found in areas more familiar to them---choosing schools, discovering the available options, negotiating transfers, and the like. There is, for example, the encouraging fact that all parents in the voucher demonstration made choices. But the trouble is that the project was organized to force choices upon everyone: Even parents whose children remained in a neighborhood school had to choose a mini-school within it.

Something can be learned, though, from the proportions of parents who chose schools outside their neighborhoods. In the first year, a negligible fraction did so, but this probably can be ascribed to the late start of the demonstration. During the second year, about 10 per cent chose non-neighborhood schools, and after that the proposition rose again to about 18 per cent —a distinct increase in parent initiative, but involving only a modest number of parents.

The choices parents made within schools are also quite illuminating. One might expect that high transfer rates among mini-schools signalled parent initiative or discontent, or both. The transfer rate within schools, for example, rose by about 11 per cent between 1973 and 1974 —not astronomical, but clear evidence that a modest proportion of parents chose innovative mini-school programs. At first, most chose traditional programs; among those who selected the more modish programs, higher-income families were considerably over-represented. The proportion of children in traditional programs did decrease by about 18 per cent, however, between 1972 and 1975.

A similar pattern characterized parents' knowledge about schools. During the first year a modest fraction did not even know which mini-school their children were enrolled in, and many more who did knew nothing else about it. In the course of the demonstration parents learned more about their children's programs, but their knowledge about the system remained fairly shallow. Most parents learned about schools from official communications, a small fraction gained information on their own, and almost all reported satisfaction with what they knew. With a few exceptions, parent involved in the Alum Rock demonstration were content to learn just as most parents do —by being told by professionals.

This is reasonably typical of American education. A small proportion of parents are active, but most are not. The voucher demonstration appreciably increased parent choice among educational alternatives, but most parents failed to become more autonomous, powerful, or involved. The existing roles may not have been entirely satisfactory, but they seem to have been sufficient to forestall much of a search for alternatives.

Programs and pedagogy

It would be a great mistake, however, to imagine that nothing happened in the voucher schools. This would make sense only if one believed that schools suffer the blahs because they are not sufficiently accountable. The absence of increased accountability did not imply stagnation; considerable change seemed to take place in many Alum Rock voucher schools.

The most obvious change was more diversity. Where before a uniform curriculum had lain over all the schools, there were now Spanish-English bilingual programs, an arts-and-crafts mini-school, several "open classroom" mini-schools, and a number of innovative approaches to reading. Some of these programs retained the regular grade-level organization of elementary schools, but others were more flexible. While some schools made few curriculum changes, others made modest revisions and still others made more serious departures. Three years after the demonstration began, voucher classrooms were certainly more different than they initially had been.

Probably the most striking change in the voucher schools was the increase in the independence of the teachers. The curriculum had previously been set by the central-office staff, but with vouchers decisions were primarily made by teachers, who even had the resources (thanks to the extra funds provided by compensatory vouchers) to support their choices. Administrators were no longer quite as important; teachers had more freedom to arrange their working conditions than before more flexibility in grouping students was possible; and teachers could create smaller working groups for themselves. The program was thus easier to revise and adapt as teachers went along.

Innovation at the school level was thereby supported and encouraged by decentralization, the mini-schools, and the compensatory-voucher monies —not by competition. If one were to speculate about innovation based on the Alum Rock experience, one would have to say that social and economic encouragement were more important than competition or political power.

But the voucher demonstration was not exactly easy for Alum Rock professionals. For one thing, it was temporary. Everyone knew things would revert to the old system in a few years, which did nothing to ease the problems of change. For another, the demonstration meant much more work: Administrative and fiscal procedures were redesigned, new budgeting systems were created, and mini-schools curriculums were established, placing greater burdens on teachers and principals. Many teachers reported that they had never worked so hard and had not expected that the demonstration would require so much effort. Especially in the early stages, there was a avalanche of meetings, and many teachers felt overwhelmed and exhausted.

Thus, although the working conditions of the teachers improved in some respects, in others they declined. There was more work and more worry, but no less teaching, no more hours in the day. And while there was more money to spend on materials and resources, teachers were not paid much more for their extra duties. They received some compensation for in-service training, but it amounted to a very modest annual salary increase over the course of the demonstration. If this was an incentive, it certainly was not awfully enticing. Indeed, the whole demonstration was a terrible tease: It offered some opportunities and encouragements to teachers, but made only marginal allowances for the personal and professional sacrifices involved,

It was no surprise, then , that as the demonstration progressed energy flagged. Teachers had less time for meetings, less patience for the demands of innovation,, less desire for the rigors of collaboration, and more appreciation of the lives they could once again lead separately and individually behind classroom doors. Because the voucher demonstration offered some encouragements for innovation, and because many professionals desired change, things began with energy, hasty improvisation, and excitement. But because the scheme had not been designed with much appreciation of the classroom experience of teachers-because it assumed that teachers should be reshaped by a stiff dose of competition- there were only partial and sometimes accidental incentives for professionals. As the demonstration moves toward a close, many innovations have begun to slip away.

Confusing symptoms with causes

One lesson of the voucher saga seems to be that if parent choice and educational alternatives make sense for public schools, it is not for the reasons contemplated by the reformers. The assumption underlying the original scheme was that schools were bad because parents were powerless, and that parents were powerless because they had been excluded by professionals anxious to protect themselves from popular control. If parents had more power —which in this case was to be gained by control of school funding— it was expected that professionals would then be accountable and that schools would thereby be better places for children. But when some barriers to parental involvement were removed, power distribution did not change appreciably.

One explanation for this may be that the existing power imbalance between parents and professionals is great enough to require even more support for parent before they can participate effectively. If this is correct , it raises questions about participatory reforms that assume that parents have been excluded and that given the opportunity to use power, they will. When they failed to, as in the case of EVAC, some observers argues that even more training, support, and professional advocacy were needed. Buy this argument redefines citizen participation: It no longer involves releasing the political energies of excluded citizens by providing greater access to power; it now consists of paying professionals to train, speak for, and support citizens. This view seems both plausible and puzzling. One is not sure whether to agree because implementation was only partial, to wonder why a larger dose would do more when a partial dose failed to help much at all, or to marvel at the need for even more professional help in the effort to overcome professional power.

The chief defect of this analysis is a confusion of symptoms and causes. There are real political imbalances in the governance of American schools, which contribute to the poor performance of political reforms to increase participation.

But the real imbalance is not political in origin. It results more from a social division of labor that encourages the specialization of work, the professionalization of roles, and the partitioning of authority. In advanced industrial societies this solidifies professional power in education, as well as discouraging active parental involvement. Parents used to have more to do with education simply because there often was not much formal schooling available. It was not uncommon in the 18th and early 19th centuries for children to get much of their education from a parent or from a job, in church, in an apprenticeship, or in other informal settings.

With the rise of schooling, education increasingly became the province of trained specialists. Professionals gain economic returns, social satisfaction, personal status, individual identity, and group power from their roles. And parents, most of whom have occupations providing similar rewards, have seen their educational role narrowed and redefined. It still involves early childhood education and help with homework in the elementary grades, but increasingly centers on insuring that children receive the right professional attention.

The growth of this division of labor had political consequences. In the early and middle 19th century, when public schools began , teachers had little status and less power: They were at the mercies of their communities. But the growth of a complex industrial division of labor weakened the bonds connecting work, family, school, and community, and eroded the forces that kept teachers in a subordinate and dependent position. Gradually, teaching-like many other occupations-has gained social definition, autonomy, and political power; community power over schools has correspondingly attenuated.

Since the imbalance in school power does not have political roots, political remedies may be marginal. Vouchers turned out so peculiarly in Alum Rock because the scheme fundamentally misconstrued the reason that power is so lopsidedly distributed in public education. As one might expect from such a misdiagnosis, the effects of the reform were perverse: Professionals gained power from an experiment in which they were supposed to lose it. Vouchers opened the door for power shifts, but they did not affect the ways in which work , authority, and child-rearing are apportioned in society. Because social realities were undisturbed by merely loosening up the political structure, the changes only enhanced the power of those who had it already.

Given this analysis, it is not surprising that all these changes occurred with little political conflict between parents and professionals. Predictably, most of the conflict was between professionals who advocated greater parent power and professionals who did not. That, after all, is what one would expect in an "expert society." The struggles were enough to make for several lively years in this small California city, but not enough to work basic changes in the distribution of political power.

More than meets the eye

At the same time, Alum Rock parents were more satisfied with their schools. This would seem perverse if one subscribed to the theory of parent power associated with vouchers: Why should parents' satisfaction increase if their power didn't? The answer, we think, is that vouchers in Alum Rock did offer benefits many parents desired, benefits that are consistent with the existing social division of labor. One of these was a somewhat greater range of educational alternatives. Some parents have strong views on the relative importance of language and culture, or on the balance among discipline, fundamentals, and individual discovery, or on the comparative significance of algebra and art. Although the mini-schools seemed to vary little in basic instructional patterns-most teachers spent about the same proportion of their time on reading and math-they did seem to offer diverse programs, this more nearly corresponding with varieties of educational opinion. It is hardly surprising that parents with views hitherto unrepresented in the curriculum appreciated the new alternatives. Their appreciation may have followed from the substance of the new programs-or simply from being offered a choice. But whatever the reason, the opportunity to choose seems to have been welcomed.

Another benefit of the Alum Rock demonstration was that these alternatives were offered by professionals. Parents had the freedom to choose from a fairly conventional range of educational possibilities, but teachers defined, devised, and implemented them. The demonstration also tended to make professionals more visible and accessible to the parents. Most important, it did all this within the limits of established roles.

This helps to explain why parents in Alum Rock were more satisfied without being more powerful: They had more alternatives and more freedom to choose, but these were provided by professionals in authoritative and familiar ways —without much work for parents.

This points to a second lesson of the demonstration: It was hard to mount a voucher test because almost everyone ignored the considerable possibilities offered teachers. Instead, vouchers were advertised as a sort of radical social surgery to improve things for students and parents at the expense of the professionals. This approach to change was certain to flop unless a substantial proportion of teachers found vouchers attractive. But the project was promoted in such a way as to suggest that vouchers would punish professionals into better performance. So it is not surprising that OEO found few volunteers for a demonstration, or that professionals in Alum Rock responded with such caution. One political consequence of the social division of labor in advanced industrial societies is that the reform of social services is unlikely to succeed unless many professionals find it attractive. Because vouchers presented a rather threatening prospect, they had few takers.

The third lesson of the Alum Rock venture is that, ironically, there is more in the idea of choice for parents and professionals than the advertising suggested. Many teachers are strongly attracted by the prospect of choosing the sort of classroom they would work in, of shaping the curriculum they would use, and of working with student who find their style attractive. There is some evidence that when teachers exercise such choices —when they are able to create alternative within the public schools— both parents and professionals are pleased with the results. Such efforts are underway in some cities (among them, Minneapolis and Cincinnati) and the reports seem encouraging. These professionally defined alternatives embody most of the main currents of thought about schooling and offer many of the specializations families desire-science, the arts culture and language, and so on. If the voucher reform had been conceived and promoted differently, it might have met with somewhat greater enthusiasm among professionals.

This hardly exhausts the lessons of the voucher story, nor does it finish the tale itself. One fascinating item concerns the effort to evaluate vouchers effectively. A major justification for the federal program in the first place was the search for scientific results to support policy decisions about whether vouchers should be expanded or discarded. Large sums of money were spent in search of the answer, but the evaluation itself seems to have played no role in decisions about the future of vouchers. Experience provided more decisive and timely evidence. But the final evaluation does offer rich testimony concerning the difficulties involved in such scientific endeavors, and it might reveal something about their potential usefulness.

Similarly, there is still a question about the impact of the voucher program beyond Alum Rock,. OEO and NIE tried to organize demonstrations in school districts all over the country: although all but one of these failed, promoting vouchers may have stimulated other efforts to increase choice and diversity. The prospect of government support for private schools may have stimulated attempts to promote diversity within the public schools, to show that alternatives were possible without resorting to nonpublic education. And all the publicity from Washington, during the last five or six years, may well have helped to legitimize diversity and choice, and create a climate of opinion in which they are more possible. It would be ironic if the primary impact of federal efforts to promote vouchers was indirect, but it would not be the first time in the history of social reform that unintended results were significant.

Nor has this article fully probed some of the more programmatic issues raised by the voucher saga-for example, the federal role in school reform. There is certainly a need for reflection concerning how federal agencies might deal with reforms like vouchers that have more appeal than support. And what of the broader implications for participatory reforms? If, as we have argued, the sort of participation most parents desire are different than those advocated by reformers. one wonders whether there are better ways to redress the imbalance of political power in education.

These and other questions are important, but must wait for a more detailed treatment of this fascinating episode in school reform. For now, it is enough to note that this scheme to promote parent power produced mixed results, and that several views are plausible. As an effort to reform the nation's schools, the voucher demonstration left much to be desired; it was an administrator's innovations, not a popular movement. Its only resources were its appeal and the ingenuity and money it advocates could produce. These were enough to keep the advocates busy, but not enough to foment a social experiment. Vouchers were intended to overturn the political power structure in local schools and put parents in the driver's seat, but the absence of popular support meant that there was really hope for success only when the opposition-the educational establishment-also liked the idea. There was only one actual test and even there local forces tended to overwhelm federal priorities. The moral, we suppose, is that bright ideas, advice, and federal funds are not substitute for political power. Reforms spun from such political gossamer have similarly fragile prospects.

But vouchers can also be viewed as an attempt to change the balance of power within schools, and in this regard we think they produced both more and less than expected. As nearly as can be discerned, parents in Alum Rock have little more power now than before the test. The promise of parent choice and power rather unsettled teachers and principals, who promptly took steps to protect their interests. The ensuing story was enough to bring tears of joy to the eyes of the most hardened political observers; Professionals in Alum Rock emerged with undiminished and probably increased power-all this resulting from an innovation designed to boost the political fortunes of parents at the expense of professionals. The voucher idea was based on a serious overestimate of popular discontent and the demand for change in education. The moral is that reforms designed to "loosen up" school systems often succeed-but with perverse political effects. This is partly because the intended victims of reforms begin with much more organization and power than the intended beneficiaries; few of the beneficiaries have the time, energy, or resources to seize the opportunities presented by the reformers. The victims naturally use their superior power and organization not just to neutralize change but also to turn it to their own advantage. Similarly, the efforts of the Ford Foundation to loosen up the schools in New York through community control enhanced the political fortunes of the United Federation of Teachers. It often helps to loosen things up, but in the ensuing looseness, those with power get more.

From the perspective of promoting diversity, the story is less gloomy : The voucher demonstration in Alum Rock increased professionals' ability to choose and design their work settings, and made it possible for parents to select among alternatives. If choice and diversity are good, then schools in Alum Rock were better places.

Finally, the Alum Rock demonstration has provided an opportunity to learn a good deal about the possibilities for alternative programs, as well as helpful evidence concerning the likely roles of parents and professionals. Some of these lessons may be indirect and perverse, but they are instructive nonetheless. The experience with vouchers point to some ways in which diversity in education can be further explored and encouraged, even though it suggests other ways that seem barren. If the voucher plan is narrowly assessed in terms of its assumptions about political participation and school reform, it must be judged something less than a resounding success. But viewed as an exploration of educational alternatives, it may prove a source of suggestive ideas and lessons.

Educational Vouchers: The Private Pursuit of the Public Purse

R. Freeman Butts

Several months ago John Gardner wrote an article for the *Chronicle of Higher Education* titled, in his felicitous fashion, "The Private Pursuit of Public Purpose" (8 January 1979). His argument centered on the need for tax policies and freedom from centralized government bureaucracies that would promote "private giving for public purposes," so that individuals and voluntary groups will be prompted to contribute as private persons to the "charitable, religious, scientific, and educational activities of their *choice*" (emphasis added.) He argued further that his protection for private action represents no sentimental aversion to large scale organization or national action that are necessary to deal with many of our problems -- including a vigorous government. But he is worried about the loss of a sense of local community, which has been badly shattered in recent years:

> In a well-designed government, there should be a wise and fitting allocation of functions between the center and the periphery. Those functions that can best be performed at the highest level of government should be performed there, while those best performed in the private sector -- or by local government -- should be decentralized.

Gardner is particularly at pains to make the point that government and the *nonprofit* private sector should *not* be viewed as adversaries but as workable partners: "There are no villains. Government is necessary to the nonprofit sector; and a vital, creative nonprofit sector is crucial to the nation's future."

I have long admired John Gardner as president of the Carnegie Corporation, as secretary of the Department of Health, Education, and Welfare, and as guiding light of Common Cause. And I must agree with much that he says. After all, I was supported for some 40 years by a private institution of higher education while I worked on behalf of public education. But I devoutly hope that John Gardner's enterprise will *not* be taken as an agency or an argument for educational vouchers. I believe that a full-scale voucher scheme will promote *private* purposes rather than *public* purposes.

If I may twist Gardner's phrase a bit, I believe that educational vouchers amount to the "private pursuit of the public *purse* ." You might say, "Why not? That is the American way." Every special interest lobbies in Washington and in the state capitals for government policies that will benefit its own particular group -- and sometimes self-interest may be clothed in arguments that private benefits promote the public interest. But I would argue that such a view is peculiarly inappropriate and even dangerous when it comes to education. I argue this from a study of history and from as assessment of the present mood of the country.

First, the historical argument -- and do not take history lightly, for it not only reveals our traditions and ideals but has embedded public education in our constitutions and governmental institutions. Now, *why* was *that* done? The basic reason why the founders of this Republic turned to the idea of *public* education is that they were trying to build common commitments to their new democratic *political* community.

Let me repeat this point. The prime purpose for a public rather than a private education was *political* : it was to prepare the young for their new role as self-governing citizens rather than as *subjects* bound to an alien sovereign or as *private persons* loyal primarily to their families, their kinfolk, their churches, their localities or neighborhoods, or their ethnic traditions. In its origin, the idea of public education was *not* to give parents more control over education, *not* to promote the individuals needs and interests of children, *not* to prepare for a better job, *not* to get into college.

Jefferson said it most eloquently just 200 years ago this year. In his revision of the laws of Virginia, Jefferson was trying to rid his society in 1779 of the economic and political props that perpetuates aristocratic privileges of status for family, kin, or social class. Jefferson thus proposed the abolition of the economic privileges of primogeniture and entail; *and* he proposed a system of public schools, governed by public officials and supported by public funds, to overcome the political inequalities and privileges inherent in private education:

> ...[O]f the views of this law none is more important, none more legitimate, than that of rendering the people the safe, as they are the ultimate, guardians of their own liberty....Every government degenerates when trusted to the rulers of the people alone. The people themselves are its only safe depositories....*An amendment of our constitution must here come in aid of the public education.* the influence

over government must be shared by all the people. (Emphasis added)

Now, 200 years later, the people of California are being asked to amend their constitution to come to the aid of *private* education.This is indeed a revolution, and its effect will be to overthrow the civic purpose of education that was the basic reason why public education was incorporated in seven of the first 14 state constitutions and eventually in all. It was seen by a wide consensus of persons ranging across the political spectrum as a necessary corrective for the several kinds of private schools that dotted the American landscape in the late eighteenth century: charity schools for the poor, tuition schools for the rich, proprietary schools run for profit, religious schools supported by subscription. Then, in the early nineteenth century, many kinds of attempts were made to channel public funds into the charity schools, the denominational schools, the private academies, and the philanthropic societies; and in the emerging public schools "rate bills' were levied upon parents who could afford to pay, while "free" schooling was often reserved for the poor. All in all, the diversity and the use of public funds for private purposes approached the situation to which present-day voucher schemes might very well return us.

If Jefferson had read and agreed with much of the voucher literature that I have read in the past decade, he might have prefaced his educational amendment to the constitution of Virginia in 1779 with the following preamble (with apologies to a certain Preamble that came along 10 years later):

We, the people of the state of Virginia, in order to
- form a more perfect *pluralism,*
- establish justice *for parents,*
- provide for the defense of *diversity,*
- promote the *private* welfare,
- insure domestic *control of education,* and
- secure the blessings of *Milton Friedman* to ourselves and our posterity
do amend this constitution on behalf of educational vouchers.

Fortunately, I believe, the founders of the Republic and the successive generations of advocates for public schools responded instead to the value claims of the democratic political community that they were trying to build and that they believed should be held in common by the citizens of the American Republic -- the values of freedom, equality, justice, and obligation for the public good.

It can be argued that private schools can just as well, if not better, develop common civic values. This is a possible argument for a society that is homogenous in religion, language, ethnicity, and cultural tradition -- or for one where there is a stable hierarchial class society in which education is a privilege of the few and where there is common agreement as to what the core of education should be (the classics, or Christianity, or Islam, or Judaism). But in a democratic society where education is intended for most of the people (if not all of them) and where there is enormous diversity of culture, of religion, of class, and of educational goals, the private schools are likely to separate and divide along homogenous lines of one kind or another and are not likely to provide the overall sense of political community needed for a viable public life. This is especially true if the government itself and public funds are used to encourage parents and families to coalesce around other like-minded families.

It was in the hope that public schools would surmount the divisiveness of the many segments in American society, while at the same time honoring pluralistic differences, that the ides of a *common* school took root in the nineteenth century and flourished so widely in the twentieth. It came to be so generally accepted that only a public school system common to all segments of society under public control could achieve the ideals of common civic community. We well know that the goals of common schooling have not always been achieved in public schools, but now Jack Coons would redefine the meaning of "common schools" in such a way that even the *ideal* would be given up. This, I believe, is the real choice before the people of California -- *not* whether parents shall have more control over the education of their children, but whether the *ideal* of a common school system devoted primarily to the task of building civic community among the vast majority of citizens shall be given up in favor of private choice.

I believe that this is a particularly dangerous time for a new "experiment on our liberties." I believe the future of the very ideal of a common national purpose is at stake, not solely with regard to public education but with regard to our whole public life. Privatism is in the saddle and galloping in a peculiarly ominous way, and a voucher system might just make the race irreversible.

I need not remind you of the mood of the 1970's stemming from a decade of Vietnam, Watergate, campus unrest, corruption in quiet place, violence and drugs, in the schools, and the whole litany if troubles. The signs are all about us: cynicism and skepticism about government; alienation from public institutions, including school administrators, bureaucracy, and militant teachers; a simplistic and self-serving complaint by big business booming with big profits about the extravagance of "big government"; the undignified scramble by politicians to echo "me too"; and now the "tax revolts" and fiscal hysteria. Just when it looked as though we might achieve fundamental school finance reforms in the interests of equity (led by Jack Coons in the *Serrano* case), Proposition 13 cut across the reform movement with its meat-axe approach to cutting property taxes, limiting governmental service, shrinking government, and adding fuel to the movement to private schools.

So we have the prospect of reduced local control over education; greatly increased state control over school finance; depressed teacher morale; monumental layoffs fought by teachers (as in San Francisco) and prospective cuts in funds that would expand California's School Improvement Programs designed to increase exactly the role of parent participation that Coons so devoutly seeks through a voucher system. All of this promises to weaken further that "well-designed government" described by John Gardner as a wise and fitting allocation of functions between the center and the periphery.

Meanwhile, at the federal level Sen. Patrick Moynihan lurks in the wings waiting for another try at tuition tax credits, which were defeated by a national coalition last year, while Sen. Jesse Helms seeks legislation to restore prayers to the public schools and prohibit the Supreme Court from interpreting the First Amendment. And Jerry Brown and Milton Friedman want to assemble a constitutional convention to amend the U.S. Constitution to keep taxes under control and budgets balanced.

In California, the state constitutional amendment fever promises a crowded agenda of initiatives on the ballot in 1980. Paul Gann's proposition would limit the growth of government spending at all levels to the percentage increase in inflation and the rate of population growth. Howard Jarvis's proposition would cut the income tax in half. Combine these two with Proposition 13 and what have we left? And Sen. Alan Robbins has led the California legislature to try to limit court-ordered school busing by legislative initiative. What all of this may do to the ideal of the public good and to the role of public education in promoting it boggles the mind.

And now comes on center stage the proposition to amend the California constitution on behalf of educational vouchers. I believe that this is one more effort to return a proper governmental function achieved over 200 years to the private markets and entrepreneurs of the eighteenth century, now multiplied many thousand fold. There is no doubt about widespread public malaise concerning public schools; there is no doubt that the fever for private schools is rising. Private secular schools, fundamentalist Christian academies, and all sorts of alternatives beckon parents of an affluent society to desert the public schools. And "cultural pluralism" has become one of the most popular terms in the lexicon of professional educators. In none of these movements do I find a well-formulated conception of the common public good nor of the obligation of schooling to try to promote a sense of civic community. Today, even the *rhetoric* of "good citizenship" as the prime purpose of the education is all but missing.

Herein lies the challenge to the education profession. In the discussion over vouchers the profession should not be perceived as taking a purely defensive stance of apology for the Establishment or of protection for special vested professional interests. It should take positive, constructive action to reassert the prime purpose of public education. Voucher advocates argue for parental control rather than official or professional of education. The profession must recognize the legitimacy of parental participation, but should argue that such participation can be most effective in the long run when it is undertaken in the open arena of the political process of public institutions rather than in private contracting and bargaining with school owners and employers. We have increasing evidence that parents and public interest groups *can* work constructively with public officials and education professionals in such cities as Seattle, Minneapolis, Indianapolis, Salt Lake City, and in many communities of California under the School Improvement Program.

We should not allow the choice facing Californians to be pictured as between the public schools as they now exist, with all of their imperfections, and some ideal vision of publicly funded private schools. The choice that a voucher proposition offers is between weakening the public schools still further by encouraging flight from them and *strengthening* the public schools by recalling then to their historic purpose of promoting the ideals of the democratic civic community. I don't see much hope of framing the discussion this way unless the profession takes the lead. We should argue for more parental participation, yes; for more cooperation with the rapidly mushrooming citizen participation movement of public interest groups, yes; for more innovation and experiment, yes.

But on the later point I believe state policy should *not* be designed to encourage families to promote any kind of education they may devise. Rather, is should encourage innovation, experimentation, and diversity of approaches to the *common goal* of developing informed, committed, and responsible citizens for a democratic political community. Competition among schools should not be simply the market value of attracting students but competition to develop the best programs of citizenship education -- including curriculum, methods, governance of schools, community participation, "hidden curriculum," and all the rest. This is the kind of competition upon which public money should be spent.

The undermining of public education can be achieved at a stroke by a constitutional amendment that will disperse public funds to all sorts of competing, specialized private-interest schools. But the *reform* of education, including public education, cannot be achieved overnight. Let's admit that. But let's covenant with the people of California that if they will defeat the voucher idea in June 1980, and if they will provide adequate funds, we *will* work to reform public education so that it will genuinely serve the highest values of the civic community. We have before us the most appropriate timetable I can think of for the revival of the civic learning.

Our deadline is June 1989 -- the two-hundredth anniversary of the First Congress elected and assembled under the Constitution framed at Philadelphia in 1787. This will give us a decade to reeducate ourselves as teachers and administrators in the historic meaning and ideals of our political community, to prepare a new generation of teachers along the same lines, to reeducate the public about the civic role of public education, and to demonstrate convincingly that public education *can* be an effective force in bringing to reality the basic values of the American civic community; liberty *and* equality *and* justice *and* personal obligation for the public good.

Of Family Choice and 'Public' Education

John E. Coons

The architect and chief proponent of California's "Initiative for Family Choice" describes the plan in some detail and claims that critic Butts has misunderstood its principles and potential.

Our critic is vague about the sins of his enemy. His indiscriminate volleys suggest that Milton Friedman conspires with Christopher Jencks and the epithet "voucher" tells us nothing—except the critic's bias. The California Initiative for Family Choice is left undescribed while missile after verbal missile is aimed at... what? As Tom Lehrer said, "Once the rockets are up who knows where they come down— that's not my department." So it is with Professor Butts.

A description of the elementary facts must, therefore, be my principal object. First, however, I will dispatch missiles of my own. They will be mercifully few, as the initiative largely speaks for itself. The setting is this. In the last five years private school enrollment in California has risen from 6% to about 12% and is expected to go higher. Historically, private schools have typically been sectarian institutions populated principally by working-class and lower-income people; Catholic schools, the most common example still enroll a higher percentage of racial minorities statewide (42%) than do the public schools (36%). However, the recent migration to private education is drawing more affluent families. The few established high-cost academies have huge waiting lists, and hundreds of new private schools are forming each year. The middle class appears to be leaving the public schools.

I say leaving the "public" schools but there is a more precise description: Affluent families are leaving the schools that have been their exclusive enclaves, They are called Palo Alto, Beverly Hills and Hillsborough. These schools have been essentially private except for the form of their financial support—property taxes deductible on the federal return. Parents chose them because they wanted a "lighthouse" district; the deed to an expensive home was their ticket of entry—the "voucher" of the upper class. Meanwhile other parents and children took what the system decided was good for them. They took it in San Francisco or in Watts; they liked it or they didn't—but they took it. They had no choice.

And that is what Professor Butts calls "public" education. It is a play on words a corruption of our language; for public is the one thing such a system is not. It was and remains a profoundly elitist, exclusive and undemocratic structure of privilege paid for by taxation—one in which the rich get choice and deductions and the poor get sent. That the name of Thomas Jefferson should be invoked to justify this servile order is a historical gaffe. The fact that excellent scholars such as Butts perpetuate the old mythology only magnifies the temptation to despair.

Butts is correct to this extent: After a century of class segregation in education, we desperately need a public school system. And we can have it once we are willing to accord every family the trust Butts reposes in the rich. The underlying principle for a public system is Jeffersonian and very simple: Ordinary people are the best managers of their own affairs. Give them good information about schools; give them the necessary resources; give them professional counsel to help them choose. But do not force them into a school picked by administrators who have never met their child. Let them decide for themselves.

Education, we are told, should enhance the sense of community. Obviously. Do we get it by blocking the hopes of nonrich families who want something different from what the administrator thinks best? Is forced assignment a good lesson in tolerance and do the poor perceive their schools as agents of a society that respects them? Has the present order produced good citizens? Butts describes his view of modern America in vivid terms:

> I need not remind you of the mood of the 1970s stemming from a decade of Vietnam, Watergate, campus unrest, corruption in quiet places, violence and drugs in the schools, and the whole litany of troubles. The signs are all about us: cynicism and skepticism about government; alienation from public institutions, including school administrators, bureaucracy, and militant teachers; a simplistic and self-serving complaint by big business booming with high profits about the extravagance of "big government"; the undignified scramble by politicians to echo "me too"; and now the "tax revolts" and fiscal hysteria.

He may be right, but who designed the education for these paragons? Coercive assignment of the non-rich has created more such social problems than it has solved; community stability and good education are nourished not by force but by choice. Families that choose their own schools do not suffer "alienation from public institutions." To the contrary they cherish and support them. People trust the society that trusts them. Their children, being linked to learning by choice, tend to feel good about their school; they participate with zest in its intellectual and social life and in the life of the society that respects their parents' decision. Such children have a better chance to learn, to succeed, and to be good citizens.

One of the parallel social goals of education is (or should be) racial integration; today it is ground under the heel of the school regime. Judges can order the integration of an urban district enrolling 30% white pupils; but, so long as the court refuses to bus across district lines or to use private schools, the judicial fiat in such cases is at best symbolic and at worst counterproductive (as is attested by last year's 30,000 white émigrés from Los Angeles public schools). If society were serious about school integration, it would insure to low-income blacks and Chicanos the same mobility enjoyed by the middle class. Minorities would be encouraged to enroll either in the public schools of other districts or in private schools. Integration could proceed beyond anything the courts will compel, and it would do so in the one way that is likely to maintain stability and to move toward a truly integrated society: freedom of choice.

The Initiative Blending Old, New

So much for argument. We must press on to examine the mechanisms chosen to foster family choice The details are crucial. Some forms of "vouchers" might indeed have pernicious effects—the greater the pity of Butts's generalities. The structure of the California Initiative for Family Choice is basically simple, but there are complexities. Some are peculiar to California, and not all can be covered here. The initiative begins by favoring the existing public schools with greater financial support (11%) than the new schools. (The initiative has no effect upon private schools that do not wish to participate in the new system.) Two new kinds of schools are created that are quite distinct from either the present public or private schools These are called "independent public schools" (IPS) and "family choice schools" (FCS). Each school is an individual nonprofit corporation—public or private; once formed, schools of each type will operate under a common set of rules, except that the FCS, being privately operated, may teach religion. When I speak of both types together here, I will call them simply "the new schools."

The principal difference between the IPS and FCS is in the way new schools are started. Each independent public school would be created by the decision of a district school board, or of a public college or university. Various incentives would move local boards to create at least some such schools. One incentive is the relaxation of important aspects of education code that restrict public schools; many California educators feel that state mandates about class size, in teacher hiring, and curriculum get in the way of reform and good teaching.

The initiative would free the new schools from much of this heavy regulation. It would not eliminate minimum requirements — the "basics" — but it would keep the legislature from imposing any greater restrictions on curriculum, hiring, and facilities of the new schools than are imposed on private schools today. In California the regulations presently affecting the curriculum and buildings of private schools are much less restrictive than those applying to public schools; and the regulations that concern hiring in private schools are even more flexible.

Private schools and their clients have found such freedom to be good for education; it might be just as good for education in the new schools— public and private. These schools could hire people for their faculties who had not attended the traditional teachers college but were simply excellent teachers. Beyond the three Rs, these new schools could decide what to teach, and they would fully control the style of instruction. No doubt some would concentrate on the basics, some on science, some on the arts; so long as they met today's standard for private schools, they could experiment with different ways to attract and serve families. Since the new schools would be able to operate in the wide range of facilities now approved for private education, their formation and operation would be much more flexible and efficient.

The governance of the new schools could take forms as diverse as those that now flourish among nonprofit corporations in the private sector. The board of directors of a school could be composed exclusively of administration, of teachers, of parents, of public trustees, or any combination of these. It could be run in a tyrannical fashion by a single headmaster. Families, like professionals, have different preferences about how a school is run and who runs it; they would be free to choose the school with a style and government that suits them.

One of the special political features of the initiative is the right of parents in a school district to petition their school board for the formation of independent public schools. If the parents of 100 children (or 30 per grade) petitioned the board for an IPS, the board would be required to honor that request, unless doing so would cause "additional cost... or substantial hardship to other pupils." Since the new schools would in general be less costly, this power of petition would be no empty right. The political process would open up in a new way to the creative energies of families. It is a pity that Professor Butts overlooked this democratic device so congenial to the American tradition of local politics. Note also that the various campuses of the University of California, the state universities, and the community colleges could create a wide variety of new institutions serving the full range of family tastes. Are such schools of choice not "public"?

The "family choice schools" would also be formed as individual nonprofit corporations, but that decision would be made by private groups or individuals. Many of today's private schools would decide to become family choice schools, especially since they would be constitutionally protected from any new regulation of curriculum, hiring, and facilities. Like the IPS, they would operate according to rules designed to support the power of the family. Those rules regarding admissions, tuition and information are especially important and should be described in detail.

Admissions and Pupil Protection

Under the initiative, every family would have the right to enroll its child or children in any of the new schools. Boundaries would be irrelevant, and the cost of transportation would be provided within reasonable limits of distance. The family, not the school, would decide who is admitted, except that single-sex schools would be permitted. The school would, of course, set and control its total size, but if a school's applications exceeded its capacity a state agency would conduct a

lottery among all of its applicants. Children would be entitled to transfer and would carry with them the pro-rated share of their educational entitlement for that year.

The open admissions rule would be tempered in one important respect. Children enrolled in the school before it joined the system would be entitled to a place, as would their siblings; it would be destructive to disrupt such existing connections. This exception concerning enrollment would be one of several devices to make the introduction of choice smooth and orderly. The system would be phased in over a period of six years. When fully in place in 1986, each of the new schools would have open enrollment every year for its beginning grade; in the higher grades, places would open up by transfers and by expansion of the school's capacity. Popular schools would presumably tend to expand or be imitated by others.

The new school could, of course, counsel its applicants; it could for example suggest to a family that the school's curriculum would not suit a particular child. The family might be persuaded to enroll elsewhere or it might not. In any case, it would hold the legal right of entry and the right to fair treatment inside the school. Once enrolled, the child could not be dismissed unless he were a serious behavior problem or unable to benefit academically from the school. In either case, the child would be entitled to legal protection and due process. And for children who were properly dismissed, an appropriate education would be guaranteed; new schools would form to serve just such children. Indeed, there would now be incentive to create schools serving every form of educational need.

Financing and Tuition

The initiative would provide financial support for the traditional public schools much as it is provided today except that all taxes would come from the state level. The use of the local property tax for schools would be eliminated, making the school portion of that tax available for other municipal services if local voters so decided.

The new schools would generate income by attracting families, each of whom would be entitled to a state certificate, redeemable for the full cost of education; its value would be set at 90% of the amount spent upon a similar child in a similar public school. Thus, if the state spent $2,000 on a normal fifth-grader in public school in an urban area, a similar child in a new school in the same area would receive a certificate worth $1,800. The legislature is also encouraged to make the certificates differ in amount according to the needs of special groups of children—the handicapped, the bilingual, those choosing a vocational curriculum, and so forth. Thus a school enrolling a significant number of children with special needs could be financially advantaged. The school could not charge the family extra tuition in any form. However, the legislature could permit differences in spending "so long as the right of every child to enroll in any school remains unaffected by his family's capacity to purchase education." Thus no child could be excluded from any opportunity because of family poverty, but various kinds of additional scholarships could be issued if the legislature saw fit. For example, low income families could be given "education stamps" redeemable for the after school services of tutors in music, the vocations, language or the arts.

Information About Schools

The information system that would be created by the initiative is unique and very important. The legislature would have the duty to assure that "sources independent of any school or school authority" provide adequate information to families about schools. The initiative is based upon respect for the judgment of all parents, but it recognizes that some will have "special information needs." Many will not speak or read English well. Some will be quite unsophisticated about education, since strangers have always decided for them. To help such families raise their level of knowledge about schools, there would not only be independent public information agencies but special grants with which to purchase private counseling services. These services would be available from professionals, independent of any school; their self-interest would be to serve only the family. The provision of reliable information to low-income families would also become an important activity of volunteer agencies, churches, private associations, and family cooperatives.

Each new school would be required to disclose relevant information about itself, including "curriculum and teaching methods, the qualifications of its teachers, and its use of resources." If a school gave false information to families or government agencies, the state certification necessary for it to receive and redeem certificates would be endangered. The information system would be the chief mechanism for monitoring the schools; they would be regulated by expanding consumer knowledge. Beyond the basic requirements the state would not decide what and how the school may teach but only what it must disclose to the public leaving it to the family to make the choice.

Costs and Shifts

The initiative would limit total statewide public spending for schools to the present level of spending adjusted for inflation. This cap would last until 1986. In 1978-79 the public schools of California spent about $9.2 billion dollars on four million children—about $2,300 per child. These figures do not include teachers retirement, depreciation, federal money and other substantial items. Of course spending varies widely from place to place. Some school districts spend about $1,000 per child; others spend $4,000. The average cost of nonpublic schools is probably half that of similar instruction in tax-supported institutions. About 450,000 pupils attend private schools. Perhaps half to two-thirds of these existing nonpublic schools would eventually participate as family choice schools if the initiative became law and an unpredictable number of new family choice schools would also be formed.

Since certificates for the new schools are set at 90% of the cost in public schools, every shift from a public school would represent a saving for the state. Nor should this 10% reaction reduce the quality of education provided; freed of the most oppressive aspects of the education code, the new schools would be able to operate more efficiently. More important, perhaps, since the system would put schools into competition for clientele, there would for the first time be an incentive for the public system itself to economize. Those schools unable to attract students would simply cease to operate. At last unwanted public institutions would have the decency to die.

This does not mean that traditional public schools would disappear. Far from it. They start with enormous advantages including the best and most expensive buildings. In addition, they would receive more money per pupil from the state; and most of them should become stronger as they learned to respond to competition. Many families would prefer the old public school simply because they're close and familiar or because they believe that heavily regulated education is better. In any case, if the old public schools should educate fewer pupils, they will educate them better because their clients will be there by choice.

There would, of course, be shifts in the ways money is spent. As children moved from traditional public schools to the new schools, a great deal less would be spent upon administration of the expensive state-mandated programs and regulations. Some of these savings would be shifted to the new information programs designed to educate parents about the variety of available schools. Some savings probably would be shifted to transportation to get the children to the schools of their choice, although the cost of transportation would depend on the patterns of choice. Most of the savings in administration would simply go into instruction; this would reverse the trend of the last decade, which saw the number of teachers and pupils fall sharply while the number of administrators increased by 10%.

A word should be said about the cost of buildings. In this respect the initiative comes at a fortunate time. There is today a great surplus of buildings in public schools because of population trends and loss of pupils to private schools. This unused space provides the flexibility that is ideal for a system of choice. The initiative empowers the legislature to assist the new schools, where necessary in creating facilities; but such help is available only where there is no appropriate space in other schools. The initiative requires all schools (except the purely private) to make excess space available for rent to other schools at cost; it thus would forbid the wasteful practice of large urban districts refusing to rent empty buildings to private schools for fear of competition.

Finally the initiative would stimulate the modification of federal aid programs to fit the new decentralized family-based system. This would require congressional action but need not increase federal dollar commitments; Congress would simply shift the existing programs to fit the new structure. This could be accomplished by modest adjustments in the federal statutes.

Religion and Ideology

The U. S. Supreme Court has never passed judgment upon any system closely resembling the California Initiative for Family Choice. In striking down various state laws designed to aid sectarian institutions, the justices have explicitly left open the validity of a general system designed to aid all families using both public and private schools There is every reason to think that it would be permissible for family choice schools to teach religion if they wished to do so.

Under the initiative all schools (except the purely private) would have to observe the distinction between teaching and coercion. A curriculum with political or religious content could be required, but no profession of belief or participation in ideological ceremony could be demanded of the student. A few religious schools view this as a barrier to participation. Most of them would welcome nonbelievers under these conditions just as they do today.

Employee Rights

Today teachers unions bargain collectively with their school districts under state law. The initiative would extend the right of collective bargaining to the new schools—public and private—but the bargaining unit for those schools would be the individual school corporation. On the one hand this extends the principle of collective bargaining; on the other it makes organizing more complex. Large and affluent teachers unions tend to prefer to bargain with one large employer rather than with many small units. It appears that some of the leadership of teachers unions will oppose the initiative because of their own institutional interests having nothing to do with the quality of education.

Individual teachers are likely to see things quite differently. Under the initiative their retirement rights and other benefits would be given protection by the legislature. More important, for the teacher who wishes to break the bonds imposed by the education code and for those teachers who might wish to start their own family choice school, the initiative represents a great opportunity. Of course much will depend in the individual case upon the quality of the teacher. Those who have performed well could now be rewarded by their schools in ways that are presently impossible. On the other hand those whose chief merit is seniority might be less well rewarded and encouraged to take up other lines of work.

Conclusion

There is pathos and irony in Freeman Butts's argument. It assumes that given the chance, anyone with good sense would desert the public schools—that the system survives solely by its capacity for economic incarceration. His conclusion? Let no one escape except the rich; subdue the remaining inmates and teach them to prefer their condition. Perfect our servile institutions and spare ordinary families the painful experience of free human decision. This he perceives as the Jeffersonian ideal.

I cannot share this paradoxical view that the brightest hope for the public schools lies in their remaining benign prisons for the lower classes. Most of these schools can survive and prosper—but only if they become a free and open choice for all. The risk they run is real, but it does not lie in the increase of freedom; the enemy they should fear is their reliance upon a captive audience. It can only drive out more of the middle class. The public school will prosper under family choice; indeed it will prosper only under family choice. By respecting the dignity of individuals and families of all income classes, this troubled institution will at last come to deserve the title to which it has so long pretended. It will at last be public.

Vouchers — Solution or Sop?

David Selden

One of today's most controversial issues is the voucher plan —a scheme designed to give students choice of school rather than requiring them to attend schools to which they are assigned. Parents would be given certificates equal to the cost of educating their children and could then spend these certificates in any public or private school with room to accommodate their children.

Opponents of the voucher plan are divided into two camps: those who believe that it will not work and those who believe it will. Those who oppose the voucher plan on grounds of impracticality have found themselves at a serious disadvantage because, a each new detailed objection has been registered, proponents of the plan have added new qualifications and safeguards designed to eliminate the objection. Those who oppose the plan as a matter of principle are raising more fundamental objections. They hold that the voucher plan is a dangerous and divisive proposal which could even destroy the public school system.

Innocence Abroad   Actually, there is no single voucher plan. One of the first to use the term was conservative economist Milton Friedman who was trying to find a way to turn the schools over to private enterprise. Later, Christopher Jencks and his associates at the Harvard Graduate School of Education saw vouchers as a way to bring about educational changes. They were and still are deeply concerned about the failure of American schools to educate underclass students, particularly those who live in the black slums and ghettos of our big cities. Jencks and others observed that while schools in nearby Boston and in other cities are overcrowded and run-down, many middle-class suburbs of those cities have underutilized school facilities.

Furthermore, the voucher advocates took heed of the central finding of the Coleman Report to the effect that the most influential element in a child's education is his social milieu. If such children could be helped to leapfrog out of the city and into suburban schools, they would thus be receiving intrinsically better educational service on the one hand an a more learning-supporting environment on the other.

Jencks and his associates further observed that throughout the nation there are a number of small, highly innovative private schools which are apparently achieving spectacular results. Yet many of these experimental schools live a hand-to-mouth existence. If a way could be found to give such schools financial security, the probability of developing useful, new educational techniques would be increased.

Hence, vouchers. What has happened to the original pure-hearted voucher concept, however, is a classic example of good intentions gone bad.

Mechanical Problems   One of the early probably encountered in making the voucher scheme viable was the obvious fact that putting an urban educational price tag on a poor kid would still leave him unable to afford a suburban school. Therefore, one of the first elements that was added to the concept was that children from poverty slum families would be given added educational green stamps, so that they could afford a more expensive education than they would get if they stayed in their urban attendance districts. This voucher override caveat introduces a vital cop-out right at the outset.

Although educational arguers concede that suburban education is better and that it costs more, they do not concede that *urban* education could be improved if more money were to be spent in the cities. The more vociferous critics of our public schools proceed from the premise that we could educate children if we, (1) really wanted to do a job, and (2) had the right idea about how to teach. They vigorously dispute assertions by teachers and their organizations that well-qualified and well-paid teachers with small classes, reasonable classroom-hour loads, ample remedial assistance, and good physical surroundings have much to do with the quality of instruction. Yet many of these same critics support the voucher plan, despite its initial concession that good education will cost more than we are now spending in slum schools.

Money alone is not a absolute determinant of educational quality. A study by the NAACP in 1969 showed that a large proportion —although not the majority by any means— of so-called compensatory education programs financed under Title I of the Elementary and Secondary Education Act proved to be educationally worthless. On the other hand, it is impossible to effect any large-scale improvement in education without having more money to hire teachers and other personnel and to invest in new schools and equipment. And if more money can be made available for education, it should be spent to improve the public school in the areas of greatest need.

The voucher bounty idea would introduce incentives for operators of private schools and, of course, for suburban school boards. Supporters of the plan pooh-pooh the possibility that the profit motive would stimulate added hucksterism in education. However, unless safeguards against profiteering were carefully drawn and enforced, voucher money would most certainly tempt unscrupulous educational entrepreneurs in the same way that the GI Bill stimulated the growth of all those electronics, watchmaking, and key punch "schools." Most of the victims of those enterprises were ex-servicemen from the underclass who were looking for educational shortcuts. The greater educational need of underclass children and their parents makes them more vulnerable to the blandishments of fly-by-night school operators.

Open Enrollment   The term voucher plan is so catchy that one almost takes for granted that this is something new, but it is not. In the early, liberal, integrationist days following the U.S. Supreme Court's 1954 school desegregation decision, many school districts adopted so-called open enrollment plans. Black children who otherwise would have been attending all-black slum schools were permitted to transfer to other schools if those schools had space to receive them. Many of these plans also provided free busing, again on a voluntary basis. While most of the open enrollment plans were theoretically "two way," it was inevitably black children who rode the bus —a segregating activity in itself.

Most open enrollment plans have been abandoned or have dwindled to insignificance. As a matter of fact, they never did enlist masses of students, and for the most part, the children who rode the bus were those with strong parental support and high motivation. These were the very children who were more likely to succeed regardless of the school they attended. They were also the very children whose presence could have provided stimulation for less striving children in their ghetto schools.

Most observers of the open enrollment plans quickly came to the conclusion that the programs were ineffective in combatting racial segregation and that very little, if any, educational gain resulted.

As an aside, the open enrollment plans, confined mostly to Northern cities, simply proved that a *little* busing would accomplish nothing; the much more extensive busing program now being followed in many Souther cities bears educational promise through its significant effect upon the social mix in schools.

Racism and Politics   Another scheme very close to the voucher idea is "freedom-of-choice," now outlawed by many court decisions. The freedom-of-choice plans were designed to *promote* racial segregation. They were based upon outright subsidies, very similar to vouchers, given to parents to trade in at the "school of their choice." Of course, black parents were not permitted to use their vouchers at white schools.

The original proponents of vouchers abhor racial discrimination, and they have again proposed mechanical regulations which would supposedly guard against use of the vouchers to promote freedom-of-choice academics. For instance, they would require that at least 25 percent of the student population be of a minority ethnic group before a school would be eligible to receive voucher students.

The proposed 25 percent safeguard illustrates another basis problem of the voucher idea. Since the plan's success seems to depend, in part at least, on federal aid, one can readily see the shape of the future. The percentage figure would loom as a major proving ground over which pro and con lobbyists would clash, just as they now struggle to influence percentages in taxes, tariffs, and oil depletion allowances.

Even if Congress passed a proper percentage, however, it still would have to be enforced. Ironically, some of those who purport to fear the specter of federal intervention in local affairs are also advocating the use of vouchers, not recognizing, presumably, the massive federal regulatory apparatus which would be necessary to prevent abuse.

European Experience   School finance systems very similar to vouchers have been in use in a number of European countries for many decades. In Belgium, Holland, and Denmark, for instance, children receive equal subsidies, regardless of the sponsorship of the school they attend —public, private, nonsectarian, or religious. Contrary to the objections usually raised, the effects of government subsidies have been far from catastrophic. While the percentage of students at religious-sponsored schools has increased somewhat, the proportion now seems to be stabilized. Furthermore, apparently the religious schools are becoming less and less sectarian and more and more like the public schools. It is predicted that there will be very little difference between the two typed of schools in five to ten years.

The European system, however, couples close supervision by the state with certain standard requirements —in staffing and equipment, for instance— which all schools must meet. Of course, all schools must teach a standard curriculum prescribed by the state, and there are single national teacher-salary schedules and pension systems.

It cannot be said that public subsidy of private schools creates illiberal, divided, and strife-torn societies, since the three countries under discussion are among the most liberal and peaceful in the world. But it must be noted that economic and social conditions in those countries differ greatly from those in the United States. First, there is no large economically deprived underclass in Belgium, Holland, or Denmark. Second, there is no large racially isolated group. Third, government is much simpler and more centralized. What seems to have become acceptable in small, middle-class, ethnically homogeneous countries under strong centralized control or supervision would not necessarily be applicable to the United States with its huge problems and deep unresolved racial, sectional, and religious antagonisms.

Incidentally, France does *not* subsidize private schools.

Religious Warfare   The dynamite which lies ready for detonation just below the surface of the voucher controversy is the growing issue of public support for religious-related schools. At several meetings called by the sponsors of the voucher plan in an effort to "clarify" the situation, the line-up of religious teams was as apparent as if they had worn colored jerseys. On the one side were those Jewish and Protestant organizations traditionally zealous in maintaining the principle of separation of church and state. On the other side were the Catholic organizations and a scattering of other denominations trying desperately to save their church-related school systems. Even though Jencks and company say that vouchers would not be used to any great extent to solve the financial plight of the church schools, spokesmen for those institutions quite obviously think otherwise.

Jencks thinks that the church schools would have a hard time meeting his 25 percent minority race qualification. Church spokesmen, however, feel that with federal support tuition for such schools could be reduced and the number of "free" students could be greatly increased, thus helping to improve racial integration in such schools and at the same time preventing their possible collapse. The religious advocates of vouchers point out that church-related schools now enroll hundreds of thousands of children who otherwise would be the responsibility of the public system. Unless these schools receive financial aid, they will be forced to curtail operations and send students flooding into already overcrowded public facilities. Vouchers seem to offer a way out.

The tuition subsidy plan now in use in New York state, which provides state funds to pay for college students to attend institutions of their choice, whether public or private, seems to be in conformity with constitutional requirements. Other scholarship plans using federal funds have also been in existence for many years without arousing successful legal objection. Even so, introduction of the voucher plan is almost certain to result in speedy legal challenge by its opponents on grounds of separation of church and state.

Several cases now in the judicial works will have a bearing on the legal status of vouchers. One of these is *Flask v. Garden,* which challenges the use of federal funds to pay for educational services conducted in religious-sponsored schools under Title I of ESEA. If the courts should decide that the use of funds in this way is unconstitutional, the legality of the voucher concept so far as the religious-related schools are concerned would be dubious indeed.

The other test case is *Lemon v. Kurtzman.* Pennsylvania now provides state aid directly to private schools —most of them church-related. A number of organizations have filed amicus briefs in opposition to the use of funds for such a purpose, but U.S. Attorney General John Mitchell announced in September, 1970, that his department would file an amicus brief on the side of the state, thus declaring in favor of such subsidies.

Polarizer   The Nixon Administration has not been slow to realize the political potentialities in the voucher controversy. Donald Rumsfeld, who was appointed by the President to become Director of the Office of Economic Opportunity (presumably on the basis that since he voted against every bill which created OEO he could not be accused of favoritism), started down the Spiro Agnew polarization trail in 1970. Rumsfield was seeking quite obviously to exploit another of those neat splitters which have become the hallmark of the current administration's political style.

By pushing the voucher plan, Rumsfield attached teachers, who are almost universally opposed, and the "liberal elements" who favor strict separation of church and state. At the same time, he declared himself in support of people who, according to cynical political analysis, are thought to be in the hard-hat category. He also gave aid and comfort to people who secretly hope vouchers will lead to a revival of the Southern freedom-of-choice plans.

In promoting the voucher plan, Rumsfeld displayed a flair for half-truths. In a speech given September 23, 1970, before the San Francisco Chamber of Commerce "Urban Roundtable," he first detailed the all too obvious defects and shortcomings of our current system of education. Then he totaled up all the money spent by all levels of government on education. In the same paragraph he threw in an observation —unsupported— that "the pupil-teacher ratio is lower today than ever in the nation's history."

What Rumsfeld left out was that the percentage of gross national product for education remained practically constant for decades and that "pupil-teacher ratio" is an almost meaningless figure. Furthermore, if the ratio has gone down, how much has it decreased? A page later in the same speech, he rejected the idea that the amount of money spent on education has much to do with the quality of education. What we need, he said, are new ideas, and he charged that the American Federation of Teachers and other teacher organizations don't want any new ideas, since they are against the voucher plan and have been against other "experiments" launched under the aegis of the OEO.

Quoting directly from Rumsfeld remarks, he stated: "They [teacher interest groups] charge that money, not new approaches, is the answer to improving educational skills." He then went on to quote President Nixon, "When we get more education for the dollar, we'll start asking for more dollars for education."

As a matter of fact, the voucher plan does not add a single new educational technique, nor can it guarantee that giving pupils more mobility will result in the development of new techniques.

Lizard or Dragon?   One of the chief objections which can be leveled fairly at the voucher idea is that it, like so many catchy educational schemes, tends to divert attention from the real and basic needs of children and the schools. Whether education is carried on by people —teachers and paraprofessionals— or by machines watched over by people, there *is* a relationship between cost and educational effort.

No one would deny that it is possible to waste school money, but all other things being equal —the educability of students, the intelligence of teachers and administrators, the social milieu in which the school must operate— the more money you spend on education, the more education is produced. It is silly, if not malicious, to suggest that money-starve school systems will have "to do better" before the great white fathers in Washington will give them more support.

Like a bright, shiny, quick-moving lizard running over a rotting log, the voucher scheme diverts our attention from the decay underneath. But what will we do if Mr. Jencks' entertaining little lizard grows up to be a fire-breathing dragon?

Vouchers: A Critic Changes His Mind
David Selden

Kids like them, teachers like them, parents like them —even I've come to like the vouchers in Alum Rock. When I was president of the American Federation of Teachers, I opposed vouchers categorically, but two visits to Alum Rock and two years of watching from the sidelines convinced me that, under the right circumstances, vouchers might open the door to a new form of learning that could go far toward humanizing the American elementary school.

Alum Rock, where the nation's first voucher experiment got under way two years ago, is not one of those well-to-do suburban districts where almost any innovation is bound to succeed. The school district lies on the eastern edge of San Jose, Calif. It is a flat, sometimes drab area of small, single-family homes, open land, and shopping centers. Many of the homes are empty now, some with foreclosure notices tacked to their doors.

There aren't many affluent people in Alum Rock. Most are poor or lower middle-class. Half of the children qualify for Title I assistance under the Elementary and Secondary Education Act. The racial-ethnic mix is roughly half Mexican-American, with the rest blacks, whites and a sprinkling of Asian-Americans.

When I first visited Alum Rock in 1973, a few months after the voucher program started, I was prepared to be critical, to look for flaws. I had been present at a meeting in Washington when Christopher Jencks unveiled his voucher plan, and I hadn't liked what I heard. Subsequently, I had written two highly critical articles about the Jencks proposal and vouchers in general.

VOUCHER ORIGINS. Some of my objections went back to the original proposal by Economist Milton Friedman in his book "Capitalism and Freedom", which suggested that the way to get government out of the education business was to give parents a check or "voucher" for what if would cost to educate each child and let the parents buy schooling on the open market. When the book was published in 1962, virtually nobody took seriously his scheme for turning education over to private enterprise.

Seven or eight years later, however, Jencks and his associates from the

Cambridge-based Center for the Study of Public Policy picked up the voucher idea as a way to permit children in the big-city black ghettos to escape the admittedly inferior schools in their neighborhoods. The Jencks model, more elaborate than the original described by Friedman, called for a bonus or "compensatory voucher " for children from poor families- to induce middle-class schools to admit them.

The Alum Rock project, now sponsored by the National Institute of Education, used compensatory vouchers for a different purpose. The compensatory vouchers the kids "carry" are pooled to provide added materials and educational services. Actually, nobody physically carries a voucher anymore - everything is done through bookkeeping - although parents are given paper certificates at the beginning of each year.

When Jencks revealed his voucher plan, the audience at the Office of Education included 50 or more representatives of organizations interested in education, many of them at the liberal end of the political spectrum. There was a stunned silence when Jencks finished his presentation.

Afterward I voiced what was probably going through the minds of many others. I reminded Jencks and federal government representatives that most of those present had spent many years trying to improve public schools and that we resented attempts to turn education over to private enterprise.

Over the next year I zeroed in on two objections to vouchers. I thought they would introduce "hucksterism" into education and that they also would violate the doctrine of separation of church and state. Neither has happened at Alum Rock.

When I last visited Alum Rock, earlier this year, the walls inside the schools were covered with posters, charts, and artwork done by the children, who reflect the informality of their school environment. Not even in the few "traditional" classrooms I observed were the children all doing the same thing at the same time. Yet there was no sense of disorder. The students all seemed to be involved in some activity in which they were genuinely interested.

The keynote was action. Everyone - kids, teachers, aides, specialists - seemed to be doing something. In this respect the so-called voucher schools were no different from any good, open classroom activity-oriented school. Behind it all, however, was a confidence that something worthwhile and good really was happening.

MINISCHOOLS. The minischool concept is the key to the success of the Alum Rock project. Although the minischool concept is not unique, of course, what gives the idea its individuality at Alum Rock is the voucher overlay. Originally, vouchers were proposed as a way to permit parents to choose from six schools, each of which would offer a separate and distinct style of education.

In actuality, devising six distinctively different but educationally valid designs proved impossible. The solution was to allow any group of teachers within a school to design a program and carry it through. Thus were born the minischools. Kids can choose any of 54 minischools until the school is filled, and they can change programs in mid-term, too. Each of Alum Rock's 14 participating elementary schools offers two to five minischool programs, focused around a theme such as basic skills, self-expression, or career arts.

They are run by teachers, with heavy parental involvement; the teachers are the ones who decide how the compensatory voucher money will be spent. They can spend the funds on materials or personnel, virtually without restriction. This emphasis on teacher control is the main reason teachers generally favor the plan.

PARENT INVOLVEMENT. The voucher concept is based on the idea that parents should have the right to determine the kind of schooling their children get.

I attended a meeting of a parents council while I was in Alum Rock. It was a refreshing change from other parents meetings I've attended. The principal wasn't even there, and school aides, who can serve on the councils, are not allowed to dominate them. Discussion came primarily from parents, and there were none of the timid questions frequently asked at such meetings. The discussion itself was practical and businesslike, dealing with such matters as the school lunch, not merely fund-raising and social events.

Great effort is made to bring parents into the school operation. The voucher project employs parent counselors, many of them bilingual, who are constantly out in the community. Parents also are employed as instructional aides. Parents I talked with were proud of their schools and their part in helping make them work.

DOES IT WORK? How do students in Alum Rock stack up on standardized achievement tests? As nearly as we can tell, after two years of the voucher plan, they are doing as well as might have been expected. After eight months they were holding their own on the Metropolitan Achievement Tests. I was told unofficially that scores will be even better on the tests given a year later, although the results have not yet been released.

Alum Rock used an "expected progress" approach to measuring cognitive achievement. That is, the kids are tested at the beginning of the, or at the end of the previous year, and eight months are added to the score. The child is expected to have learned at least that much when he takes the tests again in the spring.

Although the teachers involved are highly supportive of the plan, one national teacher leader, on the basis of first-year test scores, has called the project a failure. I think this is unfair. For decades, teachers have fought against judging teacher and school performance on the basis of pupil test scores. We should not compromise that stand in order to take a few cheap shots at a program that has many things to recommend it.

The big pluses in Alum Rock are its emphasis on teacher control, its diversity, and its encouragement of good community relation. Maybe these gains could have been achieved without vouchers. (Watching William Jefferds, Alum Rock's creative superintendent, in action gave me the impression that he could probably make any system work.) But as developed in Alum Rock, vouchers have encouraged the kind of innovation and creativity that schools, children and teachers need.

With School Vouchers Come Hucksters
Albert Shanker

Earlier this year there was a petition campaign in California for a referendum on school vouchers. The campaign failed this year, but supporters have announced that they will try again.

There have been a number of different voucher proposals. Basically, most of the schemes would give parents a voucher or check for the amount needed to pay for the cost of providing education in a public school, but parents could use the voucher to pay for educating their children at private or parochial schools as well.

If vouchers were to go into effect, there would be competition among schools in much the same way as there is now competition among toothpaste companies, auto manufactures and department stores. Chances are pretty good that schools would advertise in newspapers and magazines and over radio and television. Some enterprising schools might offer gifts to newly enrolling students in much the same way that savings banks offer such gifts to new depositors. Or, just as savings banks offer gifts to current account holders for bringing in a new depositor, students might be offered rewards for enrolling their friends!

The public can get a pretty good idea of what newspaper advertisements by the voucher schools would look like from a full-page ad that was in the *Wall Street Journal* last April 24 and in full color over four pages in the April 28 issue of *Newsweek.*. The ad, headlined "Free the Children," was part of a series paid for by the Smith Kline Corporation. An earlier ad in the series was the subject of my column last December 16. That ad was headlined "Minimum Wage, Maximum Folly." In it Smith Kline argued that minority youngsters are unable to find work because their work is not worth the minimum wage so employers who have a choice of hiring someone else at the same rate. We should get rid of the minimum wage so employers can hire minority youth for less, the advertisement argued.

Like the earlier ad which featured a picture of and editorial copy by black economist Walter E. Williams, the new one features Marva N. Collins, a black teacher who runs a private school in Chicago. According to the ad, Marva Collins was a public school teacher, became frustrated with the public schools and founded the Westside Preparatory School. There, the ad claims, some 34 children who were previously "written off as 'retarded' or 'learning disabled' are proving that only the schools are disabled.... To see 'retarded' seven- and twelve-year-olds expound on Thoreau, Dante, Aristotle and Chaucer is humbling. To know that an ill-funded one-room school has turned down a $16,000 federal grant, in order to maintain its independence, its magnificent."

That's the message. The public schools fail. Marva Collins performs miracles with children who would fail in public school. What we need "instead of government-run schools" are publicly-funded vouchers so that parents can afford to send their children to Marva Collins's school, or others like it.

The problem with the ad is that the claims made in it are mere claims. There is no evidence presented. When Marva Collins taught at Delano Elementary school, a public school with a representative group of neighborhood children, her students did not achieve higher reading scores than any other classes in school. According to colleagues, she had the normal discipline problems, and her classes were no more orderly than others. But then, after she left Delano and started her own school, miracles were performed by the same teacher with the same children, it's claimed. How? Is she using some new and special techniques? If so, and if they are indeed successful, why not share them with other teachers?

Are Collins's students really "the same"? Some of her students have returned to public school. They still show low reading achievement. Are her school's average scores raised by getting rid of poor achievers? Is she only accepting and retaining better students? Are the students really learning Plato, Aristotle, Dante -- learning to read, think, discuss? Or are the students merely memorizing passages by rote? What reading tests are being used to measure the success of Collins and her school? Who administers the tests? What precautions are being taken to assure that claimed progress is real?

In the worlds of commercial products, there are government agencies which are obliged to protect the public against false claims by advertiser and manufacturers. There are consumer magazines and testing agencies which evaluate products and claims. And government regulations require the public schools to record and report virtually everything about their students' achievement -- or lack of it. But, in the world of private and parochial school education, there are few if any of these protections. A retired public school teacher who now teaches in private schools wrote to me recently that he and his colleagues "wonder how some of the private schools have been able obtain certification," since the operating philosophy seems to be to tell parents what they want to hear. One of the rules, he says, is: "Don't be too harsh in your comments on report cards. A displeased parent may withdraw the pupil from the school. At the end of the term, promote everybody.... Remember, a satisfied customer is the best advertisement for your school."

Of course, this does not mean that public schools are all excellent--they are not. Or that private schools are all bad and practice deception--clearly not so. We should beware of false advertising in education just as we are elsewhere. Those who claim that public schools are all bad--and that private schools are *the* answer--are clearly wrong. There is a place for private schools in our society, but those claims should not be pressed to the point where public schools are destroyed.

If vouchers are adopted, and parents are faced with claims and counterclaims of school success--without the usual consumer protection--*caveat emptor*. Only in this case, instead of the loss of a few dollars on a poor product, what may be lost is a child's future.

If Teachers Get Choices......Shouldn't Parents?

Albert Shanker

School people are often cynical. They've been around long enough to know that every few years a new idea comes along that's supposed to cure all of our educational ills. They're expected to run with each new remedy even before it has had a trial run or evaluation, and if they raise even a friendly concern or question about the new cure-all idea, they're called defenders of the status quo or worse. To add injury to insult, when the cure-all doesn't live up to its sales pitch (which it never does), it's the school people who are blamed and left to clean up the mess. It's little wonder, then, that the first reaction many school people have to a hot new idea is to find all the reasons why that idea can't and won't work.

Many school people look at public school choice, our latest cure-all, in just this way. They have lots of legitimate questions about choice and find their concerns being dismissed. They know that there's lots of irresponsible hype around choice, which tells them that choice is just another fad that will come and go without doing much good and perhaps even doing some harm.

This attitude is understandable but it's unfortunate. Our schools are in bad shape. Changes, big changes, are needed. Public school choice, by itself, is not the big change we need. But it may be that we can't get the big changes we need without choice.

Take the example of school-based management/shared decision making - one of the most positive recent developments in school reform. The idea is simple: Stop running schools like a centralized bureaucracy in which all orders come from above. Encourage individual schools to take initiative and think through what works or does not work for their students. Let them run themselves on the basis of these judgments instead of following uniform rules and regulations that no longer connect with real schools and children.

But in order for this to happen, local and state school boards will either have to repeal hundreds of regulations or be willing to grant individual schools exemptions from these regulations. Similarly, teacher unions will need to adopt procedures to allow the faculties of individual schools to modify or lift contractual rules that are hindering rather than helping their professional goals. This needs to be done because if all the current rules and regulations are kept in force, no school can break out of the bureaucratic lockstep, and school-based management/shared decision making will be just another empty public-relations phrase.

But will school management and unions be willing and able to do this? Probably not so long as students (and teachers) are compelled to remain in their assigned schools. How, for example, would school authorities handle parent complaints? When schools are all subject to the same requirements and do things pretty much the same, the answer is easy. The school official tells the parent, "I'm sorry you don't like this particular policy or practice, but we decided that this way was the best for everybody. They're not doing anything different in your child's school. That's the way it's done in all our schools."

But what if that particular school system had adopted school-based management/shared decision making? What if the parent complained about something being done in her child's school that was different from what was being done elsewhere?

The school official might answer, "According to the best new management and educational thinking, it's best to have school decisions made by the people at the individual school level. No one really is sure of what gets kids to be successful, so each of our schools is looking for answers and trying different things."

What if the parent persists, " I don't like what they're trying in my child's school. And if all the schools are doing things differently, what right do you have to force my kid to go to a school that I don't like? As long as all the schools operated under the same rules and regulations, I didn't question you when you told me where my kid had to go. But if principals and teachers can now choose to do things in very different ways, why can't I, a parent, have a choice about which of these different schools I want for my child?" Why not indeed?

School people who view school-based management/shared decision making as their first real opportunity to make some real changes in their schools should be prepared to give parents their first real opportunity to choose their child's public school. We can't force parents to try something different and unproven for their children if they don't want to, even if we believe that the old way of doing things wasn't doing their children much good. We can't say school people should be allowed to exercise judgment and deny that to parents. And if we do, we shouldn't be surprised if school authorities call a halt to school change efforts the first time a parent complains.

By the same token, choice proponents have to stop talking as if choice, by itself, will cause schools to improve. It won't - unless schools have a real opportunity to redesign themselves. That opportunity means school-based management/shared decision-making. This, in turn, means a mutual willingness on the part of school management and unions to get out of the business of telling people at the school level how and when to do things (except when it comes to issues like health, safety, civil rights and student and employee exploitation).

State and local school boards should set goals, provide incentives and monitor progress. They should empower school-level professionals to invent much better ways of educating students and hold them accountable. Never again should we hear professional say," I think this would work, but they wouldn't let me do it." But the only way school boards will ever consider such bold moves is if they are politically shielded, if they can say to complaining parents, "We respect what they're doing in that school, but if you don't like it you can take your child to a different school."

There needs to be a marriage between public school choice and school-based management/shared decision making if either one of them is going to work.

Educational Vouchers: Regulating
Their Efficiency and Effectiveness

Arthur E. Wise and Linda Darling-Hammond

From the time of Adam Smith to the time of Ronald Reagan, the idea of injecting market forces into public education has fascinated economists, reformers, and politicians. Competition and choice to be promoted by educational vouchers or tuition tax credits are concepts periodically advanced to improve education. Often proposed, frequently reinvented, and never fully tested, vouchers and tax credits embody theory and rhetoric that can be seductive. As recently as winter 1983, the Reagan administration proposed converting federal compensatory aid into vouchers. And as recently as spring 1983 the Senate once again was considering tuition tax credits. At this writing, they are plans whose time has not come. We can be sure, however, that they embody ideas whose time for being proposed will come again . . . and again.

Proponents of vouchers and tax credits argue that a competitive market approach to the provision of schooling will increase school quality—or at least parental satisfaction with their children's schools—and improve the efficiency of public spending on education. Their arguments are directed at the perceived shortcomings of public school systems and are built on assumptions about how the introduction of private market mechanisms will overcome these problems. Because there has been no true test of vouchers, we are left to examine the advocates' predictions in the light of historical and contemporary knowledge about schooling in America.

The public schools have evolved to their current form to accommodate various forces: legislative desire for financial accountability, state interest in prescribing minimal equity and quality standards, interest group pressures, and more. The forces have shaped a school system that serves public and personal interests through a bureaucratic (somewhat centralized, somewhat uniform) apparatus. To believe that the forces that have shaped American education will disappear with the introduction of vouchers is naive. Indeed, some underlying pressures will be exacerbated by vouchers. Hence, we must anticipate that these forces will generate legislation, regulation, and bureaucratization intended by the political system to control education. The unknown factor is the extent to which market accountability will substitute for bureaucratic accountability in the political system. Against this unknown factor must be arrayed another unknown. How much more (or less) will the political system regulate private providers than it has its publicly elected providers?

The Goals of Education

One fundamental outcome assumed by voucher advocates is that under any voucher plan the state will have less control over education and, conversely, parents will have more choice over the type of education their children will receive. An extension of this reasoning leads to another presumed outcome: that the education received will serve the best interests of the child. Below we examine these assumptions, along with the assertion that a voucher system will lead to more efficient and effective delivery of educational services. We explore the questions of efficiency and effectiveness with respect to four goals of education important for the state and a fifth goal important for individual consumers:

(1) socialization to a common culture;
(2) inculcation of democratic values and preparation for exercising the full rights of citizenship;
(3) preparation of students for further education, training, and occupational life;
(4) equal opportunity; and
(5) provision of education in the best interests of the child.

The degree to which each of these goals is attainable by the workings of the marketplace will greatly influence the extent to which state control over education may be relinquished.

Socialization and Preparation for Citizenship

We consider the goals of socialization and preparation for citizenship jointly because they often are viewed as linked. As Levin (1979) notes:

> A major function of the public schools is the transmission of a common language, heritage, set of values, and knowledge that are necessary for appropriate political functioning in our democratic society. (p. 15)

The common curriculum and a (not always realized) commitment to heterogeneity of student populations are efforts of the public schools to meet these goals. Clearly, the marketplace freely operating will not produce either common teachings or heterogeneity in those who are taught. The primary appeal of vouchers is that they would allow those whose philosophical, pedagogical, political, or religious views differ to band together in schools that satisfy their tastes along any of these dimensions.

But a common educational experience is not, in the minds of some voucher proponents, necessarily linked to the ability of students to later function in a democratic society. Coons and Sugarman (1978) argue that the public schools, because they aim to socialize children in a particular way, can never be neutral and, therefore, deprive the student of opportunities to develop autonomy, a desirable quality in democratic citizens. Family choice schools would foster autonomy, they say, because "there may be a linkage between tribal ways and the path to independent moral judgment .... Even where particular values seem narrow and one-sided, a child's engagement with them at a crucial stage in his development might secure his allegiance to that ideal of human reciprocity which is indispensable to our view of autonomy" (p. 35).

Thus, they dispense with the goal of socialization to a common culture by arguing its irrelevance to preparation for democratic life. There seems little dispute that an unregulated voucher scheme would be an ineffective and inefficient means for socializing children to a common culture and set of values. Were there sufficient public concern about this likely consequence, regulations prescribing certain common subject matter or course content would certainly emerge. Many states already regulate private schools in this manner for this reason, although requirements are generally minimal (Lines, 1982). Whether state restraint in this regard is because the spending of state funds is not at stake is a question we treat later.

Some argue that the socialization functions of schooling are among the oppressive, essentially undemocratic mechanisms of the corporate state that Americans are (or should be) ready to cast aside (see, generally, Carnoy, 1975). That argument, whatever its validity, does not allow us to dispense so easily with the question of what education will best prepare students for full political participation in the society. To Coons and Sugarman's not ineluctable argument for autonomy we may counterpose Levin's argument for tolerance as a precondition to political competence.[1] Levin (1979) observes that the tolerance toward dissenting viewpoints that is necessary "for a democracy in which controversial issues must be addressed and resolved continually" (p. 17) emerges from opportunities for exposure to constructive conflict and controversy. Such exposure seems unlikely in a system where parents choose schools that reinforce their own views.

We cannot resolve here the questions of whether autonomy or tolerance is more important for political preparation or empowerment, whether the two are related to each other, or whether either is more or less likely in a world of family choice schools. We can, however, move beyond the issue of what values are explicitly taught or addressed in schools (and what their effects may be) to the issue of what group of students receives the teaching. As James (1982) notes:

> The latter [issue] involves deciding what is the most legitimate criterion by which to organize children for learning basic skills and for entering the economy, the democratic polity, and adult society .... Our rules for bringing students together in schools are a political matter that precedes pedagogy and policy .... Schools teach some of the most deep-seated and lasting lessons of social life by the ways in which they bring children together, regardless of what is taught in the classroom. It could hardly be otherwise, since patterns of inclusion reflect quite accurately the school's relation to community and society .... This is true because it is through direct experience that children learn about the conventional rules of human association in their society .... Whatever else children learn in school, they learn about democracy as the word is to be understood where they live. (p. 609, italics in original)

If we accept that there is a relationship between demonstrated inclusiveness and democratic understanding, we must conclude that where bureaucratic efforts to stem exclusion have only partially succeeded at providing children with an experience of inclusive democracy, market mechanisms are sure to fail. The decades of controversy over segregation along lines of social class, ethnicity, ability, gender, and physical/mental health will not evaporate with the introduction of family choice. Some families' choices will then, as now, result in the exclusion of others. No recourse will exist for those excluded unless the market is regulated. The question is not only one of equal access, which we treat more fully below, but of the state's interest in encouraging those who would not prefer to be grouped together to nonetheless share a collective association. Even with substantial regulation of financial supplementation and access, vouchers unlikely would prove a more efficient or effective means of promoting a democratic understanding based on inclusiveness than do publicly governed means for associating children. In fact, to the extent that regulation of vouchers seeks to counteract preferences for private association, the very foundation of the voucher concept is weakened.

Preparation for Further Education, Training, and Occupational Life

The preceding criteria for evaluating vouchers are based on a view of education as primarily a public good. If we meet voucher proponents on their own ground, we must also give considerable weight to the private benefits of education. Although academic preparation serves both public and private needs, it is far easier justified as a benefit to the individual than are the social and political objectives discussed above.

One of the generally offered rationales for vouchers is that the competition they will induce will lead to greater educational quality. There are several possible definitions for this imprecise term:

(1) The quantity of educational resources available in a school;

(2) the educational processes employed in a school;

(3) the extent to which education results in the attainment of specified outcomes or competencies;

(4) the extent to which education results in the development of those aspects of a student's potential desired by the student or his or her family.

Some voucher proponents would leave all these elements of quality to the marketplace, relying on family choice to support the better schools and to eliminate the less desirable ones. The eventual emergence of better quality, in this view, depends on (1) a closeness between producers and consumers so that preferences can be translated into services, (2) the existence of the "perfect information" system that economists are so fond of assuming, (3) equal access to good quality schools (however defined), and (4) a consonance among public wants, public needs, and available products (Arons, 1971). Pacheco (1980) argues that

> [I]t is a fundamental mistake to equate the presence of alternatives with either higher quality or what the public wants. It may be a serious mistake to equate public wants with public needs. All that might be guaranteed by a voucher scheme is that some sort of educational options would exist, not necessarily those that families want or need. Like commercial TV, the public may be faced with a plethora of 'alternatives,' none of which are particularly good or attractive. (p. 24)

In the worst case scenario, unregulated vouchers could result in at least certain classes of parents not being able to secure the quality of education they want for their children. This would be true under the various definitions of quality if the entire voucher system were to be underfunded by the state, if parents did not have adequate information to make sound decisions about school options, if the marketplace did not produce desired educational options in all neighborhoods, or if the educational resources, processes, or philosophies selected by parents were not to result in the learning outcomes they desire. Furthermore, if tuition and admissions policies are unregulated, low-income parents and those parents of children with whatever the excluded characteristics might be from schools practicing selective admissions (ability, gender, ethnicity, language dominance, etc.) would have fewer opportunities to choose the quality of education they want for their children. To avoid any one of these potentially undesirable consequences, the state would have to become involved in policies about the state financing and private supplementation of vouchers, the extent and accuracy of the information system for parents, the location of educational alternatives of various types, the technology of education, and/or the admissions policies of schools.[2]

The question still remaining is whether market accountability will serve to satisfy public needs to know whether children are being adequately prepared for further education, training, and occupational life. Will parents know when adequate preparation is being offered? Will they have options when they are dissatisfied? Will their individual decisions taken collectively satisfy the state's needs for an educated citizenry? The state very likely will want to exercise some control over this aspect of accountability. Many states already require that private schools meet some of the course requirements of the public school system. In addition, many states have enacted minimum competency tests to ensure that public school students are adequately prepared. The notion that these tests or other standardized achievement tests might be used to measure the quality of private (as well as public) schools has been advanced by some voucher advocates and others concerned with preventing state regulation of the curricula of private schools (e.g., see Coons & Sugarman, 1978; Lines, 1982). Such outcome measures, they reason, might serve as a substitute for other, more intrusive, accountability measures.

There are, of course, many potential problems with this solution to the problem of knowing whether voucher schools are effective. First, the more difficult and extensive tests are, the more likely they are to drive the curriculum in all schools. To the extent that they homogenize curricula and, perhaps, even teaching methods, they undermine the diversity that vouchers are meant to offer. If the tests are minimal, on the other hand, they will not be very informative to those who want to know how effective the schools are. There is the additional possibility, of course, that such tests are not the best indicators of the quality of education, or that they even undermine the pursuit of other educational goals.

There is another problem with the use of test scores as a substitute for other measures of school quality. If people accept such a measure as an accurate indicator of what the school does, the perceptions of school quality as an extension of student body composition that have hampered integration efforts along all the dimensions discussed earlier would be strengthened. The segregative effects of such perceptions would be exacerbated. Schools that serve low-achieving students would be viewed as inadequate institutions. Institutions would have little incentive to locate in neighborhoods where students have been ill served in the past, or to accept such students as part of the student body.

The alternatives that exist require either regulation of voucher schools in the ways we've mentioned or faith that parents will have adequate information to choose wisely, adequate options to choose from, and that their decisions will somehow converge with the state's definition of an adequately educated citizenry. At the nexus of the argument for vouchers, though, is the concept that the parents' choice of an education serving the best interests of the child need not converge with state goals. There is also a nebulous quality to the concept of equal opportunity incorporated into voucher schemes. Can the parents' view of the best interests of each child be served while equal opportunity is also ensured? Below we examine how the dialectic between Green's "best" and "equal" principles might be framed under vouchers.

Equal Opportunity and Best Interests of the Child

There are two major ways in which the "best" and "equal" principles might collide under vouchers. One is if a parent's definition of what is best for his or her child encompasses an educational setting that, by its nature, must exclude some other children. The other is if a parent's definition of what is best for his or her child limits the child's own opportunities according to some other, possibly valid, definition. The first instance where the dialectic comes into play poses questions of equal access. The second poses the more fundamental question of who knows what serves the best interests of the child.

The question of equal access is addressed in part in the preceding section. It might be resolved in part by providing equal vouchers with no private supplementation (or vouchers scaled to financial or educational need), requiring an extensive information system, providing free transportation, and requiring nondiscriminatory admissions. However, no voucher scheme envisions totally open admissions or equal educational opportunity as it has come to be defined in the public sphere. To require exclusive preparatory schools to admit any student, for example, would contravene the notions of institutional diversity and rights of private association that undergird voucher conceptions. Furthermore, to require all voucher schools to provide services to the handicapped or to limited English-speaking students—in the way that courts have defined programmatic equal access—would divert many schools from what they see as their institutional mission and would visit upon the private sector much of the regulation that some feel has impaired the efficiency of the public sector.

Voucher proponents would leave the task of educating students who don't fit in elsewhere to the public schools or to new voucher schools that might emerge to fill their particular needs. Given the fact that combined public and private services in lower-income neighborhoods have been found over and over again to be both quantitatively and qualitatively inadequate (e.g., see Dimond, Chamberlain, & Hillyard, 1978; Rich, 1979), we find it difficult to swallow the assumption that equal opportunity will be better served by the marketplace than it has been (however haltingly) served by public efforts. Were a voucher scheme to emerge with a provision that guaranteed access to the capital needed to start schools where they were needed, we might choke a little less on the equal opportunity assumption. We would still, however, have to grapple with the substantive aspects of equal opportunity that touch upon different notions of the best interests of the child.

Arguing that parents may not always choose education that serves the best interests of their children has a paternalistic ring to it that is uncomfortable. Nonetheless we advance this argument because it is not entirely clear that the appeal of family choice is grounded in a completely realistic view of families or of the social good. The family choice approach is based on assumptions that parents always have the best interests of their children at the forefront of their concerns; that parents know what type of education will serve those interests; and that parents have the information and access necessary for them to select the education they seek.

While most parents want what is best for their children, parents vary in the amount of time, attention, and expertise they can bring to bear on educational and other decisions pertaining to their children. Reliance on the family as the single best entity for pursuing the child's welfare is as dangerously one-sided as relying solely on public institutions or officers to be caring and knowledgeable about what the child needs. Parents may not always recognize their children's potential. And parents may not know how to choose an educational experience that will fulfill their children's potential.

If we can assume that some means for translating professional knowledge to parents can be devised, we must return to the question of whether parents will be empowered by enough information about school choices and by access to schools of their choice to act on decisions they have made. Will parents' well-informed choices in the best interests of their children be met by a responsive, honest, informative, and equally accessible marketplace? Is a voucher sufficient empowerment absent other forms of accountability? Without many of the safeguards we have discussed, we would have to say "probably not." While some diversity would undoubtedly be encouraged by vouchers, with benefits for many children and parents, those who are ill informed, who are unwilling or unable to "shop around," or who are barred by geography or personal characteristics from the schools they would otherwise choose will not reap the benefits of the new marketplace.

This outcome might seem little different from what many parents and children experience in the current, largely public educational system. And, in fact, the degree to which many public schools seem ineffective and unresponsive to many children might suggest that if some children benefit from vouchers, those who remain ill served at least will be a smaller portion of children than is now the case. The fundamental trade off is that with vouchers we would buy, on faith, more, perhaps better, options for some while in many ways relinquishing public accountability for all. We would rely on consumerism to ensure quality and equality, and we would forego knowledge of whether state economic, political, and social goals are being well served. To be sure, some voucher plans contain many proposals for overcoming the expected inefficiencies of vouchers at achieving these goals. These proposals will regulate the educational system in ways similar to the current regulation of public schools. What is not clear is whether regulating the private marketplace will prove to be more effective and efficient in the long run than the current system for ensuring public control of a public school system.

Legislation, Regulation, and Bureaucracy under Vouchers

Vouchers are intended to deregulate schooling. The rhetoric is to release schools from the progressive and oppressive bureaucratization that has constrained parental choices. Yet, at minimum, a set of regulations will be required to specify the financial component of the plan. Regulations concerning the value of the basic voucher and rules concerning public, private, and familial supplementation or nonsupplementation will need to exist. A state-level bureaucracy will need to be created to administer the financial component of the plan. Under certain voucher systems, the agency may have to have the capacity to monitor the financial plans of schools, families, or other private agencies.

Rules for defining a "school" will also need to be developed; the state may need to be able to monitor schools to determine that they meet the minimum definition of a school. Beyond minimum regulation lie such areas as personnel and admissions. There may be no personnel qualification requirements, existing requirements for private school teachers, or existing public school teacher requirements. There may be no admissions policies, nondiscrimination policies, or policies favoring integration. There may be no curriculum requirements, curricular prescriptions, or curricular proscriptions.

Voucher advocates are likely to understate the quantity of regulation and bureaucracy required to implement a system of vouchers. It is noteworthy that the California Initiative required nearly two pages of fine-print additions to the California Constitution. Constitutional provisions and amendments are generally sparely worded. Less noticed was the change implied in the functioning of the California Department of Education (Levin, 1979). The Department would need to relate not to 1,040 school districts but to a much larger number of individual schools and the 5,000,000 students who attend them. Many locally administered functions would need to be handled on a statewide basis. The state would need to classify individual students, track them, monitor their attendance, and adjudicate conflicts between family and school. In short, the state bureaucracy would likely increase in size and in certain responsibilities.

While vouchers might be enacted tabula rasa, it is likely that two forces would increase the quantity of regulations (and attendant bureaucracy) over time. These are accountability and interest group pressures.

Accountability

Under a voucher system, the schools would still be publicly financed, if privately provided. Under the present state/local system for financing and providing public education, state legislatures have shown a remarkable interest in financial and educational accountability. This is so despite the fact that schools are operated under the supervision of local school boards. Perhaps because state legislatures provide state aid or perhaps because they do not trust local school boards, state legislatures have embraced a variety of financial and educational accountability legislation. The legislation has ranged from pure accountability systems to planning-programming-budgeting systems to minimum competency testing (Wise, 1979). Under vouchers, the state legislature would be appropriating funds to individual schools. Indeed, the sum, if the system operates statewide, almost will double the sum now appropriated (since local funding will not exist and private funding will be largely subvented).

Each year the state legislature will have to decide whether it is appropriating the "right amount" for education. As it gropes to determine the answer to this question, it will raise questions about the effectiveness of the educational system, about the adequacy of the last year's appropriation, about equity in the system, and so on. These are precisely the kinds of questions that legislators now raise about education and that give rise to fiscal and educational accountability legislation. Whether the legislature will be able to resist asking "hard questions" about the very largest item in its budget would remain to be seen. Market accountability will mitigate some of the pressure. However, an aging, nonparent and fiscally conservative population— adults who are not in a position to judge the quality of schooling immediately and who have no direct interest—may still be inclined to ask "hard questions."

As alluded to above, state legislatures have often acted paternalistically toward local school boards. They have prescribed the minimum qualifications of teachers that school systems may hire. They have prescribed textbooks, courses, class size, contact hours, and so forth. They have begun to require state monitoring of local school output through state-administered tests. In short, they have acted to supplant local decisionmaking in areas where they judge local decisionmakers to be deficient. State paternalism is not new; it also shows no sign of abating. If state legislatures have been unwilling to delegate full control to locally elected officials (or officials appointed by elected local officials), will they be willing to delegate full control to privately owned and operated schools? Perhaps market accountability will suffice. More likely, state legislatures will, from time to time, believe that they have a better idea.

Interest Group Pressures

All types of interest groups have secured legislation favoring their interests. While vouchers appear likely to decentralize operational control, they centralize financial and other controls over schools. The potential power of central government will increase.

To some extent, the availability of schools of choice should remove the perceived need of some interest groups to secure legislation to alter the schools in their preferred direction. Those who want prayer in the schools can enroll their children in religiously oriented schools. Those who favor or disfavor sex education can make the appropriate enrollment decision. Those who believe in evolution or creationism can act accordingly. The question is whether the availability of choice would function as an escape valve for those with strongly held views. Would interest groups find the local school market responsive to their desires? Would they seek state assistance to counteract a lack of desired services? Or would interest groups wish to impose their needs or views on all schools to ensure the availability of what they seek? If so, the strengthened state role in education would present the clear mechanism.

Interest groups obviously range beyond curricular choices. Organized teachers, administrators, teacher educators—the members of the education establishment—may perceive the need to protect their own interests through legislation. They may perceive the need to regulate their sense of good educational practice. Civil rights groups may want to ensure that admission and expulsion decisions are fairly made. Patriotic groups may wish to see that schools do not teach subversive ideas. Fiscal conservatives may want to ensure that public funds are not squandered on basket weaving and the like. All of these groups will have a more direct pipeline to the state than is currently the case, should the marketplace disappoint them.

Conclusion

It is not enough for voucher advocates to espouse the virtues of competition and choice. They must be prepared to explain how schools under vouchers will achieve the states' goals efficiently and effectively. They must be prepared to explain how we will achieve public and private purposes in private settings with public money. And they must be prepared to explain how the bureaucratic means for achieving these goals will prove more flexible and responsive than those that have already evolved to serve the public's demands for accountability and equity.

The forces that have led to pluralistic, public decisionmaking concerning education will not disappear under vouchers. Some who are dissatisfied with their current options will be content with the new choices available to them. Others will find the choices open to them still inadequate. To the extent that the state tries to resolve disappointments or perceived inadequacies through regulation, the bureaucratic apparatus associated with public schooling will reemerge, only it will grow at the state rather than at the local level. To the extent that the state leaves the child's right to choice in education to the vicissitudes of the marketplace, litigation will be the means for solving problems of market failure or of perceived violations of rights. Lawmakers will still need to balance rights of private association with rights to equal opportunity. They will need to weigh the students' rights to "appropriate" education or choice alongside the state's fundamental interest in education.

These issues will be made more complicated by public funding of the private sector. The potential need for regulation that we have described is a symptom of a more fundamental problem with the voucher concept: the achievement of public goals through the private market. Under the current system of financing schools, we resolve tensions between public and private interests by pursuing pluralistic goals through public decisionmaking in the public sector and by allowing individualistic goals to be pursued in the privately funded and operated private sector. Private control over the public interest has been avoided over the course of this nation's history by linking accountability for the pursuit of public goals to public funding of institutions. Public funding of the private sector without the public accountability that accompanies pluralistic decisionmaking is unlikely to occur.

Notes

1 A critique of Coons and Sugarman's argument (1978) that voucher schools will produce greater autonomy in students and, hence, prepare them for fuller participation in society is offered in Pacheco (1980).

2 The Alum Rock voucher experiment illustrates how some of these potential problems might occur. First, the single most important determinant of parents' school choices was proximity to the home, even when free transportation was provided. Thus, to the extent that schools of different kinds cluster in different kinds of neighborhoods, access to similar quality school experiences may be constrained by geography. Furthermore, even after extensive bilingual publicity about the voucher program in Alum Rock, a substantial fraction of the parents did not even know it existed; a much larger proportion did not have accurate information about the voucher program or the specific schools. Parents of low-income and lower educational attainment were less well informed than other parents. Finally, parents' program choices resulted in clusterings of students by family background factors like income, education, attitudes, and childrearing values (Bridge & Blackman, 1978).

References

Arons, S. Equity, option, and vouchers. *Teachers College Record,* 1971, 72 February, pp. 337-364, 357.

Bridge, R.G., & Blackman, J. *A study of alternatives in American education, Vol. 4: Family choice in schooling.* (R-2170/4). Santa Monica, Calif.: The Rand Corporation, April 1978.

Carnoy, M. (Ed.). *Schooling in a corporate society.* New York: David

McKay, 1975.

Coons, J.E., & Sugarman, S. *Education by choice—the case for family control.* Berkeley: University of California Press, 1978.

Dimond, P.R., Chamberlain, C., & Hillyard, W. *A dilemma of local government: Discrimination in the provision of public services.* Lexington, Mass.: D.C. Heath, 1978.

James, T. Tuition tax credits and the pains of democracy. *Phi Delta Kappan*, May 1982, p. 609.

Levin, H.M. *Educational vouchers and social policy.* Stanford, Calif: Stanford University, Institute for Research on Educational Finance and Governance, July 1979.

Lines, P.M. State regulation of private education. *Phi Delta Kappan*, October 1982, pp. 119-123.

Pacheco, A. *Educational vouchers and their implications for equity.* Stanford, Calif: Stanford University, Institute for Research on Educational Finance and Governance, January 1980.

Rich, R.C. Neglected issues in the study of urban service distributions: A research agenda. *Urban Studies*, 1979, 16, 143-156.

Wise, A.E. *Legislated learning: The bureaucratization of the American classroom.* Berkeley: University of California Press, 1979.

Educational Vouchers:
A Viable Option for Urban Settings?

Andrew B. Sandler and David E. Kapel

One of the most persistent issues in American education is the question of how and where the family should be involved in the schooling of its children. Because of the continued growth and expansion of urban public school systems, critics have suggested that education is becoming increasingly bureaucratic and unresponsive to the needs of parents and/or the children. Critics have also raised the joint issues of public school monopolies and the quality of education (Everhart, 1982). It has been argued that these monopolies have reduced accountability of those who administer large urban school systems; consequently, the critics believe that the quality of education in the public schools has been reduced. As a result, questions have been raised as to who should control urban schools. Should it be school personnel and legislators or should it be the consumer, that is, the parents? Richard Elmore (1986) raises the question in terms of demand side (student and parental empowerment) and supply side (education control, organization, and management). This controversy has produced suggested options to reform the present system. These options would allow parents more input into their children's education.

One such proposal for educational reform to emerge in the past twenty years has been educational vouchers. The purpose of this paper is to delineate the social and economic consequences that voucher plans will have on education in urban areas. At the present time, vouchers have been proposed in Minnesota, Colorado, South Dakota, and Louisiana. In Louisiana, where 56% of students attend schools within urban areas (Bureau of Research, 1987), this issue has been debated hotly, as evidenced by three state senate bills and by the Right to Learn Program proposed by the Louisiana Association of Business and Industry. Vouchers have also been promoted by candidates in the 1988 presidential election as a means of social reform. The authors believe that educational vouchers cannot be implemented effectively and will, in fact, create new problems for urban areas. In particular, the following arguments will be made:

1. Vouchers could weaken or destroy urban public school systems.

2. Vouchers are not feasible from an economic standpoint.
3. Vouchers could lead to greater racial, economic, and social isolation of
   children.
4. There are other methods that introduce choice into the system which can be considered as alternatives to educational vouchers (Elmore, 1986; Governors'
   1991 Report on Education, 1986; Kapel and Pink, 1978).

PHILOSOPHY OF VOUCHER PROPOSALS

Educational vouchers entitle local boards of education to issue to parents tickets
or "vouchers" worth the full or partial cost of educating a child in public schools.
Parents then select a school, among participating public and private schools, to
spend the voucher for the school's educational services. This philosophy differs
from the present system in which state and local tax money is distributed directly to
public schools. As the parents have the option to use their voucher at a public
school or nonpublic school, they also can select a school without regard for
geographical limitations.

While there are many proponents of educational vouchers, the leading figures in
this controversy are John Coons and Stephen Sugarman, law professors at the
University of California at Berkeley. The basic assumptions of vouchers can be
found in their book, *Education by Choice* (1978). They cite three major advantages
of vouchers: (1) increased parental influence and choice in their children's
education: (2) equity in education for poor and minority students; (3) improvement
in the quality of education. At the heart of the voucher debate is the question of
where authority should rest when decisions are made about each child's education.
Proponents of vouchers believe that the family is the ideal educational decision
maker.

It is argued that vouchers will increase parental choice by promoting
competition among private and public schools. According to the voucher's free
market approach, schools that are not subscribing [sic] to will be forced to meet
parental expectations and standards or face the possibility of extinction. In addition,
proponents predict that new schools will open in response to the political, religious,
and academic preferences of parents. Also, it is hypothesized that vouchers will
enable the poor to send their children to the public or private schools that higher
socioeconomic children current!y attend; it is assumed that these schools are the

"better" schools. According to voucher proponents, the notion of choice holds the promise of extending those educational options to poor families that the rich now enjoy.

HISTORY OF EDUCATIONAL VOUCHERS

The voucher plan was originally proposed in 1955 by Milton Friedman, an economist at the University of Chicago. Friedman's plan was to increase choice to parents through vouchers, and to minimize government interference (e.g., no regulations regarding instructional content), while also assuring that no laws were being violated.

Most voucher models since 1955 have been variations of Friedman's plan. Models were proposed by Jencks (1966), Sizer and Whitten (1968), and Coons and Sugarman (1978). In the late 1960s and early 1970s, the Nixon administration launched a serious effort to establish several experimental voucher projects. The Office of Economic Opportunity (OEO) designed and sought to implement a voucher experiment in a large urban area. By 1973, six school districts received OEO funds to study the feasibility of implementing full voucher systems. Of the six, only Alum Rock could be persuaded to attempt a voucher system. The system implemented was a modified version of the original OEO plan (Van Geel, 1978).

The Alum Rock School District served approximately 10,000 children in a low-income section of San Jose, California. (The population in 1978 was approximately 55% Mexican-American, 10% black, and 35% other ethnic groups.) For five years (1972-1978) some of the Alum Rock public schools (K-8) tried voucherlike systems (Bridge, 1978).

In year 1, seven schools in Alum Rock began the voucher system. Each offered three to five "minischool" programs that varied in curriculum objectives. In year 2, six additional schools joined the project, and in year 3 another school joined. In year 4, parents were allowed to choose minischools from different school buildings for their children. Free transportation was provided to children who needed it. In year 5, the district switched to a limited open enrollment scheme that greatly restricted parents' choices (Bridge, 1978).

Although the Alum Rock experiment expanded parent choice, it never contained some key components of a competitive, market system. For example, nonpublic schools were not included in the program. Teachers received no rewards for their productivity. Finally, the administration acted to constrain competition between minischools through means such as prohibiting advertising (Bridge, 1978; Cohen and Farrar, 1977).

To date, there has not been a voucher experiment of similar magnitude to Alum Rock. There have been limited voucher programs in Maine, Vermont, and Nebraska. Implementation of vouchers in these states has predominantly taken place in white, small-town or rural areas that rank within or above the national averages in education achievement tests. It should be stressed that these experiments did not take place in large urban areas with heterogeneous, poor populations. Because of the size and multifaceted educational problems in urban areas, one cannot assume that the results of vouchers in Maine and Vermont would be similar to those in states with much different population demographics.

The Minnesota legislature adopted an open enrollment program that allowed students the right to attend any public school in the few school districts that had volunteered for the program. In May 1988, Rudy Perpich signed a bill phasing in open enrollment over two years, beginning in 1989, for all 435 of the state's public school districts. Students will be able to attend any public schools, where there is room, and if transportation can be arranged by their parents. Supporters of the program say that the program will force schools to improve; critics believe that the affluent, at best, will benefit and, at worst, the voucher system will begin to undermine public education (Cassel, 1988).

Salganik (1981) and Wise and Darling-Hammond (1984) noted that there has been no true test of vouchers. The voucher proposals described above, as well as the Alum Rock experiment, are the most widely cited voucher examples in the literature. For practical evidence that vouchers can work, proponents have turned to very limited voucher experiments.

DISCUSSION OF VOUCHER ISSUES

Implications for Public Schools

Any debate over educational vouchers must examine closely what will happen to public schools should the system be fully implemented. Critics of the voucher system question whether private/parochial schools and public schools can compete in an open market without serious side effects to public schools. These critics have hypothesized that vouchers will lead to major changes in the public schools (Levin, 1979; Garibaldi, 1985). In order to examine this issue, it is necessary to look at the social benefits of education in relationship to the pressures that will occur if voucher systems come into effect.

Levin (1979) noted that "a major function of the public schools is the transmission of a common language, heritage, set of values, and knowledge that are necessary for appropriate political functioning in our democratic society" (p. 16). To a large extent, schools attempt to prepare the young for their role as self-governing citizens by exposing them to a common curriculum and a heterogeneous peer group. Butts (1979) stressed the fact that the founders of the Republic turned to the idea of public education for political reasons. He wrote that, "in its origin, the idea of public education was not to give parents more control over education, not to promote the individual needs and interests of children, not to prepare for a better job, not to get into college" (p. 7).

Levin (1979) points out that the voucher approach would violate these premises as soon as public funds were dispersed to a variety of competing schools with individual interests and goals. In the United States, where there is a large diversity of culture, religion, and educational goals, it seems likely that the private schools will divide along homogeneous lines that will not reflect the overall sense of political community envisioned by the founders of this country. The possibility exists that vouchers will stratify students so that they do not have the opportunity to experience the diversity of backgrounds and beliefs that contributed to the democratic process. In addition, educational vouchers that include sectarian schools might be challenged on constitutional grounds since it might be difficult to separate secular and religious instruction, as funded by the tuition (Total Community Action, Inc., 1987, p. 17).

Proponents of vouchers argue that competition between public and private schools will force the public schools to increase the quality of education provided. In order to have fair competition, all aspects within the marketplace have to be equal. Unfortunately, it is difficult to equalize competition between private and public schools.

By necessity, public schools are heavily regulated because there is a need for accountability of the tax dollar. Public schools are forced to operate within strict guidelines to receive federal and state money. In contrast, private schools are not required to operate by the same rules (e.g., private schools are not required to transport students to and from school). Few private schools contain special education programs. Although the requirements that public schools must follow certainly have merits, they also increase economic costs.

Public schools operate under laws mandating that they educate all children. Children attend public schools with abilities ranging from gifted to severely retarded. At the present time, many private schools operate with admission guidelines that prohibit entrance to children operating below normal ranges of abilities. We can only hope that public schools will not become places for students that no one else wants or knows how to educate. Unfortunately, the possibility exists that a voucher system will segregate these difficult-to-educate youngsters into public schools that are not motivated to improve.

Butts (1979) described educational vouchers as the "private pursuit of the public purse" (p. 7). Since a program of increased aid to nonpublic schools is likely to divert funds from public schools, any benefits of greater public assistance to nonpublic schools must be weighted against the loss of financial benefits to public schools. Muller (1982) admitted that competition from nonpublic schools could create public school improvement because public schools would be forced to evaluate themselves more closely. However, public school improvement would be hampered by diminishing funds. The total educational budget is not likely to be increased and a voucher program would have to divert funds from public schools.

Before vouchers occur, one needs to consider whether schools with poor reputations in a community deserve to operate. If a voucher system is implemented, safeguards will need to be placed within the system ensuring that competition between public and nonpublic schools is equalized over time. Given the assumption that nonpublic schools have an unfair advantage over public schools in the open market, the possibility exists that public schools perceived as "less desirable" by consumers could lose large numbers of students as soon as the vouchers are distributed. Because school funding is based on the number of students enrolled, many public schools with the potential to meet parental demands in a competitive market may be forced to close before given the opportunity to change. Within this scenario, poor school districts could lose schools that have value to many residents (e.g., because of location and because school facilities benefit the community).

Besides money, other kinds of support for public schools will diminish in a voucher system (Muller, 1982). At the present time, middle-class parents who desire to improve their children's education provide much of the resources, time, and money to effect change in the public schools. If these parents have greater incentive to send their children to nonpublic schools, they will work toward increasing the quality of education in the nonpublic schools. In the long run, it could be this new lack of interest in public schools by the middle-class parents that may be the most harmful side effect of educational vouchers.

Vouchers and Choice

Implicit in the argument for educational vouchers is the desirability of allowing parents more choice in educational decision making for their children. Proponents stress the fact that vouchers will increase options for parents because new and varied schools will open, and parents will be given the financial resources to take advantage of them (Coons, 1979). Also voucher advocates assume that state will have less control over education; conversely, parents will have more choice over the type of education their children will receive.

Although on the surface vouchers appear to remedy the constraining features of public education, they fail to deal with other powerful realities of society. The following discussion will point out such realities.

All voucher plans raise the issue of information dissemination (Puckett, 1983). In order for parents to make informed choices about their children's education, detailed information about all schools must be available. Puckett argues that "dissemination of information to the disadvantaged, those who need it most, may constitute a major problem" (p. 12). Wealthy parents have greater access to information resources than poor parents do. Even in the Minnesota open-admissions program, observers believe that "just as in the regular marketplace, there is going to be a bias in favor of the most affluent, informed consumers.... There is no reason to think that market forces will help out the poor and disadvantaged" (Cassel, 1986, p. 6). Families cannot make informed choices until they are made aware of the options. A good voucher plan must incorporate a scheme to provide low socioeconomic populations with adequate information. In addition, because of the inadequate reading skills of some parents, considers [sic] need to be made to ensure that they understand these choices.

The Alum Rock experiment illuminated what might happen if voucher systems were adopted. Bridge (1978) summarized the results from surveys Alum Rock parents conducted in the fall of years 1, 2, 3, and 5 of the voucher demonstration. In general, low-income parents and those with less formal education were less well informed than other parents. Socially advantaged people had more accurate information about the schools. They had access to more information sources and as a result knew more about alternatives. Despite the fact that a variety of information sources existed, Wise and Darling-Hammond (1984) noted that after four years of bilingual publicity about the voucher system (i.e., use of newspapers, mailings, radio announcements, neighborhood meetings, and information counselors) a quarter of the parents did not even know that this information existed; a much larger proportion did not have accurate information about the voucher program.

Geographic consideration reduces the number of viable options for families within a voucher system. Many parents prefer to send their children to schools close to home regardless of the academic attractiveness of alternative schools. Bridge (1978) asked parents to explain why they chose a particular program in the second year of the Alum Rock project. Over 70% of those who responded cited the geographic location of the school as the primary determinant; 31% cited the desire to keep siblings or friends together in the same program. In every single ethnic group and in every single survey year the majority of parents agreed that "for most parents, how close a school is to home is the most important reason for choosing a school for their children to attend." School location has become a more important factor as a result of a recent United States Supreme Court decision that children *do not* have a constitutional right (under the United States Constitution) to an education. Therefore, school districts can legally charge parents to bus their children to school (*Kadrmas v. Dickinson Public Schools*, 1988). The exception to this decision *may be* in states that include the right to a free public education in their constitution. However, it does appear that most states will be able to charge parents to bus children to school, thus adding an additional, and depending on distance, a significant cost to the education process. Nonaffluent parents will feel this cost and will make location an increasingly important factor in selecting schools.

The influx of vouchers into the educational system will not take place in a vacuum. Many of the forces that shaped education historically are not going to disappear because voucher legislation is passed. Public schools have always reflected the cultural, political, and economic changes occurring on the broader social context. A crucial point, often neglected by voucher advocates, is that the government will never cease to influence educational policy because a large amount of state and federal money is spent on education.

In order to determine efficiency and quality of schools, some form of accountability in the system will have to exist. It seems likely that the accountability introduced into the voucher system will reflect the public school values that the new system is attempting to modify. One example is the fact that many voucher proposals (including Louisiana Senate bills in 1985, 1986, and 1987) contain requirements that all schools eligible to receive and redeem vouchers must administer a national standardized test and make the results available to the public. Thus, it seems likely that schools will have to resort to the common curriculums and teaching methods to produce scores to satisfy state requirements and to attract students. In the end, the possibility exists that the expected curricula diversity, providing parents with many options, will not be available.

Other special interests will also merit consideration. Cohen and Farrar (1977) pointed out that in Alum Rock the voucher system did not create a situation in which professionals lost power to parents. In fact, the opposite occurred. Before the experiment was half over, school administrators changed the market aspect of vouchers to suit their needs. The first step was to restrict demand by making it impossible for schools to expand indefinitely. Schools only had to maintain enrollments at capacity levels so that additional strain did not occur. School principals, because they feared the consequences of competition, banned the use of advertising of schools. Teachers who left a voucher school for reasons associated with the experiment were given priority in assignments to other schools. All of these steps reduced the free market aspect of vouchers and protected the interests of the educational professional.

Although voucher proposals make promises of increased educational choices for parents, the preceding discussion points out that only *constrained* choices will be available to the public. The free market approach to education can be written into the legislation; however, experience indicates that it may never work the way it was intended.

Vouchers and Equity

When vouchers were first proposed, one trademark of education was the equality of educational opportunity. During this period, attention shifted from improving educational opportunities for the majority of children to improving education for the disadvantaged. As with other social programs of this progressive period (e.g., Head Start, Follow-Through), vouchers promised to protect the poor and minority students from educational discrimination and to increase the educational opportunities of this population. This section will examine whether vouchers will be able to carry out these lofty goals.

The free market taking place in a voucher proposal assumes that everyone will have the same opportunity to acquire quality education. True equality of education implies that an individual has opportunity to receive a quality education regardless of race or social class. It is unrealistic to assert that such a situation exists today, and the possibility exists that under a free market approach the disparity between the poor and the rich will increase.

At the present time there is no evidence to suggest that schools operating in a market system will be responsive to the needs of the poor and minorities. The failure of the market to give rich and poor consumers equal resources to purchase privately produced goods and public services makes it doubtful that things will be different when applied to education. For example, goods sold in stores located in poor neighborhoods are frequently higher in price than they are in stores located elsewhere. Landlords whose property is located in slums are often accused of being unresponsive to the needs of their tenants.

One common theme of this paper is that special interests of individuals and groups will interfere with the quality of education that could be available in a competitive market system. Even though new schools will open in response to educational vouchers, there will probably be far fewer sellers of educational services to the poor. In to minimize finances, schools will be developed most frequently in geographical areas that do not contain heavy populations of children with health and learning problems. As we have already seen, the Alum Rock experience teaches us that geographical location is a crucial feature of the marketplace. Levin (1969) wrote, "if the previous experience of the slums can be used for prediction, few if any sellers of high quality educational services at competitive rates will locate in the ghetto. Not only is there no Saks Fifth Avenue in Harlem; there is no Macy's, Gimbels, Korvettes, or Kleins." (p. 8).

Most voucher proposals do not have stipulations mandating participation in the program. The successful private schools will decline to accept vouchers because of the administrative requirements accompanying the state funds. Thus, low-income, minority students will not have increased opportunity under a voucher approach to attend selective, high-achieving private schools.

Schools that do participate in the voucher system will still have the opportunity to refuse students on the basis of low achievement or poor academic ability. Schools will not be able to refuse students if they are unable to pay the tuition but they could be rejected if scores on admission exams do not meet the school's criteria or if previous performance in other schools has been substandard. In addition, even if low-achieving students are admitted, what is to keep private schools from expelling them once it is established that they are not achieving at "acceptable levels"? If standardized tests are used as a means of advertising school quality to the public, it seems likely that the students who score below the mean will not be welcome. By definition, 50% of all students have to fall below the norm on standardized tests. Will schools in this competitive atmosphere want to attract and keep those students who do fall below the norm? The children most "damaged" by poor public school education will be the least likely to meet the admission requirements of many of the private schools.

Even though most voucher proposals indicate that nonpublic schools participating in the program must charge tuition equal to the value of the state stipend, there is a lack of detail about how other types of expenses will be paid (e.g., uniforms, class trips). Low-income families who barely have money for food and clothing probably will not be able to afford these extra expenses even if school tuition is paid. This lack of income also has the potential of polarizing student bodies.

Vouchers and Quality of Education

One argument frequently used by those who favor the voucher is that competition will improve the quality of education in America. This improvement will occur, according to voucher advocates, because competition will force some schools to shut down due to declining enrollment and will create incentives for existing schools as well as new schools to become more responsive to consumer demand. Although it is a given that competition for students will occur in a voucher system, one needs to question whether this competition will lead to an improved educational product.

Within a voucher system, successful schools might be defined as those with full enrollment. However, it is tenuous to assume that a school is providing quality education just because it is popular with parents. Voucher proponents make claims about quality education; however, the term *quality education* is controversial and not easily defined. Some schools with empirical evidence supporting their effectiveness (e.g., low dropout rates, high achievement test scores) may have difficulty attracting students because of factors such as location, ethnic makeup, and limited advertising budgets.

The meaning of quality education is partly dependent on the needs and background of the consumer in a voucher system. Levin (1979) notes that parents typically pursue child-rearing patterns that reinforce their own values and class position in society. These values will come into play in a voucher system when parents select the schools that their children attend. Levin makes the following arguments:

> Parents will choose those school environments that they believe will maximize the probability of success as defined within the context of their experience. The working-class child will be provided with schooling that will reinforce working-class orientations while children from higher classes will attend schools that will orient them toward the upper echelons of the occupational hierarchy. (p. 19).

Levin cites research suggesting that working-class parents will select highly structured schools for their children that emphasize a high degree of discipline, concentration on basic skills, and obedient behavior. Higher socioeconomic parents, on the other hand, are more likely to pick schools that will emphasize flexible schooling with a curriculum devoted to problem solving and development of communication skills. This phenomenon occurred at Alum Rock. Parents program choices resulted in clusterings of students by family background (i.e., income, education, and attitudes) (Wise and Darling-Hammond, 1984). Parents with higher socioeconomic status were more likely to chose innovative programs (Salganik, 1981).

Even if new schools open, there is no historic evidence to support the assumption that the marketplace will improve. One salient example is the plight of air transportation. When airlines were deregulated, many new airlines were formed. At present, most of these new airlines have folded or have been incorporated into larger, more established air carriers. Although fares went down for a while, we are now seeing a trend in which the cost of air travel is escalating. In addition, there is considerable controversy regarding the decreased safety of air travel and the increase in flight delays and cancellations.

As has been stated, unregulated vouchers may not result in increased educational options for poor families. Even for middle-class families, there is no guarantee that schools will improve. Pacheco (1980) argued that:

> It is a fundamental mistake to equate the presence of alternatives with either higher quality or what the public wants. It may be a serious mistake to equate public wants with public needs, All that might be guaranteed by a voucher scheme is that some sort of educational options would exist, not necessarily those that families want or need. Like commercial TV, the public may be faced with a plethora of alternatives, none of which are particularly good or attractive. (p. 24)

One inherent problem with vouchers is that many nonpublic schools are filled to capacity due to the parental perception that they provide quality education. These schools would not be able to add many new students even if they were motivated to do so. What probably would happen in a voucher system is that some nonpublic schools not perceived as providing quality education (e.g., those currently operating without full enrollment) would be able to attract students from families who want their children out of the public schools. The question that must be asked is how are these previously unpopular schools going to improve the way they educate children when they have even more students. The possibility exists that vouchers will simply shift the enrollment figures within public and nonpublic schools. There is no guarantee that dedicated teachers and competent administrators are going to suddenly appear on the scene and improve the way many existing schools educate their students.

Implicit to the voucher is the assumption that private schools are more efficient and of better quality than public schools. This is not always the case, however, as evidenced by the millions of parents who choose to keep their children in public schools for a variety of reasons. Sullivan (1982) disputed the act that private education is always more cost effective. In order to explore this issue it is necessary to consider that the private sector is really composed of two distinct elements: a small (15%) independent component whose per pupil expenditures are much higher than most public schools and a larger (85%) church-affiliated sector with very low reported expenditures. When these expenditures are analyzed, some important factors emerge. First, many costs of church-affiliated schools do not appear in their budgets (e.g., donations to the schools). Second, a significant part of the expenditure differences are for public school services not directly provided by private schools (e.g., transportation).

Willms (1982) noted that policy decisions should not be based on the assumption that private schools produce better achievement outcomes than do public schools. A data review of 30,000 sophomores in 1,000 schools resulted the following conclusion: There is no evidence that the performance of a child an academic course of study would improve by a shift from the public to the private sector.

Economic Considerations

Consideration of a voucher proposal must include a review of the economic ramifications. The most obvious economic concern is that money currently being used for public school education will be used to also finance children attending private schools. In Louisiana, the Right to Learn proposal would hand to parents a voucher equal to $1,200 for each elementary school student and $1,500 for each high school student. These amounts would result in an increased education budget. In the 1986-87 school year 136,222 Louisiana students (14.68% of all students attending school in this state) were enrolled in nonpublic schools; almost 74% of the nonpublic school enrollment (100,318 students) is found in the urban communities of the state. In the two largest urban parishes (counties), nonpublic enrollment accounts for 28% (Orleans) and 31% (Jefferson) of the total number of children attending schools (Bureau of Research, 1987).

Private school attendance is already a major consideration in Louisiana. If one assumes that each voucher is worth $1,300, then the state will be required to come up with an additional $17,708,860 for those already attending private schools. That money would come from the public school budget. Even though many students would leave the public schools to attend private schools, the public school structure would still be intact (e.g., central administration, school buildings, maintenance of buildings). Therefore, public schools would still require funding. The total budget needs would not be reduced dollar for dollar by the reduction in student enrollment.

There are additional hidden costs not accounted for in this Louisiana proposal. The Right to Learn program states that "students attending schools of choice would be eligible for the same state-funded transportation assistance currently provided in state law for private and parochial schools." With the advent of additional schools and increased opportunities, to go to schools outside of the neighborhood, it is reasonable to assume that transportation costs would rise dramatically. The problem becomes compounded in large cities lacking transit systems. A large percentage of students will rely on school buses in order to attend school. These huge costs are not reflected in the Right to Learn proposal.

Another example of hidden cost is the increased number of administrators that would be necessary. A whole new bureaucracy would be created to implement and monitor the system. In order to provide information to parents, a variety of costly methods similar to those utilized in the Alum Rock experiment would be needed. Information about schools would have to be distributed to parents to ensure equal opportunities to learn about the choices available. We might require state agency personnel to make annual inspections of voucher schools to ensure that the information they distribute to parents is accurate. Until these factors are budgeted into a voucher proposal, it is not realistic to assume that states in dire financial straits, such as Louisiana, will be able to absorb the cost.

Parents of students already attending nonpublic schools also have reason to be wary of a voucher system. Schools that charge tuitions higher than the voucher will lose money on all the new admissions who are low-income voucher residents. In order to recoup the losses, these schools might be forced to raise tuition. Voucher programs will have to provide built-in safeguards to prevent the inflation of tuition in participating schools.

ALTERNATIVE OPTIONS

Families want more input on school operations (Governors' 1991 Report on Education, 1986). Unfortunately, advocates of vouchers assume that choice cannot be introduced to families without dismantling the present educational system. Viable alternatives to vouchers have been proposed to improve the responsiveness of schools. In contrast to vouchers, these approaches focus on working within public schools so that parents, teachers, administrators, and government officials interact constructively. Some of these plans are briefly summarized below.

Kapel and Pink (1978) noted that the present structure of schools, especially in urban areas, is not always responsive to the needs of the community. Unfortunately, professional educators often avoid community involvement in decision making:

> In short, the educator senses a loss of power as a result of community input. The view, while popular, is totally dysfunctional because it overlooks the fact that the schools are legally the responsibility of the community. Philosophically and legally the school belongs to the people, not the central administration, the principal, or the teachers. What is urgently needed to defuse the contemporary confrontation between the "people" and the "professional educator" is a plan for decentralization that directly involves community decision making within a framework that promotes a shared power base with a viable system of checks and balances. (p. 24)

Kapel and Pink proposed a model designed to decentralize urban schools and allow direct community decision making. The crucial aspect of the model is the implementation of a local decentralized school board comprised of 12 to 14 members selected randomly from the parents of the children attending the school. Each school would have its own school board, and each school board would have its own school. These school boards would have broad decision-making authority. Thus, all parents would be given an equal opportunity to participate in the educational system. The goal of this plan is the reduction of distance between parents and educational decision makers to allow entire educational community involvement in the educational process.

A major flaw within voucher proposals is the fact that low-socioeconomic parents whose children attend voucher schools far away from home will not have sufficient input. In contrast to Kapel and Pink's solution, vouchers have the potential to reduce parent input because of the difficulty in getting to the school. More effective solutions are needed to involve parents in school activities. Parents will feel more involvement if the public schools already in existence create programs to include parents in classroom and administrative decision making.

One component of the Governors' 1991 Report on Education (1986) was recommendations to increase the amount of cooperation between home and school. These recommendations were as follows:

1. State education departments should work closely with school districts, universities, and organizations such as the PTA. State education departments need to provide technical assistance by encouraging instruction in effective parent-involvement techniques to be included in preservice and recertification training programs of all teachers and administrators.
2. A climate should be created for greater parent involvement (e.g., publicizing and rewarding parent involvement programs that deserve wider recognition).
3. Incentives should be provided to school districts that implement cooperative programs.
4. Opportunities for students should be expanded by adopting legislation that permits families to select from among kindergarten to twelfth grade public schools in the state. High school students should be able to attend accredited public postsecondary degree-granting institutions during their junior and senior years.

Choice can be introduced into the public school system by increasing the use of public magnet schools that specialize in particular areas of curriculum (e.g., fine arts). These magnet schools could be educational alternatives within the public sector.

Another approach to choice is to increase within program alternatives, such as college prep programs, advanced placement courses, vocational and career courses/programs, greater variety of general education courses, and greater use of a variety of creative courses to meet individual needs. Elmore (1986) suggests that there is no simple causal relationship between choice and the academic performance of students. However, there should be further experiments with choice because (1) there are currently many limitations of present local centralization (present school organization), (2) choice itself reflects inherent democratic values, and (3) educators and parents should be brought together to engage in creative activities to solve serious educational problems (Elmore, 1986, p. 31).

CONCLUSIONS

We have examined ways in which vouchers could impact education. Despite the claims made by voucher advocates (e.g., improvement in both the quality and efficiency of education, increased opportunity for low-socioeconomic families to educate their children), the voucher system has many problems that must be reviewed closely before its implementation.

The most serious reservation concerning vouchers is the fear that our public school system will decline as the emphasis on education shifts to the private sector. Economic as well as human resources will be drained from public education. The public schools could become the depository [sic] for students that no one else wants to educate.

Vouchers will not provide the choice promised. Factors such as transportation, the need for the state monitoring of schools, standardized testing, geographic concerns, and refusal by many nonpublic schools to participate have the potential to make a voucher system as constraining as our current public system. The realities of the marketplace will probably limit the number of poor children who will be able to change schools and benefit from vouchers. It is likely that vouchers will lead to larger educational inequalities between those children of the middle class and those of the poor.

A voucher system has never been fully implemented in an urban setting. There is no empirical evidence supporting advantages to this educational approach. Vouchers could destroy urban public schools. Changes in the present structure are necessary and required; the solutions are not readily apparent. As Elmore (1986) stated, "The existing system of local centralization may indeed create serious problems for the performance and responsiveness of schools. But neither of the two extreme alternatives to this system—a private market for education or a complete monopoly—is defensible in theory or in practice" (p. 6). Innovative plans involving cooperative efforts between parents and public school decision makers appear to be the best approach to solving the problems that face education today.

Acknowledgements. Funds for this work were provided, in part, by a grant from the League of Women Voters (New Orleans Chapter).

REFERENCES

Bridge, G. (1978). Information imperfections: The Achilles' hell of entitlement plans. *School Review* 86: 504-529.

Bureau of Research (1987). *Louisiana School Directory*. Baton Rouge, LA: Louisiana Department of Education.

Butts, R. F. (1979). Educational vouchers: The private pursuit of the public purse. *Phi Delta Kappan* 61: 7-9.

Cassel, A. (1988). Minnesota's free market in education. *The Philadelphia Inquirer*. Vol. 318, no. 179, p. 1ff.

Cohen, D. K., and Farrar, E. (1977). Power to the parents?—The story of educational vouchers.
Public Interest 48: 72-97.

Coons, J. E., and Sugarman, S. D. (1978). *Education of Choice*. Berkeley University of California Press.

Elmore, R. F. (1986). *Choice in Public Education*. Center for Policy Research in Education Santa Monica, CA: The Rand Corporation, Rutgers University, Wisconsin Center for Education Research.

Everhart, R B. (ed.) (1982). *The Public School Monopoly*. San Francisco: Pacific Institute for Public Policy Research.

Friedman, M. (1955). The role of government in education. in R. A. Solo (ed.), *Economics and the Public Interest*. New Brunswick, NJ: Rutgers UniversityPress.

Garibaldi, A. (1985). Pros and Cons of Educational Vouchers. New Orleans, LA: *Total Community Action* Inc.

Governors' 1991 Report on Education (1986). *Time for Results*. National

Governors' Association Center for Policy Research and Analysis.

Jencks, C. (1966). Is the public school obsolete? *The Public Interest* 2: 18-27.

Kadrmas v. Dickinson Public Schools (1988). 86-7113.

Kapel, D. E., and Pink, W. T. (1978). The schoolboard: Participatory democracy revisited. *The Urban Review* 10: 20-34.

Levin, H. M. (1969). The failure of the public schools and the free market remedy. *The Urban Review* 1: 1-16.

Levin, H. M. (1979). *Educational vouchers and social policy.* (Program Report No. 79-B12). Stanford, CA: Institute for Research on Educational Finance and Governance.

Muller, C. B. (1982). *The public interest in education. Social and political considerations.* Stanford CA: Institute for Research on Educational Finance and Governance. Winter.

Murnane, R. J. (1984). Comments on Arthur E. Wise and Linda Darling-Hammond's "Education by voucher." *Educational Theory* 34: 49-50.

Pacheco, A. (1980). *Educational vouchers and their implications for equity.* (Program Report No. 80-A2). Stanford, CA: Institute for Research on Educational Finance and Governance.

Salganik, L. H. (1981). The fall and rise and educational vouchers. *The Education Digest* 6-10, December.

Sizer, T., and Whitten, P. (1968). A proposal for a poor children's bill of rights. *Psychology Today* 58.

Sullivan, D. (1982). *Comparing public and nonpublic schools. The difficulty of measuring efficiency.* Stanford, CA: Institute for Research on Educational Finance and Governance. Winter.

Van Geel, T. V. (1978). Parental preferences and the policies of spending public educational funds. *Teachers College Record* 29: 339-363.

Willms, D. (1982). *Is there a private school advantage? Measuring differences in student achievement.* Stanford, CA: Institute for Research on Educational Finance and Governance. Winter.

Wise, A. E., and Darling-Hammond, L. (1984). Education by voucher: Private choice and the public interest. *Educational Theory* 34: 29-47.

The Urban Review   1988 Agathon Press, Inc.   Vol. 20, No. 4.

Vouchers Are A Viable Option for Urban Settings
A Response to Andrew B. Sandler and David E. Kapel

Margaret D. Tannenbaum

Introduction

Sandler and Kapel (1988) conclude their article "Educational Vouchers? A Viable Option for Urban Settings?" by saying that "The most serious reservation concerning vouchers is the fear that our public school system will decline as the emphasis on education shifts to the private sector." With this statement they expose one of their basic underlying assumptions with which this author would like to take issue —that, given a choice among public and private schools, an overwhelming proportion of parents would flee the public schools. It is just as likely that those parents not satisfied with the public school their children currently attend would send them to another **public** school. In fact, according to a survey conducted in the Spring of 1989 (Tannenbaum) only an additional 6% of parents said they would send their children to private school if they had the opportunity.

This statement by Sandler and Kapel reflects a failure on their part to examine the question of why parents, especially urban minority parents, currently send their children to private, usually Catholic, schools. Further, although they purport to repudiate vouchers on the grounds of their lack of potential for providing choice and equity and improving the quality of education, their arguments make a number of unwarranted assumptions and predictions. What's more they give short shrift to the question of the right of parents to select the site of schooling for their children in light of the overwhelming power of the state to mandate this schooling for such a large portion of children's lives. Finally, in their discussion of the implications of the implementation of a voucher system for public schools and economic considerations, they fail to take account of the changes that would eventuate if a voucher system were implemented.

Historical background

Before dealing with any of these problems, it is necessary first to make some additions and corrections to their history of educational vouchers, at the same time, sharpening up the distinction between the terms 'voucher' and 'schools of choice.'

Although the Alum Rock experiment from 1971 to 1976 was described as a voucher plan at the time (Sandler and Kapel, p. 269), it is now more accurate to describe it as a system of schools of choice. There are two basic distinctions between vouchers and schools of choice. A voucher system would include private schools; a system of schools of choice would include only public schools (Raywid, 1989; NJ State Department of Education, 1988). Secondly, in a system of schools of choice, the money would continue to go directly and only to the public schools, whereas in a voucher system the parents would receive a voucher worth a certain amount of money which they could use to purchase services in either a public or private school. On this definition, then, not only is the Alum Rock experiment mislabeled, but so is Minnesota's state-wide plan permitting parents to choose any public school to which to send their children.

Although Sandler and Kapel discuss some of the shortcomings of the Alum Rock experiment --nonpublic schools not included, no rewards for teacher productivity, advertising of schools prohibited, they fail to mention that it was very difficult for the Office of Economic Opportunity to find a school district willing to take the federal government's initial offer of $5 million (eventually $9 million) to run the project because of the opposition from teachers' unions (Rand, 1981). In fact, the only way Alum Rock would agree was with the assurance that teachers whose programs were not selected would be placed in non-teaching positions for the duration of the experiment. Thus, not only was there no external competition from nonpublic schools, the opportunity for rewards and sanctions that would accrue from internal competition was minimized.

No history of the discussion of providing parents with options for schooling for their children (which is what Sandler and Kapel are really discussing, not just vouchers in the strict sense) is complete without a description of the Montclair School system because it is the primary example of how providing parents with options will maximize both equity and excellence Begun as a limited magnet program to meet the demands of the federal government to desegregate a system with a nearly 50% minority (43% black) population (Fitzgerald, 1989), Montclair now has district-wide schools of choice from K to 8 and several distinct "houses" spread out across their high school campus. In the little over a decade since

Montclair launched their first magnet schools, academic achievement scores of minority students have risen impressively, a fact not to be ignored in the discussion of how a choice system would bring about equity. Overall average Iowa test scores for grades 2 through 8 have risen from the 61st to the 94th percentile, with the greatest gains at the 7th and 8th grade levels --43rd to 94th percentile (Montclair Public Schools, Handout, 1989). Montclair's average SAT score in 1987 was 944, 38 points above the national average (*Montclair Times,* 1987).

Prior to dealing with the issues raised at the beginning of this paper, it is necessary to address one additional conceptual concern —Sandler and Kapel's use of the set or related terms 'free market,' 'market system,' 'open market,' 'marketplace,' which appear at least ten times throughout their fifteen-page article. No where do they define these terms or use them in such a way that it can be clearly understood how or why a voucher system would succeed or fail because it exemplifies a "free market" approach or that the education of children would be improved or impeded if a voucher system were implemented.

Finally, their statements that "In order to have fair competition, all aspects within the marketplace have to be equal," and "...it is difficult to equalize competition between public and private schools" (p. 271) are just not true. If all aspects in a competition were equal, there would —by definition— be no competition. That one "wins" (or succeeds while others fail) means that some aspect was unequal, or there would be no point in having competition. And the difficulty (read here, in context, "impossibility") of equalizing competition between public and private schools is not, as Sandler and Kapel claim, with making the public schools more equal to the private by removing some of the constraints on student selection and program requirements that the public schools now face. The authors have failed to distinguish the two levels of inequality between the public and private schools --structural and educational. Although public schools exist by virtue of a monopolistic state-funded structure, they provide a lower quality of education (or at least no better, depending on your view of the 1981 Coleman data, (Coleman, 1981) than private schools, the majority of which (85%) are in the "church-affiliated sector with very low reported expenditures" (p. 271). Currently schooling operates in a fixed market, a monopoly. If we wish to equalize the access of public and private schools to clients, obviously a voucher system would be the way to achieve such equalization. This author will further argue that this would be more likely than any other system to equalize the quality of education received, i.e., raise the quality of public education to that of private, as defined by higher academic achievement scores and increased parental and societal satisfaction with the schools.

Implications for Public Schools

It is necessary to begin to deal with Sandler and Kapel's claims and predictions by first dealing with the issue of parents' right to select schools for their children. Arguments they present by Levin and Butts (p. 270) regarding what reasons "the founders of the Republic" had for turning to the idea of public education must be discussed in historical context. During the latter half of the nineteenth century when state-by-state mandatory attendance and child labor laws were being passed, few children attended school or shared in "the common culture." At that time the right of the state to mandate such attendance was widely questioned by ordinary people. Today, no one would question it, not even voucher proponents. Nor would anyone question the purpose of this schooling --a literate citizenry. What is questioned is the right of the state to mandate the form and content of and value context (given that education cannot be carried on value-free) in which schooling is carried on. With a state monopoly, the argument goes, there is absolutely no incentive for the providers of a service to make any attempt to meet the real differences in learning needs of potential clients. Nor is there any accountability for outcomes because -- for financial reasons-- the majority of these clients have no option, are constrained to take the services from state-designated providers, like it or not. That you provide parents with options for the schooling of their children in no way precludes achieving the goal of "preparing the young for their role as self-governing citizens" (p. 270). Butts writes as though giving parents more control over education, providing for (not "promoting") the needs and interests of children, preparing for a better job, and getting into college are not all part of "preparing the young for their role as self-governing citizens." In fact, to deny parents and young people the right to select among options for schooling can be seen as one sure way to impede their becoming self-governing.

Now, to deal with some of the specific claims made by Sandler and Kapel.

They propose that "...it seems likely (in a "voucher approach") that the private schools will divide along homogeneous lines that will not reflect the overall sense of political community envisioned by the founders of this country. The possibility exists that vouchers will stratify students so that they do not have the opportunity to experience the diversity of backgrounds and beliefs that contributed to the democratic process" (p. 271). Taking these statements in reverse order, they fail to acknowledge that the very possibility they predict regarding students' experience is the currently prevailing state of affairs, as can readily be shown by both the recent court decision invalidating the Kentucky state school system (*Gloucester County Times*, 1989) and the ongoing *Abbott v. Burke* case in New Jersey (McCoy, 1989). Children are presently segregated by attendance zones based on residence, which usually results in stratification based on class. This will remain the case as long as we continue with our present monopolistic system of schooling.

Sandler and Kapel argue that to increase funding to nonpublic schools (though such action may —through competition— bring about improvement in public schools) would, of necessity, decrease the amount of money available for public school improvement. There are two important points they fail to consider here. First, the assumption that more money equals better schooling and less money equals worse schooling on a one-to-one ratio is unwarranted. It is much more complex than that.

Certainly one of the explanations for the quality of schooling provided by the 85% of church-affiliated private schools at roughly half the cost of that in public schools is that parents' empowerment in having chosen these schools brings with it a sense of investment in its outcomes that is worth more than many dollars in bringing about academic achievement. This is not to say that there is not a bottom dollar level below which expenditures cannot go (as argued in *Abbott v. Burke*) if a quality education is to be provided.

Secondly, the authors fail to consider the fact that we are obligated as a society to educate all children and if those currently in private schools were to attend public schools, the total amount of money available for schooling, as well as per-capita expenditure, would diminish. From simply an economic perspective, it makes good sense to implement a voucher system.

Vouchers Would Reduce Inequity

In this section of their paper, Sandler and Kapel make two major erroneous assumptions and several lesser questionable claims. Their statement that "The free market taking place in a voucher proposal assumes that everyone will have the same opportunity to acquire quality education (p. 274)," embeds both erroneous assumptions.

First, despite much discussion in the literature, our society does not have a clear notion of what "the same opportunity" of equality of educational opportunity would be in the real world where there is a wide diversity of needs, interests, and abilities among children. However, this does not keep us from realizing that, whatever equality of educational opportunity might be, we currently have widespread major **inequality** of opportunity. Our goal, then, is to **reduce inequality**, which is much more real, realistic, and realizable than chasing the chimera of equality.

With the reduction of inequality as our agenda, we can then list some of the kinds of inequality that currently exist and ask if the voucher system would be likely to reduce them. At least three **measurable** forms of inequality in our present monopolistic school system come to mind —opportunity to select one's school, per-capita expenditure, and student achievement scores. By definition the voucher system would equalize the first two and, as indicated earlier by the Montclair data, we have reason to believe that parent choice would result in improved achievement scores for those now at the lowest levels.

The second erroneous assumption contained in the authors' above-quoted statement is that 'quality education' has a single definition and is not subjective to the perspective of the individual or group making the judgement. In fact, in their discussion of vouchers and quality of education further on, they make this very point themselves. Although most of us would want to assume that minimally what we mean by 'quality education' is a basic level of literacy and numeracy, whether these are better acquired through and applied to literature, science, business, athletics, or human relations varies widely. And whether they are learned in a structure that is individualistic and oriented to the written word or group-based and focused on the spoken word does not necessarily determine the quality of education received.

There are at least four related predictions regarding the likelihood of increasing equity (i.e. reducing inequity) through a voucher system for which Sandler and Kapel offer no evidence (p. 275):

(1)."...there will probably be far fewer sellers of education services to the children of the poor."

(2). "The successful private schools will decline to accept vouchers because of the administrative requirements accompanying the state funds."

(3). "Schools that do participate in the voucher system will still have the opportunity to refuse students on the basis of low achievement or poor academic ability."

(4). "Low-income families who barely have money for food and clothing probably will not be able to afford these extra expenses (e.g. uniforms, class trips) even if school tuition is paid."

These predictions must be examined and responded to collectively. The first three deal with the operation of the system and how schools in it are likely to act, the last with the response of clients. In the first place, it would make sense to design the system in such a way that academic or other requirements for admittance are permissible only at the secondary level and only where they are demonstrably related to the focus of the program at that school. And this would not be far out of line from the present system of private schooling. Sandler and Kapel write this entire section as though the 15% of private prep schools were the majority of private schools and not that 85% of church-affiliated schools, many of them inner-city Catholic schools which are eager for students and presently provide the only option for many low-income and minority families.

Secondly, there is no reason why we could not increase both incentives and rewards for academic success with the hard to educate. If indeed —as we have every reason to believe— children from low-income and minority families cost more to educate than those from middle class families, then their vouchers should be worth proportionately more. Further, when the results of schooling in terms of academic achievement are examined, there is no reason why bonuses cannot be given to those schools and teachers performing beyond expected levels. And we do not have to, as Sandler and Kapel suggest, use norm-reference standardized tests to make these determinations. With criterion-referenced tests, it is possible for 100% of the students to achieve at or above expected levels.

Finally, how the system is structured will affect how clients respond. For those low-income families who cannot afford the extra expenses of uniforms, class trips, transportation, etc., we could easily provide subsidies in much the same way we currently subsidize school lunches for those very same families.

It cannot be denied that, although some families may not —for whatever reason— take advantage of choice available in a voucher system, inequality of opportunity is reduced just by virtue of the fact that choice is **available**. It can be viewed as triage. Undoubtedly there are those families that will be at an advantage in **any** system and those for whom **no** system will improve their lot in life, but there is a substantial majority in the middle for whom educational vouchers would provide an opportunity to select the environment in which their children would be schooled that could make the difference between success and failure. And this "third" of the population would continuously expand into the bottom "third" as empowerment through choice became more fully understood.

Vouchers Would Increase Choice

Although increase in choice as one form of reduction of inequity was discussed in the previous section, it is necessary to respond to Sandler and Kapel's three distinct reasons for questioning whether choice would be increased in a voucher system.

(1). Dissemination of information. Once again they focus on everyone in a system's having equal access to and use of information, which would just never be the case. However, providing choice and making special efforts to help "the poor and disadvantaged" receive and act on information about available options is certainly a do-able task. Further, such an information-providing system would be a much better state of affairs than currently prevails in most states (with the exception of New Jersey, which is now issuing school report cards, providing the public with information about the schools their children attend in comparison to other schools and state norms).

(2). Geographic considerations. No one doubts, or is surprised at, the fact that for the majority of parents the closeness of a school to their home would be the primary consideration in selecting a school, especially for parents of elementary children. However, if the program of the closest school does not meet a child's needs, many parents —if they could— would consider sending their children to the next closest school. Many small and medium-sized communities have more than one elementary school and whether a child attends one a half mile or a mile and a half from home is usually no big deal geographically. What's more, in urban areas, where a voucher system would have the most promise for increasing choice and reducing inequity, public transportation systems drastically reduce the problem of geographic considerations. In addition, that the courts have ruled, as Sandler and Kapel point out, that school districts can legally charge parents to bus their children to school doesn't mean this will become a wide-spread reality.

(3). Accountability. This is the strangest argument that Sandler and Kapel make for why vouchers would not increase choice. They claim that "In order to determine efficiency and quality of schools, some form of accountability in the system will have to exist" (p. 273). They predict that this accountability would be likely to be achieved through the use of standardized tests which would drive all curricula to sameness rather than diversity. Without disputing their prediction about how accountability would be determined, it must be pointed out that they ignore two blatant realities.

First, children can be taught to read well whether they are being taught to read model airplane assembly directions or *The Wind in the Willows*. Uniformity of ends in no way entails uniformity of means. Just as importantly, the scenario they described is what presently exists in our monopolistic system that, in many cities and states, claims all the children in a particular grade should be in a specified place in their math books at a designated time each day.

Sandler and Kapel conclude their section on vouchers and choice with the following statement: "Although voucher proposals make promises of increased educational choices for parents, the preceding discussion points out that only *constrained* choices will be available to the public" (p. 274). This implies that there is some system such that there would not exist constrained choices. It just ain't so! The point is that a voucher system would reduce the constraints that presently exist by providing alternatives for many families who do not now have them.

Vouchers have greater potential for improving the quality of education than any other single proposal

Sandler and Kapel begin their discussion in the section on vouchers and the quality of education with a straw man. "Within a voucher system, successful schools might be defined as those with full enrollment" (p. 276). They attack this view by arguing that 'quality education' cannot be equated with popularity, saying that "The meaning of quality education is partly dependent on the needs and background of the consumer in a voucher system." Although anyone would have to agree that full enrollment is a sign of a certain form of success, no one would claim that it is the equivalent of quality education, as is implied by the authors.

Next, having made the statement that there is no universal definition of 'quality education,' Sandler and Kapel proceed to suggest that we will not achieve quality education because different types of parents would, in a voucher system, select different forms of education for there children, **a statement which assumes a state of affairs they just negated.** They continue to assume that the term 'quality education' has common coinage when they quote Pacheco (p. 277), who denies that the presence of alternatives equals higher quality, as though he does know what equals higher quality.

They continue this section with a loosely argued paragraph that attempts again to show that full enrollment does not equal quality (as some people, we don't know who, might perceive), proposing that "What would probably happen in a voucher system is that some nonpublic schools not perceived as providing quality education (e.g. those currently operating without full enrollment) would be able to attract students from families who want their children out of the public schools" (p. 277). That this would take place is certainly questionable, but if it did, one could assume that those parents perceived the nonpublic schools in which they placed their children as offering a higher quality of education than the public schools from which they removed them. Sandler and Kapel go on to say "the question that must be asked is how are these previously unpopular schools going to improve the way they educate children when they have even more students (p. 277)," **as though unpopularity could be equated with lack of quality.**

In conclusion to this section, Sandler and Kapel cite a data review by Willms that shows "There is no evidence that the performance of a child in an academic course of study would improve by a shift from the public to the private sector" (p. 277). This fails to undermine the claim that a voucher system could lead to the improvement of the general quality of education on at least two grounds. First, it focuses on the individual rather than the aggregate in determining improvement as measured by academic outcomes. Secondly, it addresses only the performance of those in the academic course of study, those most likely to be succeeding whether they are in public or private schools. Generally speaking, these are not the clients for whom vouchers would make a difference in the quality of education they could acquire for their children.

Alternative Options

Sandler and Kapel offer as their primary alternative option to vouchers a system of site-based management in which each school would have its own elected school board with broad decision-making authority. There is no reason why this proposal could not be put into place in a system of vouchers or schools of choice. In fact, given that traditional district lines would become increasingly meaningless as parents chose to send their children to school in other districts, site-based management might be the only sensible form of school governance.

Conclusions

In conclusion, it is important to note that the many different proponents of vouchers have a wide variety of primary justifications for defending such a system. As West (1981) has indicated, the model proposed by Friedman (1978) focuses on improving the quality of education through vouchers, while that endorsed by Jencks (1970) and Sizer (1969) aims to bring about equality in our educational system. Although these goals are not mutually exclusive, how one implements a system of choice will certainly be affected by which of these two is the primary goal.

Then there are those who argue that providing choice is good in and of itself because children and families are different and the very essence of the democracy is found in providing for and fostering this diversity. This argument is usually coupled with the idea that the family is in the best position to decide what is in the interest of the child and care enough to see that it is brought about, and therefore ought to be given the means to make choices in education that the voucher system would provide.

Finally, it is important to emphasize that not merely public schools of choice, but a voucher system which includes those schools presently labeled 'private', is necessary to fully realize the meaning of being educated in the democracy for the democracy. Sandler and Kapel propose that "...educational vouchers that include sectarian schools might be challenged on constitutional grounds since it might be difficult to separate secular and religious instruction, as funded by the tuition" (p. 271). In the first place, once the government is giving money in the form of vouchers to parents to purchase schooling, there will be no "tuition" charged, or else all schools could be described as charging tuition. Historically charging of tuition has been one of the primary differences between public and private schools. The other difference has been control over admissions. In a voucher system, those schools presently labeled 'public' would have more control over admissions than they now do and those labeled 'private' would have less if they wish to be eligible to receive vouchers. Thus, two of the major differences between public and private schools would disappear.

But, of course, this is not the primary focus of Sandler and Kapel's remarks; it is the Establishment Clause of the First Amendment, which states "Congress shall make no laws establishing religion...." They suggest that a voucher system would provide public funds to support sectarian instruction. This fear must be examined in light of two considerations. In the first place, in a voucher system, unlike most current forms of aid to private schools, the money will be given to individuals, not to institutions. Secondly, our present form of mandatory attendance at a school in a monopolistic state-provided system can be seen as both a violation of the Establishment Clause as well as a violation of the Free Exercise Clause of the First Amendment, which continues "Congress shall make no laws establishing religion, nor prohibiting the free exercise thereof."

Establishment first. It can be argued that, in light of the fact that education cannot be conducted as a value-free enterprise and that any system of values must be grounded in basic underlying assumptions about the worth of human beings and their relationship to the universe (metaphysics), it is impossible not to have some form of establishment in schooling supplied by the state. This concern, in its more popularized form, takes the position that in the early 1960's with the Supreme Court rulings in *Schemmp/Murray* (1963) and *Engle v. Vitale* (1962) which removed mandatory prayer and Bible-reading from the schools, we went from Protestant establishment to one based on secular humanism. For example, teachers no longer tell Johnny not to steal his neighbor's pencil because he will be punished by God for doing so, but because he would not want his neighbor to steal his. In any case, it is argued, that justifications for behavior must be value-based and, as long as children's behavior conforms to that expected in a democratic society, the choice of values given to justify behavior should be the parents', not those established by the state. Forcing parents to school their children in state-run, tax-supported schools is a form of establishment. This can also be seen as a violation of the Free Exercise Clause in that it is thereby impossible for parents to afford to send their children to schools that endorse their own value systems and they are, thus, prohibited from the free exercise of their religion.

Moving from the philosophical to the practical, there are several economic and educational reasons why a voucher system makes good sense. As explained above, increasing financial support for private schools that already exist would be far less costly than attempting to educate in public schools all of the children now in private schools. Secondly, the extensive bureaucracy visualize by Sandler and Kapel is not a necessity. It is conceivable that the decentralization occurring in a system of vouchers coupled with site-based management could bring about a savings in salaries of costly central administrators. It is probable that transportation would cost more. But if children are in schools chosen by their parents and, as they get older, by themselves, the likelihood that they will succeed academically and vocationally, thereby reducing the long-term costs for welfare and crime to society, is greatly increased. Many inner city Catholic schools now educate a higher proportion low-income and minority **non-Catholic** students than surrounding suburban public schools for substantially less than those public schools (West, 1981). Supporting this activity is a sound financial and educational investment.

Sandler and Kapel conclude by pointing out that a voucher system has never been fully implemented in an urban setting. This, of course, is true. They go on to say "There is no empirical evidence supporting advantages to this educational approach" (p. 281). This is not true. Data regarding improvement in the academic achievement of minority students in Catholic schools (Greeley, 1982) and in systems of choice such as Montclair (*Montclair Public Schools; Composite,* 1989) represent a substantial advantage, especially in urban settings, from this educational approach. What's more, the very fact that a voucher system has never been fully implemented in an urban setting should keep Sandler and Kapel from coming to any hard conclusions about the consequences of implementation.

REFERENCES

Coleman, James; Thomas Hoffer; and Sally Kilgore (1981). *Public and Private Schools.* Washington D.C. National Center for Education Statistics.

Engle v. Vitale, 370 U.S. 421 (1962).

Esposito, Frank J. (1988). *Public School Choice: National Trends and Initiatives.* Trenton, NJ: New Jersey State Department of Education

Fitzgerald, Mary Lee (1989). Presentation to Conference for members of the New Jersey School

Boards Association.

Friedman, Milton (1978)."The Voucher Idea: Selling Schools Like Groceries." *N Y Times Magazine:* 22-23 ff.

The Gloucester County Times (June 1989). "Kentucky Court Wipes Out State School System."

Greeley, Andrew M. (1982). *Catholic High Schools and Minority Students.* New Brunswick: Transaction Books.

Jencks, Christopher (1970). "Giving Parents Money for Schooling: Education Vouchers." *Phi Delta Kappan:* 52:49-52.

McCoy, Craig R. "Arguments to Begin in School Funding Case." *Philadelphia Inquirer.* June 1989.

Montclair Public Schools; Composite: Elementary, Middle and High Schools (1989). Unpublished Handout.

Montclair Times (1987). Editorial Comment.

Raywid, Mary Anne (1989). *The Case for Public Schools of Choice.* Bloomington, IN: Phi Delta Kappa Educational Foundation.

Rand Corporation (1981). *A Study of Alternatives in American Education.* Washington: National institute of Education, Seven Volumes.

Sandler, Andrew B. and David E. Kapel (1988). "Educational Vouchers: A Viable Option for Urban Settings?" *The Urban Review.*

School District of Abington Township v. Schempp and *Murray v. Curlett*, 374 U.S. 203 (1963).

Sizer, Theodore (1969). "The Case for a Free Market." *The Educational Frum.*

Tannenbaum, Margaret (1989). *A Survey of the Perceptions of and Attitudes About Schools of Choice of Teachers, Administrators, Board Members, Parents, and Secondary Students in Public and Private Schools.* Unpublished.

West, E.G. (1981). "Choice or Monopoly in Education." *Policy Review.*

The Uncertain Prospects for Educational Vouchers

Dwight R. Lee

The most effective thing we could do to improve the quality of education in America is to make educators compete for the consumer's dollar. As long as educational consumers have to pay taxes to support public schools, whether they send their children to these schools or not, and have little choice in the public schools their children do attend, our public school professionals will continue to view their students as captive clients. Our public educators have taken advantage of this situation by paying less attention to the concerns of their customers and more attention to perquisites of their profession.

There is a simple and effective way of reforming public education so that the tonic of competition would invigorate educational policy: the institution of an educational voucher system.[1] Although educational vouchers would significantly improve the quality and efficiency of education, in an important respect the voucher proposal is a rather modest one. Government would still be the primary source of financial support for education, but with this support taking the form of vouchers or tax credits given to consumers rather than to the schools.[2] Under a voucher plan schools would be provided by private individuals responding to the publicly financed, but consumer controlled, demand for education.

The key to understanding the advantages of the voucher approach is the additional control this approach would give to the consumers of education. Under the current arrangement consumers of public education have some control, but not much. This control has to be exercised indirectly through political influence rather than directly through market decisions on whether or not to patronize a particular supplier. It is well known that the diverse interests of consumers are difficult to aggregate and transmit through the political process. Even strongly-felt consumer demands often fail to translate into effective political demands since wielding political influence requires a level of organization consumers seldom achieve. In contrast, suppliers of a publicly provided service, such as education, are well organized through professional associations with a dominant interest in decisions affecting their professional prosperity. This makes it relatively easy to transmit supplier-oriented concerns through the political process. Not surprisingly, it is public school professionals who, under current arrangements, have the greatest control over educational programs and policies.

This situation would change quickly under a voucher system. Consumers would find it easy to transmit their educational demands effectively through the exercise of market choices. Educational professionals would find that they had to either provide a service of the type and quality desired by the consumer, at a competitive price, or experience a loss of patronage. Educational quality would improve, educational costs would decline, and educational consumers would be better off.

It does not require clairvoyance to predict the response of public school professionals to such a shift in control. Educators whose interests are attached to existing public school arrangements quite accurately see proposals for educational vouchers as a major threat to be opposed at all cost. There is little hope of convincing the public school educators that vouchers are the best way of realizing the goals of educational quality which they so vociferously support. Few responses are more natural than the sincere belief that those things which threaten our private interests also threaten the public interest. In the effort to achieve genuine educational reform it simply has to be accepted that the public education lobby will oppose the voucher system.

In order to lay the foundation for a more detailed discussion of the current problems with the public schools, and to explain how the source of these problems creates obstacles to genuine reform, it will be helpful to consider an analogous, but hypothetical situation.

The Tale of Tax Mart

Imagine a successful movement to have all local governments establish grocery stores for the purpose of providing, at no charge, a proper diet for everyone. The cost of this service would, of course, be paid for through higher taxes. The stated rationale for this movement would be that nutrition is too important to be left to the whimsy of an uninformed public, and the new arrangement would enhance the well-being of all by giving nutritional experts more control over our diets. People could continue shopping at private food stores if they chose to do so, but they would still have to pay the same amount of taxes to support the provision of public food. Almost everyone, having to pay anyway, would assume initially that it was to their advantage to get their food at the local Tax Mart.

This arrangement would immediately reduce the competitive pressures operating in the retailing of food. If costs went up because salaries were increased, more administrators and specialized nutritional consultants were employed, and more professional conferences and workshops were attended, there would be little concern that consumers would shift their patronage to private stores. The additional costs would not be reflected in prices observed on the grocery shelves. Instead they would show up in higher tax payments that would have to be paid regardless of where one did his shopping. Tax Mart professionals would also face little pressure to stock a large variety of food in order to appeal to the diverse taste of consumers, to offer convenient hours, or to provide fast and courteous checkout. Service could decline significantly before it would pay the consumer to purchase food at private stores and in effect pay twice. In short, those working for Tax Mart would, under the new arrangement, be able to devote more attention to doing the things they thought were important and less attention to doing the things their consumers thought were important.

As long as public grocery stores are locally financed and controlled, however, there would still be some noticeable influence exerted by the consumer. The cost of the public grocery stores would have a significant impact on the local government's budget, and attempts to pass inefficiencies along to the taxpayer in the form of higher taxes would be noticed, at least by some. Also, it is easier for a group of concerned taxpayers to have an impact on local politicians, who can be voted out of office by relatively few voters, than is the case with politicians elected by larger constituencies. Moreover, it is easier to vote with your feet at the local level than at the state or national level. If local taxes become too great a burden, or local service too much a disappointment, it is easier to move from one local jurisdiction to another than from one state, or country, to another. But it is really not necessary for people to move out of a locality due to high tax rates in order for taxpayer mobility to exert some control over local politicians. People are constantly moving from one region of the country to another for reasons that have nothing to do with local tax rates. In deciding exactly where to settle, however, there will typically be several local political jurisdictions from which to choose. In such cases the local tax rates and the quality of the local governmental services will often be decisive considerations in the location decision. Local governments that want to maintain their tax base will have to keep their activities at least somewhat responsive to the citizen consumer.

Those who administer and work for Tax Mart would not be unaware of the restrictions imposed upon their professional discretion by total reliance on local financing. Clear advantages would be seen in obtaining state and federal financing. One advantage, from the Tax Mart perspective, is that state and federal funding would greatly diffuse the tax burden imposed by Tax Mart operations. This would serve to further weaken the incentive and the ability of those who are paying the bill to exert control over the type and quality of the service being provided. Also, by allowing local taxpayers to shift part of the burden of paying for their food to others, state and federal financing would make it easier to obtain local support for expanding local Tax Mart operations. Of course, taxpayers in each locality would end up paying for part of the public food services received by those in other localities. But this fact will do little to dampen demand for local service since each taxpayer would recognize that the amount he has to pay for the Tax Marts serving others will be unaffected by the size of the Tax Mart serving him.

State and federal financing of local services also reduces the control citizens can exercise over the taxing and spending proclivities of local politicians by voting with their feet. More state and federal funding inevitably means more state and federal taxes, taxes that are unaffected by the choice among political jurisdictions within a particular state. The larger the overlay of state and federal taxes, the less the relative difference in tax burdens between jurisdictions with high local taxes and those with low local taxes. So higher state and federal taxes to finance the local Tax Mart would likely mean greater support from local taxes as well. The private interests of those employed by Tax Mart, as well as the other special interests that benefit from Tax Mart activities, would be well served by moves to centralize the financing of the local public grocery stores.

The arguments for more centralization, however, would not be made in private interest terms. Rather, proposals for more state and federal financing would be presented as desperately needed measures for advancing the public interest. For example, it would be argued that more centralized financing is needed to provide those who live in poorer political jurisdictions the same quality of public food service as that received by those living in wealthier jurisdictions. Public interest statements of this type are always used to camouflage special interest proposals in such a way as to make them more acceptable politically. The success of this type of camouflage both helps explain, and is explained by, the advantage narrowly focused interests have over widely diffused interests in the political process. Because the rather concentrated interests of the Tax Mart professionals, and of their special interest allies, would be advanced by more state and federal financing, one could expect movement in this direction to take place despite the fact that it would work against the general interests of taxpayers and consumers.

As the financing of local Tax Marts became more centralized, the tendency toward higher costs and a lower quality of service would become more pronounced. Additional layers of bureaucracy would provide employment opportunities for more public food professionals. And additional professional certification would be required of these professionals as they looked for highly visible barometers attesting to their expertise. Entry level positions would require undergraduate degrees which feature such courses as Meat Management, Deli Display, Psychology of the Food Consumer, and the History of Eating. Salary increases and promotion would be based on graduate credits obtained from in-service courses, or on the successful completion of a masters degree or Ph.D. in Public Food Administration. Before long a significant percentage of those who work as public food professionals would have advanced academic degrees.

College professors who teach these courses, and who lobbied for making them a requirement, would recognize that public funding for grocery stores is the primary source of the demand for their services. These educators would join their students as special-interest advocates who believe strongly that the public food establishment is essential to the nutritional well-being of the country.

Other special interests would also find it tempting to use public food policy for realizing advantages, or promoting causes, that would be difficult to do in the absence of politically concentrated power. The more centralized the political control, the more impact single issue groups will have if they are successful politically. And the more centralized the control, the fewer levers these single issue groups will need to control in order to be a success.

One group, for example, may feel strongly that public grocery stores should not carry foods that have religious significance, as this would violate the constitutional separation of church and state. This group may be successful in getting Kosher foods, Christmas cookies, and Easter candy banned from all Tax Marts. Another group would feel that allowing people to shop in the neighborhood Tax Mart promotes racial segregation. This group may be successful at pushing legislation which results in many shoppers having to use a public grocery store on the other side of town. One can be sure that the egg lobby, the pork lobby, and the beef lobby will be trying to use their political muscle to influence Tax Mart policy in ways that favor their products. Political opposition can be expected, however, from a coalition of the health food lobby and the animal rights activists who, if they got their way, would restrict the selection at Tax Mart to such things as stone-ground granola bread, prune juice, bean sprouts, unflavored yogurt, lima beans, and brown rice. Product selection and store policies would soon have little to do with the exercise of consumer choice in the market place. Increasingly people would find that the only effective way to exert influence would be to engage in political combat. The provision of food would become a socially divisive issue as emotional conflict dominated Tax Mart policy. The voice of the placid fellow who just wanted a better selection of pork and beans and his favorite six-pack of beer would be ignored.

Indeed, the service would decline to the point where some consumers would begin shopping at private grocery stores. The ability of private stores, charging full price for their products, to compete successfully against the fully subsidized Tax Mart would be undeniable evidence that the consumers' interests were being given scant attention in the tax-supported stores.

As the evidence became unmistakable that Tax Mart was failing to provide acceptable service, many reforms would be considered. Most of the suggested reforms would involve more federal government funding, more control over professional qualifications by the National Public Food Workers Association, or stricter educational requirements for public food professionals, as the best way to improve service and restore the public's confidence in Tax Mart. There would be a few, however, who would recognize these suggestions as more of the same policies that caused the problems in the first place. These reformers would see the advantage in shifting control over food decisions away from government and back to the consumer. They would see the answer to many of the problems facing the public grocery stores in a bold new program called Universal Food Stamps (UFS). While accepting the prevailing view that food is of such national importance that the government should finance a minimum acceptable level of food consumption for everyone, UFS advocates would see no reason why the food actually had to be provided by the government. Rather, once people received their governmentally supplied food stamps they could spend them anywhere they chose. As private grocery stores competed against the Tax Marts (which no longer received direct public financing) for these food stamps, it would be argued that the quality of food would improve, as would the selection and the service.

In comparison to the other suggested reforms, however, the UFS suggestion would receive little serious attention. And most of what it did receive would be negative. Those whose careers were tied to existing public food arrangements, along with those who had been successful at promoting their causes through public food policy, would, quite correctly, see UFS as a threat to their wealth and political influence. Of course, the arguments made against the UFS proposal would mask the private interests being protected behind a rhetoric of public interest concerns. We would be told that the implementation of UFS would destroy the public food system as private stores would spring up only in the rich suburbs where rich patrons could supplement their food stamps, leaving financially starved remnants of the public stores to serve those in the poor neighborhoods. Shopping segregation would once more rear its ugly head as people would put the convenience of their neighborhood stores ahead of higher social goals such as racial integration and harmony. Also, if left to the capriciousness of individual choice, the public would soon be taken in by slick advertising and would begin polluting their bodies with junk foods. The public food lobby would see no end to the social havoc which would be caused by the UFS approach to food financing.

With the exception of a few academics there would be little vocal support for the UFS proposal. Most consumers of food would be ignorant of, and apathetic toward, public food policy, and few of them would have any real understanding of how a UFS policy would actually work. It would be difficult to find a special interest group which would find it worthwhile to expend its political influence in support of the Universal Food Stamp program. The Association of Private Grocery Stores would be the most likely lobbying group to lend political support to the UFS reform, but more likely its members would be fearful that government money coming their way in the form of food stamps would soon be followed with government controls that would leave them worse off.

The best the UFS advocates could hope initially to maneuver through the political process would be a local experiment for the purpose of gauging the feasibility and effectiveness of the food stamp approach. Unfortunately, the design and implementation of this experiment would necessarily be carried out by government, and be subject to the influence of those special interest groups which oppose UFS. The result would be so many special interest restrictions on the experimental food stamps that little would be learned except that they do not work anything at all like the UFS advocates had argued they would. For example, criteria would be imposed that would restrict the use of food stamps in existing Tax Marts. There would be no mechanism for rewarding personal achievement in those stores that attracted food stamp customers or for penalizing those in stores which lost customers. Food stores which did find favor with the consumer would not be able to expand to satisfy the demand, with excess demand being rationed over all stores by the authorities. Furthermore, restrictions would be imposed on the use of food stamps for the purpose of promoting an ethnic mix in the grocery stores which the authorities considered appropriate.

Predictably, the food stamp experiment would be judged a failure by those who saw consumer choice as a threat. The dominance of these interests in the political arena would remain a major obstacle to the hope that food stamps would be implemented on a wide scale. Even if food stamps were implemented widely, this would likely indicate nothing more than that the dominant special interests had decided that they could better secure their positions and promote their crusades through food stamps than through existing arrangements. Since the special interests could never accomplish their objectives with a "clean" food stamp system, the danger would be that any politically viable UFS would impose just as many restrictions on consumer choices as the Tax Mart System it would replace.

The Moral of the Story

The tale of Tax Mart is in fact directly analogous to the situation as it actually exists in the field of education. Education, apparently being too important to be left to the private decisions of the consumer, has been entrusted to professional educators. These professional educators, who are chosen by government agencies and paid with tax revenues, provide education at no cost to all children from kindergarten through twelfth grade.[3] Consumers of education can, of course, attend private schools, but this requires that they pay twice for education since tax obligations are not reduced if the private option is chosen.

The observable implications~of stymied competitive pressures in education are the same as those in the hypothetical case of food retailing. For example, the student-teacher ratio is lower in public schools than private schools, and is currently dropping.[4] It is the rare private school that requires teaching certificates, but it is easy for private schools to dismiss those who prove to be incompetent, something that is almost impossible to do in the public schools once a teacher has tenure. Public schools are becoming increasingly top-heavy with administrators and special-help professionals. For example, the number of classroom teachers in the public schools as a percentage of the instructional staff has declined from 96 percent in the early 1930s to 86 percent in 1983.[5] Even after allowing for inflation, the cost per student in the public schools has increased more than fivefold.[6]

Furthermore, and as one would expect, protection against competition has also had adverse effects on educational quality. The dramatic drop in the average SAT score, declining from almost 1000 in 1963 to slightly under 900 today, is well known. And this decline has been most pronounced among students who attend public schools. It has been argued by public school supporters that this difference reflects nothing more than the fact that the public schools are required to take everyone while the private schools are at liberty to admit only the better students. But the facts suggest strongly that, if this provides an explanation at all, it is a very incomplete explanation. According to one recent study, 60 percent of the parochial private schools do not expel a single student during a given academic year, and in the inner city of many major metropolitan areas, the majority of the students of these parochial schools are black. The important difference between the public and private schools are explained by such considerations as the following: private school students are 50 percent more likely to put in an hour's worth of homework each night than are public school students; 70 percent of all private school students are enrolled in an academic program compared to 34 percent of public school students; a third year of language is taken by 14 percent of the private school students compared to 6 percent of the public school students; chemistry is taken by 53 percent of the public school students but by only 37 percent of the public school students; geometry is taken by 84 percent of the private school students and by only 53 percent of the public school students.[7] It is difficult to avoid the conclusion that, on average, private schools provide better education than do public schools, and they do so at lower cost.[8]

Just as in the Tax Mart example, a highly decentralized system of public schools does allow for some competition; the public education lobby, however, sees its interests served by greater centralization. This can be accomplished by increasing the size of school districts or increasing the amount of financing these districts receive from state and federal governments. Public educators have favored both of these centralizing moves, and with noticeable success. Since the early 1930s, the number of school districts has declined from 130,000 to 16,000.[9] Before the 1930s, local government provided over 80 percent of school financing, with state governments providing the remainder. The local share has declined steadily ever since, with the state share taking up most of the slack. Although the proportion of public school financing provided by the federal government is still small, this proportion has also been increasing in recent years. In 1983, only 42 percent of the public school bill was financed by local governments, with the states financing approximately 50 percent and the federal government supplying the remaining 8 percent.[10] And the pressure from the public school lobby continues for yet more funding from the state and federal governments. For example, the National Education Association (NEA) has drafted and lobbied for what it calls the "American Defense Education Act" which, if passed, would authorize $10 billion in federally financed block grants to local school districts.[11]

Lacking the competition needed to forge a meaningful connection between the performance of public school teachers and the economic reward they receive, other measures of merit have to be relied upon. From the perspective of those in the education industry, an ideal measure is one which is easily quantifiable and lends apparent credibility to the claim of professionalism. Academic success, as measured by the degrees acquired or number of post-graduate credits earned, serves nicely in this regard. Not surprisingly, academic credentialism is the most important consideration, after seniority, in determining pay raises for public school teachers. Over 50 percent of all public school teachers today hold master's degrees.[12] Unfortunately, there is little incentive for anyone to effectively monitor this degree-granting process in order to ensure that educational quality is being maintained. If anything, the incentives all go in the other direction. Graduate courses in education requiring little or no intellectual effort on the part of the student provide an easy way for school administrators to evaluate personnel, a painless path to more "prestige" and pay for public school teachers, and a rationale for the existence of departments of education which are lowering the average academic quality of colleges around the country.[13]

The interest administrators and professors in departments of education have in maintaining public education as it is now structured is obvious. If the survival of individual elementary and secondary schools was made to depend on their ability to satisfy the consumers' demand for quality education, then the survival of college departments of education would depend on their ability to turn out graduates with solid intellectual skills. Few departments of education, as they are now staffed and structured, would survive with this requirement.

Neither have the opportunities offered by political, rather than consumer, control of the public schools gone unnoticed by other special interest and single issue groups— groups that possess power disproportionate to their membership

size when operating through the political process. The public schools have
provided a tempting target for a whole host of groups which appreciate the
advantages government compulsion has over persuasion in the effort to advance
particular goals and points of view. And once one group begins pushing its agenda
through the public schools, hostile reactions from those with equally strong
opposing views are inevitable. It should surprise no one that the public schools
have been turned into battlegrounds over such socially divisive issues as prayer,
sex education, creation versus evolution, racial balance, and the censorship of
"dirty" books. With education policy being buffeted with such emotional issues,
there can be little wonder at the strong evidence indicating that education has been
neglected in the public schools.

Neither can there be any wonder, given the decline in the quality of education
provided in the public schools, that many parents are sending their children to
private schools even though this means paying for education twice. In recent years
over 5 million elementary and secondary students have been attending private
schools. This represents almost 11 percent of the student population.[14] This is
clear and compelling evidence that the educational demands of a large segment of
the public are being ignored or poorly served by the public schools. Also revealing
are the results of the Gallup surveys of the public's opinion of education. Since
1974 respondents have been asked to rate public schools by the standard school
grading scale of A through F in the annual poll. The top two categories, A and B,
were chosen by 48 percent of the respondents in 1974. By 1977 this percentage
had declined to 37 percent, where it has held fairly constant. At the other end of the
scale, the percentage assigning the public schools grades of D or F rose
consistently through the late 1970s.[15]

Clearly there is widespread sympathy for reform of public education. For the
most part, however, this desire for reform has not focused on proposals that call
for fundamental changes in current arrangements and practices. Coming as it does
from the rather diffused interests of the education consumer, the desire for reform
may well be satisfied for the time being with platitudes such as a "national
commitment to excellence in education." And certainly any move that goes beyond
platitudes and toward genuine educational reform is sure to be opposed vigorously

by the organized, and politically influential, public school lobby.

Consider the response to the one suggestion for real reform in education that has been put forth—the voucher proposal. Despite the fact that educational vouchers have the potential for transferring control over educational decisions back to the consumers, only a small percentage of the population is even familiar with the voucher concept. Although almost all parents are concerned about the education of their children, with educational policy being determined through the political process most parents quite rationally feel that they can have little influence on the type of education their children receive in the public schools. Rational ignorance and apathy best explain the impact, or lack of impact, the general public has had on public school policy. Advocates of the voucher approach had assumed that Catholic schools, which now face the heavily subsidized competition of the public schools, would provide organized support for vouchers. This has turned out to be incorrect. The view of the Catholic schools seems to be that the opportunity to compete for governmentally financed vouchers would come at an unacceptably high price—extensive government regulations and controls.[16] It would be hard to argue that the Catholic schools are wrong in this judgment. The public school lobby has resisted strongly, and effectively, any move toward the voucher approach, including localized experiments with vouchers. In those very few cases in which a voucher experiment has been permitted, so many regulations and restrictions were applied that private schools were either disqualified from participating, or chose not to participate.

Of the federally funded voucher experiments, the one that ran the longest and which has been deemed most successful was conducted in Alum Rock, California. But, as one might expect, restrictions were placed on these vouchers which minimized the competitive pressures they imposed on public school professionals, and which attempted to promote social objectives that had little to do with education. Teachers, for example, did not have to worry about loss of income if their enrollments declined. They were given priority in teaching jobs at other schools and given makeshift work at full pay until such jobs were available. On the other hand, teachers who succeeded in attracting additional students were not rewarded with higher salaries. Those schools which parents preferred were not able to expand to meet the extra demand. Those students who did not get their first choice were simply assigned to other schools. A local employee certification council required that any private school had to satisfy a host of standards on such things as teacher education requirements, pay and fringe benefits, and faculty-student ratios. This made it effectively impossible for a private school to enter into competition for the vouchers. In addition, the vouchers were addressed to the issue of income distribution, with financial incentives for schools to enroll poor children and restrictions on parents' ability to supplement their voucher. The concern over racial balance in the schools resulted in further restrictions on the Alum Rock vouchers.[17] Experimental educational vouchers have been anything but the "clean" vouchers the advocates of the voucher approach have in mind.

Whether we are considering the hypothetical case of Tax Mart or the reality of our public school system, the logic of special interest politics remains the same. Once decisions are transferred from the market place to the political arena the interests of suppliers soon dominate the interests of consumers.

What are the prospects for the enactment and implementation of a voucher system which actually transfers control from the professional educator to the consumer? From the discussion so far it would be easy to conclude that the prospects are bleak. The same political influence that has allowed the public education lobby to manipulate educational policy to its own advantage will be used to oppose meaningful reform, since reform would threaten those advantages. The special interest political power of the public education lobby is extremely strong and can easily cause one to despair of any hope for genuine educational reform. But the special interest influence of the public school establishment is a dark cloud which has a silver lining.

The political success of special interests almost always depends upon a facade of public interest. If that facade is penetrated the ability of politically organized groups to capture private benefits at public expense is severely limited. This suggests that advancing the goal of educational reform through vouchers requires more than sound economic arguments on the educational benefits vouchers would provide. Such arguments, while valuable at one level, will do little at the political level to overcome counterarguments by the public school establishment if the public perceives only noble motives behind those arguments. The public school lobby is well aware of the advantage image can have over substance in politics, and it has been very good at presenting an image of the existing system of public education as essential to the wellbeing of our country and resting on the shoulders of dedicated public servants making heroic personal sacrifices for the sake of our children.18 The political effectiveness of the public school lobby would begin to weaken with the recognition that behind the public interest rhetoric are the special interest pressures of power politics.

It is this view of the vulnerability of the public school lobby that has motivated the current essay. The emphasis has been on the private interest motivations that lie behind the political opposition to educational vouchers rather than on the advantages of educational vouchers themselves. These advantages are real and significant, and deserve the extensive discussion they have received elsewhere. But mounting a strong offense will be futile if the defense is even stronger. The enormous strength of the public school lobby's defense against educational vouchers has had nothing to do with the logic of their arguments and everything to do with their ability to hide their special interest politics behind a facade of public interest rhetoric. Weakening that defense requires piercing that facade and exposing the pubic education lobby for what it is—an organized special interest using political influence to realize private gain at public expense.

1. See Milton Friedman, "The Role of Government in Education," in Robert Solow, ed., *Education and the Public Interest* (New Brunswick: Rutgers University Press, 1955).
2. For the purpose of this paper there is no advantage in distinguishing between the voucher approach and the tax credit approach to the financing of education, and henceforth we will simply refer to vouchers.
3. Not to mention the fact that, for those who qualify, education continues to be provided at little or no charge at both the undergraduate and graduate levels of college.
4. See Phil Keisling, "How to Save the Public Schools," *The New Republic*, November 1, 1982, 27-32.
5. See Milton Friedman's *Newsweek* column, December 5, 1983.
6. Ibid.
7. These figures are found in Keisling, 27.
8. This is roughly the conclusion reached by James S. Coleman, Thomas Hoffer, and Sally Kilgore in their book, *High School Achievement: Public, Catholic, and Private Schools Compared* (New York: Basic Books, 1982). This book is the subject of the article by Keisling.
9. See Friedman, *Newsweek*, December 5, 1983.
10. See Denis Doyle and Chester Finn Jr., "American Schools and the Future of Local Control,"

The Public Interest, Fall 1984, 77-95.

11. The official designation of the bill is H.R. 5609, 98th Congress, 2nd session. For the NEA's perspective on the bill see "NEA Creates ADEA Momentum," NEA Today, December 1983, 8.

12. See Thomas Toch, "How To Attract Better Teachers," *Journal of Contemporary Studies,* Summer 1984, 59-67.

13. As one would expect, there is tremendous special interest resistance to any move that would weaken or circumvent this teacher education process. See, for example, Virginia Inman, "Certification of Teachers Lacking Courses in Education Stirs Battles in Several States," *Wall Street Journal::* 6 January 1984, 23.

14. See Donald E. Frey, *Tuition Tax Credits for Private Education: An Economic Analysis* (Ames: Iowa State University Press, 1983), 8.

15. Ibid., 105.

16. See Denis P. Doyle, "The Politics of Choice: A View From the Bridge," 227-55, in *Parents, Teachers, and Children: Prospects for Choice in American Education* (San Francisco: Institute for Contemporary Studies, 1977).

17. See E. G. West, "The Prospects for Educational Vouchers: An Economic Analysis," in Robert B. Everhart, ed., *The Public School Monopoly: A Critical Analysis of Education and the State in American Society* (San Francisco: Pacific Institute for Public Policy Research, 1982), 369-91.

18. There are, of course, many dedicated and competent individuals working in our public school system, and so the above characterization of public school employees is not a complete distortion. Successful political propaganda always has to have some connection with fact. But this characterization of the existing public school system ignores the private interest motivations which underlie the politics of public school policy.

It should be noted in passing that dedicated and competent teachers and administrators have nothing to fear from educational vouchers. Indeed they would do better under a voucher approach since the ensuing market competition for their skills would create a system of genuine merit pay.

SECTION II: MAGNET SCHOOLS

INTRODUCTION

The articulation of the concept of 'magnet' —i.e., a school with a theme which attracts students to it— emerged during the 1960s in response to efforts to desegregate American schools. In many instances, especially in large cities, magnet schools were created to try to avoid involuntary busing. In a certain sense, however, as long as there has been organized schooling, there have been magnet schools. Any time anyone set up a school organized around a particular theme, it was, though the term may not have existed in earlier times, a magnet. Thus, any vocational school, Montessori program, school of science and technology or performing arts is a magnet school. It remains, however, for the purposes of most discussions, magnet schools are usually found in urban areas and are established to implement segregation.

There is little doubt that magnet schools have been successful in the sense that the students fortunate enough to be accepted into them (as there are almost always more applicants than seats available) are more likely to receive an education with which they are satisfied than those left behind in undistinguished urban public schools. However, one of the major problems with establishing magnets, especially in large urban school systems, is that they tend to draw off from the neighborhood schools the "best" —i.e., most knowledgeable, most motivated, most likely to succeed— students with the most ambitious parents, leaving behind —as opponents of magnets have so often labeled them— "the dregs."

HISTORICAL BACKGROUND

In the 1970s magnet systems to accomplish the goals of desegregation were established in a number of cities, including Houston, Boston, Los Angeles, East Harlem, Rochester, St. Louis, Milwaukee, and Montclair, NJ. Milwaukee's system was interdistrict, involving the cross enrollment of students from the surrounding suburban districts. St. Louis, after the failure of intradistrict magnets to substantially desegregate the city's schools, was transformed into an interdistrict system in the 1980s. In addition, during the 1970s, Dade County, FL, initiated a county-wide magnet system that has continued to grow since that time. During the 1980s Tucson, Chicago, and Prince George's County, MD, also developed magnet programs aimed at reducing school segregation.

One school system which has avoided the problem of magnets draining the most motivated students away from neighborhood schools is Montclair, NJ, all of whose schools, at both the elementary and secondary levels, are magnets. As a result, there is no school in which the students are "left behind." Every school has a theme and every parent/guardian must select a school for his/her child.

In the early 1970s Montclair, with a very segregated 49% minority population, was placed under a federal court order to desegregate its schools. Recognizing all the political problems involved in cross-district busing, the superintendent of schools introduced a magnet system. Inasmuch as minority parents were no more eager than others to send their elementary children to schools outside their neighborhoods, the plan was to site in each of two areas a school most likely to draw students from the opposite area. In 1977, in the predominantly white middle class section of town, Montclair established a back-to-basics school, which minority parents were more likely to select for their children, and in the predominantly minority lower class section of town, they established a gifted and talented school, to which white middle class parents were most likely to want to send their children. In the next decade Montclair gradually added magnets to the system until it was fully "magnetized," thus achieving a full system of schools of choice. Currently there are seven elementary schools, two middle schools, and a high school with four "houses" to which families can choose to send their children. The neighborhood school as it has traditionally been understood no longer exists in

Montclair; the entire township is the neighborhood for every school.

Although magnets in recent decades were introduced primarily as a way to desegregate schools, it is illuminating to consider their virtues as a way of organizing schooling in their own right. The idea that a group of people —teachers, administrators, and other staff members— would develop a curriculum and system of delivery around a theme they commonly hold as valuable is very energizing. Whether these themes are substantive —such as technology, science, world cultures— or organizational —such as back-to-basics, Montessori, open classrooms, a logical assumption is that individuals' choosing the context in which they work is very likely to increase their level of commitment. At the same time, it is reasonable to expect that parents' and students' choosing these schools would have a similar effect —increased commitment to their success— meaning higher levels of achievement for the students who attend these schools. What is crucial, it would appear, is that an entire system is magnetized.

Overview of Articles

In the selections that follow, descriptions of some of the most prominent magnet systems have been selected for inclusion. These include St. Louis Milwaukee; Montclair, NJ; and District 4 in East Harlem, NY. Several articles address the issue of the value of using magnets as a means to achieve the goals of desegregation. The section concludes with a summary description of a sampling of large-system magnet programs throughout the country prepared by Frank Esposito for the New Jersey Department of Education.

In a pair of articles E. T. Foote and Bruce La Pierre give first-hand accounts of their involvement in the beginning of St. Louis' desegregation plan using magnet schools. Foote, a Civil Rights attorney practicing law and teaching at Washington University in 1980, was asked by Judge Jim Meredith, who had at times helped Foote teach, to help him implement the school desegregation order that had just been issued by the Eighth Circuit Court of Appeals. Foote then describes the interactions of the citizens' committee, of which he was chair, in working with St. Louis and twenty-three surrounding districts to develop a voluntary desegregation "plan ratio," basically a benign quota. La Pierre picks up the story at this point and explains his role, as Special Master for the purpose of negotiating a settlement among the parties (the school districts), in gaining agreement among all of the districts to the three principal components of the settlement: provisions for voluntary interdistrict student transfers, the establishment of magnet schools and the improvement of the quality of education in the city schools, and provisions for major capital improvements.

In "Champion of Choice," John Fund interviews Polly Williams, the black state representative who began in Milwaukee the nation's first experiment in education vouchers for low-income children to be used in private as well as public schools. Williams responds to questions regarding busing, the liberal versus conservative agendas, her own background, and urban problems, concluding with a comparison of a choice system to having the opportunity to get a second opinion when one is sick.

In "The Montclair Model," from a summary report prepared for the Educational Testing Service, Beatrice C. Clewell and Myra F. Loy provide a history of the implementation of district-wide magnets in Montclair, discuss the major impact the program has had on racial balance and test scores for both minority and non-minority students, concluding with an analysis of why magnets have been so successful in Montclair.

In "Central Park East: An Alternative Story," Deborah Meir, the chief architect of the four-school system in Central Park East and principal of the high school, describes how District 4 in New York City has become one of the most innovative and successful school systems in the country. She begins with the fact that "...one of our primary reasons for starting the school...was out of personal desire for greater autonomy as teachers," decries the failure of the rest of New York City to "break out of the traditional mold," and concludes with the challenge that "...the current reform mood offers an important opening —if we can resist the desire for a new 'one best way.' We cannot achieve true reform by fiat."

This section concludes with two articles addressing the issue of magnet schools and desegregation. Of the three authors who raise the question of whether magnets will increase desegregation, two say no and one says yes. Stanley Trent, in "School Choice for African-American Children Who Live in Poverty: A

Commitment to Equity or More of the Same?" begins with his own childhood experiences in black schools and goes on to argue from historical and sociocultural perspectives that the Bush Administration's emphasis on achieving excellence through choice was misguided because "equity for minority groups has never occurred as a by-product of a focus on excellence."

By contrast, Christine Rossell, in "The Carrot or the Stick for School Desegregation Policy?" reports that the results of a study she conducted indicate that school choice through magnets had positive outcomes, claiming that "a desegregation plan based primarily on voluntary transfers to magnet schools produced greater long-term interracial exposure than a mandatory reassignment plan with magnet components, in part because of the greater white flight from the mandatory plans."

Toward Voluntary Desegregation:
The Beginnings of the St. Louis Plan

Edward T. Foote II

(Adapted from a speech)

I spent more than a year of my life working on the St. Louis case. Rather than give you a detailed legal account of where we were and where we are and where we might be going, what I'd like to do is to try to give you something of the human drama and history of this case.

During my time on the case, I had the privilege of working with some of the greatest people I will ever know. Each of us has to look at it in the context of our own backgrounds. Whether we're white or black, or a lawyer, or an educator, or a demographer, or whatever, we come to a case like this within the individual contexts of our experiences as American citizens. You can't escape it. And so, I've thought that it might be of passing interest to you to know how I got involved in this case.

I grew up here. The terrible irony I regret to recall is that when I was a teenager in this town, some people, who later became lifetime friends of mine, could not travel with me or attend school with me. My life went on. I went away to college, did some other things, and ended up a journalist in Washington, D.C. in the early 1960s during the extraordinary, explosive days of the Civil Rights Movement. I covered John F. Kennedy—his presidency, and his assassination. I knew Dr. King. I was there as a young reporter with 500,000 people on the grass in front of the Lincoln Memorial for the "I Have a Dream" speech. And I covered, as a reporter and during law school, the rising drama of the Civil Rights Movement that culminated in the great legislation of the Civil Rights Acts of 1964 and 1965.

I came to St. Louis to practice law beginning in 1966. I had the good fortune of later trying cases before a judge named Jim Meredith, testing the meaning of the Civil Rights Act of 1964.

And then I went on and I started teaching, and guess what I chose to teach? Civil Rights. What else? And as I taught Civil Rights, I chose the desegregation cases as a vehicle to try to understand, and help my students understand, the meaning of equal protection in American society. One of the people I used to ask to help me teach on occasion was Judge Meredith because he was then sitting on the school desegregation case.

In the spring of 1980, the telephone rang at my office at Washington University and Judge Meredith said that the circuit court of appeals, after nine years of litigation, had found the city of St. Louis school system to be segregated in violation of the Constitution of the United States, and had ordered that desegregation be completed by next fall. Judge Meredith asked, "Will you help me?" I said, "Yes, of course."

And then began the most extraordinary six weeks of my young life, because I was appointed to chair a committee of citizens, ten were black and ten were white—all kinds of people, some of the greatest people I'll ever know. It didn't matter who sat on my right or my left, because we became a circle by the time we were through. Minnie Lidell, who brought the case, was one of us and on my left (or was it right?) was Jerry Anne Adams—two wonderful mothers, one white and from South St. Louis, the other black, from North St. Louis. The ironies were fantastic.

Our job was to work with the superintendent and the school board in the shaping of a desegregation plan for St. Louis. We were to try in our imperfect way to represent the citizens of this town, to go out to every school, to answer the telephone, to read the mail, to talk with the black ministers, to talk to the media, to listen, to hold public hearings, to try to understand. We gave the school board our advice. And by the time six weeks were over, we had spent 84 hours together as a committee, not to mention the countless number of hours that we spent individually doing our assigned work. We'd met a total of 30 times. We filed our report. The school board filed its plan. The one thing about which every one of us around that room agreed was that we were there in order to better the lives of children in our community. So we did our work, put ourselves out of business, said thanks a lot, and that was the end of that committee.

That was the first chapter. The court adopted a variation of the plans that were coming in and that was the beginning of the next phase of desegregation in this city. The court knew a pigeon when it saw one. It said, "Foote doesn't have enough to do." So I was asked to chair the first desegregation monitoring committee and I was pleased to do that.

As the court approved the desegregation plan for this city, it did so in a long order, as courts do. In that order, the court looked on to the next phase. The next phase, as everybody knew, was, "All right, you're doing something in the city—what are you going to do about the entire metropolitan area?" And in the court's order were two paragraphs which students of this case now know very well, paragraph 12A and paragraph 12C. 12A, to keep it simple, was a paragraph in the court's order that said to the parties: "Try to find a voluntary solution, one that people can agree to." And 12C, to keep it simple also, was: "What might happen if the voluntary thing didn't work?" It was the mandatory side of it.

This order symbolically reflected the two fundamental concepts of American life: individual freedom in a free society, and the clarion calls from the beginning for equality, which may require the restriction of some freedoms. Freedom and equality define the tension that exists, in a society like ours, between the rights of the individual and the needs of everyone. 12A, to keep it overly simplified, in a sense stood for freedom to choose. And 12C stood for the possibility of a court-ordered solution that would apply to the entire metropolitan area.

During the summer and the fall, the St. Louis monitoring committee set about the task of implementing the first desegregation order in this city's history. To sum up a very long story, because of the work of the parties, the lawyers, the court, the educators, the school board, and everybody involved—this city desegregated itself without violence. It did so in a period of months, not years. It did so with many problems, and when I say desegregated, believe me, I'm very well aware of what the ratio was and is. But at least the city came up with an order that the court said was constitutionally permissible, and then got on peacefully with the business of educating students.

The monitoring committee met once a week for months and months, and tried to help the process continue. The committee also took up paragraph 12A, the possibility of some kind of voluntary plan that had to do not with one school district, but with 23 school districts.

In the summer of 1980, I began to work with the court in seeking a plan that could combine the best of freedom and equality, some kind of solution for this metropolitan area that no city had ever done before in the tremendously volatile years since Brown. I talked to a lot of people. One thing led to another. As the fall moved toward winter, here was the status of the case: On the one hand, there was increasing talk of including the county districts in more litigation on the theory that the county was constitutionally in violation. They had not been found so, don't forget. They've not been found so to this day.

On the other hand, very quietly, the court asked me with another hat on to try to see if I couldn't work with the parties to come up with a so-called voluntary 12A solution. By December, there had been no voluntary plan. The state had filed a voluntary plan, as did the city. But the court basically said to everybody, "Go back to work. You haven't gotten it done right."

Meanwhile, the series of quiet conversations with several key players continued. I travelled to Washington and talked to the Justice Department. In St. Louis, I spoke to the school board and its lawyers. Later, I spoke with the state attorney general and then with the lawyers for the county school districts.

What I was asked by the court to do, and tried to do, was to bring the parties together, to find a mutually acceptable alternative to a mandatory court order. Can you imagine? To bring 23 separate school districts, 23 separate school boards, together in a plan that would not only be educationally sound, but constitutionally acceptable?

Well, Judge Meredith, I'm sorry to say, got sick and. withdrew from the case in December of 1980. Judge Hungate replaced him. That slowed things down some. In January, the NAACP and the School Board, for their reasons, decided to file the papers to bring the county into the case. That chilled the discussions a little bit. Those who were critical—and I'll give both positions—said, "We might have settled this thing in a few weeks if you hadn't sued the county." Those who favored that said, "Had you not sued the county or tried to sue the county to bring them in the case there would not have been the stick hanging over the carrot to keep the voluntary discussions going." Who knows which side was right. Maybe the historians will tell us. In any event, the discussions that were moving along very well, slowed down a lot.

Then the court said, "All right, Foote, you've been talking about the possibility of settling this case and I've ordered you to go out and try to settle it, and it hasn't happened. You have from March 4, 1981 to March 27, 1981 to present to this court a plan for voluntary interdistrict settlement of this case." I continued working. For three, wild, wonderful weeks it got very, very busy.

But what we did—I say we; I happened to be the scrivener but only that—was to come up with a plan that I did present to the court on March 27, 1981. And then I did what one would expect. I had worked for a year and a half on this cause. I had made nobody happy. I had made a lot of people mad. So, I left town. It seemed the rational thing to do.

The voluntary plan in the city of St. Louis, basically the "old way" of mandatory measures, is not a 100 percent success. But it's very clear that this city is a better place in a lot of ways. The voluntary aspects of the St. Louis County plan may be not only a new way of moving through a terribly difficult phase of desegregation, but may in retrospect be seen to have ushered in a new era of constitutional litigation for these cases. Time will tell.

The plan that we came up with, essentially the plan that three years later was adopted by the court, was based on several principles. Number one: it had to meet the needs of the Constitution of the United States. Number two: it had to meet the needs of children, black children and white children, in so far as it was within our power to do so. Number three: it had to meet these needs in a way that was voluntary. That is, the choice of school to decrease segregation was made by the individual students or their parents, not by the court or anybody else. What it did, in effect, was to open up thousands upon thousands of seats in white or predominately white school districts in the county for black children from the segregated schools in the city to attend by their choice, and with a great deal of assistance from the state. We came up with what we called the "plan ratio," basically a benign quota. On the basis of the overall population ratio in the entire metropolitan area, which was approximately 20 percent black at the time, we said we'd allow some latitude on either side and the plan ratio for each school became a minimum of 15 percent and a maximum of 25 percent black students. So we were able to say to the county school districts, if they wanted to hear it, you take up to that amount, no more. We were able to say to what is now 10,000 black students, who were still attending fully or predominantly segregated black schools on the north side of this town after the so-called segregation order, here's an alternative that before, didn't exist. And we were able to say to the whole community, if this plan is implemented well, you do not have to spend the next five, ten, 20, 30 years litigating these issues.

And now I've come back and have spent many hours looking at yellowed newspaper clippings, remembering the work, the joys, the heartaches, the exhaustion, the all night sessions, remembering a photograph, which is on my desk and will always be, of that first committee of 20 people, half black and half white, holding hands and singing, "We Shall Overcome."

We haven't yet, but we will.

The St. Louis Plan: Substantial Achievements — and Unfulfilled Promises

D. Bruce La Pierre

In this article I'd like to focus on four points:

• an overview of the settlement process and some comments, limited by confidentiality requirements, about the reasons why the case was settled;

• an explanation of the principal provisions of the Settlement Agreement as adopted by the parties and modified and approved by the courts;

• a brief analysis of the implementation of the Settlement Agreement, which is now in its fourth year. The record here with respect to voluntary interdistrict student transfers from the city to suburban school districts and with respect to district-wide Quality Education programs is one of substantial achievement. Unfortunately, the special Quality Education programs for the all-black city schools have not been implemented completely, and the record with respect to magnet schools and capital improvements of city school facilities is one of unfulfilled promises and refusals to compromise.

• The incomplete implementation of the special Quality Education programs for all-black schools, paralysis in the interdistrict magnet program, and the total failure of the capital improvements program threaten the final success of the Settlement Agreement. More importantly, the unfulfilled promises about Quality Education, magnet schools, and capital improvements deny, depending on the standard of measurement, some 21,444 to 24,446 black children in all-black city schools the remedy contemplated by the Settlement Agreement. Because some very significant promises have not yet been honored, some of my comments are critical, perhaps harsh, and I am going to close with some strong, perhaps unpopular, recommendations.

As Tad Foote's article discusses, the District Court recognized that its May 1980 order approving the intradistrict plan would leave some 30,000 black students (approximately two-thirds of all black students in the city schools) in all-black schools, and it ordered the State, the City Board, and the Department of Justice to explore interdistrict remedies. In Paragraph 12(a), the court ordered these three parties to develop a "voluntary, cooperative plan of pupil exchanges" between the city and suburban schools. In Paragraph 12(c), the court also ordered the three parties "to develop and submit...a suggested plan of interdistrict school desegregation necessary to eradicate the remaining vestiges of government-imposed school segregation in the City of St. Louis and St. Louis County." The two plans ordered by the court were quickly dubbed the 12a voluntary plan and the 12c mandatory plan. A 12a plan was originally submitted to the court in the spring of 1981. Although the parties did not reach an agreement on this plan, it was the basis for an order entered by Judge Hungate on July 2, 1981. This order proposed a plan for voluntary student exchanges between city and suburban schools that would be funded by the State, and Judge Hungate invited the 23 suburban St. Louis school districts to participate.

In August 1981, after only five of the 23 suburban school districts agreed to participate in the court's 12a plan, Judge Hungate stayed any interdistrict litigation against these five school districts as long as they participated in good faith, and he took two steps toward a mandatory interdistrict remedy for the 18 non-participating districts. First, the court resumed the previously suspended consideration of mandatory interdistrict relief under Paragraph 12c by ordering the State, the City Board, and the United States to file 12c plans and by setting a hearing for these plans in March 1982. Second, the court approved the initiation of the interdistrict school desegregation case by granting, in part, prior motions of the City Board and the NAACP to join the nonparticipating suburban school districts.

With the failure of the court's 12a plan to involve all of the suburban school districts and the shift to consideration of a mandatory interdistrict remedy either under Paragraph 12c or after litigation and findings of interdistrict violations, all hope of a voluntary settlement of this metropolitan school desegregation case seemed to be lost. After entry of Judge Hungate's August 1981 orders, questions about the court's power to impose a mandatory interdistrict plan occupied center stage during the fall of 1981 and winter of 1982. The public's attention was riveted on the proposed 12c plans that called for consolidation of the suburban districts with the city schools, a uniform tax rate, and mandatory reassignment of students between city and suburban schools.

On February 25, 1982, the Eighth Circuit entered a judgment on appeals from

Judge Hungate's August 1981 orders, and this judgment set the framework for a final resolution of the interdistrict case. The Eighth Circuit's opinion settled three important points. First, it settled the relationship between 12c plans and the interdistrict litigation. On the one hand, the court held~that 12c plans rested on the State's established intradistrict violation and were limited to measures that either had no direct effect on the suburban districts or involved only voluntary actions by the suburban districts. The Court suggested that under paragraph 12c, the district court could order the State:

  • to improve the quality of education in all-black city schools;
  • to establish magnet schools in the city or in the suburban school districts with their consent; and
  • to provide additional incentives for voluntary interdistrict student transfers.

On the other hand, the Eighth Circuit held that mandatory interdistrict student transfers and school district consolidation could be ordered only after completion of the interdistrict litigation, and on a finding either that the suburban school districts had contributed to segregation in the city schools or that the State, through its control over the suburban schools, had contributed to city school segregation. Second, the Eighth Circuit upheld Judge Hungate's voluntary 12a plan, and ruled that the State must pay the costs of voluntary interdistrict student transfers.

Finally, and most importantly, the Eighth Circuit implicitly held that the State was liable for the full costs of any voluntary interdistrict desegregation plan solely on the basis of its previously established intradistrict constitutional violation.

The Court specifically held that the State, on the basis of its established responsibility for segregation of the city schools, "can be required to take those actions which will further the desegregation of the city schools even if the action required will occur outside the boundaries of the city school district." In short, the Court held that the State could be required to take actions both inside and outside the city school district as a remedy for its intradistrict violation. This last holding proved to be the key to the settlement.

At the beginning of the 1982-83 school year, the situation was as follows:

• Fifteen of the 23 suburban school districts had agreed to participate in Judge Hungate's 12a voluntary plan, and the interdistrict litigation against them had been stayed.

• Trial of the interdistrict case against the State and the seven remaining suburban school districts was scheduled to begin on February 14, 1983.

• The district court had tentatively approved a 12c plan that suggested that school district consolidation and mandatory busing would be the remedy if liability was established.

Against this background, I published an article in the fall of 1982, arguing that the interdistrict desegregation case could be settled.

In October 1982, Judge Hungate called my cards and appointed me Special Master for the purpose of negotiating a settlement among the parties—the original Liddell plaintiffs, the NAACP, the City Board, which was a defendant in the intradistrict case and a plaintiff in the interdistrict case, 23 suburban school districts, the State of Missouri, the Department of Justice, the City of St. Louis, and St. Louis County.

The Settlement Process

For the first four months of my appointment, I conducted what can be best described as "shuttle diplomacy." I met individually with all the parties to learn their positions and demands and to exchange ideas and proposals. On the eve of the interdistrict liability trial, I met throughout the day and long into the night with most of the parties. At the eleventh hour, I concluded that there was now sufficient movement to create a genuine possibility of settlement, and I asked Judge Hungate for a delay so that we could work out an agreement. The court granted a one-day postponement and directed that all parties begin meeting with me in a room in the courthouse immediately. I met with all the parties as a group for the first time that day, and we continued around-the-clock meetings for the next three days. The meetings were hectic, exhausting, and often contentious, but we hammered out an agreement in principle. Although at times it appeared that our efforts would founder, the lawyers for the interdistrict plaintiffs—Liddell, the NAACP, and the City Board—and for the 23 suburban school districts ultimately succeeded in drafting a final Settlement Agreement.

I am not at liberty to discuss the negotiations in detail, but I can suggest the basic reasons why the parties were willing to explore settlement. From the plaintiffs' perspective, they had to consider the delay inherent in litigation, the risk that they could not prove liability, and the risk that even if they proved liability, the finding of constitutional violations would not be sufficient to support a comprehensive remedy including school district consolidation and substantial mandatory interdistrict student transfers. From the defendant suburban school districts' perspective, they had to consider that if the case went to trial and they lost, Judge Hungate's tentatively approved 12c plan presaged school district consolidation and substantial mandatory transfers of white students into the predominantly black city schools. Given these risks, the Liddell, NAACP, and City Board plaintiffs, and the 23 suburban school district defendants agreed that the Settlement Agreement, which I will describe in a moment, was a better alternative than trial.

As you probably know, some of the parties—the Department of Justice, the City of St. Louis, and the State—refused to join the Settlement. The DOJ declined to endorse the Settlement Agreement completely when it was presented to the District Court. Throughout the negotiations, DOJ waffled—sometimes supportive of our effort, sometimes disruptive. The City of St. Louis actively opposed the Settlement Agreement. Although the Settlement Agreement provides substantial benefits for the children in city schools, the City apparently believed that the financing provisions of the Settlement Agreement would divert tax resources from the City's coffers to the school board's treasury. The State of Missouri was and is the principal opponent of the Settlement Agreement. Although the State initially played a constructive role in my shuttle negotiations, it ultimately withdrew from active negotiation when it became apparent that the State would have to foot most of the bill for the Settlement Agreement.

We tried hard to persuade the State to join the Settlement Agreement, and if the State had joined, many of the problems of implementation could have been avoided or reduced. Unfortunately, but understandably, the State deemed the costs too high. As a political matter, it is easier to complain about costs imposed by a court order than it is to explain costs that appear to voters' eyes to have been assumed voluntarily by signing a settlement. Fortunately, the State's refusal to participate was not significant as a legal matter because the Eighth Circuit had held, over a year before the settlement was reached, that the State could be required to take actions both inside and outside the city school district as a remedy for its intradistrict violation.

The Terms of the Settlement

The three principal components of the settlement are:

- provisions for voluntary interdistrict student transfers;
- the establishment of magnet schools; and
- the improvement of the quality of education in the city schools and provisions for major capital improvements.

One preliminary, and crucial, point is that all interdistrict student transfers are voluntary. The 16 suburban school districts district operating under a desegregation order either of a court or of the state board of education will have its racial balance impaired by the operation of a program of student choice. Districts may refuse to release and may decline to admit students where compliance would be impaired.

Champion of Choice
Shaking Up Milwaukee's Schools
Polly Williams

Interviewed by
John H. Fund

This fall the Milwaukee Public Schools begin the nation's first experiment in education vouchers for low-income children. Polly Williams, the Wisconsin state representative who made it happen, was inspired by an idea proposed three decades ago by Nobel Laureate Milton Friedman and promoted in recent years by conservatives in the White House and state legislatures. To gain approval for the plan, Williams formed a coalition with her Republican colleagues against the liberal establishment. Yet Williams is a Democrat who twice served as Jesse Jackson's state campaign manager.

Under the choice plan, a five-year pilot project, about 1,000 low-income children will receive vouchers of up to $2,500 that can be used at nonsectarian private schools. The money, which will be subtracted from the city's public-school budget, will mean new opportunities for students and greater competition for the state system. If the program works, other states —some of which already allow students to choose among public schools— can be expected to follow suit.

Born in Belzoni, Mississippi, Williams move to Milwaukee with her family at age 10. She attended the city's public schools but later sent her four children to a local private school known for its high standards and insistence on parental involvement. At 52, she is completing her fifth term as a legislator.

John H. Fund, an editorial writer for the *Wall Street Journal*, interviewed Williams at a hotel in downtown Milwaukee.

Reason: What obstacles did the education establishment throw up to stop your choice plan?

Williams: They tried everything to stop me. After they were convinced choice couldn't be stopped, they tried to hijack the issue and came up with their own version of choice. It basically created another bureaucracy which would have supervised the whole choice process and strangled it. The Milwaukee Public Schools would have selected the students for the choice program, not the parents. Students would have been picked if they met enough of the seven negative criteria they set up. If you were in a family of alcoholics, had a brother in prison and a pregnant teenage sister, and were inarticulate, you would have been a perfect candidate for their choice plan. In other words, a program they hoped would fail. This fake choice plan was the product of a white, do-good liberal legislator named

Barbara Nostein. Liberals backed her; they weren't for my bill. We finally won when we got 200 parents to testify for three hours in favor of my bill. In good conscience, my colleagues could not vote against those parents.

Reason: The Milwaukee Public Schools spend $6,000 a year per student on education. That's a lot of money.

Williams: Well, that money isn't going to the kids. It's going to a system that doesn't educate them and to a bunch of bureaucrats. A lot of the money goes out the tailpipes of buses, trucking kids halfway across town so they can sit next to white kids. The average ride for a Milwaukee kid is 45 minutes. That has nothing to do with education.

Reason: Why is busing still used in Milwaukee after all these years? I understand the court order has lapsed.

Williams: They have destroyed or failed to build new schools in the innercity. If busing ended tomorrow, there would be 40,000 kids downtown and 20,000 places in school for them. They have built new, fancy magnet schools next to the suburbs to entice white kids across the city line in buses. They are busing kids from one black elementary district in this area to 104 different schools. A group of African-American parents is going to propose we modify this busing madness and start building schools kids can walk to again.

Reason: These magnet schools—can blacks go to them?

Williams: Not many. Even if they are in African-American neighborhoods they are largely filled with whites from the suburbs. People attack my plan for subsidizing private schools. Well, these magnet schools are private education at public expense. I simply say that my black parents want the same choice they do. None of the people who oppose my plan lack choice in education themselves. They have no idea what the lack of choice in education means, the damage it does when you have to go to an inferior school that will trap you for life.

Reason: Why do white liberals insist on busing instead of choice?

Williams: It's more feel-good politics for them. They think their kids are having a neat cultural experience by going to school with African-American kids. But they don't want to really relate to them; they just want to take them out to the playground with their kids so they can point to some black kids and say, "See, those are different people you should be nice to." It reminds me of a zoo. It has nothing to do with education. The theory is that if black kids sit next to white kids, they will learn better; it's insulting. I thought these people were liberals!

Reason: You castigate liberals a lot. But aren't you a liberal Democrat?

Williams: Labels do not tell you much about me. I'm not a liberal; I believe in what works. I often vote against the state budget because there are things in there I don't think should be funded.

White liberals feel guilty about blacks, and they do things to convince themselves they are helping blacks. It's feel-good politics, which is really just helping themselves. Poor people become the trophies of white social engineers.

We have to be saved from our saviors. They have been feeding us pablum for so long, we are finally tired and demand some real meat. We want self-sufficiency, self-determination, and self-reliance, not a handout.

Reason: How do you get along with your colleagues in the legislature?

Williams: I am respected and listened to, but I must tell you that I have a better rapport with conservative Democrats and Republicans than I do with my liberal colleagues. We all agree on self-determination for minorities, and they aren't so obsessed with guilt and giving away money. I get along fine with Jack Kemp and Newt Gingrich.

Reason: Do you think they are sincere in wanting to help blacks?

Williams: I don't care. I think they are, but they don't have to be. They just have to sincerely want to push my agenda.

Reason: Suppose a conservative legislator came to you and said: "Polly, these welfare programs are a mess. Let's change them to a voucher approach. But to get Republican votes, I have to cut 30 percent of the budget out. The rest goes in cash payments directly to the poor, and they choose how to use it." What would you say?

Williams: I would go along with that. The money is wasted now, and I think it couldn't be more wasted if people spent it themselves. This paternalistic idea that poor people can't make choices is ridiculous. Poor people are some of the best shoppers, most skilled at stretching a dollar, you'll ever see.

Reason: You fell on hard times for a while. What happened?

Williams: I divorced in 1971, and our family income fell from $20,000 a year to $8,000 a year. I had to go on public assistance for a while. I didn't like it, and neither did my kids.

Reason: Why?

Williams: They were embarrassed. They were raised to think there was a real stigma to public assistance. They would refuse to go shopping with me when I used food stamps. After I got back on my feet, I finished college at night school. I became very active in community organizations, and eventually, in 1978, I ran for the state legislature. I lost, but I came back and won in 1980.

Reason: What impact did segregation have on you?

Williams: In the South it was always understood that you were different. You would only be served in a store after all the white people had been served. In Milwaukee, I remember trying to buy something and standing aside when a white person came up to the counter. The clerk asked me what I wanted and served me first. It was a culture shock. There was discrimination here, but it wasn't a way of life.

Reason: Judging from your comments on busing, I take it you don't think much of integration?

Williams: Integration comes in time for those who want it. A lot of African-Americans, including myself, don't believe in it. We had a civil rights revolution so we would have an equal chance at the good things in life, not to blend into white society.

Reason: What are your views on affirmative action?

Williams: Well, in theory I could see some affirmative action if it went to the people who really needed it—at the very bottom. But it never does that; it goes to people who don't need it, who can make it largely on their own. And it carries with it the stigma that whatever position you succeed in getting, people think you got there because of favoritism. That can be very destructive.

Reason: What is your opinion of those black politicians, such as the mayors of Baltimore and Hartford, Connecticut, who say that the costs of the drug war are too high?

Williams: I agree with them that we have to decriminalize drugs. Three things would happen. We would make sure innocent people are no longer gunned down by drug gangs. And we would take the profit out of selling that poison. Right now, 80 percent of the cocaine money comes from yuppies. They are the ones consuming it, and they drive into our neighborhoods to buy it.

The business leaders of any major city are also willing to keep the status quo. Look at the banks, car dealers, and condo projects. Drug money is in all of them. Lastly, ending the drug war would mean the police would no longer have an excuse to come in and dominate black neighborhoods.

Reason: You were Jesse Jackson's campaign manager in Wisconsin. What does he think of choice in education?

Williams: He has never told me I shouldn't be doing this. When he has been asked, he has simply said he doesn't know enough to comment. I think he would agree with what I am doing here.

Reason: The Milwaukee papers have been very critical of your plan. So has most of the white establishment and the NAACP. Why do you think that is?

Williams: The Milwaukee papers used to be among my biggest supporters. I was their darling. Then I started asking questions and speaking up in the legislature. They didn't like that. They have been awfully unfriendly lately. A cartoon in the paper showed me with a bandit mask on holding up a public school official and demanding he surrender money to this fat, white guy from the private schools. If that isn't a cheap stereotype, I don't know what is.

The NAACP—I don't know why they oppose the plan. I guess they are just too tied in with the old system and way of doing things. This choice plan does nothing for the local power structure. It helps the people that everyone forgot—poor, innercity kids who want a better life.

Reason: What do you say to those who think you are out to destroy the public schools?

Williams: I want the public schools to work. I think they should work at $6,000 a year per student. Maybe if they had some competition they would have an incentive to work better. But if teachers and school bureaucrats are so worried about losing their jobs, why don't they just go out and do them a little better?

Reason: Tell us about the private schools that will participate in the choice program.

Williams: There are about six to eight schools that want to join. For many it is a sacrifice, since we had to compromise and make the voucher only $2,500 a year, and parents cannot supplement the voucher with their own money. Many of these schools have costs of $3,000 or $3,300 a year.

My kids went to Urban Day School, which was started as a nonreligious school by some Catholic sisters. All of these schools are nonreligious, so there is no separation of church and state problem. They all have different races going to them.

Urban Day and the others go up to the eighth grade, and there is real discipline and learning there. Many kids who leave them and go on to public high school are shocked at the differences. Still, some 90 percent of kids who go to any of these schools finish high school, and most go on to college. They also tend to stay out of trouble.

And these schools do more than provide a good education. They help instill pride in the African-American heritage through history and other courses the public schools aren't interested in.

Reason: Why did you insist on a plan to let kids attend private schools? Why not just improve the public schools?

Williams: We've tried to do that for years, and the best we get is, "Well, we're the experts, you are just parents." We're tired of that excuse. Look, if you go to a doctor and you stay sick, at some point don't you have a right to a second opinion? The choice plan is our second opinion. The folks who run the poverty industry in this town are worried that kids will get a better education at schools that cost half the amount they spend on the public schools. In their shoes, I'd be worried too.

The Montclair Model

Beatriz C. Clewell

Myra F. Joy

Montclair, New Jersey provides an interesting model of an urban school district that has achieved success in desegregating its schools through a voluntary magnet school plan based on choice, while enhancing educational programs, improving student achievement, and providing program diversity. The environment in which the plan was implemented has both urban and suburban characteristics and contextual factors that might be expected both to help and hinder support for a desegregation plan. This section describes the Montclair Magnet Plan and provides the findings of an evaluation conducted recently of the effectiveness of the plan in meeting its goals.

Demography of Montclair

Montclair is an urban school system located 12 miles from New York City. It is primarily a residential community in which most of its working population commutes to New York or Newark. Its median income of $30,635 in 1980 was substantially above the state average of $22,906. Approximately 40 percent of its residents hold college degrees.

Montclair's Black population has increased from 24 percent in 1960 to 29 percent in 1980, but Black representation in the public schools in 1980 was 45 percent and close to 49 percent in 1988. Despite high taxes, Montclair continues to attract both minority and non-minority families, many from nearby New York and Newark, who want the advantages of the suburbs along with the amenities of an urban area. Minority families moving into Montclair are very supportive of the school system. Some non-minority families continue to opt for private and parochial schools. About one of five of the community's school-age children attends a private or parochial school, compared with the national average of one of ten.

*(Tables, figures, and appendices omitted. Text edited to reflect omissions.)

History of Desegregation Efforts

Despite the urban flavor of Montclair, housing patterns have, until recently, been relatively segregated, causing a racial imbalance in school enrollments, which reflected the population of the neighborhoods. The magnet school plan was adopted in 1976 to address the segregation, under threat of losing state education funds. The adoption of this plan followed trial of at least seven other plans that included forced busing. These earlier proposals caused much conflict and turmoil, accelerating White flight and thereby increasing the proportion of minority enrollments in the schools. The 1976 plan included developing several magnet schools and redrawing some district boundaries. Montclair was given a year for planning by the state during which time a Citizen's Task Force was established to provide input for the plan and to talk with parents and teachers to enhance support. The plan included establishment of a gifted and talented program in a predominantly minority school to attract White students and a fundamental program (a traditional structured program emphasizing the basics) designed to attract Black students in a predominantly White school.

The plan, with some modifications in 1979 and 1982, worked well for about five years, at which point some racial imbalance was occurring. By 1985, due to a gradual enrollment decline, an increase in minority enrollments, and the choice of many affluent White parents to send their children to private schools, the stability of the plan was threatened. Furthermore, some parents had become concerned about the inequity of the resources between magnet schools and those without special programs, "neighborhood schools." To address these concerns, and prevent resegregation of schools, the magnet plan was broadened in 1985. The new plan eliminated all neighborhood schools by designating all Montclair schools as magnet schools (except the one district high school). This basic plan is the one currently operating, although programs have been added and refined over the years as needed. District resources across schools are now equalized. Montclair recently received a grant to refine and expand some programs, develop some initiatives to enhance academic performance, and continue to upgrade staff training.

The Montclair Schools

Montclair has a total building enrollment of 5,104 students, of which 49 percent are minority; 43 percent are Black. The school system contains six elementary schools, two middle schools, and one high school. The average teacher-pupil ratio in the elementary grades is 1 to 20; in the middle schools, 1 to 16.2, and in the high school, 1 to 14.6. The special focus programs are gifted and talented, fundamental, international, science and technology, and a recent Montessori program within one of the fundamental schools. All schools, however, have a basic core curriculum that is consistent across grade levels.

Procedures

To study the effectiveness of Montclair's plan in terms of providing racial balance across schools and providing educational quality and diversity in programs through use of choice, the researchers used a case study approach, combining quantitative data (such as standardized test scores, enrollments, and census data) and qualitative data collected through reviews of reports and other documents and interviews with knowledgeable informants. The original study was conducted in 1987, with a follow up in the summer of 1989. The major part of the data collection was accomplished through interviews with and observation of individuals in the schools—principals, teachers, students, and parents—and central office staff, members of the board of education, and individuals in the community.

How Choice Works

Montclair's magnet system is considered a voluntary plan in that parents and students select a school, rather than being assigned to one. The school district provides transportation for all students. Every elementary school has over half its student body bused, indicating that a majority of parents are selecting a school outside their neighborhood. Among elementary schools, Bradford and Edgemont have the largest proportion bused (78.6 percent and 71.8 percent respectively in 1988-89). Both are considered "fundamental schools," and are located in predominantly White neighborhoods. Edgemont has a Montessori program as well. The schools with the largest enrollments from the neighborhood (the lowest portion bused) are Watchung (a racially mixed neighborhood) and Northeast (which is predominantly White). Mt. Hebron Middle School has a higher portion of its student body bused than Glenfield Middle School (80 percent vs. 62 percent).

Montclair's plan relies totally on choice to achieve racial balance. Parents select the school they wish their child to attend and register that choice with the central office. So long as racial balance in the schools is maintained and the school is not over enrolled, the child will be assigned to the school of choice. Individuals moving into the district in mid-year may be assigned to a school on the basis of available space, and those who register late may not get their first choice. Over 95 percent of parents get their first choice of schools.

Based on the interviews, the researchers found that parents believe they have total choice in selecting schools and like the concept of choice. However, parents select schools for many different reasons. Parents at the fundamental and gifted and talented schools talked about program and style, including school climate, environment, and leadership. They selected schools they felt appropriate for their child's needs. Another consideration, however, is location—many parents select the school closest to them. One trend that central office staff noted is that there is a lot of transferring to another school when students reach the third grade. Parents may want to keep their child close to home for prekindergarten through second grade and to see how the child performs in school before actually selecting a program. By the time their child is in third grade, the parents have some basis on which to make a choice. Another basis for choice is the principal and staff in a particular school. Facilities, size of the school, and atmosphere were also mentioned. At the middle schools, many believe t~e major choice is on style, since the curriculum of the two schools is similar. It was clear from the interviews that most parents were informed about the different programs and differences in the schools. Several principals indicated that parents are less likely to complain about a school and are more involved with its programs if they select it. Montclair parents are involved in the schools, and were part of the decision-making process when new programs were planned.

Freedom of choice has created a certain degree of competition among the schools. Since unsatisfied parents have alternatives, principals must make sure their programs are working well and produce good results. In several schools where enrollments dipped, principals were replaced and new programs started to improve the school.

One drawback to a choice plan, cited by teachers and principals, is that parents may not always make the most appropriate choice for their child. They may choose the gifted and talented school because it sounds impressive, rather than because it is most suited to their child's needs. Also, even though information is available to parents, many do not read it or take advantage of visiting days at the schools to get the information they need to select a school. School district personnel work closely with all pre-kindergarten teachers in the town, including Head Start teachers, to tell parents when and how to register and provide them with information. Despite these efforts, some parents, particularly those of Head Start students, are still late signing up and may not get their first choice.

The next section of the paper reviews Montclair's program against three criteria: racial balance, improving the quality of education for all students, and increasing program diversity.

Racial Balance

Montclair's magnet plan was developed and implemented to desegregate its schools. In 1975, one year before development of the plan, overall minority enrollment in elementary schools was 43 percent. There were several schools with extreme racial imbalance: Bradford (24 percent minority); Edgemont (28 percent minority); and Glenfield (74 percent minority). With implementation of the plan, which also included closing two schools, Montclair was able to achieve a better racial balance among all schools. By 1977, Bradford, the first fundamental school, went to 46 percent minority enrollment and Edgemont to 33 percent; Glenfield was closed. Nishuane and Hillside, which became gifted and talented schools, both achieved racial balance with enrollments of 49 percent minority and 51 percent non-minority.

During the next few years, although there was some shifting of enrollments, the racial balance was maintained. Since 1986, enrollments have stabilized and racial balance has been maintained. The total minority elementary school enrollment in 1988 was 48 percent. The range of each school's enrollment in 1988-89 was between 46 percent and 52 percent.

Middle school enrollments showed a similar pattern. Hillside, the most segregated school, was closed, and Mt. Hebron and Glenfield were able to maintain racial balance in their enrollments. In 1989, total middle school enrollment was 53 percent minority and both Mt. Hebron and Glenfield's minority enrollments represented that same proportion of minority students.

Thus the racial mix in every school is well-balanced, even though total enrollments may have increased or decreased. It is important to note also, that because there is a substantial minority population in the school system, every school is able to have a critical mass of minority students to prevent them from being a small isolated group.

When the researchers conducted the follow-up in 1989 they also looked at the socio-economic level of each school by obtaining data on the proportion of students eligible for free and reduced school lunch in each elementary and middle school. The range in 1987 was 6.4 percent in Glenfield to 27 percent at Edgemont, with a district average of 13.5 percent. All but two schools were within four percentage points of the district average. In 1988, the district-wide average increased to 19.2 percent, but all schools, except Bradford and Edgemont at 29 percent, were within six percentage points of the district average. These figures indicate that Montclair's schools, with a few exceptions, are relatively well-balanced on this measure of socio-economic status.

Integration in the classroom. An important aspect of achieving racial balance is to assure that there is racial integration within the classrooms and that resegregation does not occur at that level. In elementary schools, classes are grouped heterogeneously and efforts are made to assure good racial and gender balance. Enrollments in every grade level at every school are carefully monitored. At the middle schools and high school, it is more difficult to determine racial balance at the classroom level, since students change classes and choose electives, but homeroom assignments are carefully monitored.

One area cited where racial balance has not occurred is in the honors and advanced classes, especially at the middle and high schools. Minority students are underrepresented in these classes. The district is addressing this problem through a bridge program at the middle schools and an early bridge program at the elementary level to identify high potential but underachieving minority students and provide them with academic enrichment and reinforcement. In one school, the principal personally monitors standardized test scores to spot potentially bright students who have been overlooked. In that school there is good minority representation in the advanced classes.

General racial climate. The researchers found good racial relations among staff and students in the schools. Maintaining racial balance among staff and providing positive minority role models is given a high priority by the school system. Approximately 28 percent of supervisors and administrators and 29 percent of education professionals (teachers, counselors, etc.) are minority. Overall, the researchers found good relations between Black and White staff and no indications of problems or tensions. Teachers of different races seemed at ease with each other and worked well together. Teachers also indicated that they felt at ease with students of another race, although some found it difficult to work with a diversity of students.

In every school visited, students of different races mixed well, both in classrooms and during lunch or playing together on the playground. Although in the high school, and to some extent in the middle schools, all-Black or all-White groups of students were observed, there were interracial groups as well. The magnet schools are believed to contribute to formation of interracial friendships by bringing together students from many different neighborhoods, helping students to form new friendships in school based on mutual interests and classroom assignments. Many of the students interviewed indicated that one of their three best friends was of a different race.

There was also a conscious effort in the district to promote cultural understanding. Posters and displays showed balance and representation of races and gender. Black History Week and Martin Luther King's Birthday were used as opportunities to enhance awareness of the contribution of Black people in all areas. Where there were special activities—sports, safety patrol, class officers and the like —both Black and White students participated. In one school the principal made a special effort to encourage minority students to run for student council.

Improving Quality for All Students

In addition to achieving racial balance in the schools, the quality of education provided through a choice plan is a crucial factor in assessing its effectiveness. Performance in reading and math as measured by Iowa Test of Basic Skills (ITBS) scores has improved since implementation of the magnet schools in 1977. The percent scoring below grade level in math and reading has declined at all grade levels. Additionally, the mean percentile scores in math and reading show a general upward trend from 1984 to 1983. These achievement data indicate that Montclair students are performing well and that academic performance has improved since implementation of magnet schools as measured by the ITBS.

Although many factors may have contributed to the improvement in test scores, the data indicate that implementation of the magnet schools has not caused a decline in reading and math achievement levels, and may have been a factor contributing to improved performance. Certainly, the stability brought about by the magnet system after a period of turmoil in the schools is believed to have been a factor contributing to better performance.

Despite the achievement gains and overall academic performance of Montclair students, the data show differential performance between minorities and nonminorities. Montclair has been making special efforts to increase the performance of students who are underachieving in basic skills through such efforts as the local bridge program and state Basic Skills Improvement Program (BSIP). The district has also recently received funding to implement several new initiatives that start in lower grades to improve basic skills performance of students.

School climate. The researchers found a favorable school climate and a comfortable environment for learning. All buildings were clean, well kept and in good condition and appeared to be a secure environment for the students. Most schools had a "firm, but not rigid" norm of behavior that conformed to the district behavior code, although some schools were more strict and structured than others. Behavior problems were usually not serious and there was no vandalism or violence in the schools.

Most principals have a relaxed and informal relationship with both teachers and students. Their doors are always open and they seemed to know students by name. Principals clearly set the tone for the schools. Assignments and school programs are not static and principals are held accountable for the performance in their schools.

Principals and teachers at all schools visited were aware of and supportive of their school's stated goals and for the most part felt their particular school was fulfilling its goals. The fundamental schools, with an emphasis on basics, had a more structured, disciplined (yet, in most cases, friendly) atmosphere and the gifted and talented schools, with more flexible curricula, were more relaxed and informal. This difference also met the desires of parents, who often selected a school on the basis of atmosphere and style.

Generally, students expressed satisfaction with their school, their teachers, and what they were learning. Students knew the rules and believed they were fair. They indicated that teachers expected good performance, and were available for extra help when students needed it.

In most schools, teachers were satisfied with the leadership, working environment, and quality of education provided. All teachers were supportive of the magnet system and its goals. They indicated the system's main advantages were the choices it offered and the diversity of programs and learning opportunities to suit a child's need.

Curriculum and instruction. Curriculum review and careful monitoring of programs have been an on-going process to help assure the effectiveness and attractiveness of the magnet schools. In 1985 there was a comprehensive review and revision process that involved members of the school board, central office staff, building staff, and parents. The curriculum was standardized across schools and grade level objectives were set for all subjects, so that all schools share a common core curriculum and have additional emphases according to special focus.

Principals can select their teaching staff. With implementation of the first magnets there was substantial turnover to place many of the best teachers in the magnets. Since that time, staff have become more stable at schools. Staff are very professional and well-trained; most have taken credits beyond the bachelor's degree. Teachers and principals set high expectations for students and believe all students can succeed.

Diversity of Programs. Both teachers and parents cited the diversity of programs as a major attraction of the Montclair school system. Parents feel that there are differences across schools and that they can choose a school based on the needs of their child.

The initial magnets were a fundamental school and two gifted and talented schools, one for pre-kindergarten through second grade and one for second through fifth grades. The gifted and talented schools do not have admission requirements, but rather have the philosophy that all students are gifted and talented in some areas. There are special advanced courses for the students who are more talented academically and other courses for students in their special talent. Since 1977, an additional fundamental magnet has been developed, with a basic arts program which has an affiliation with Lincoln Center. The original fundamental school has added a junior great books program. The other elementary magnets include an international program, with an emphasis on foreign languages and a science and technology magnet, with a strong emphasis on environmental sciences. In the last two years Montclair has made additional efforts to enhance programs and provide new equipment in these latter two schools. The most recent magnet is a Montessori program, housed within one of the fundamental schools. Parents have been very active in expressing the desire for new programs and the need to enhance others, and it has been partially as a result of various parents' advisory committees that many changes in programs came about.

The major difference between middle schools is on the basis of style, but programs continue to change there as well. A recent change in principals at one of the schools will undoubtedly lead to some changes in style and atmosphere at that school.

Factors Contributing to Montclair's Success

Montclair has been successful in implementing a magnet school plan that relies on choice to achieve racial balance and provide a quality education for all students through a diversity of programs. Its success is due to many factors including the type of school district and community as well as leadership and careful planning.

Montclair is different from many urban districts in several ways. First, it is a smaller school district than many that have tried to desegregate through magnet schools. It is not at all clear that larger districts would be able to employ all the same tactics that Montclair has used. Transportation is somewhat easier to provide than in many larger districts. Montclair provides transportation beyond what the state reimburses, in order to make all programs accessible to all students, so that parents actually do have total choice in selecting a program without concern about transportation. The relatively small size of Montclair also made communication with the community and publicizing the plan easier. School officials were able to meet with small groups throughout the community.

Montclair is also a suburban setting, so that many of the problems that were occurring concomitantly with early desegregation plans and that may have contributed to White flight did not occur there. Montclair was able to eliminate all neighborhood schools and make all its schools magnets with some special program, thereby avoiding the problems that are caused when magnets attract the best students into a few schools, leaving the non-magnets to cope with the lowest achievers. Moreover, once the initial magnets had been established, resources were equalized across the schools. School assignments are voluntary and based on choice, a factor that has been found to be important in achieving greater racial balance through magnet plans (Rossell & Clarke, 1987). Because of the district's size, selection of school and registration are manageable.

Montclair's population is generally supportive of diversity and racial balance in the schools and places importance on maintaining a quality education for students. Montclair's population has relatively high levels of income and education. Such individuals are generally more supportive of equity goals and education programs than populations of lower educational and occupational status (Dye, 1968). Moreover, a large proportion of the Black population is professional and well educated, so there is not as large a gap in terms of income and education between the Black and White population as occurs in some places.

Many of the new arrivals to Montclair come because of the schools and because they want a diverse population and many of the amenities of urban life in a suburban setting. Although only 18 percent of the current population have children in the public schools, the community is supportive of the schools and is willing to pay the high taxes necessary to support the school system. Much of this support can also be attributed to efforts of the superintendent in building community support and showing that the schools are careful in their use of resources.

The success of Montclair's plan, however, involved more than just favorable predisposing circumstances and population characteristics. The individuals responsible for planning and implementing the plan helped to produce a favorable environment and engender support for the system. The opposition to the previous plans in effect, particularly the forced busing, helped develop community interest and involvement in the plan. The actions of both the superintendent and the board of education during this period further increased the probability of success.

Research has suggested that community involvement in the planning of magnets contributes to their effectiveness in achieving maximum desegregation (Blank, 1984). Careful planning for appropriate programs also contributes to success in implementing magnet schools (Asher, 1985). The superintendent in Montclair increased community support and involvement during the planning phase by publicizing the magnet plan and forming a Citizens Advisory Task Force to participate in the planning process. Parents and community members are still involved in various task forces and the schools have formal mechanisms for parent input. Many of the program changes since 1977 have come about as a reaction to the concerns of parents.

The superintendent who developed and first implemented the magnet school plan undertook a thorough study of existing magnet school programs. He placed programs and resources strategically to achieve maximum desegregation, developed a sound implementation strategy, and obtained release time for a team of staff people to assist in the planning and implementation of the program. This last strategy was considered by some who were involved in the planning process to be a crucial factor in the plan's success. The Montclair Board of Education supported the superintendent's actions by voting for the resources to accomplish the plan and by endorsing the plan and its implementation.

Specific components of the plan that were at least partially responsible for its success were the placement of the gifted and talented programs in the predominantly minority schools and the fundamental programs in the predominantly White schools. Research has shown these strategies to be effective in achieving desegregation since White parents are attracted to gifted and talented programs, whereas minority parents prefer the fundamental programs (Fleming et al., 1982; Levine & Eubanks, 1980; Rosenbaum & Presser, 1978; Royster et al., 1979). Extensive renovation of the predominantly minority schools in Montclair also enhanced their attractiveness to White parents, as has been shown to be the case in other research (Levine & Eubanks, 1980; Rossell, 1985). Elimination of attendance zones, accomplished in 1985, has also been shown to contribute to the success of magnet plans in small school districts (Rossell & Clarke, 1987).

Strong leadership at the district level is essential to the continued effectiveness of a magnet school plan (Blank et al., 1983). The present administration in Montclair continues to assure the success of the system by monitoring school enrollments and racial balance. Careful monitoring has prevented resegregation as shifts in population demographics occur. New programs have been developed as needed and other programs enhanced to improve their drawing power. The system is not static, but always adjusting as needed.

The magnet schools, under the leadership of their principals, continue to preserve their reputation for excellence, their positive teacher-student relationships, and their high levels of interracial interaction, all considered necessary,v for such a plan to succeed.

Lessons Learned

What can be learned from the success of Montclair's magnet plan? As mentioned above, the district possesses some characteristics that favor success. There are, however, other manipulable factors that also contributed to the plan's success. These were present at the various stages of development and implementation of the magnet plan:

Planning Stage

• Careful planning to ensure optimal program selection and placement.

• Strong and intelligent leadership to map the strategy for achieving implementation and increasing community support and involvement.

• Community involvement to increase support for the plan.

Initial Implementation Stage

• Gradual introduction of the magnets.

• Elimination of all attendance zones.

• Strategic placement of programs.

• Provision of transportation to all programs.

• Ensuring the attractiveness of all programs and buildings.

• Fostering continued parent involvement.

• Careful placement of staff.

• Effective leadership.

Continued Implementation

• Careful monitoring of enrollment patterns and programs.

• Refinement of programs as needed.

• Continued emphasis on encouraging parent involvement.

• Evaluation.

• Effective leadership.

Obviously, depending on demographic and other characteristics of the district, not all of the above elements can be achieved in all districts. For example, the elimination of all attendance zones might be more difficult in a larger school system. Other elements, however, such as community involvement and support, strong leadership, and careful planning and monitoring can be components of magnet plans in any district, no matter how different from Montclair.

The body of research on magnet school plans and programs suggests that of the school choice plans that have been implemented and evaluated, magnets present the best mechanism for achieving quality education, racial balance, and diversity of program offerings as well as parental choice. According to Esposito (1988), of all the choice systems in his study, choice within a district made up mostly or entirely of magnet or alternative schools seemed to bring about the most positive results. (Esposito cites Montclair, together with Community District 4 in New York City and Cambridge, Massachusetts as the most impressive.)

The Montclair experience as well as others have provided concrete examples of magnet plans that have been effective in meeting diverse educational goals over a period of time. Although it is acknowledged that no one choice model is best for all types of communities, much can be learned from successful models such as the Montclair school district magnet plan.

References

Alkin, M. C. (1983, April). *Magnet school programs evaluation; Assessing a desegration effort.* Paper presented at the annual meeting of the American Educational Research Association, Montreal.

Alves, M. J., & Willie, C.V. (1987). Controlled choice assignments: A new and more effective approach to school desegregation. *The Urban Review, 19*(2), 67-88.

Ascher, C. (1985, December). *Using magnet schools for desegregation: Some suggestions from the research* (ERIC/CUE Trends and Issues Series Number 3). New York, NY: ERIC Clearinghouse on Urban Education, Teachers College, Columbia University.

Blank, R.K. (1984, December). The effects of magnet schools on the quality of education in urban school districts. *Phi Delta Kappan.*

Blank, R. K., Dentler, R.A., Baltzell, C.E., & Chabotar, K. (1983, September). *Survey of magnet schools: Analyzing a model for quality integrated education.* Report prepared for the U. S. Department of Education, Washington, DC: James H. Lowry and Associates.

Bortin, B. H. (1982). *Magnet school programs: Evaluation report, 1980-1981* (Milwaukee ESAA Title VI). Milwaukee, WI: Milwaukee Public Schools, Department of Educational Research and Program Assessment.

Bridge, R. G., & Blackman, J. (1978). *A study of alternatives in American education, Volume IV: Family choice in schooling* (Report No.R-2170/4 - NIE). Santa Monica, CA: The Rand Corporation. (ERIC Document Reproduction Service No. ED 206058)

Cappell, F.J. (1981). *A study of alternatives in American education, Volume VI: Student outcomes in Alum Rock* (Report No. R-2170/6 - NIE). Santa Monica, CA: The Rand Corporation. (ERIC Document Reproduction Service No. ED 216426)

Carrison, M.P. (1981, January). Do magnet schools really work? *Principal, 60* (3), 32-35.

Clewell, B.C., & Joy, M.F. (1987, May). *Evaluation of the Montclair Magnet School System.* Princeton, NJ: Educational Testing Service.

Comerford, J. P. (1980, September-December). Parent perceptions and pupil characteristics of a senior high magnet school program. *Integrated Education 18*(5-6), 50-54.

Davenport, S., & Moore, D. R. (1988). *The new improved sorting machine,* Chicago, IL: Designs for Change.

Dorgan, M. (1980), August). Integration through magnet schools: Goals and limitations. *Integrated Education, 18* (1-4), 59-63.

Dye, T.R. (1960). School desegregation and school decision-making (pp. 107-121). In M. Gittell & A. G. Hevesi (Eds.), *The politics of urban education.* New York, NY: Frederick A. Praeger Publishers.

Epstein, J. (1980), April). *After the bus arrives: Resegregation in desegregating schools.* Paper presented at the annual meeting of the American Educational Research Association, Boston, Massachusetts.

Esposito, F.J. (1988). *Public school choice: National trends and initiatives.* Trenton, NJ; New Jersey State Department of Education.

Eyler, J., Cook, V.J., & Ward, L.eE. (1983). Resegregation: Segregation within desegregated schools. In C. H. Rossell & W. D. Hawley (Eds.), *The c onsequences of school desegregation* (pp. 126-162). Philadelphia, PA: Temple University.

Fleming, D. S., Blank, R.K., Dentler, R.A., & Baltzell, D. C. (1982. *Survey of magnet schools, Interim Report.* Chicago, IL: James H. Lowry and Associates.

Gallup, P. (1986). *Phil Delta Kappan, 68,* 43-59.

Joy, M.F., & Clewell, B. C. (1988, April). *Evaluation of a magnet school system: A case study approach.* Paper presented at the annual meeting of the American Educational Research Association, New Orleans.

Larson, J. C. (1981). *Takoma Park magnet school evaluation; Part II, Final Report.* Rockvile, MD: Montgomery County Public Schools.

Levine, D. U., & Eubanks, E. E. (1980, January-August). Attracting nonminority students to magnet schools in minority neighborhorhoods. *Integrated Education, 18* (1-4), 52-58.

McMillan, C.B. (1980). *Magnet schools: An approach to voluntary desegregation.* Bloomington, IN: Phi Delta Kappa Educational Foundation.

Metz, M.H. (1986). *Different by design: The context and character of three magnet schools.* New York, NY: Routledgee and Kegan Paul.

National Governors Association. (1986). *Time for results: The Governors 1991 report on education.* Washington, DC: National Governors Association.

New York State Magnet School Research Study. (1985, January.) *Magnet schools, school improvement, equity, and school-parent/community relations.* Prepared for the New York State Education Department by MAGI Educational Services, Inc.

Rasmussen, R. (1981). *A study of alternatives in American education. Volume III: Teachers' responses to alternatives* (Report No.R-2170/3-NIE). Santa Monica, CA: The Rand Corporation.

Raywid, M.A. (1982) *The current status of schools of choice in public secondary education.* Hempstead, NY: Project of Alternatives in Education, Hofstra University.

Raywid, M.A. (1985, Winter). Family choice arrangements in public schools: A review of the literature. *Review of Educational Research,55*(4), 435-467.

Rosenbaum, J.E., & Presser, S. (1978, February). Voluntary racial integration in a magnet school. *School Review, 86* (2), 156-186.

Rossell, C.H. (1979, October). Magnet schools as a desegregation tool: The importance of contextual factors in explaining their success. *Urban Education, 14* (3), 303-320.

Rossell, C.H. (1985), April). What is attractive about magnet schools? *Urban Education, 20* (1), 7-22.

Rossell, C.H. (1987, October). The Buffalo Controlled choice plan. *Urban Education, 22* (3), 328-354.

Rossell, C. H., & Clarke, R.C. (1987, March). *The carrot or the stick in school desegregation policy?* A report to the National Institute of Education. Boston, MA: Boston College.

Rossell, C. H., & Glenn, C.L. (1988). The Cambridge controlled choice plan.*The Urban Review, 20,*(2), 75-94.

Royster, E.C., Baltzell, D. C. , & Simmons, F.C. (1979, February). *Study of the Emergency School Aid Act magnet school program* (AAI#78-112). Report prepared for the Office of Education, Department of Health, Education and Welfare, Cambridge, MA: Abt Associates, Inc.

Smith, H. V. (1978). Do optional alternative public schools work? *Childhood Education, 54,* 211-214.

Thomas, M. (1978). *A study of alternatives in American education. Volume II: The role of the principal* (Report No. R-2170/2-NIE). Santa Monica, CA: The Rand Corporation.

Weber, L.J., McBee, J.K., & Lyles, J.H. (1983, April). *An evaluation of fundamental schools.* Paper presented at the annual meeting of the American Educational Research Association, Montreal.

Yin, R. K. (1984). *Case study research: Design and methods.* Applied Social Research Methods Serices, Volume 5). Beverly Hills, CA: Sage Publications, Inc.

Zerchykov, R. (1987). *Parent choice: A digest of the research.* Boston, MA: Institute for Responsive Education. (ERIC Document Reproduction Service No. ED 283 270).

Central Park East: An Alternative Story

Deborah Meier

In the spring of 1991, Central Park East will graduate its first high school students. Some of them will have been with us since they were 4 years old. From age 4 to age 18, they will have attended a school—located in East Harlem in the midst of New York City's District 4—that many observers believe is as good as any school in the public or the private sector. A progressive school in the tradition of so many of New York's independent private schools, Central Park East is firmly fixed within New York's school bureaucracy. As its founding principal, I remain both ecstatic and amazed. Have we really succeeded?

For most of us on the staff and for many of our parents, well-wishers, and friends, the success of Central Park East is a dream come true. A rather fragile dream it has been, tossed by many of the ill winds of this city's tumultuous politics. Today, however, we appear to be sturdier than ever. It would take an unusually strong storm now to uproot us or break us—or even to bend us very much. We were surrounded by a lot of people— within the district and citywide—who would offer strong support if needed.

But it wasn't always so. We have had our share of luck, and we owe a great deal to many different people over the years. We know, too, that our success depended on the success of a districtwide effort to create a whole network of alternative schools. We are, in fact, just one of nearly 30 "options" that are available to families in District 4, aside from the regular neighborhood-zoned elementary schools.

In the fall of 1974 Anthony Alvarado, the new superintendent of District 4, initiated just two such alternatives: our elementary school and a middle school, the East Harlem School for the Performing Arts. Each year thereafter the district supported the launching of several more alternative schools—generally at the junior high level. These schools were rarely the result of a central plan from the district office, but rather tended to be the brain children of particular individuals or groups of teachers. They were initiated by the people who planned to teach in them.

It was the district's task to make such dreams come true. The details differed in each case. Most of these schools were designed around curricular themes—science, environmental studies, performing arts, marine biology. But they also reflected a style of pedagogy that suited their founders. They were always small and, for the most part, staff members volunteered for duty in them. Finally when the alternative schools outnumbered the "regulars," Alvarado announced that henceforth all junior high schools would be schools of"choice." By 1980 all sixth-graders in the district chose where they would go for seventh grade. No junior high had a captive population.

On the elementary school level, neighborhood schools remain the norm, though the district handles zoning rather permissively. The only schools of choice on the elementary level are the Central Park East Schools, the East Harlem Block School (founded in the 1960s as a nonpublic, parent-run "free" school), and a network of bilingual elementary schools .

Today, Central Park East is, in fact, not one school but a network of four schools: Central Park East I, Central Park East II, and River East are elementary schools that feed into Central Park East Secondary School, which enrolls students from grades 7 through 12 and is affiliated with Theodore Sizer's Coalition of Essential Schools.

The Central Park East schools were founded in 1974, during a time of great educational grief in New York City—just before the schools were forced to lay off more than 15,000 teachers and close elementary school libraries and at a time when the spirit of hope was crushed out of the parent movement and out of the struggles for decentralization, for teacher power, and for structural change. Progressive educators suffered particularly, both because people began to claim that "openness" was "through" (and discredited) and because many of the young teachers and programs that had carried the progressive message were hardest hit by the layoffs.

In the spring of 1974, when Alvarado invited me to build a school in one wing of P.S. 171, it seemed a most unlikely offer. School District 4 served a dismal, bitterly torn, largely Hispanic community. Still, I accepted. Who could refuse such an offer? After struggling for years to make my beliefs "fit" into a system that was organized on quite different principles, after spending considerable energy looking for cracks, operating on the margins, "compromising" at every turn, the prospect that the district bureaucracy would organize itself to support alternative ideas and practices was irresistible. I was being offered a chance to focus not on bureaucratic red tape, but on the intractable issues of education—the ones that really excited me and many of the teachers I knew.

But this was not a time for having large visions, and I didn't want to be disappointed. I met with Alvarado, began to collect some experienced teachers to help launch our effort, and gradually began to believe that he meant what he said. He offered to let us build a school just the way we wanted. The total allocation of funds (per-pupil costs) would have to be comparable to what was spent on any other school, and our teachers would have to meet the usual requirements of the city, the state, and the union contract. Nor could we be exempt from any city or state regulations. Beyond that, however, the district would support us in doing things our own way.

We began very small and very carefully. First there was the question of "we." Creating a democratic community was both an operational and an inspirational goal. While we were in part the products of what was called "open" education, our roots went back to early progressive traditions, with their focus on the building of a democratic community, on education for full citizenship and for egalitarian ideals. We looked upon Dewey, perhaps more than Piaget, as our mentor.

Virtually all of us had been educated in part at City College's Workshop Center under Lillian Weber. We came out of a tradition that was increasingly uneasy about the strictly individualistic focus of much of what was being called "open.

We were also unhappy about the focus on skills rather than content in many of the "modern," innovative schools—even those that did not embrace the "back-to-basics philosophy. Many "open" classrooms had themselves fallen prey to the contemporary mode of breaking everything down into discrete bits and pieces—skills—that children could acquire at their own pace and in their own style. In contrast, we were looking for a way to build a school that could offer youngsters a deep and rich curriculum that would inspire them with the desire to know—that would cause them to fall in love with books and with stories of the past; that would evoke in them a sense of wonder at how much there is to learn. Building such a school required strong and interesting adult models—at home and at school—who could exercise their own curiosity and judgment.

We also saw schools as models of the possibilities of democratic life. Although classroom life could certainly be made more democratic than traditional schools allowed, we saw it as equally important that the school life of adults be made more democratic. It seemed unlikely that we could foster democratic values in our classrooms unless the adults in the school also had significant rights over their workplace.

We knew that we were tackling many difficult issues at once. Because of political considerations, planning time was insufficient, but the district tried to make up for this by being extra supportive. Looking back, we were so euphoric that we had the energy of twice our numbers .

We purposely started our school with fewer than a hundred students—in kindergarten, first grade, and second grade only. At the superintendent's request, we recruited outside of the usual district channels, in part so that we wouldn't threaten other schools in the district and in part because one of Alvarado's goals was to increase the pupil population of the district and thus guard against school closings.

Families came to us then, as they still do today, for many reasons. Philosophical agreement on pedagogy was probably the least important. Many families came because they were told by Head Start teachers or principals that their children needed something different, something special. In short, many families came to us because experts claimed that their children would have trouble in traditional schools. Some came because their children were already having trouble in other schools or because older siblings had had trouble in neighborhood schools in the past.

Some families came to us because they had heard us speak and just liked the way we sounded—caring (they told us later), often, friendly, committed. Some came because they had friends who knew us professionally, and some came because they were looking for a different kind of school for philosophical reasons. Yet even among those who chose us because of our presumed beliefs, there was often confusion about what those beliefs were. Some thought for example, that this would be a parent-run school, and some thought we didn't believe in any restrictions on children's freedom.

In fact, one of our primary reasons for starting the school—although we didn't often say it—was our personal desire for greater autonomy as teachers. We spoke a lot about democracy, but we were also just plain sick and tired of having to negotiate with others, worry about rules and regulations, and so on. We all came together with our own visions—some collective and some individual — of what teaching could be like if only we had control. Ours was to be a teacher-run school. We believed that parents should have a voice in their children's schooling, and we thought that "choice" itself was a form of power. We also believed that we could be professionally responsive to parents and that, since the school would be open to parents at all times and the staff would be receptive, there would be plenty of opportunity to demonstrate our responsiveness.

Good early childhood education, we believed, required collaboration between the school and the family. This was a matter not only of political principle but also of educational principle, and it motivated us from the start to work hard to build a family-oriented school. We wanted a school in which children could feel safe. Intellectual risk-taking requires safety, and children who are suspicious of a school's agenda cannot work up to their potential. To create a safe school, we needed to have the confidence of parents, and children needed to know that their parents trusted us. It was that simple. Hard to create, perhaps, but essential.

We stumbled a lot in those early years. We fought among ourselves. We discovered that remaining committed to staff decision making was not easy. It was hard, too, to engage in arguments among ourselves without frightening parents and raising doubts about our professionalism. We were often exhausted—sometimes by things that mattered least to us.

By the end of the second year, I had made some crucial decisions regarding the organization and structure of Central Park East. These involved my leaving the classroom to become a somewhat more traditional principal. We have never entirely resolved the tensions over who makes which decisions and how. But the staff continues to play a central role in all decisions, big and small. Nothing is "undiscussable," though we have learned not to discuss everything—at least not all the time. This has actually meant more time for discussing those issues that concern us most: how children learn, how our classes really work, what changes we ought to be making, and on what bases. We have also become better observers of our own practice, as well as more open and aware of alternative practices.

As we have grown in our understanding and in practical skills, we have also reexamined the relationships between school and family. Today, we understand better the many, often trivial ways in which schools undermine family support systems, undercut children's faith in their parents as educators, and erode parents' willingness to assume their responsibilities as their children's most important educators.

Although we have not changed our beliefs about the value of "naturalistic" and "whole-language" approaches to teaching reading, we have become more supportive of parents whose "home instruction" differs from ours. We give less advice on such topics as how not to teach arithmetic or how to be a good parent. We listen with a more critical ear to what we say to parents, wondering how we would hear it as parents and how children may interpret it as well.

As we became more secure with ourselves and our program, the district was expanding its network of alternative schools. In the fall of 1974 we were one of two. Within a half-dozen years there were about 15 "alternative concept" schools, mostly on the junior high level, where schooling had most glaringly broken down.

The district also dispensed with the assumption that one building equals one school. Instead, every building in the district was soon housing several distinct schools—each with its own leadership, parent body, curricular focus, organization, and philosophy. Most of the new junior highs were located in elementary school buildings. Former junior high buildings were gradually turned to multiple uses, as well. Sometimes three or more schools shared a single building. As a result, the schools were all small, and their staffs and parents were associated with them largely by choice.

By the late Seventies, Central Park East was so inundated with applicants that the district decided to start a small annex at P.S. 109. The district's decision was probably also motivated by the availability of federal funds for the purpose of school integration. While Central Park East has always had a predominantly black (45%) and Hispanic (30%) student population, it is one of the few district schools that has also maintained a steady white population, as large as about 25%. (The population of District 4 is about 60% Hispanic, 35% black, and 5% white.)

In the beginning, this ratio came about largely by chance, but the 25% white population in the school has been maintained by choice. In general, the school has sought to maintain as much heterogeneity as possible, without having too many fixed rules and complex machinery. The school accepts 211 siblings, as part of its family orientation. After siblings, priority goes to neighborhood families. In other cases, the school tries to be nonselective, taking in most of its population at age 5 strictly on the basis of parental choice, with an eye to maintaining a balanced student body. Well over half of the students have always qualified for free or reduced-price lunches, and some 15% to 20% meet the state requirements for receiving special education funds.

In 1980 the annex opened in P.S. 109 and served the same purposes and the same population as Central Park East I. Although the new school was about a mile and a half southeast of Central Park East I, it began as an "annex," serving two classes of 5- and 6-year-olds. Within a few years it was big enough to be designated a separate school. The parents and staff members selected their own director, Esther Rosenfeld, but they decided to continue to proclaim their connection to Central Park East I by calling their school Central Park East II. And the two schools continue to handle recruitment decisions jointly, to share staff retreats, to plan their budgets jointly, and sometimes to share specialists.

The demand for spaces still far outstripped available seats, and, a few years later, the district decided to start a third school. This time the new director, Shelley Price, and her staff decided to call themselves by a new name: River East. They opened in the old Benjamin Franklin High School building beside the East River. The old high school had been closed, largely because of district pressure. It reopened as the Manhattan Center for Math and Science, and it housed in addition to River East, a small junior high school and a new high school.

Thus by 1984 Central Park East had become three schools, each designed for about 250 students, each with its own individual style and character, yet united in basic ways. Then, in 1984, at the 10th anniversary celebration of our founding, Theodore Sizer congratulated the school for its impressive history and asked, "Why not a Central Park East secondary school?" Why not keep the good things going through the 12th grade?

We agreed. Our own study of our sixth-grade graduates persuaded us that starting a secondary school was a good idea. Some of our critics had said that a secure and supportive elementary school would not prepare students to cope with the "real world." Our study of our graduates had proved them wrong. Regardless of race or social class, our graduates had handled the real world well. They had coped. The statistics we compiled amazed even us. Only one of our graduates, who were hardly an academic elite, had left school prior to earning a high school diploma. Furthermore, half of our graduates had gone on to college.

But our graduates had stories to tell. And their stories were not stories about being educated, but about survival. They told us stories that confirmed what Sizer had written about U.S. high schools in Horace's Compromise. But the stories our graduates told us were generally far worse than those Sizer chronicled, since he was often describing wealthy or middle-class schools.

We began negotiations with the district and with the city. In the fall of 1985 we opened the doors to Central Park East Secondary School, which serves grades 7 through 12. We are now back where we began, starting something entirely new. However, circumstances are not exactly the same as they were when we began Central Park East I. For one thing, we cannot avoid public exposure even as we muddle through our first years. Then, too, the obstacles that block the path of reforming a high school are harder to budge than those that face elementary schools.

For instance, the idea that an "alternative" high school means a school for "difficult" kids is firmly entrenched in the tradition of New York City high schools, and the anxiety about preparing students for the "real world" is more pressing than in elementary schools. Moreover, the Regents exams, course requirements, college pressures, and the usual panic about dealing with adolescents and their problems combine to make the task even more complex—especially in light of New York's recently adopted Regents Action Plan, which runs counter to everything we and the Coalition of Essential Schools believe. With its increased number of required courses and standardized examinations and its greater specificity about course content, the Regents Action Plan leaves far less room for initiative and innovation at the school level. Another barrier is the dearth of experience with progressive education at the secondary school level. There is little for us to learn from and not much of a network of teachers or teacher education institutions that can provide us with support, ideas, and examples.

But we have a lot going for us, too. We have our three sister elementary schools to lean on and draw support from. We have the Coalition of Essential Schools and a growing national interest in doing something about the appalling quality of many public secondary schools. And, under its current superintendent, Carlos Medina, the district continues to support the idea of alternative "schools of choice" for all children, all parents, and all staff members. We have also been receiving invaluable support from the citywide high school division and the alternative high school superintendent, who oversees a disparate collection of small high schools throughout New York City.

The oddest thing of all is that the incredible experience of District 4 has had so little impact on the rest of New York City. Here and there another district will experiment with one or another of our innovative practices. But few are willing to break out of the traditional mold. Generally, their alternative programs are mini-schools, with relatively little real power as separate institutions and without their own leadership. Often they are open to only a select few students and thus are resented by the majority. Sometime.. they are only for the "gifted' (often wealthier and whiter) or only for those having trouble with school.

There are many possible explanations for this state of affairs, and we keep hoping that "next year" our ideas will finally catch on. Perhaps the fact that next year keeps moving one year further away suggests that many parents and teachers are satisfied with the status quo at their local elementary schools or that junior high passes so quickly that a stable constituency of parents cannot be built.

But the high schools, which remain the responsibility of the central board in New York City, are clearly in a state of crisis. The dropout rate is appalling, the fate of many who do not drop out officially is equally devastating, and the decline in college attendance by black and Hispanic students is frightening. Perhaps the time has come for progressive education to tackle the high school again, to demonstrate that giving adolescents and their teachers greater responsibility for the development of educational models is the key ingredient.

The notion of respect, which lies at the heart of democratic practice, runs counter to almost everything in our current high schools. Today's urban high schools express disrespect for teachers and students in myriad ways—in the physical decay of the buildings, in their size, in the anonymity of their students, and in the lack of control over decisions by those who live and work in them.

Although the reasons for the recent national concern over high schools may have little to do with democracy, the current reform mood offers an important opening—if we can resist the desire for a new "one best way." We cannot achieve true reform by fiat. Giving wider choices and more power to those who are closest to the classroom are not the kinds of reforms that appeal to busy legislators, politicians, and central board officials. They cannot be mandated, only facilitated. Such reforms require fewer constraints, fewer rules—not more of them. They require watchfulness and continuous documenting and recording, not a whole slew of accountability schemes tied to a mandated list of measurable outcomes.

Do we have the collective will to take such risks? Only if we recognize that the other paths are actually far riskier and have long failed to lead us out of the woods. Like democratic societies, successful schools can't be guaranteed. The merits of letting schools try to be successful are significant. But allowing them to try requires boldness and patience—not a combination that is politically easy to sustain.

School Choice For African-American Children Who Live In Poverty: A Commitment to Equity or More of the Same?

Stanley C. Trent

I remember vividly a day during the mid-1960s when my parents called my brother and me to the kitchen table for a family conference. They had just received a letter from the school board office indicating that a free-choice school plan was in effect. This plan would give parents the opportunity to send their children to one of several segregated, White schools in this rural Virginia district. In this way, county school board officials could document that they were moving toward gradual school desegregation. The question from our parents was, "Which school do you want to attend?"

Being the oldest sibling still in school, I quickly announced, "I don't want to go to no White school." My younger brother concurred, my father signed the form indicating that we wished to remain in our same school, and that was the end of our family conference. We returned outside and continued to shoot some hoops.

I have wondered often how my parents might have reacted had I requested to attend one of the White schools, one that was far closer to my house than the Black school I attended. In all honesty, I believe that such a request would not have resulted in a change of where my father marked the "X" on the choice sheet. After all, we attended a Black elementary school that enjoyed an outstanding reputation. Because the school was located near a historically Black university, we were exposed to many cultural events and activities that were not even accessible to White students who attended neighboring schools. Parents at the school, many of whom were employed by the university, had worked with teachers and administrators to build a very strong, supportive parent-teacher association.

The faculty and staff were an active and vital part of our community. By virtue of their ethnicity and their life experiences, they possessed a sense of awareness about those aspects of our culture, our language, and our behavior that had to be honored and incorporated into our learning experiences. I suspect that these were some of the reasons why my parents allowed us to remain in a segregated school setting.

Perhaps, though, at the heart of this choice was my parents' fear that enrollment in one of the White schools would place us in physical, psychological, and emotional danger. They feared that our mere presence in one of the newly integrated schools would aggravate and intensify the hatred that had maintained our segregated communities, our segregated existence, for centuries. I am sure that they recalled the newscasts of the 1950s that showed the anxiety, humiliation, and fear felt by the Little Rock Nine as they walked down human corridors of national guardsmen who allowed them entrance into Central High School.

At any rate, they decided to take the safe route and protect the well-being of their children. A few Black parents sent their children to White schools, but the majority opted to maintain the status quo. Some 4 years later, the freedom of choice program was abandoned, Black schools were either closed or converted into annexes, and the majority of Black students were enrolled in the previously all White schools.

At this time, Brown v. the Board of Education (1954) was over 10 years old, yet the sociopolitical overtones that hovered over African-American parents forced many to make choices that resulted in the continued segregation of southern schools.

Now, in 1992, many educators and policymakers are once again promoting public school choice as a means to improve the quality of education for all children. However, based on past practices, it appears that such a policy will only result in the continued denial of equal access and quality education for African-American students. Federal government priorities have shifted from access and equity to excellence; and programs designed to meet the needs of minorities, the economically disadvantaged, and the educationally disabled are criticized by government officials, policymakers, and practitioners. Attempts to dismantle, amalgamate, deregulate, and revoke funding for these social programs are being promulgated by federal officials (Kauffman, 1989; Kauffman & Hallahan, 1990; Moran, 1984).

Still, despite these cuts in federal funding, school choice is being proposed as a central policy alternative to overcome what is argued to be the bankruptcy of the public schools. Choice proponents contend that the reform can be achieved by two basic means—choice within public education and a voucher system to support choice options in private schools. Public choice is defined as, "the deliberate differentiation of public schools, permitting students and their families to select the type of school each youngster will attend" (Raywid, 1987, p. 763). Raywid defines vouchers as a system whereby parents are given funds to purchase schooling for their children within the private sector.

Although much controversy exists over the implementation of such plans, particularly voucher systems, the Bush administration remains staunch in its position that choice will restore excellence to an inadequate public education system. Moreover, federal government officials contend that education will be at its best for all of America's children because the competition stimulated by choice will spur school improvement and choice will cause parents to be psychologically invested in the schools where they send their children. As stated in America 2000 (1991),

> If standards, tests and report cards tell parents and voters how their schools are doing, choice gives them the leverage to act. Such choices should include all schools that serve the public and are accountable to public authority, regardless of who runs them. New incentives will be provided to states and localities to adopt comprehensive choice policies, and the largest federal school aid program (Chapter 1) will be revised to ensure that federal dollars follow the child to whatever extent state and local policies permit. (p. 12)

When I analyze this movement that invests the future of educational reform to the states and localities, I find myself asking the question, "How will school choice benefit African-American students who live in poverty?" As an African-American educator, there are perhaps two viewpoints that might characterize my answer to this question. On one hand, I might conclude that freedom of choice will serve to free African-American children and their parents from the inequities that now exist within public education. Because prior policies (e.g., Brown, Education for All Handicapped Children Act) have not resulted in significant, widespread, long-lasting change for targeted constituents, implementation of choice programs will force schools to clean up their acts. African-Americans, as well as all other parents, will have the option of sending their children to private or public schools that offer state-of-the-art instructional approaches and above-average standardized test scores. Those schools who do not satisfy constituents will be simply forced out of business.

However, based on my knowledge of past treatment of African-Americans, I am unconvinced that choice will improve significantly the quality of education for low-income students of color who are not successful in school. In fact, this move to establish competitive public and private schools will be less fruitful than past reforms that were designed to address the critical needs of these children.

I have come to this conclusion because freedom of choice is an integral part of a movement that lays the responsibility of educating children squarely in the hands of states and localities. History has taught us that when this occurs, those constituents who are not a part of the community of the preferred are the ones whose concerns and needs are neglected and ignored (Astuto & Clark, 1992; Futrell, 1989; Moran, 1984; Wayson, Mitchell, Pinnell, & Landis, 1988). What we have failed to realize is that society as a whole has been the source of illness, and our misdiagnoses of social problems have resulted in prescriptions that produced negative side effects and the perpetuation of the ailment that policy advocates and policy developers sought to remedy. For example, the Education for All Handicapped Children Act (EHCA) was enacted to insure a free, appropriate education to children with disabilities. However, implementation of this policy has also resulted in the disproportionate placement of minority students in remedial tracks and special education. Based on this analysis, I assert that if we truly desire to create quality and equity in education, we must examine problems in service delivery from a historical and a sociocultural perspective. I provide support for this argument in the remainder of the article.

The Education Of African-American Children: A Historical Perspective

Intellectuals ought to study the past not for the pleasure they find in so doing, but to derive lessons from it.

—Cheikh Anta Diop (quoted in Bell, 1986)

A historical examination of the education of African-American students reveals that they have had to endure hardships and disadvantages more intensely than children who are members of other ethnic groups. Perhaps one of the most comprehensive perspectives provided on this issue is presented by Comer (1989). Comer demonstrated the fact that Europeans and Asians who immigrated to this country enjoyed continuity in their respective cultures. Although they too experienced prejudice and discrimination, their religion, language, customs, and traditions allowed them to maintain links with the old country and at the same time make smoother adjustments to life in America. Comer distinguished between the life experiences of Blacks and European and Asian immigrants and illustrated the many disparities that existed for Blacks between 1900 and the 1940s:

> The first wave of these immigrants came to America before the 1900s when one could be uneducated and unskilled and still provide for one's family. Between the 1900s and the 1940s, their children were able to gain the modern level of education and training that enabled them to function in the economic mainstream of that era. The stable families that emerged from that generation gave their children the kinds of experiences that allowed them to function well in the postindustrial period from 1945 to the present in which a high level of education and training is necessary. (p. 133)

On the other hand, Blacks, Hispanics, and Native Americans experienced quite different histories. Their lives were characterized by what Comer referred to as cultural discontinuity. For Blacks, during the institution of slavery, "There was loss of the African institutions, the loss of the belief systems that guided and supported functioning, and the loss of the sense of belonging and of personal adequacy that occurred upon their introduction to American society" (Comer, 1989, p. 133). Also with slavery, there came a loss of independence, a sense of inferiority, and a sense of powerlessness. Even after emancipation, African-Americans were still denied access to the mainstream of American life. Education, the vital element that made the difference for so many Americans, was not available to the vast majority of African-Americans. As Comer (1989) commented,

> As late as 1940, when the rest of America was being educated and prepared for a future in which high-level education would become extremely important, four to eight times more money was being spent on the education of White children than Black ones in the eight states that held 80 percent of the nation's Black population. (p. 134)

Finally, Comer (1989) made two observations that are critical to understanding the emergence of the Black middle and lower class. As late as the 1950s, Blacks found refuge and safety in communities that were established as a result of forced segregation. Because they were skilled laborers, a disproportionate number of Blacks were able to acquire economic and educational status for their children that moved beyond the accomplishments of their predecessors and their contemporaries. An interesting, but not surprising, phenomenon occurred. According to Comer, "Many of the well-functioning families began to have fewer children. Families that did not function well, almost by definition, did not limit the numbers of children; thus, the least well-functioning families had the most children" (p.135).

Comer's explanation helps us understand better the nature of the circumstances that caused a disproportionate number of Black families to become economically disadvantaged. These factors contributed greatly to the stress experienced by poor Black families, and these sociocultural stress factors persisted throughout the desegregation years.

Desegregation: The Promise of Forty Acres and a Mule

As the 1960s approached, America found itself in the middle of another wave of educational reform that influenced the schooling of many children. During the late 1950s through the mid-1960s, despite the passage of Brown v. Board of Education, the country was preoccupied with Russia, the space race, science, and technology. Unfortunately, the focus on equity never had time to develop fully because of the National Defense Education Act (NDEA) and its focus on excellence in science and mathematics. Hence the focus on equity and educating the masses that characterized the progressive movement gave way to a movement that supported improved educational programs for White America's most capable learners. Excellence, not equity, became the priority of the day (Clark, Astuto, & Rooney, 1983; Cuban, 1990; Lazerson, 1983).

Still, because they feared losing federal funds, state and local educational agencies developed plans (e.g., the freedom-of-choice plans) that presumably illustrated their willingness to comply with federal mandates. However, to a large degree, these plans represented merely the states' and localities' subtle insistence that segregation and inequities in educational programs for African-American children would remain the law of the land. Mizell (1968) provided reasons for the failure of freedom-of-choice plans during this period:

> Freedom of choice has proved to be ineffective because the burden has been primarily on the Negro parents and it is only with their decision to send their children to predominantly white schools that these institutions have been desegregated. School officials must understand that Negro citizens see through the sham of freedom of choice and they feel no obligation to bear this burden which allows school authorities to evade their responsibility to abolish the dual school systems. (p.20)

Mizell failed to realize that school system officials were indeed aware of Black parents' understanding of their ulterior motives. Although many of these schools had better facilities, newer textbooks, and more comprehensive curricula, Black parents did not wish their children to attend schools where teachers and administrators would perceive them as being inferior, would have low expectations for them, would not understand the uniqueness and soundness of their language patterns and styles of presentation, would not have accurate knowledge of their history, and would not see the value and significance of their communities.

When schools were finally desegregated in large numbers, these suspicions and perceptions on the part of Black parents were confirmed, and many saw their fears come to life as they witnessed the damaging effects of desegregation on their children. In analyzing the influence of the state and local implementation of desegregation policy on the achievement of Black students, Irvine and Irvine (1983) concluded that desegregation resulted in a breakdown of interactions between different institutions that served to preserve, to some degree, the security and well-being of Black children. These authors' analyses parallel closely those of Comer (1989). More specifically, Irvine and Irvine (1983) speak from a sociocultural context and relate how changes in interpersonal and institutional dynamics affected the performance of Black students. At the interpersonal level, the disappearance of Black teachers and administrators affected negatively the self-esteem and self-awareness of Black children. Irvine and Irvine reviewed the literature on teacher expectations of Black students and concluded that in general, White teachers reported lower expectations of Black students than did Black teachers (Beady & Hansell, 1981; Eyler, Cook, & Ward, 1982; Gay, 1975; Massey, Scott, & Dornbusch, 1975).

From an institutional perspective, the Black school served as an institution of strength, hope, and security for the community. Black principals and teachers were, to a large extent, in control of what happened at Black schools. White central office administrators paid little attention to these schools as long as major problems were kept to a minimum. With the implementation of large-scale desegregation plans, Black schools were the ones that were dismantled. Black teachers and administrators were the ones who were reassigned, demoted, or in some cases dismissed.

Irvine and Irvine (1983) noted that "the number of role models declined; in their stead, there were placed teaching and administrative staffs that were either foreign or overtly hostile to the black students" (p. 418). Those students who were not bicognitive, bicultural, and bidialectic became at risk for below-average school achievement (Anderson, 1988).

Special Education and the Continuation of Inequity

During the 1960s and the 1970s, a new set of advocates sought to gain access and equity for their children who heretofore had been either denied access or served inappropriately in public school settings. Just as African-Americans had done before them, White, middle-class citizens formed advocacy groups and pushed government officials to act on behalf of their children. As a result, several pieces of legislation were enacted, one of the most prominent being the EHCA. Some of the specifications of EHCA included "an active search to locate all handicapped children excluded from public education, nondiscriminatory diagnostic procedures, individualized education programs, adequate due process procedures for all handicapped children, and placement in the least restrictive environment for learning" (Lazerson, 1983).

Interestingly enough, while these newly organized groups advocated pull-out services in public school settings, civil rights advocates began to question the legitimacy of the growing practice of placing low-income Black children into programs for the mentally retarded. Many have attributed this overrepresentation to the cultural bias in special education testing procedures (Clark-Johnson, 1988; Duffey, Salvia, Tucker, & Ysseldyke, 1981; MacMillan, Hendrick, & Watkins, 1988; Mercer, 1974; Tucker, 1980). In addition to invalid testing procedures, the same factors that contributed to the lack of academic achievement of Black children after desegregation (e.g., expectations of White teachers and administrators, decrease in number of Black teachers and administrators, a desire to maintain segregation within desegregated schools, lack of understanding about the Black community) directly influenced the disproportionate placement of these children into special education programs (Chinn & Hughes, 1987; Lazerson, 1983; McIntyre & Pernell, 1985; Reschly, 1984). Lazerson (1983) discussed the nature of this phenomenon:

> From its origins, special education was tied to views of racial inferiority; without the ethnic and racial antagonisms of World War I years, special education would have received only the most minimal attention. The racial biases that made minorities the most likely candidates for placement in inadequate special education classes continued into the post-World War II period. Indeed, the biases played much the same role they had before: public education and special education expanded simultaneously, in the 1950s and 1960s, allowing school systems both to incorporate large numbers of nonwhite pupils into the schools while simultaneously segregating them within the schools. (p.40)

The history of the education of African-American children identifies clearly those factors that have interacted to create a disproportionate number of Black children who are classified as economically disadvantaged, educationally disabled, or both. In fact, in identifying children who are educationally disadvantaged, Pallas, Natriello, and McDill (1989) state that "minority racial/ethnic group status is perhaps the best known factor associated with being educationally disadvantaged" (p. 17). In addition, these authors report that these students perform substantially below White children in reading and writing, live in households with incomes below the poverty level, live in homes where the primary caretaker is the mother, and live with mothers who are poorly educated. Moreover, according to the National Black Child Development Institute (1986), (a) nearly one of every two Black children lives in poverty; (b) almost two thirds of young Black children live in homes relying on some form of public assistance; (c) Black children receive poorer health care than do White children; (d) an affluent suburban White child is more likely to participate in a gifted and talented program than is a Black child in the inner city; and (e) nationally, the dropout rate for Black youth is almost 28%, approaching 50% in some areas. Currently, many reformers (including the Bush administration) contend that the wide-scale implementation of school choice programs will correct these inequities that have been embedded in American society for over three centuries.

AMERICA 2000 and the Push for Choice

. . . What you seen
Wasn't no dust of changes rising.
It was the dust of sameness settling.

— Sterling Plump (quoted in Bell, 1986)

The government document entitled America 2000 (1991) sets the tone for drastic restructuring and reform of education—or does it? The following national goals are identified in the document. Goals are to be met by the year 2000.

1. All children in America will start school ready to learn.

2. The high school graduation rate will increase to at least 90 percent.

3. American students will leave grades four, eight, and twelve having demonstrated competency in challenging subject matter including English, mathematics, science, history, and geography; and every school in America will ensure that all students learn to use their minds well, so they may be prepared for responsible citizenship, further learning, and productive employment in our modern economy.

4. U.S. students will be first in the world in science and mathematics achievement.

5. Every adult American will be literate and will possess the knowledge and skills necessary to compete in a global economy and exercise the rights and responsibilities of citizenship.

6. Every school in America will be free of drugs and violence and will offer a disciplined environment conducive to learning. (p. 9)

In the report, a four-part strategy is outlined that it is argued will allow America to meet these goals. Included under these strategies are American achievement tests, presidential citations for educational excellence, presidential achievement scholarships, a national report card, and business and school partnerships. Except for the paragraph cited earlier in this article, there is little information devoted to public school choice. Moreover, although private schools are not mentioned specifically anywhere in this section, the implication is quite clear. The developers of this policy proposal assert that parental choice among public and private schools will create schools that will accept low-income Black students with disabilities, honor cultural diversity, and actively seek to remedy social conflicts that exist currently between the parents of these children and the public schools. There are no specific references in the document that outline how these critical issues will be addressed. I must conclude that this plan will only create situations in which those who already reap the benefits of quality education will benefit even more. In his reaction to *America 2000*, Kaplan (1991) shared this opinion:

> As an educational strategy, *America 2000* is a plan for Middle Class America, where pride in academic achievement still runs high much of the time and most people like their community's schools. That some of these schools are performing below expectations is lamentable, but jettisoning them in order to conform to a market-driven, private-school-oriented vision of schooling in a responsible democratic society is palpable nonsense. And very dangerous. (p. 36)

Another unlikely assumption embedded in America 2000 and the policy of school choice is the belief that low-income minority parents will send their children to private or public schools that maintain better-than-average grades on the national report card. There is already evidence that private-school choice is a simplistic solution that will not work. Ascher (1986), for example, found that although Black enrollment in private schools is increasing, those Black children who do enroll "are from better educated black parents than are those children of similar socioeconomic backgrounds attending public school" (pp. 138-139).

Ascher also identified misconceptions about Black children who attend private schools. She found that the commonly expressed notion that Black students enrolled in private schools outperform their counterparts enrolled in public schools is erroneous. She concluded that the two groups are not comparable because they differ significantly in socioeconomic status and educational background of parents. Also, low-income-serving Catholic schools tend not to offer higher level courses (e.g., calculus, German, French) as often as do high-income-serving Catholic schools. In terms of quality of programming, Ascher (1986) reported the following:

> There is evidence that the higher the percentage of black students in a private school, the more likely are the class size and pupil-teacher ratio to be large. Factors such as the level of teacher training, the number of years teachers have taught, and the materials available also appear to decrease as the number of black students increases. (p.143)

Ascher's review of the literature on Black students in private schools also revealed that multicultural education was not incorporated into the curriculum of many of the schools.

School choice policies espoused in *America 2000* also fail to address the school/community relationship and parental involvement referred to by Comer (1989). The document states that

> rich parents, white and non-white, already have school choice. They can move, or pay for private schooling. The biggest beneficiaries of new choice policies will be those who don't now have any alternative; with choice they can find a better school for their children or use that leverage to improve the school their children now attend. (America 2000, 1991, p.31)

What the framers of this document fail to acknowledge is that middle- and upper-middle-class parents are the ones who are in the position to take advantage of educational policy and due process safeguards (Darling-Hammond & Kirby, 1985; Lynch & Stern, 1982; Maddaus, 1988; Weiler, 1974). Maddaus (1988), for example, found that although lower-middle-income parents in two neighborhoods were more likely to send their children to schools other than neighborhood public schools, low-income parents were more likely to send their children to inadequate neighborhood schools because of lack of information and lack of access. Lynch and Stern (1982) conducted a study to determine the extent to which poor Hispanic and African-American parents participated in the development of their child's special education program. Results indicated minimal involvement. These parents cited factors such as transportation, work schedules, and lack of babysitting services as being roadblocks to more active participation. Whether the school is public or private, if parental and community concerns are not considered and honored, if the community is not considered as legitimate and viable, if positive relationships are not established between school personnel, parents, and other community members, then the chances of invoking positive change are minimal.

SUMMARY AND CONCLUSIONS

Our nettlesome task is to discover how to organize our strength into compelling power.

—Martin Luther King, Jr. (quoted in Bell, 1986)

As we assess the appropriateness of choice as a policy option that will bring about educational equity for African-American children who live in poverty, we must consider several factors. First of all, we must remember that the vehicle of school choice has never worked to increase educational opportunities or educational attainment for African-American children. Furthermore, the Bush Administration's plan for education reform—which includes school choice as an option—espouses excellence in education without addressing the needs of children who are at risk for school failure. We must remember that equity for minority groups has never occurred as a by-product of a focus on excellence.

Finally, one might conclude from this writing that I believe that the lack of positive outcomes as a result of federal mandates points to a realization that such interventions are ineffective and unnecessary. Such a conclusion is a far cry from what I believe. As the demography of this country continues to change, federal involvement is needed more than ever to mandate and monitor redistributive policies designed to protect the rights of neglected groups. However, we must seek ways to insure that our policies, service delivery models, implementation practices, and evaluation and research designs are synthesized in ways that will promote true equity in education for all children.

We must move beyond the belief that solutions emanating from simplistic, cause-effect relationships will bring about positive changes in education and quality of life for undeserved populations. The sociocultural and sociopolitical factors that have been embedded in American society for centuries must be addressed directly if policy implementation is to have any chance of dismantling a system of stratification along the lines of race, ethnicity, and socioeconomic status in this country.

To start, policymakers, researchers, and educators must begin to develop policies and practices that will better prepare nonminority teachers and administrators to deal effectively with diversity in the classroom from both instructional and sociological perspectives. We must also begin to develop policies and programs that will result in the recruitment and retention of African-American teachers and administrators, teacher educators, and educational researchers. Perhaps one of the most neglected areas in educational reform is that of home-school relations. The development and implementation of programs designed to increase parental involvement and cooperative community-school relationships must become a major focus of policymakers and researchers. To implement these and other policies, more funds and incentives must be provided from the federal government.

Although we must continue to focus on quantative research designs and analyses to determine efficacy, we must also focus more intensely on qualitative procedures that will help us to identify those process variables that will lead to a better understanding of why our innovations succeed or fail. If we can take a broad perspective on how to assess, problem solve, implement, and evaluate what we do in the name of equity, then we can plot a new course that will yield more positive, widespread, and long-lasting results. In the process, we may find that these positive outcomes may be realized in increasing numbers of our nation's nonchoice public schools.

References

America 2000: An education strategy. (1991). Washington, D.C: U.S. Department of Education.

Anderson, J.A.(1988). Cognitive styles and multicultural populations. *Journal of Teacher Education*, 39, 2-9.

Ascher, C. (1986). Black students and private schools. *Urban Review*, 18, 137-145.

Astuto, T.A., & Clark, D.L. (1992). Challenging the limits of school restructuring and reform. In A. Lieberman (Ed.), *The ninety-first yearbook of the National Society for the Study of Education* (pp. 90-109). Chicago: University of Chicago Press.

Beady, C. H., & Hansell, S (1981). Teacher race and expectations for student achievement. *American Education Research Journal*, 18, 191-206.

Bell, J.C. (Ed.).(1986). *Famous Black quotations and some not so famous.* Chicago: Sabayt.

Brown v. Board of Education, 347 U.S. 482 (1954).

Chinn, P.C., & Hughes, S. (1987). Representation of minority students in special education classes. *Remedial and Special Education*, 8(4), 41-46.

Clark, D.L., Astuto, T.A., & Rooney, P.M. (1983). The changing nature of federal education policy in the 1980's. *Phi Delta Kappan*, 65, 188-193.

Clark-Johnson, G. (1988). Black children. *Teaching Exceptional Children*, 20, 46-47.

Comer, J.P. (1989). Child development and education. *Journal of Negro Education*, 58(2), 125-139.

Cuban, L. (1990). reforming again, again and, again. *Educational Researcher*, 19(1), 3-13.

Darling-Hammond, L., & Kirby, S.N. (1985). *Tuition tax deductions and parent school choice; A case study of Minnesota* (report No. R-3294-NIE). Santa Monica, CA: RAND. (ERIC Document Reproduction Service No. ED 273 047)

Duffey, J.B., Salvia, J., Tucker, J., & Ysseldyke, J. (1981). Nonbiased assessment: A need for operationalism. *Exceptional Children*, 47, 427-434.

Eyler, J., Cook, V., & Ward, L. (1982, March). *Resegregation: Segregation within desegregated schools.* Paper presented at annual meeting of the American Education Research Association, New York.

Futrell, M.H. (1989). Mission not accomplished:Education reform in retrospect. *Phi Delta Kappan*, 71, 8-14.

Gay, G. (1975). Teachers' achievement expectations of classroom interactions with ethnically different students. *Contemporary Education*, 46, 166-172.

Irvine, R.W., &Irvine, J.J. (1983). The impact of the desegregation process on the education of Black studies: Key variables. *Journal of Negro Education*, 52(4), 410-422.

Kaplan, G.R. (1991, may 22). Watch out for America 200: It really is a crusade. *Education Week*, pp. 36, 27.

Kauffman, J. M. (1989). The regular education initiative as Reagan-Bush policy: A trickle-down theory of education of the hard-to-teach. *Journal of Special Education*, 23, 256-278.

Kauffman, J.M., & Hallahan, D.P. (1990, October 24). The politics of special-education "backlash." *Education Week*, pp. 25, 27.

Lazerson, M. (1983). The origins of special education. In J.G. Chambers & W. T. Hartman (Eds.), *Special education policies: Their history, implementation, and finance* (pp. 15-47). Philadelphia, PA: Temple University Press.

Lynch, E. W., & Stern, R. (1982). Perspectives on parent participation in special education. *Exceptional Education Quarterly*, 3, 56-63.

MacMillan, D. L., Henedrick, I. R., & Watkins, A.V. (1988). Impact of Diana, Larry p., and PL 94-142 on minority students. *Exceptional Children*, 54, 426-432.

Maddaus, J. (1988). Families, neighborhoods and schools: Parental perspectives and actions regarding choice in elementary school enrollment. *Dissertation Abstracts International*, 49, 477-A. (University Microfilms No. 88-06, 952).

Massey, G. C., Scott, M.V., & Dornsbusch, S. M. (1975). Racism without racists: Institutional racism in urban schools. *Black Scholar*, 7, 10-19.

McIntyre, L. D., & Pernell, E. (1985). The impact of race on teacher recommendations for special education placement. *Journal of Multicultrual Counseling and Development*, 13(3), 112-120.

Mercer, J. R. (1974). A policy statement on assessment procedures and the right s of children. *Harvard Educational Review*, 44, 125-141.

Mizell, M. H. (1968). The south has genuflected and held on to tokenism. *Southern Education Report*, 3, 19-21.

Moran, R. M. (1984). Excellence at the cost of instructional equity? The potential impact of recommended reforms upon low achieving students. *Focus on Exceptional Children*, 16(7), 1-12.

National Black Child Development Institute, Inc. (1986). 1986 *NBCDI annual report*, Washington, DC: Author.

Pallas, A. M., Natriello, G., & McDill, E. L.(1989). The changing nature of the disadvantaged population: Current dimensions and future trends. *Educational Researcher*, 18(5), 16-22.

Raywid, M. A. (1987). Public choice, yes: Vouchers, no! *Phi Delta Kappan*, 68, 762-769.

Reschly, D. J. (1984). Beyond IQ test bias: The national academy panel's analysis of minority EMR overrepresentation, *Educational Researcher*, 13(3), 15-19

Tucker, J. A. (1980). Ethnic proportions in classes for the learning disabled: Issues in nonbiased assessment. *Journal of Special Education*, 14, 94-105.

Wayson, W. W., Mitchell, B., Pinnell, G. S., & Landis, D. (1988). *Up from excellence: The impact of the excellence movement on schools.* Bloomington, IN: Phi Delta Kappa Educational Foundation.

Weiler, D. (1974). *A public school voucher demonstration*: The first year at Alum Rock (Report No. R-1495-NIE). Santa Monica, CA: RAND.

THE CARROT OR THE STICK
FOR SCHOOL DESEGREGATION POLICY?*

Christine H. Rossell

The relevance of the public-choice model of decision making for school desegregation is tested by comparing the desegregation effectiveness of voluntary plans, which depend on parents choosing magnet schools, to mandatory reassignment plans, which "force" parents to send their children to desegregated schools. A desegregation plan based primarily on voluntary transfers to magnet schools will produce greater long-term interracial exposure than a mandatory reassignment plan with magnet components, in part because of the greater white flight from the mandatory plans. In short, the public-choice model of decision making is more successful in producing interracial exposure than the command-and-control model.

Opposition of the American public and its leaders to what is popularly termed "forced busing," combined with highly publicized white flight from mandatory reassignment plans (see Coleman et al., 1975; Rossell, 1975-1976, 1978c), has prompted local administrators, the federal government and the courts to search for alternatives. The most popular alternatives-magnet school plans-have been based on the concept of attracting students rather than forcing them to attend desegregated schools.

The use of magnet schools to attract students as an alternative to forced busing has its intellectual foundation in public-choice theory. Public-choice theory is the application of microeconomic theory to problems within the public domain. The presumptions are that the behavior of citizens is similar to that of consumers in a market system and that they will act in their own self-interest (Downs, 1957; Olson, 1965; Tiebout, 1956; Friedman, 1962; Friedman and Friedman, 1981; Buchanan and Tollison, 1984). In the public-choice model, the government agency seeks to

---

AUTHOR'S NOTE:*This work could not have been completed without the invaluable assistance of Ruth Clarke in managing the data collection, data coding, file construction, and generation of indices and enrollment data. Nor could it have been completed without the cooperation and generosity of the administrative personnel in the school districts in this sample. The research was supported by grant NIE-G-83-0019 from the National Institute of Education and a Filed Initiated Studies Program grant, as administered by the Office of Research, OERI, U. S. Department of Education.*

* Figures have been omitted and text edited to reflect this omision.

change the behavior of the target group by restructuring, rather than bluntly limiting, the environment of choice. The targeted individuals have the freedom to choose among a wide range of actions and are expected to act in a manner that is economically most advantageous to them —as if they were operating in a market place— but they are encouraged through positive and negative incentives to pick actions that are consistent with the desired social goals.

In a magnet school plan, schools that need to be desegregated are selected to have magnet programs.[1] Not only is more money spent on these schools, but the curriculum is altered so that it has a special theme or focus. The magnet school theme is publicized widely, and parents are actively and aggressively recruited. When such a magnet school program is implemented in a segregated neighborhood school system, the primary assumption is that parents will evaluate the educational program of the neighborhood school and that of the desegregated magnet school in rational, programmatic terms. The corollary assumption is that the additional money being allotted and the special theme of the school will be sufficient incentives for large numbers of parents to choose the magnet schools.

Although numerous scholars have recommended the use of incentives to induce voluntary desegregation (Meadow, 1976; Bullock, 1976; Orfiedl, 1976; Armor, 1979; Rossell and Hawley, 1982), the efficacy of the public-choice model for desegregation has been questioned in most of the literature. The general conclusion, even in the most recent writings, is that voluntary plans do not work (Rossell, 1978a,b 1979, 1983; Orfield, 1978, 1988; Royster et al., 1979; Rossell and Hawley, 1983). For example, in a recent review of the research, Hawley and Smylie (1986; 282) cited studies published through 1983 and concluded that

wishful thinking to the contrary and occasional anecdotes notwithstanding, wholly voluntary strategies are only partially successful in reducing racial isolation...those based primarily on voluntary strategies...have limited impact on levels of racial isolation throughout the system, particularly in districts with substantial proportions of minority students.

Similarly, the Fifth Circuit Court of Appeals concluded in 1987 in *United States v Pittman by Pittman* that a voluntary plan with magnet schools proposed for the Hattiesburg, Mississippi, school district "did not meet the constitutional test for dismantling a long established dual system. Magnet schools should be a supplement to a mandatory desegregation plan based to a reasonable extent on mandatory reassignment and pairing and clustering of schools" (p. 390) and that "burdening black parents with the obligation of choosing schools is unworkable in fact and contrary to the law" (p.388).

Thus the dominant model of policymaking in the school desegregation literature and in the courts is the command-and-control model. In this model citizens are assumed to be recalcitrant, and compliance must be mandated. Directions and prohibitions are drafted with a limited, specific range of actions. For school desegregation policy this takes the form of specific assignments of specific students to schools where their attendance will desegregate that school. The command-and-control model is assumed to be more effective in achieving the goal of desegregating a school system because citizens are either too consumed by racial prejudice stemming from early childhood socialization to act in their own self-interest or no school district would be able to afford the kind of incentives that would be necessary for benefits to outweigh costs in the minds of parents whose early childhood socialization weights the costs of desegregation heavily. Given the assumptions, even if evasion (that is, white flight) occurs, the net benefit from a command-and-control approach will still be greater than if one relies on voluntary transfers.

Presented here is the most recent evidence on the question of whether the public choice model or the command-and control model is more effective in desegregating a school system: The desegregation effectiveness of voluntary plans with magnet schools (the public-choice model) is compared to that of mandatory plans with magnet schools (the command-and-control model). The sample is 20 school districts, 18 of which were originally studied by Abt Associates (Royster et al., 1979; Rossell, 1979). This study differs from previous research on this subject in three ways. First, this is the first study in which the long-term impacts of voluntary and mandatory plans are compared. In this sample, the average desegregation year is 1974 and the last data are for 1985. The quasi-experimental design of this study includes at least 31 years of postimplementation data. Although Rossell (1979) and Royster et al (1979) concluded that magnet mandatory plans produce more desegregation than magnet-voluntary plans, each of these studies was limited by having only one year of postimplementation data. Yet, it is often the case that the long-term impact of a policy is very different from the short-term impact (see, for example, Salamon, 1979).

Second, most of the authors in this field have failed to distinguish between the source of the order and the degree of parental choice. Here, the source of the order refers to whether a plan is board ordered or court ordered. The extent of parental choice determines whether a plan is called voluntary or mandatory because the most important factor affecting white flight is parental choice, not the source of the order (Rossell, 1983). In this sample, 56% of the voluntary plans are court-ordered and 36% of the mandatory plans are board-ordered.

Third, in even the most recent studies comparing the relative effectiveness of magnet-voluntary plans with magnet-mandatory plans, researchers have used dependent variables that I believe to be inadequate. The most common inadequate dependent variable is a standardized measure of racial balance, such as the index of dissimalarity.[2] The formula is as follows:

$$D = 1/2 \sum \frac{W_i}{W} - \frac{B_i}{B},$$

where W is the number of whites, or any other ethnic or racial group, and B is the number of blacks or any other ethnic or racial group. The index of dissimilarity represents the proportion (or percentage if multiplied by 100) of black students who would have to be reassigned to white schools if no whites were reassigned, in order to have the same proportion in each school as in the whole school district.[3] The index ranges from 0 (perfect racial balance —that is , no black students need to be reassigned) to 100 (perfect racial imbalance —that is, 100% of the black students would need to be reassigned, if no whites were reassigned, in order to have perfect racial balance).

Another way of measuring the contact between the races is by determining interracial exposure-specifically, the proportion white in the average minority child's school.[4] The measure is calculated as follows:

$$Smw = \frac{\sum_k N_{km} P_{kw}}{\sum_k N_{km}},$$

where k stands for each individual school, and, thus, N_{km} is the number (N) of minorities (m) in a particular school (k), and Pkw is the proportion (P) white (w) in the same school (k). Because the proportion white in the average minority child's school increases with racial balance reassignments but decreases as the white enrollment decreases, it yields the interracial exponent or net benefit, of desegregation reassignments.

Racial balance, by contrast, is an inadequate goal because it ignores white reactions to desegregation that influence how many whites are coming into contact with minorities. This is as true of the precise racial balance measures such as the index of dissimilarity, as it is of the more imprecise racial balance standards used by the courts, such as the requirement that all schools be within plus or minus 15 or 20 percentage points of the district's mean proportions.

Thus the index of dissimilarity, or any other measure of racial balance is less comprehensive than the index of interracial exposure, because interracial exposure includes racial balance, but racial balance does not include interracial exposure. Racial balance can be achieved with very little interracial exposure, but interracial exposure cannot be achieved without significant racial balance. If whites and minorities are evenly distributed among schools there will be a higher percentage white in the average minority child's school, that is, more interracial exposure will occur than if each race goes to separate schools. Interracial exposure is also, however, a function of the properties of whites and minorities in the school system - the level of interracial exposure for the average minority child can be no higher than the proportion white in the school system.[5]

This becomes clearer if we consider the example of a hypothetical segregated school system with six schools as follows:

	Minorities	Whites
	100	0
	100	0
	100	0
	0	100
	0	100
	0	100
Sum	300	300
% of Total	50.0	50.0

Virtually all supporters of school desegretion would prefer a plan that produced the following outcome A, with considerable racial balance and 245 white students remaining, to a plan that produced outcome B with perfect racial balance but only 6 white students remaining.

OUTCOME A			OUTCOME B	
Minorities	Whites		Minorities	Whites
50	20		50	1
50	45		50	1
50	40		50	1
50	50		50	1
50	45		50	1
50	45		50	1
Sum 300	245		300	6
% of Total 55.0	45.0		98.1	1.9

Although outcome B shows only one white in each school, the racial inbalance score is 0- that is, perfect racial balance-and all schools are within plus or minus 15 or 20 percentage points of the school district's proportions (98% minority and 2% white). There is, however only 2% white in the average minority child's school. Thus outcome B illustrates a case of perfect racial balance but very little interracial exposure.

Outcome A, by contrast, produces an index of dissimilarity of 8.8 - that is more racial imbalance occurs than in outcome B. One school (17% of the total number of schools) in outcome A is racially imbalanced by the or minus 15 or 20 percentage point criterion, wheras in outcome B, non is racially imbalanced by that standard. Nevertheless, outcome A has 44.2% while in the average minority child's school. Thus, if racial balance were the goal, the intuitively least desirable plan, that in which there was only one white in each school, would be selected. If interracial exposure were the goal, however, the intuitively most desirable plan, the one with 44.2% white in the average minority child's school, would be chosen.

The inadequacy of racial balance measures thus stems from the fact that they hold changing demographics constant. Because white flight is a function of the characteristics of a school desegregation plan (see Rossell, 1983, 1988; Wilch and Light, 1987), using interracial exposure as a dependent variable enables one to specify plan characteristics that will minimize the costs and maximize the benefits of desegregation. Unfortunately, in most studies, including the recently released U.S.

Commission on Civil Rights Study by Welch and Light (1987), researchers have used racial balance as a dependent variable because it is easier to use —one does not have to control for the redesegregation percentage white as it is necessary with interracial exposure.[6] Wilch and Light's conclusion that mandatory plans produce more racial balance but also more white flight than voluntary plans reveals little that is not already known.[7] The most important question not addressed in that and similar reports is, "What is the net benefit of these two countervailing tendencies - racial balance transfers and white flight?" Interracial exposure, unlike racial balance, can be used as a measure of this net benefit. Moreover measuring the outcome of a school desegregation plan as interracial exposure rather than racial balance also is supported by the social science research that shows the educational and social benefits of desegregation to be derived from the percentage white in the average minority child's school rather than the uniform distribution of the races (Mahard and Crain, 1983; Braddock et al. 1984; Crain and Strauss, 1985).

CLASSIFYING PLANS INTO
MAGNET-VOLUNTARY AND MAGNET-MANDATORY

Essentially, two types of desegregation plans incorporate the use of magnet schools: magnet-voluntary and magnet-mandatory (see Rossell, 1979). A magnet-voluntary plan is one which desegregation primarily is accomplished through voluntary transfers. Typically it is charactized by white parents choosing from among a number of magnet schools and minority parents choosing from among a number of white schools that may or may not be magnet schools. If the white school is not a magnet, the transfer is called a majority-to-minority transfer.[8]

A magnet-mandatory plan, on the other hand, is one in which desegregation is accomplished primarily through mandatory assignment of students to other race schools. In such plans, the magnet schools are educational options that have the purpose of reducing conflict and increasing parental satisfaction. Although participation in the desegregation plan is not voluntary (as is the magnet-voluntary plans), participation in the magnet school portion typically is.

In the magnet-voluntary plans, therefore, desegregation is driven by the choice system, and transfers primarily are voluntary; these plans thus exemplify the public-choice model of decision making. In the magnet-mandatory plans, the desegregation plan is driven by the assignment system, and transfers primarily are forced; these plans thus exemplify the command-and-control model of decision making in which government commands, and citizens or organizations are expected to obey.

The school districts in this sample and the extent of magnet school participation are listed in the appendix.[9] The districts are grouped according to whether their plan is primarily voluntary (Buffalo through Tacoma) or primarily mandatory (Boston through Tulsa). For both types of plans, the averge desegregation year is 1974; the earliest year is 1968 and the latest year is 1977. Note that the magnet-voluntary plans analyzed in this study are comprehensive. Of the school districts with voluntary plans, 55% were ordered to desegregate by a court after a finding of intentional segregation. In all cases the goal was to desegregate the entire school district, and in all but two (San Bernardino and Cincinnati), the desegregation goals were implicit and ambitious. The average number of magnet schools in the districts with voluntary plans is 28, comprising one-third of the schools and enrolling one-third of the students in the district.

The average number of magnet schools in the districts with mandatory plans by contrast, is only 10, comprising about 13% of the students. Of the school districts with mandatory plans, 64% were ordered by a court to implement them, which is only slightly more than the percentage court-ordered among the districts with voluntary plans.

None of the voluntary desegregation plans in this sample is entirely voluntary-all use some additional, minimal, mandatory techniques such as selected school closings and contiguous rezoning, particularly at the secondary level. Nevertheless, none of the voluntary plans analyzed here has an explicit mandatory backup, although presumably those ordered by a court have implicit mandatory backup.[10]

Similarly, no mandatory desegregation plan is entirely mandatory. In some cases magnet programs have been used to desegregate schools that have become resegregated through white flight, deliberately avoiding additional mandatory reassignments. In other areas, such as Boston, magnet programs were placed in schools in which desegregation could not be accomplished by mandatory means because of extreme white resistance,[11] and in other schools around the city to reduce white flight and resistance.

As suggested in this brief discussion, although the school districts have been classified into two exclusive categories for analytical purposes - mandatory and voluntary - it may be more accurate to describe the mandatory-voluntary dimension in terms of a continuum. Because of this and because these plans have changed somewhat over time, exactly how to classify them will always be in dispute.[12]

Characteristics of the sample

Although only nine comprehensive magnet-voluntary school desegregation plans are included in this sample, they represent two-thirds of the school districts with such plans in the 119-district sample (see Rossell, 1990) from which the 20-district subsample is drawn. The sample includes all of the school districts in the Abt Associations study (Royster et al., 1979) plus San Bernandino and Cincinnati. Originally, Abt Associates chose their sample on a random basis after stratifying the potential population of school districts among two major dimensions: (1) according to the percentage minority in the school district population and (2) according to whether the desegregation plan utilized a magnet-voluntary or a magnet-mandtory structure (which was verified by telephone). School districts were selected randomly from among the sites in each category.

The resulting sample of of 20 school districts is quite varied in terms of most population characteristics, ranging from the huge, predominantly minority Houston school district to the tiny, predominantly white Montclair school district. Table 1 shows the average school district and community characteristics for voluntary and mandatory plans.[12] Mandatory desegregation plans are in communities that, before desegregation, were smaller in population and percentage minority and higher in income and education than those in which voluntary plans were implemented.[13] In other words, in this sample the districts with voluntary plans are at a small desegregation disadvantage with regard to social characteristics in comparison to districts with mandatory plans. The districts with voluntary plans also had less interracial exposure before desegregation, but more racial balance than those with mandatory plans. None of these differences, however, is statistically significant.

Table 1: Average Predesegregation School District and Community Characteristics with Voluntary and Mandatory Plans

Average

	Mandatory	Voluntary
Community Characteristics		
City Population	377,675	472,330
Percent white city 1970	80.6	78.1
Income 1970	8,178	7,320
Minority income 1970	5,428	5,477
Education 1970	12.2	12.0
Minority education 1970	10.9	10.9
SMSA white population change 1970-1980	13.3	3.0
School District Characteristics		
Percent white T-2	73.2	64.0
Enrollment T-1	74,088	82,159
White enrollment change T-1	-4.5	-3.7
White enrollment change T-2	-3.0	-4.7
White enrollment change T-3	-2.8	-3.7
White enrollment change T-4	-2.7	-4.1
Interracial exposure T-2	44.3	40.8
Year of desegregation plan	74	75
Racial imbalance T-2	57.9	52.8

FINDINGS
White Flight

Of all the forms of white response to school desegregation, white flight is probably the most important because it directly affects interracial exposure. Although the issue of white flight from mandatory desegregation plans has been hotly debated since Colemen et al. (1975) charged that mandatory desegregation plans were counterproductive (see Rossell, 1975-76), in only two studies (Smylie, 1983; Welch and Light, 1987) have voluntary and mandatory plans been compared specifically. Not surprisingly, mandatory plans were found to produce more white flight.

As with the original Abt sample, the school districts within the categories voluntary and mandatory are classifeid into those above and below 30% minority before desegregatiion. School districts with more than 30% minority are thought to have significantly greater long-term white flight that is detrimental to interracial exposure (Coleman, 1977; Rossell, 1978a; 31,1978b; Armor, 1979; Farley et al., 1980; Ross et al., 1982; Smylie, 1983). Moreover, because interracial exposure is limited by the predesegregation percentage white, dividing the districts into those above and below 30% minority before desegregation makes the voluntary and mandatory plans more comparable for the purposes of an interrupted time series. (Ultimately I group this division when I analyze interracial exposure in a pooled crossectional analysis with the predesegregation percentage minority as one of the control variables.)

Because all of the school districts in this sample have magnet schools as a component of their plan, the analysis presented here is a test of the effect of voluntary versus mandatory reassignment of white students. Put another way, this is a test of whether placing magnet programs within a mandatory plan will make these plans comparable in white flight to voluntary plans with magnet schools.

These data indicate that in school districts above 30% minority, that mandatory desegregation plans with magnet schools produce greater white enrollment loss than do the voluntary plans with magnet schools, not only in the implementation year, but in subsequent years. In the implementation year, the loss is 5.5% for the districts with voluntary plans and 12.7% for the districts with mandatory plans, despite the fact that before desegregation, the districts with mandatory plans had less white enrollment decline.

The pattern for school districts with less than 30% minority is different before desegregation but similar after desegregation. The districts with mandatory plans have, on average, more predesegregation white enrollment loss than those with voluntary plans. Nevertheless, the gap between the two widens dramatically with the implementation of desegregation, so that the districts with voluntary plans have a loss of 1.4%, and the districts with mandatory plans have a loss of 6.9%. It is only in the eighty year of desegregation that the two trend lines cross and remain essentially the same for the next three years.

Hence a difference exists between the two groups of school districts —those above and those below 30% minority. In the school districts below 30% minority, the white enrollment change trend lines of the voluntary and mandatory plans eventually cross around the eighth year, although the school districts with mandatory plans never recover the much greater white enrollment loss they incur in the previous years, contrary to Rossell (1978a), Farley et al. (1980), and Wilson (1985),[18] but similar to Welch and Light (1987). In the school districts above 30% minority, however, those with voluntary plans —less white enrollment loss than the districts with mandatory plans have during the entire postdesegregation time period.

The total white enrollment loss for districts with greater than 30% minority is 37% for those with voluntary plans and 55% for those with mandatory plans. This is a significant difference between the two. The total white enrollment loss for districts less than 30% minority, but contrast, shows a much smaller disparity between mandatory and voluntary plans —34% for those with voluntary plans and 41% for those with mandatory plans. In short, districts with mandatory plans, although they include magnet schools, incur more white enrollment decline with desegregation than do districts with voluntary plans.

INTERRACIAL EXPOSURE

Although these data are interesting, they are an insufficient criterion for selecting alternative desegregation plans. Considering just the costs of school desegregation plans is not only constitutionally unacceptable, but senseless from the perspective of policy analysis. If one were to consider only white flight costs, the desegregation alternative chosen would always be "do nothing," because that produces the least white flight. Therefore, from both a constitutional and a policy analysis standard, one must consider both the costs and the benefits of desegregation reassignments.

As previously discussed, the measure that enables one to do this is interracial exposure - the percentage white in the average minority child's school. Although school districts with voluntary plans had a lower predesegregation percentage white, they nevertheless had more predesegregation interracial exposure than did those with mandatory plans, within the two categories of percentage minority.

In school districts above 30% minority, the magnet-voluntary plans produce a significant increase in interracial exposure from a level of 32.8 to 36.2 in the implementation year, but both the increase and the absolute level of exposure are greater for the mandatory plans, in which interracial exposure increases from 29.1 to 38.0. By the fourth year of desegregation, however, the trend lines for the two types of plans meet. By the fifth year, the districts with voluntary plans surpass the mandatory plans, and the gap continues to widen. Although all school districts have decreasing interracial exposure after the implementation year, the trend line of the districts with mandatory plans is much more negative than that of the districts with voluntary plans. In the tenth year, the school districts with voluntary plans have a level of interracial exposure of 35.0, whereas those with mandatory plans have a level of interracial exposure of 29.4.

There is a similar pattern for school districts with less than 30% minority. Again, the school with voluntary plans had greater predesegregation interracial exposure than those with mandatory plans, but both had a large increase with the implementation of their desegregation plans. In the school districts with voluntary plans, interracial exposure increased form 62.7 to 68.1, and in the districts with mandatory plans, interracial exposure increased form 57 to 69.1. The districts with voluntary plans, however, surpassed those with mandatory plans by the third year of desegregation, and as with the school districts with above 30% minority, the gap between the two types of plans increased over time. In the tenth year, the school districts with voluntary plans had a level of interracial exposure of 63.6.

Therefore, regardless of whether a school district is above or below 30% minority, the districts with mandatory plans do better in the implementation year and for a few years after, but the districts with voluntary plans surpass them within two to four years, and the disparity continues to grow. Ultimately, the voluntary plans produce more interracial exposure.

RACIAL IMBALANCE

Not only do the districts with voluntary plans produce more interracial exposure, they also produce similar levels of racial imbalance. Although the districts with mandatory plans consistently do better than the districts with voluntary plans in achieving racial balance, the difference between them is fairly small, beginning around the third year of desegregation for school districts less than 30% minority and around that fourth or fifth year of desegregation for school districts above 30% minority. They both produce an average level of racial imbalance between 30 and 35 somewhere between the fourth and sixth year of desegregation - a level that indicates systemwide desegregation but allows for court-approved deviations. By the tenth year, the school districts greater than 30% minority have a level of racial imbalance of 31.7 in those with voluntary plans and 32.2 of those with mandatory plans. In the school districts less than 30% minority, the level of racial imbalance is 28.9 in the districts with voluntary plans and 27.1 in the districts with mandatory plans. In short, even by the traditional limited criterion of racial balance, the voluntary plans ultimately do at least as well as the mandatory plans.[20]

Table 2: Predicting Postimplementation Interracial Exposure (Smw)

	Average	r	b	Beta	SE b
Smw Postimplementation	48.624				
Voluntary	0.441	-0.22	-3.690**	-0.10	1.707

Percentage white T-1	68.608	0.88*	1.016*	0.82	0.065
Smw T-2	42.407	0.80*	0.248*	0.26	0.059
Percent white enrollment change T-2	-4.000	0.55*	0.985**	0.12	43.167
Enrollment	66,105.492	-0.45*	8.05e-7[a]	-0.00	1.75e-5
Year of plan	74.118	-0.04	2.193*	0.31	0.297
City/County education, 1970	12.083	0.34**	-8.308*	-0.26	1.404
Time	4.390	-0.09	-0.882*	-0.13	0.200
Time x Voluntary	1.987	-0.17	0.903*	0.13	0.302
SMSA changes - whites, 1970-1980	9.178	-0.20	-0.030	-0.04	0.028
Constant			-84.655		
r2			0.912		
df			184		

a. The term e-7 means to move the decimal point 7 places to the left.
*Signficant at the .001 level or better; **significant at the .05 level or better.

NET BENEFIT

Table 2 contains a pooled cross-sectional time-series analysis of the extent of interracial exposure produced by desegregation,[21] controlling for whether a plan is voluntary or mandatory, the predesegregation percentage white, interracial exposure, white enrollment change, total enrollment, the year of the plan, the city or county educational level, the time period (0,1,2,3. . .9), an interaction effect (time period times voluntary), and change in the standard metropolitan statistical are (SMSA) white population from 1970 to 1980. For the purpose of this study, this is a test of the effect on interracial exposure of a voluntary plan, controlling for demographic variables that might also affect interracial exposure. This equation shows that voluntary desegregation plan produce significantly more interracial exposure overtime than do mandatory desegregation plans, controlling for possible confounding factors. The b coefficient for the many effects and the interaction effects can only be interpreted by solving the equation for those variables. This equation tells us that a voluntary plan at T+9, holding all other variables constant, would be expected to have a level of interracial exposure 4.4 percentage points about that of a mandatory plan. [22]

In addition, interracial exposure is positively related, as would be expected, to the predesegregation percentage white, predesegregation percentage white enrollment change, the predesgregation interracial exposure, and the year the desegregation plan was implemented. Postimplementation interracial exposure is negatively related to the city or county educational level and to the time period. There is no relationship between interracial exposure and the total district enrollment or change in the white population in the SMSA from, 1970 to 1980. Moreover, all of these relationships conform to logic. This equation explains 91% of the variance in postimplementation interracial exposure and is quite robust. The coefficients change little when the data are analyzed without the predesegregation adjustments to Montclair and Houston,[23] when the entire postimplementation time period is analyzed with missing data for some districts and years,[24] and when Buffalo's postdesegregation interracial exposure is fixed at the 1980 (before mandatory reassignments) level.[25]

This equation can be solved for any point in time. Starting with the highest point (T+1), the voluntary plans produce a level of interracial exposure of 49.65, and the mandatory plans produce a level of interracial exposure of 52.43. By T+9, the tenth year, the voluntary plans have virtually the same level of interracial exposure as at T+1 —49.86— but the level of interracial exposure of the mandatory plans has dropped to 45.42, a decline of 7 percentage points. Thus this equation indicates that, on average, the voluntary plans have been brought to a halt to the normal decline in interracial exposure resulting from the declining white birthrate. The mandatory plans have not.

However, more decline is seen over time in interracial exposure in the school districts greater than 30% minority than in the entire sample. In an equation including only school districts greater than 30% minority (see Rossell, 1990), the gap in interracial exposure between voluntary and mandatory plans is 4.9 points, and the decline from the highest point (T+1) to the --nth year (T+9) is 2.7 points for the voluntary plans and 10 points for the mandatory plans. A decline of 2.7 is about what you would expect from the normal demographic white enrollment decline.

In a hypothetical school system with a mandatory plan and 80,000 students, of whom 40,000 are white, the 4.4 percentage gap in interracial exposure between all of the voluntary and mandatory plans represents about 6,800 fewer white students coming into contact with minorities. The 4.9 percentage gap in interracial exposure between the voluntary and mandatory plans in school districts greater than 30% minority represents a loss of about 7,600 whites coming into contact with minorities in the same hypothetical school system. Exactly how one values this difference is, of course, dependent on a number of assumptions and other values. Nevertheless, I believe most supporters of school integration would prefer voluntary plans over mandatory plans when confronted with such information, all other things being equal.

THE GREATEST INTERRACIAL EXPOSURE
IS PRODUCED BY PROVIDING INCENTIVES

According to the analysis presented here, the public-choice model works for school desegregation. When asked to choose between their neighborhood school and a superior magnet school, sufficient numbers of parents will select the magnet school, thus making plans based primarily on such choices superior in producing interracial exposure to those based primarily on mandatory reassignment. But part of the reason why the magnet-voluntary plans ultimately produce more interracial exposure is that the mandatory plans produce more white flight, and adding magnet schools to a mandatory reassignment plan does not reduce the white flight enough to make it competitive with a voluntary plan over the long term.

Even when magnet schools are included as educational options, school districts with mandatory desegregation plans begin to resegregate shortly after the implementation year at a rate that is much faster than that of school districts with voluntary plans.[26] About the third or fourth year of desegregation, the two trend lines cross, and the magnet-voluntary plans produce greater than or less than 30% minority and regardless of the extent of predesegregation interracial exposure. In this sample, however, none of the mandatory desegregation plan has more interracial exposure in the tenth year of desegregation than if no plan at all had been implemented.

Although the finding that voluntary plans produce more interracial exposure over time than mandatory contradicts several decades of school desegregation research, it must be emphasized that the voluntary plans analyzed in this report are qualitatively different from the old southern freedom-of choice plans or northern one-way majority-to-minority programs. They are different from these plans in that incentives are provided to motivate whites to act in a socially desirable manner. They also are different in that the choice plans analyzed here are not complete "marketplace solutions." Racial controls are imposed on transfer, and although perhaps not necessary, most of the school districts had racial balance goals. Some also did some minimal redrawing of attendance zones and mandatory transfers.

The whites in this study also are different from the whites of the 1960s when freedom-of-choice plans consistently failed. Currently 93% of white Americans support the principle of school integration; in 1959, less than 40% did. Because white attitudes have changed over time, we would expect voluntary plans to be more successful. Thus one way to look at magnet schools is that they provide white parents with an incentive to act rationally - that is, in a manner consistent with their current support for integration.

This suggests that the public-choice model and the command-and-control model are each linked to a model of individual decision making. If the command-and-control model of policymaking had been more effective than the public-choice model, the implication would have been that, on this issue, most citizens are primarily motivated by racial attitudes formed in early socialization, as many social scientists have argued (Erbe, 1977; Kinder and Rhodebeck, 1982; Sear et al., 1979, 1980; Weidman, 1975; Caditz, 1975, 1976; Kinder and Sears, 1981; Miller, 198; Jacobson, 1978; McConahay, 1982: Gatlin et al., 1978). Incentives (at least as currently structured) will not lure students out of their neighborhood schools to desegregated magnet schools, and thus they have to be "forced" to go. The success of the public-choice model of policymaking, on the other hand, implies that many parents are rational on issues of desegregation and race and that they will embrace the socially desirable goal of school integration when incentives are provided. The conclusion that opposition to forced busing is just another from of racism (Erbe, 1977; Kinder and Rhodebeck, 1982; Sear et al., 1979, 1980; Weidman, 1975; Caditz, 1975, 1976; Kinder and Sears, 1981; Miller, 1981; Jacobson, 1978; McConahay, 1982; Gatlin et al., 1978) and that as a result, individuals would not enroll their children in even high-quality desegregated schools may have been true once, but it is no longer. Surveys conducted in Yonkers and Savannah in 1986 indicated that those white parents most opposed to forced busing of white students are those most likely to volunteer for a magnet school (Rossell, 1986a, b).

However, neither the "racism" model not the "self-interest" model can be used to explain satisfactorily all behavior in this area. Some of the more interesting questions that cannot be addressed in the aggregate analysis presented here are why some parents believe it is in their self-interest to enroll their child in magnet school and others do not. The motivation to enroll their child in a magnet school may be a combination of self-interest and altruism for many parents. For others, it may be solely a matter of self-interest or even that magnet schools are the lesser of two evils when the neighborhood school becomes desegregated by majority-to-minority transfers or neighborhood transition. Regardless of the exact nature of the individual calculation, the data presented in this analysis refute the notion that racism is so deeply embedded in American society that school desegregation plans cannot be tailored to take into account the interests of white parents and still desegregate schools.

NOTES

1. Segregated white schools that are already quite attractive may have nothing special done to them on the assumption that they can be desegregated by minority student transfers under a majority-to-minority transfer program with transportation provided.

2. The measure originates with Duncan and Duncan (1955), but it has been most closely associated with Taeuber and Taeuber (1965). It has been used in numerous studies of school and residential racial imbalance since then. Some examples are Farley (1981), Farley et al. (1980), Van Valey et al. (1977), Welch and Light (1987).

3. It is also the sum of (1) the proportion of black students who need to be reassigned to white schools and (2) the proportion of white students who need to be reassigned to black schools, to have the same proportions as in the whole school district. the specific proportions of each group adding up to the index are a function of racial proportions and prior segregation.

4. This measure has been used in several more recent studies of school desegregation to assess desegregation nationally (Farley, 1981; Orfield, 1982; Orfield and Monfort, 1986) and to estimate the outcomes of alternatives desegregation plans (Ross, 1983; Rossell, 1978a,b, 1979, 1985, 1990).

5. It is possible, however, to have a higher percentage white in the average Hispanic or Asian or black child's school than exists in the school district.

6. An example of how not to use interracial exposure can be seen in Orfield (1998:28). Here he lists for 24 "cities" the percentage white (incorrectly labeled the percentage *of* whites) in the school of the typical black student in 1980 and whether there was a mandatory busing plan. There is no control for the predesegregation percentage white. The "cities' with a high percentage white in the average black child's school tend to be those with mandatory plans. They also are largely countywide, southern school districts that were about 80%-90% white before desegregation. The cities with a low percentage white in the average black child's school tend to be those with voluntary plans. They also are, with one exception, big cities that were about 30%-45% white before desegregation. Needless to say, this is an incomplete and misleading "analysis" without the control for predesegregation percentage white.

7. Surprisingly, the average difference in reduction in racial imbalance between major voluntary plans and the mandatory plans is only 6 percentage points for the entire desegregation time period (Welch and Light, 1987:55). This is a far cry from the early 1960s in the South, when mandatory plans reduced racial imbalance by 20 to 50 points more than voluntary plans.

8. In a majority-to-minority transfer program, students can transfer from any school in which their race is the majority to any school in which their race is the minority. Although such programs are open for students of any race, typically only minority students participate.

9. Because the magnet school participation data depend partly on information obtained from the school districts, Table 1 contains data only through 1982. This limitation does not affect the rest of

the analysis, however, which includes 1985 enrollment data.

10. In Buffalo, for example, the court ordered mandatory reassignment of 15% of the students in 1981, after five years of successful voluntary desegregation.

11. A white enclave, East Boston, was excluded from the mandatory reassignment portion of the plan, and only magnet schools were placed there.

12. For example, although this study builds on the 1979 Abt Associates study (Royster et al., 1979), I disagree with their classification of three school districts. They classified Dallas, Texas, as having a voluntary plan, and I classify it as mandatory. They classified Racine, Wisconsin, as having a voluntary plan, and I classify it as mandatory. They classified Montclair, New Jersey, as having a mandatory plan, and I classify it as voluntary. For a detailed discussion of the justification for these changes, see Rossell(1990).

13. Two of the school districts in this sample (Montgomery County, Maryland, and Louisville-Jefferson County, Kentucky) are countywide school districts, and therefore their population characteristics are for the county, not the city.

14. This is measured as white enrollment in one year minus white enrollment the previous year, divided by white enrollment the previous year and multiplied by 100 to create a percentage.

15. The implementation year for the voluntary plans is the year that the first magnet programs were established. Most of these school districts, however, had already had majority-to-minority transfer programs for several years prior to that. The implementation year for the mandatory desegregation plans is the year of the major plan. If there is a court-ordered plan, it is usually that year. The only exception to this occurs when a significant plan with mandatory white reassignments precedes a court-ordered plan (as in Stockton). Although this rarely happens, the prior plan would be considered the major plan.

16. Data were estimated for all measures for San Bernandino T+8 and T+9 and San Diego and Des Moines T+9 by averaging the change in the last two years for which there were data. For white enrollment change, T-3 data were also estimated for Cincinnati, Portland, and Dallas from the T-2 white enrollment change.

17. This comparison, however, is less reliable than that for school districts above, 30% minority because only two school districts that have less than 30% minority have voluntary plans- Portland, Oregon, and Tacoma, Washington.

18. In these studies the researchers did not distinguish between voluntary and mandatory plans. The finding that school desegregation plans recover their implementation year losses may be, in part, a function of the failure to distinguish between voluntary and mandatory plans, as well as an inability to control adequately for the predesegregation trend in southern, county wide school districts.

19. Because mandatory reassignment plans were dismantled in Houston and Montclair (a very limited one in the case of Houston) and were replaced with voluntary plans, the predesegregation data for these cities are adjusted slightly to eliminate the effect of the prior mandatory plans implemented in 1970 in Houston and 1969 and 1971 in Montclair. This small adjustment is necessary because the later voluntary plans did not build on them but replaced them. (see Rossell, 1990).

20. See note 7 for a similar finding by Welch and Light (1987).

21. The postimplementation time period is T+0 to T+9, and missing data are not filled at, as in the interrupted time series. A pooled, cross-sectional analysis increases the n by treating each year as a separate case.

22. For voluntary plans the equation for Smw in the tenth year (T+9)= -84.655 - 3.690(1)+ 1.106968.608) + .248(42.407) + .98480(-4.0)+ .000000805(66105.492 = 2.193(74.118)- 8.308(12.0830 -.882(9) + .903(9) - .03(9.178). This produces an index of 49.86 in the tenth year (T+9). For mandatory plans, the equation for Smw in the tenth year (T+9) is the same exception that the dummy variable "voluntary" is zero, so it drops out. The interaction effect also drops out

since zero times anything is zero. This produces an index of 45.52 in the tenth year. The difference between the two is 4.4 points. A quicker way to determine the difference is simply to look at the variable "voluntary" and the interaction effect. The two variables together add up to 4.4 points. Therefore, voluntary will produce 4.4 points more than mandatory plans.

23. The b coefficient for voluntary is -1.061 and for time x voluntary .947.

24. The b coefficient for voluntary is -3.434 and for time x voluntary .979.

25. (See note 9.) With Buffalo's interracial exposure from 1981 on set at the 1980 level, the b coefficient for voluntary is -4.359 and for time x voluntary is .879.

26. The *implementation* year superiority of the mandatory plans, however, is the primary reason why Rossell (1979) and Royster et al. (1979), with one year of postimplementative data, concluded that mandatory plans produce greater interracial exposure.

REFERENCES

ARMOR, D.J. (1979) "White flight and the future of school desegregation," pp. 187-226 in W.G. Stephan and J.R. Feagan (eds.) School Desegregation:

BRADDOCK, J., II, R. CRAIN, and McPARTLAND (1984) "A long-term view of school desegregation: some recent studies of graduates as adults." Phi Delta Kappan 66: 259-264.

BUCHANAN, J.M. and R.D. Tollison [eds.] (1984) The Theory of Public Choice - II. Ann Arbor: Univ. Of Michigan Press.

BULLOCK, S. (1976) "Desegregating urban areas: is it worth it?," pp. 123-142 in F. Levinsohn and B.Wright (eds.) School Desegregation: Shadow and Substance. Chicago: Univ. of Chicago Press.

CADITZ, J. (1975) :"Dilemmas over racial integration: status consciousness vs. direct threat." Soc. Inquiry 45: 463-476.

COLEMAN, J.S. (1977) "Population stability and equal rights." Society 14: 34-36.

COLEMAN, J.S., S.D. Kelly, and J.A. MOORE (1975) Trends in Segregation, 1968-1973. Washington, DC: Urban Institute.

CRAIN, F and J. STRAUSS (1985) "School desegregation and black occupational attainments: results from along-term experiment." Baltimore, MD: John Hopkins University, Center for Social Organization of Schools.

DOWNS, A. (1957) An Economic Theory of Democracy. New York: Harper & Row.

DUNCAN, O.D. and B. DUNCAN (1955) "A methodological analysis of segregation indexes." Amer. Soc. Rev. 20:210-217.

ERBE, B.M. (1977) "The Politics of school busing." Public Opinion Q 41: 113-117.

EARLEY, R. (1981). Final Report, NIE Grant No. G-79-0151. Ann Arbor: University of Michigan, Population Studies Center.

EARLEY, R., C. WURDOCK, and T. RICHARDS (1980) "School desegregation and white flight: an investigation of competing models and their discrepant findings." Sociology of Education 53: 123-139.

FRIEDMAN, M. (1962) Capitalism and Freedom. Chicago: Univ. of Chicago Press.

FRIEDMAN, M. and R. FRIEDMAN (1981) Free to Choose. New York: Avon.

GATLIN, D., M. Giles. and E. CATALDO (1978) "Policy support within a target group: the case of school desegregation." Amer. Pol. Sci. Rev. 72: 985-995.

HAWLEY, W. and M.A. SMYLIE (1986) "The contribution of school desegregation to academic achievement and racial integregation," pp. 281-297 in P. Katz and D. Taylor (eds.) Eliminating Racism: Means and Controversies. New York: Pergamon.

JACOBSON, C.K. (1978) "Desegregating rulings and public attitude changes: swhite resistance or resignation?" Amer. J. Sociology 84: 698-705.

KINDER, D.R. and A. RHODEBECK (1982) "Continuities in support for racial equality, 1972 to 1976." Public Opinion Q. 46: 195-215.

KINDER, D.R. and D. O. SEARS (1981) "Prejudice and politics: symbolic racism vs. racial threats to the 'good life.' " J. Of Personality and Social Psychology 40: 414-431.

MAHARD, R.E. and R.L. CRAIN (1983) "Research on minority achievement in desegregated schools." pp. 103-125 in C.H. Rossell and W.D. Hawley (eds.) The Consequences of School Desegregation. Philadelphia:Temple University Press.

McCONAHAY, J.B. (1982) "Self-interest versus racial attitudes as correlates of antibusing attitudes in Louisville." J. of Politics 44:   692-720.

MEADOW, G.R. (1976) "Open enrollment and fiscal incentives,: pp. 1243- 156 in F. Levinsohn and B. Wright (eds.) School Desegregation:Shadow and Substance. Chicago: Univ. Of Chicago Press.

MILLER, S. (1981) "Conflict: the nature of white opposition to mandatory busing." Ph.D. dissertation, University of California, Los Angeles.

OLSON, M. (1965) The Logic of Collective Action. Cambridge, MA: Harvard Univ. Press.

ORFIELD, G. (1976) Desegregation and the Cities, the Trends, and the Policy Choices Washington, DC: Brookings Institution.

ORFIELD,G. (1978) Must We Bus? Segregated Schools and National Policy. Washington DC Brookings Institution.

ORFIELD,G. (1982) Desegregation of Black and Hispanic Students from 1968 to 1980. Washington, DC: Joint Center for Political Studies.

ORFIELD,G. (1988) "School desegregation in the 1980's." Equity and Choice 4 (February) 25-28.

ORFIELD,G. and F. MONFORT (1986) "Are American schools resegregating in the Reagan era? a statistical analysis of segregation levels from 1980 to 1984." National School Desegregation Project, University of Chicago. (unpublished)

ROSS, J.M. (1983) The Effectiveness of Alternative Desegregation Strategies: The Issue of Voluntary Versus Mandatory Policies in Los Angeles." Boston: Boston University. (unpublished)

ROSS, J.M., B. GRATTON, AND R. CLARKE (1982) School Desegregation and White Flight Reexamined: Is the Issue Different Statistical Models? Boston: Boston University. (unpublished)

ROSSELL, C.H. (1975-1976) "School desegregation and white flight." Pol. Sci. Q. 92: 675-696.

ROSSELL, C.H. (1978a) Assessing the Unintended Impacts of Public Policy: School Desegregation and Resegregation. Boston: Boston University. (unpublished)

ROSSELL, C.H. (1978b) "The effect of school integration on community integration." J. of Education 160 (May); 46-62.

ROSSELL, C.H. (1978c) "White flight: pros and cons." Social Policy 9 (November/December) 46-51.

ROSSELL, C.H. (1979) "Magnet schools as a desegregation tool: the importance of contexual factors in explaining their success." Urban   Education 14: 303-320.

ROSSELL, C.H. (1983) "Applied social science research; what does it say about the effectiveness of school desegreagtion plans?" J. of Legal Studies 12: 69-107.

ROSSELL, C.H. (1985) "Estimating the net benefit of school desegreagtion in reassignments." Educational evaluation and Policy Analysis 7 (Fall): 217-228.

ROSSELL, C.H. (1986a) "Estimating the effectiveness of a magnet school desegregation paln for the the Yonkers Shcool Disrtict." A report prepared for the U.S. District Court in the case of U.S. and NAACP v. Yonkers Board of Education et al., March 17.

ROSSELL, C. H. (1986b) "Estimating the effectiveness of a magnet school desegreagtion plan for the Savannah-Catham County School District." A report prepared for the U.S. District Court in the case of Stell and U.S. v. the Board of Public Education for the City of Savannah and the County of Chatham, September 23.

ROSSELL, C.H. (1988) "Is it the busing or the blacks?" Urban Affairs Q. 24 (September) 138-148.

ROSSELL, C.H. (1990) The Carrot or the Stick for School Desegregation Policy: Magnet Schools or Forced Busing? Philadelphia: Temple Univ. Press.

ROSSELL, C.H. and W.D. HAWLEY (1982) "Policy alternatives for minimizing white flight." Educational Evaluation and policy Analysis 4: 772-796.

ROSSELL, C.H. and W.D. HAWLEY [eds.] (1983) The Consequences of School Desegregation. Philadelphia: Temple Univ. Press.

ROYSTER, E.C., D.C. BALTZLL, and F.C. SIMMONS (1979) Study of Emergency School Aid Act Magnet School Program. Cambridge, MA: Abt Associates.

SALAMON, L. (1979) "The time dimension in policy evaluation: the case of the New Deal land-reform experiments." Public policy 27: 129-183.

SEARS, D.O., C.P. HENSLER, and L.K. SPEER (1979) "Whites' opposition to 'busing': self-interest or symbolic politics?" Amer. Pol. Sci. Rev. 73: 369-384.

SEARS, D.O., R.R. LAU, T.R. TYLER, and H.M. ALLEN, Jr. (1980) "Self-interest v. symbolic politics in policy attitudes and presidential votings." Amer. Pol. Sci. Rev. 74: 670-684.

SMYLIE, M.A. (1983) "Reducing racial isolation in large school districts: The comparative effectiveness of mandatory and voluntary desegregation strategies." Urban Education 17: 477-502.

Taeuber, K. and A. Taeuber (1965) Negroes in Cities. Chicago: Aldine.

Tiebout, C. (1956) "A pure theory of local expenditures" J. of Pol. Economy 64: 416-424.

UNITED STATES v. PITTMAN BY PITTMAN (1987) 808 F.2d 385.

VanVALEY, T.L., W.C. ROOF, and J.E. WILCOX (1977) "Trends in residential segretion: 1960-1970." Amer. J. Of Sociology 82: 827-844.

WEIDMAN, J.C. (1975) "Resistance of white adults to the busing of school children." J. of Research and Development in Education 9 (Fall): 123-129.

WELCH F. and A. LIGHT (1987) "New evidence on school desegregation." Report prepared for the U.S. Commission on Civil Rights. Los Angeles: Unicon Research.

WILSON, F.D. (1985) "The impact of school desegregation programs on white public school enrollment, 1968-1976." Sociology of Education 58: 137-153.

THE NEW IMPROVED SORTING MACHINE:
A RECENT STUDY

Frank Esposito

Cambridge, Lowell, and Fall River, Massachusetts, New York City's East Harlem District 4 and Montclair, New Jersey are the only school systems to date that have created public school choice systems by designating every school as a magnet or specialty school.

Most often, districts create a few magnets targeting certain groups for racial or ethnic desegregation, while maintaining neighborhood schools zoned for attendance. Most magnets have some kind of admissions policies if only to guarantee desegregation. The effects of academically selective school admissions criteria in a choice system have been questioned by researchers .

In a two-year study (preliminary report released April 1988) of Chicago, Philadelphia[1], Boston and New York's school systems, Suzanne Davenport and Donald R. Moore concentrated on admission to selective versus non-selective high schools. Davenport and Moore found a six-tier school system in these cities.

Schools in the upper tiers "operate as separate virtually private schools, while those at the bottom tier, catering almost exclusively to low-income students, provide essentially custodial care" (Davenport and Moore, The New Improved Sorting Machine, Designs for Change, Chicago, 1988).

Six Tier High School Systems

Schools highest on the tier admit the highest scoring students based on competitive exams. Boston has 3 exam schools, Philadelphia 2, Chicago 2, New York 4. (Davenport and Moore, 1988: 3b-3c). Selective magnet schools sometimes have admissions requirements that rival those of exam schools. Selective vocational schools often have academic requirements less stringent than selective magnets.

---

[1]Philadelphia public schools have an extensive magnet program offering more than 100 schools or special programs from which to choose. Students who are not accepted into the magnets attend their neighborhood schools. Students can attend any magnet school in the district as long as the student meets entrance criteria and does not upset the racial balance of the school.

The last three types of schools on the tier are non-selective moderate, moderate-low and low-income schools that have minimal or no selection criteria. These schools serve 50 to 70 percent of all students in the systems studied by Davenport and Moore. Schools with the lowest-income students are predominantly black or Hispanic.

Davenport and Moore found that certain qualities of selective magnet schools and programs can negatively affect the functioning of non-selective schools.

1. Selective schools attract the most successful students, often leaving non-select schools to deal with the most serious learning problems.
2. Selective schools are often granted special prerogatives to select staff that are not allowed to neighborhood schools.
3. Selective schools are often given extra resources and increased flexibility in using them. These schools most likely have better and more attractive facilities than non-selective schools.
4. Because they have specific enrollment limits, these schools are able to plan more effectively.
5. Students who "don't work out" in selective schools are often sent back to neighborhood schools.
6. "Because selective schools create a "system-wide" focus on high achievers, non-selective schools were forced to compete for these students to enhance their own reputation rather than improving education for the majority of students in the system." (Davenport and Moore, 1988)
7. Lastly, educators tend to see students not accepted into selective schools (unless they attend an exceptional neighborhood high school) (Davenport and Moore, 1988: 10) as "losers, uneducable and not deserving to be educated." Students, in turn, often feel this way about themselves. (Davenport, Interview, 1988)

Among their recommendations, Davenport and Moore suggest that students should have the right to apply to a selective school based on their interests. The enrollment of these schools should mirror the makeup of the city.

Schools should have to justify entrance requirements and keep them at a minimum, randomly choosing from minimally qualified students.

This study shows that monitoring of choice systems involving specialty schools is crucial to ensure equity. If schools are allowed free reign in admission criteria, academic and racial segregation may result. For low-income students, choice based on selective schools may hurt educationally and emotionally by grouping them as undesirable students in undesirable schools.

Effectiveness of Magnets on Student Achievement and Desegregation

When properly designed, magnets have provided high quality education in urban school districts, according to the findings of a "Survey of Magnet Schools: Analyzing a Model for Quality Integrated Education," (a two-year study of the effectiveness and status of magnet schools prepared by James H. Lowry and Associates, September 1983). One-third of the 45 magnets used in 15 urban school districts in the survey received high ratings in instructional quality, curriculum design, student-teacher interaction, student learning, and use of resources.

High quality magnets do not require highly selective methods of student admission, the study found. The magnets served average— as well as high- ability students. Only 14 of 45 magnets used achievement test scores, grade point averages or other highly selective admittance standards.

Of the 32 magnet schools that reported achievement test scores, 40 percent had average reading and math achievement scores 10 points above their district averages. Twenty percent had average scores 30 points higher than district averages for the grade level. (Survey of Magnet Schools, 1 983).

Average daily attendance, dropout, suspension and transfer rates show that magnets have more positive outcomes than district averages, which may be a function of voluntary enrollment and self selection.

Researchers found that magnet school achievement is strongly related to the innovative leadership of the school principal, (Survey of Magnet Schools, 1983:28) a high degree of coherence of the theme, teaching styles, and staff to form a strong program identify and district commitment. Magnet programs received slightly more funding over the two-year period.

Districts with high quality ratings for their magnet schools also frequently had a high level of community involvement from parents, businesses, universities and community organizations. Involvement ranged from program planning and design to writing curriculum, providing part-time teachers and arranging for special equipment or facilities.

The analysis states that 40 percent of urban districts which develop magnet schools as a means to desegregation have positive results. Full racial and ethnic desegregation was achieved in two-thirds of the magnets. The remainder were districts in which desegregation was not a program objective.

A 1987 evaluation of the all-magnet system in New Jersey's Montclair School District by the Educational Testing Service found that the Iowa Test of Basic Skills showed an improvement in academic performance since the implementation of a magnet program. Both black and white students were performing above the national average.

The magnets created a "good learning environment in which students of diverse backgrounds feel comfortable and are able to learn. We found evidence of strong leadership, happy students, and generally satisfied teachers." (Educational Testing service, Montclair, 1987:ii)

The impact of creating alternatives within the public school system was positive and added excitement to the schools, researchers wrote.

Montclair parents liked the idea of choice. Communications increased between parents and the schools through involvement in the "school, PTA, school review committee and other volunteer efforts."

As often associated with magnets, some parents perceived unequal resources in the schools. Black parents expressed concerns about achievement gaps between black and white students, underrepresentation of blacks in high school honors classes and a lack of attention to raising minority scores in Basic Skills Improvement Plans. (Educational Testing Service, 1987).

Montclair achieved its desegregation goals. The schools and classrooms were racially balanced. ETS found that the magnets created an integrated environment. A weakness in the system was that greater number of minorities were present in compensatory education classes and fewer minorities were in honors classes. Encouragement of minority enrollment in advanced classes increased the representation in this area.

A 1984 study of New York State's 41 magnet schools in eight districts (state or federally funded) by MAGI Educational Services Inc. found that New York's magnets provide quality education and promote racial/ethnic balance.

In summary, the report found that State Pupil Evaluation Programs test results revealed statistically significant increases in student performance after the introduction of magnet schools in the mid 1970s. These improvements were not because of changes in racial composition or selective enrollment patterns, the report stated. The majority of magnets had higher achievement test scores than their district averages. Fifty-eight percent performed better in reading while 65 percent were better in math. Nearly one-quarter surpassed their district averages by more than 10 normal curve equivalent points, a statistically and educationally important difference (MAGI Educational Services, New York State Magnet School Research Study Final Report, 1984).

Research indicates that magnets encouraged students' interest in learning. Ninety-eight percent had higher attendance rates than their district averages. Nearly three-quarters had dropout rates below the district averages. (MAGI Educational Services, 1984). Magnets had a strong program identity, with clear goals and a rich curriculum that offered choice and diversity to parents and students (MAGI Educational Services, 1984).

Parent participation in magnets was exceptionally high. In nearly half of the magnets, 50 percent or more parents regularly participated in school activities. In 30 percent, three-quarters or more parent were active participants. Ninety-eight percent of the parents said they were satisfied or very satisfied with magnets. The same percentage said they would recommend their magnets to other parents and the majority perceived that the magnets provided a better education than other schools. (MAGI Educational Services, 1984).

Magnets had positive school climates with strong leadership, cohesiveness, teacher-directed learning and sound working relationships. They were characterized by high levels of communication Magnet teachers were confident in their schools and in the concept of magnets. Teacher turnover rates were low and 80 percent of teachers rated their magnets as superior to non-magnets. More than 90 percent said magnets successfully met the needs of students for whom they were intended. (MAGI Educational Services, 1984).

Magnets reduced racial isolation in that high minority schools' average minority enrollments dropped to 54 percent in 1983 from 90 percent in 1973. Low minority schools' average minority enrollment increased by 26 percent in 1983 from 28 percent in 1973. The current racial composition in magnets reflected the district-wide average at the time of the study despite large discrepancies before magnet implementation. (MAGI Educational Services, 1984).

Positive Characteristics of Magnet Schools

Robert Arnove and Toby Strout of Indiana University's School of Education wrote that "the element of choice is important. In most cases, along with the right to choose a program has come the opportunity to participate in some degree in the design, operation and evaluation of the programs" (Arnove and Strout,1977/1978: 24). Magnets that include parents in the decision-making process have made them more "amenable to the desegregation process," according to Arnove and Strout.

Proponents argue that not only do parents become more involved in the schools, but community and business leaders share their expertise with students through lectures, work opportunities or field trips related to magnet themes.

Some magnet school systems allow teachers to choose their schools. Teachers who choose the magnet school in which they teach are more likely to be interested in the academic theme of the school and hopefully play a leadership role in the design and implementation of a thematic curriculum.

Some experts say options provide better matches of students' interests with educational programs. Smaller numbers in magnet programs allow a more personalized education. Magnet school teachers say they have developed relationships with students which have given them a greater understanding of students' needs and learning styles. (Raywid, 1984).A family atmosphere often develops in these schools which leads to greater collegiality among students, teachers, administrators, parents and the community. (Ibid.)

Magnets have also been linked with reduced school violence and vandalism, improved pupil attendance and more positive student attitudes toward school (News In Brief, Office of Educational Research and Improvement, 1988, U.S. Department of Education).

Negative Characteristics of Magnet Schools

By their nature, magnet schools can also create problems in a public school choice system.

Some magnets establish entrance requirements because the demand for admission is so great. However, research studies indicate this limits choice to only certain children. Requirements including prior achievement, conduct and demonstrated interest largely limit programs to white middle-class students (Arnove and Strout, 1978). Research shows that minorities and low-income students can increase their academic achievement through magnet programs but (if they are denied access) there is little chance for improvement (Nathan, interview, June 28, 1988).

Selective magnets can be elitist schools. Academic magnets such as science, math or technology may "cream off" top students from other schools and weaken academic balances. Sometimes, magnets are selective simply by the nature of their themes.

Magnets can be extremely costly and may drain the resources of other schools, stripping them of their educational resources.Magnet school teachers may have to be retrained to teach the theme, which can strain budgets and evoke negative feelings for those teachers who have no interest in the magnet.If teachers are allowed to choose the school in which they want to teach, controversy may result if teacher placement is largely based on seniority, but not necessarily on capability.

The paperwork involved with choice can become an administrative burden and may be costly if additional personnel are hired.Sometimes magnet school themes are not actualized because of poor planning, haste or lack of resources. Themes in a choice plan must be actualized. Choice cannot exist unless schools differ, offering an array of programs from which to choose (Raywid, Educational Options Conference, 1988).

Racial resegregation may occur unless a magnet system is strictly monitored. In some districts, school buildings housing several magnets became more racially integrated, but actual classes were more segregated (Arnove and Strout, 1977).

While many districts use magnets and choice as tools to try to achieve racial desegregation, others are using parental choice in a greater variety of ways. Among these are choice to achieve program quality, involve parents more directly in the schools and to provide greater competition between schools.

Bibliography

Aikin, Wilford M. 1942. "This We Have Learned: In the Story of the Eight-Year Study," *The Education Digest* 7(9) May: 29-32.

Alves, Michael J. and Charles V. Willie. 1987. "Controlled Choice Assignment: A New and More Effective Approach to School Desegregation ." *The Urban Review*. 19(2): 67-88.

Arnove, Robert and Toby Strout. 1978. "Alternative Schools and Cultural
    Pluralism: Promise and Reality." *Education Research Quarterly*. 2(4): 74-95.
    _____. 1981. "Magnets As Alternatives to Mandatory Busing." *Changing
    Schools*. 7: 2-4.

Barth, Roland. 1988. "Principals, Teachers, and School Leadership." *Phi Delta
    Kappan*. May: 639-642.

Bell Associates. *Parents' Attitudes Toward The Cambridge Public Schools*.
    Cambridge, MA: September 13, 1988.

Bennett, William J. 1988 "Providing Choice." *American Education Making It
    Work: A Report to the President and the American People*. April: 46-48.

Blank, R., R.A. Dentler, D.C. Baltzell, and K. Chabotar. 1983. *Survey of
    Magnet Schools Final Report*. Washington, D.C.: James H. Lowry and
    Associates.

Boyer, Ernest. 1985. *High School: A Report on Secondary Education in
    America*. New York: Harper and Row.

Bridge, R. Gary and Julie Blackman. 1978. *A Study of Alternatives in American
    Education, 4: Family Choice in Schooling*. Santa Monica,   California:
    Rand Corporation.

Burns, Leonard T. and Jeanne Howes. 1988. "Handing Control to Schools: Site-
    Based Management Sweeps the Country." *The School Administrator*. August:
    8-18.

Cambridge School Committee. 1981. *Desegregating The Schools: A Civic
    Responsibility*. Cambridge, MA.

Carnegie Forum on Education and the Economy. 1986. Task Force on Teaching
    As A Profession. *A Nation Prepared*, New York: Carnegie Corporation.

Catterall, James. 1987. "The Supply and Demand For Private Education." *Journal
    of Education Finance*, 13(2). Fall: 205-215.

Chubb, John E. and Terry M. Moe. 1986. "No School Is An Island. Politics,
    Markets and Education." *The Brookings Review*. Fall: 21-28.

Clewell, Beatriz Chu and Myra Ficklen Joy. 1987. *Evaluation of the Montclair
    Magnet School System*. Educational Testing Service.

Clinchy, Evans. 1987. *A Consumer's Guide to Schools of Choice*. Boston MA:
    Institute For Responsive Education.

_____. 1987. "Fall River's Move toward Equity." *Equity and Choice.* 3(3). Spring : 35-40.

_____. 1987. *Planning For Parent Choice: A Guide to Parent Surveys and Parent Involvement in Planning for Parent and Professional Choice in the Public Schools.* Boston, Ma : *Institute For Responsive Education.*

Coleman, James S. 1985. "Schools and the Communities they Serve ." *Phi Delta Kappan.* April: 527-532.

_____.and Thomas Hoffer. 1987. *Public and Private High Schools: The Impact of Communities.* New York: Basic Books.

Collins, Roger L. 1987. "Parents' Views of Alternative Public School Programs: Implications for the Use of Alternative Programs to Reduce School Dropout Rates." *Education and Urban Society.* 19 (3). May: 290-302.

Conner, Daryl R., Alvin Toffler, et al. 1988. "Chords of Change." *World Summer: 35-43.*

Coons, John E. and Stephen D. Sugarman. 1978. *Education by Choice: The Care for Family Control.* Berkeley, CA: University of California Press.

Cooperman, Saul, Joel Bloom, and Peter Bastardo. 1986. *Effective Schools: An Annotated Bibliography.* Trenton, NJ Department of Education.

Comer, James. 1988. *Partners in Learning.* Trenton: N.J Department of Education.

Corcoran, Thomas B. and Barbara J. Hansen. 1983. *The Quest for Excellence: Making public Schools More Effective.* Trenton, NJ: NJ School Boards.

Cremin, Lawrence A. 1976. *Public Education.* New York: Basic Books.

Cuban, Larry. 1988. "You're on the Right Track, David." *Phi Delta Kappan .* April: 571-572.

_____.1988. "A Fundamental Puzzle of School Reform."*Phi Delta Kappan.* January: 341-344.

Daley, Suzanne. 1988. "On The Road Back: Alvarado Vitalizing A School District." *New York Times.* July 18:B5.

Davenport, Suzanne and Donald R. Moore, 1988. *The New Improved Sorting Machine.* Designs for Change. Chicago, Illinois.

DeClue, James. 1988. "The St. Louis Case: A Personal View." *Equity and School.* New York: Random House.

Dennison, George. 1969. *Lives of Children: The Story of the First Street School.* New York: Random House.

Doyle, P Denis. 1977. "The Politics of Choice: A View from the Bridge." În James S. Coleman, et al. *Parents, Teachers and Children: Prospects for Choice in American Education.* San Francisco: Institute for Contemporary Studies.

Eilber, Charles R. 1987. "The North Carolina School of Science and Mathematics." *Phi Delta Kappan.* June: 773-777.

Elmore, Richard F. 1986. *Choice in Public Education.* Center for Policy Research. New Brunswick, NJ.

Eurich, Alvin C. 1969. *Reforming American Education: The Innovative Approach to Improving Our Schools and Colleges.* New York: Harper and Row.

"Fall River's Plan Pioneers Against Segregation by Languages." *New York Times.* March 22, 1987.

Fantini, Mario D. 1973. *Public Schools of Choice.* New York: Simon and Schuster.

_____. 1974. *What's Best for the Children?* Garden City, NY: Anchor Press/Doubleday.

_____ and Milton A. Young. 1970. *Designing Education for Tomorrows Cities.* New York: Holt, Rinehardt and Winston.

_____. 1975. *The People and Their Schools: Community Participation.* Bloomington, IN: Phi Delta Kappa.

Finn, Chester E. Jr. 1985. "Toward Strategic Independence: Nine Commandments for Enhancing School Effectiveness. *Phi Delta Kappan.* 65(8): 518-524.

_____ and Denis P. Doyle. 1984. "American Schools and The Future of Local Control" in *Public Interest.* No. 77, Fall: 77-95.

_____. 1985. Education Choice: Theory, Practice, and Research, testimony before Senate Subcommittee on Intergovernmental Relations, Committee on Governmental Affairs: October 22.

_____. 1985. "Teacher Unions and School Quality: Potential Allies or Inevitable Foes? *Phi Delta Kappan.* January: 331-338.

_____ and Diane Ravitch. 1988. "No Trivial Pursuit." *Phi Delta Kappan.* April: 559-564.

Fiske, Edward B. 1988. "Parental Choice in Public Schools Gains." *New York Times.* July 11: A1, B6.

Fizzell, Robert L. 1987. "Inside A School of Choice." *Phi Delta Kappan.* June: 758-760.

Flax, Ellen. May 4, 1988. "Arizona House Adopts Measure to Mandate Statewide Choices". *Education Week.* 7 (32): 13.

Foote, Edward T., II. 1988. "Toward Voluntary Desegregation: The Beginnings of The St. Louis Plan." *Equity and Choice.* February: 30-33.

_____. 1962. *Capitalism and Freedom.* Chicago: University of Chicago Press.

Friedman, Milton and Rose Friedman. 1980. *Free To Choose: A Personal Statement.* New York: Harcourt Brace Jovanovich.

Frymier, Jack. 1986. "Legislating Centralization." *Phi Delta Kappan.* May: 646-648.

Futrell, Mary Hatwood. 1985. "Chester Finn and Quality Education." January: 339-340.

Garber, Darrell. 1987. "Tuition Exemptions: An Experiment in Vouchers," *Journal of Education Finance* 13(2): Fall: 167-173.

Gilley, J. Wade and Kenneth A. Fulmer. 1986. *A Question of Leadership or To Whom Are the Governors Listening?* A Report of the Center for Policy Studies in Education. Fairfax, Virginia: George Mason University.

Glenn, Charles. 1985. "The Significance of Choice for Public Education." *Equity and Choice* VOL. 1(3). Spring: 5-10.

_____. 1986. *Family Choice and Public Schools: A Report to the State Board of Education.* Massachussetts Department of Education: June.

_____. 1986. "New Challenges: A Civil Rights Agenda For The Public Schools." *Phi Delta Kappan.* May: 653-656.

_____. 1987. "The New Common School." *Phi Delta Kappan.* December: 290-294.

_____. 1988. Parent Choice and American Values. Unpublished paper: 21 pages.

Goodlad, John I. 1984. *A Place Called School*. New York, NY: McGraw-Hill.

———. 1983. "Improving Schooling in the 1980's: Toward The Non-Replication of Non-Events." *Educational Leadership*. April 4-7.

Goodman, Paul. 1960. *Growing Up Absurd*. New York: Vintage Books.

———. 1964. *Compulsory Miseducation*. New York: Vintage Books.

Grant Gerald. 1982. "The Elements of A Strong Positive Ethos." *NASSP Bulletin*. March: 85-90.

Graubard, Allan. 1972. *Free The Children: Radical Reform and The Free School Movement*. New York: Random House.

Gregory, Tom. 1985. "Alternative School As Cinderella." *Changing Schools*, 13(3): 2-4.

Gutek, Gerald L. 1986. *Education In The United States: An Historical Perpective*. Englewood Cliffs, NJ: Prentice Hall.

Healy, Ann Macari. "Volunteer Program Helps Cut Linguistic Barriers in Schools." *Providence Journal-Bulletin*. September 8, 1987, C-1.

Hentoff, Nat. 1966. *Our Children Our Dying*. New York: Viking Press.

Herdon, James. 1968. *The Way It Spoozed to Be: A Report On the Classroom War Behind the Crisis in Our Schools*. New York: Simon and Schuster.

Holt, John. 1964. *How Children Fail*. New York: Putman.

Jenks, Christopher, et al. 1970. *Education Vouchers*. Cambridge, Massachusettes: Center for the Study of Public Policy.

Johnson, Dirk. 1988. "Catholic Schools Reach Out To Save Poor and To Borrow." *New York Times* September 13: A1, A25.

———. 1988. "Illinois Legislative Moves to Give Parents Control of the Chicago Schools," *New York Times*. July 13: B7.

Johnson, Thomas H., Moderator and a panel of experts, "Chords of Change." 1988. *World*. Summer: 35-43.

Katz, Michael B. 1971.*School Reform: Past and Present*. Boston: Little, Brown and Company.

Kearns, David T. 1988. "An Education Recovery Plan For America." *Phi Delta Kappan*. April: 565-570.

_____ and Denis P. Doyle. 1988. *Winning The Brain Race: A Bold Plan To Make Our Schools Competitive.* San Francisco: Institute For Contemporary Studies.

Kohl, Herbert. 1967. *36 Children* New York: New American Library.

Kolderie, Ted. 1988. "The Essential Principles of Minnesota's School Improvement Strategy." *Equity and Choice.* Winter: 47-50.

Kozol, Jonathan. 1988. "A Report Card on America's Schools After 20 Years." *The School Administrator.* October: 13-14.

_____. 1967. *Death At An Early Age: The Destruction of The Hearts and Minds of Negro Children in the Boston Public Schools.* Boston: Houghton Mifflin.

_____. 1982. *Alternative Schools: A Guide for Educators and Parents.* NY: Continuum. (in other editions called *Free Schools*)

LaPierre, K. Bruce. 1988. "The St. Louis Plan: Substantial Achievements and Unfulfilled Promises." *Equity and Choice.* February: 34-44.

Leonard, George. 1968. *Education and Ecstasy.* New York: Delta.

Leonard, Steven C. 1987. Boston's Equity Challenge." *Equity and Choice.* Fall: 59-63.

Leslie, Connie et al. "Giving Parents A Choice." *Newsweek.* September 19, 1988: 77-81.

Lieberman, Ann. 1988. "Teachers and Principals: Turf, Tension, and New Tasks." *Phi Delta Kappan.* May: 648-653.

Lowell Public Schools. 1987. *Lowell Voluntary Revised Desegregation and Educational Improvement Plan.* Lowell, MA: June.

Maeroff, Gene I. 1988. "Blueprint For Empowering Teacher." *Phi Delta Kappan.* March: 473-477.

MAGI Educational Services, Inc. 1985. *New York State Magnet School Research Study Final Report.*

Mahon-Lowe, Kathryn. 1986. Organizational Effectiveness of Alternative and Traditional Schools. Ph.D. Thesis. Fordham University.

Manley-Casimir, Michael E. 1982. *Family Choice in Schooling: Issues and Dilemmas.* Lexington, Massachusetts: Lexington Books.

McLaughlin, Milbrey Wallin and Patrick Shields. 1987. "Involving Low Income Parents in the Schools: A Role for Policy? *Phi Delta Kappan,* October: 157.

McNeil, Linda M. 1988. "Contradiction of Control." Part I, January; 1988. Contradiction of Control." Part II. *Phi Delta Kappan.* February: 432-438. February. *Phi Delta Kappan,* January: 333-339.

Mecklenburger, James A. 1988. "Neither Schools Nor Photocopiers Are Flawless." *Phi Delta Kappan.* April: 574-575.

Meier, Deborah. 1987. "Central Park East: An Alternative Story." *Phi Delta Kappan,* June: 753-757.

_____. 1987, "Success In East Harlem." *American Educator.* Fall: 34-39.

Metz, Mary Haywood. 1986. *Different by Design* New York: Routledge, Keagan, Paul.

_____. 1986. "In Education, Magnets Attract Controversy," *NEA Today* January: 54-59.

Miller, Harry L. and Marjorie B. Smiley 1967. *Education in Metropolis,* New York: Free Press.

Minnesota Department of Education. 1987. *Post Secondary Enrollment Options Program Final Report,* St. Paul, MN.

_____. 1985. *The Condition of Education.* St Paul, MN.

_____. 1988. *Alternative Programs in Minnesota Schools.* St. Paul MN.

_____. 1988. *Enrollment Options Program, Parent Survey, 1987-88, Overall Results Summary.* St. Paul, MN.

Mueller, Van D. 1987. "Choice: The Parents' Perspective." *Phi Delta Kappan.* June: 761.

Nathan, Joseph [Joe]. 1983. *Free To Teach: Achieving Equity and Excellence in Schools.* New York: Pilgrim Press.

_____. 1985. "The Rhetoric and The Reality of Expanding Educational Choices." *Phi Delta Kappan.* March: 476-480.

_____. 1987. "Results and Future Prospects of State Efforts to Increase Choice Among Schools." *Phi Delta Kappan.* June: 746-752.

_____. Progress, Problems and Prospects with State Choice Plans, unpublished paper, October, 1988.

National Commission on Excellence in Education. 1983. *A Nation At Risk: The Imperative for Educational Reform.* Washington, DC: U.S. Government Printing Office.

National Education Association. 1985. *What Research Says About Effective Schools.* Number 1. Washington, D.C.

_____. and National Association of Secondary School Principals. 1986.*Ventures in Good Schooling.* August.

National Governors Association. 1986. *Time For Results: The Governors 1991 Report on Education.* Washington, D.C.: National Governors Association.

National School Public Relations Association. 1981. *Good Schools: What Makes Them Work.* Arlington, Virginia.

Nault, Richard L. and Susan Uchitelle. 1982. "School Choice in the Public Sector: A Case Study of Parental Decision Making" in Michael E. Manley Casimir. *Family Choice in Schooling.* Lexington, Massachusetts: Lexington Books.

Neill, A.S. 1960. *Summerhill: A Radical Approach To Child Rearing.* New York: Hart Publishing Company.

O'Connell, Martin. 1988. *Fertility of American Women: June 1987.* Current Population Report. Wahington, D.C.: U.S. Bureau of Census.

Olson, Lynn. 1987. "Less is More." *Education Week.* 6(21), February 18: 1, 22-24.

Orfield, Gary. 1988. "School Desegragation in the 1980's" *Equity and Choice.* Vol. 4, February: 25-28.

Palmer, Parker J. 1987. "Community Conflict and Ways of Knowing." *Change.* September/October: 20-25.

Penkalski, Janice and Linda Wagar. 1988. "School Reforms Under Scrutiny." *State Government News.* 31(8): 8-11.

Perlez, Jane. "Year of Honor in East Harlem Schools." *New York Times.* June 27, 1987: 29,52.

Phi Delta Kappa. 1980. *Why Do Some Urban Schools Succeed? The Phi Delta Kappa Study of Exceptional Urban Elementary Schools.* Bloomington, Indiana.

Postman, Neil and Charles Weingartner. 1973. *The School Book.* New York: Delacorte Press.

Powell, Arthur G. and David K. Cohen. 1985. *The Shopping Mall High School: Winners and Losers in the Educational Marketplace.* Boston, MA: Houghton-Mifflin.

Pratte, Richard. 1973. *The Public School Movement: A Critical Study.* New York: David McKay Company.

Quie, Albert H. 1987. More 'Choice' is Key to Public-School Reform. *Education Week.* 4(34).

Rand. 1974. *A Public School Voucher Demonstration: The First Year at Alum Rock: Summary and Conclusions.* National Institute of Education. Santa Monica, CA.

Ravitch, Diane. 1983. *The Troubled Crusade: American Education, 1945-1980.* New York: Basic Books.

Raywid, Mary Anne. 1983. "Schools of Choice: Their Current Nature and Prospects." *Studies of School.* 684-688. June: 684-688.

_____. 1983. "Alternative Schools As A Model for Public Education." *Theory Into Practice.* 22(3).

_____. 1984. "Synthesis of Research on Schools of Choice." *Educational Leadership.* April: 71-78.

_____. 1985. "The Choice Concept Takes Hold."*Equity and Choice.* Fall: 7-13.

_____. 1985 "Family Choice Arrangements in Public Schools: A Review of The Literature." *Review of Educational Research,* 55(4). Winter: 435-467.

_____. 1985. "Keeping At-Risk Youth in School." *State Education Leader.* Spring: 4-6.

_____. 1986. "Success Dynamics of Public Schools of Choice." *Content, Character and Choice in Schooling: Public Policy and Research Implications.* Washington: National Council on Educational Research.

_____. 1987. "Alternate Routes to Excellence." *National Forum,* Phi Kappa Phi. Summer: 25-28.

_____. 1987. "Drawing Educators to Choice."*Metropolitan Education.* Fall (3): 35-47.

_____. 1987. "Excellence and Choice: Friends or Foes?" *The Urban Review.* 19(1): 35-47.

_____. The Mounting Case For Schools of Choice. unpublished paper. May 1988.

Rich, Dorothy. 1987. *Schools and Families: Issues and Actions.* Washington, D.C.: National Education Association.

_____ and Spencer Rich. "One Parent Families Found to Increase Sharply in U.S." *Washington Post.* May 15, 1985.

Reid, Linda. 1986-7. *Final Report: Magnet Schools.* Rochester City School District.

Riley, Richard. 1986. "Can We Reduce the Risk of Failure?" *Phi Delta Kappan.* November: 214-219.

Rosenholz, Susan J. 1985. "Political Myths About Education Reform: Lessons From Research on Teaching." *Phi Delta Kappan.* January: 349-355.

Sarason, Seymour B. 1983. *Schooling In America: Scapegoat And Salvation.* New York: Free Press.

Schrag, Peter. 1967. *Village School Downtown: Politics and Education - A Boston Report.* Boston: Beacon Press.

Seeley, David S. 1981. *Education Through Partnership: Meditating Structure and Education.* Cambridge , MA: Ballinger Publishing Company.

Sexton, Porter W. (1985). "Trying To Make It Real Comapred To What? Implications of High School Dropout Statistics." *Journal of Educational Equity and Leadership.* 5(2), Summer: 92-106.

Silberman, Charles E. 1970. *Crisis in the Classroom: The Remaking of American Education.* New York: Random House.

Sirotnik, Kenneth A. and Richard W. Clark. 1988. "School-Centered Decision Making and Renewal." *Phi Delta Kappan.* May: 660-664.

Sizer, Theodore R. 1973. *Places for Learning, Places for Joy: Speculations on American School Reform.* Cambridge, MA: Harvard University Press.

_____. 1984. *Horace's Compromise: The Dilemma of The American High School.* Boston: Houghton Mifflin.

Smith, Kenneth. 1988. "A Comprehensive Strategy to Help At-Risk Students." *School Leader.* July/August: 34.

Smith, Vernon H. 1974. *Alternative Schools: The Development of Options in Public Education.* Lincoln, Nebraska: Professional Educators Publications, Inc.

_____. 1978. "Optional Alternative Public Schools" in Arthur J. Newman *In Defense of the American Public School.* Berkeley, CA: McCutchan Publishing Co.

Snider, William. 1987. "The Call For Choice: Competition in the Educational Marketplace." *Education Week.* June 24: C1-C24.

Spring, Joel. 1982. "Dare Educators Build A New System?" in Michael E. Manley-Casimir, ed., *Family Choice In Schooling: Issues and Dilemmas.* Lexington, MA: Lexington Books.

Stedman, Lawrence C. 1988. "The Effective Schools Formula Still Needs Changing: A Reply to Brookover." *Phi Delta Kappan.* February: 439-442.

Stern, Joyce D. and Marjorie O. Chandler. 1988. *The Condition of Education: Elementary and Secondary Education.* National Center for Education Statistics. Vol. 1.

Summerhill: For and Against. 1970. New York: Hart Publishing Company.

Surwill, Benedict J., editor. 1984. *A Critical Examination of American Education: A Time for Action.* Billings, Montana: Eastern Montana College.

Toffler, Alvin. 1970. *Future Shock,* New York: Random House.

————. Daryl R. Conner, et al. 1988. "Chords of Change."*World.* Summer: 35-43.

U.S. Department of Education. 1985. *Justice and Excellence: The Case For Choice in Chapter 1.* Washington, D.C.

Walberg, Herbert J. 1984. "Families As Partners in Educational Productivity." *Phi Delta Kappan.* 65(6). February: 397-400.

————. 1988. Educational Productivity and Choice, unpublished paper, February.

Warren, Jim. 1976. "Alum Rock Voucher Project." *Educational Researcher.* March: 13-15.

Wehlage, Gary, and Robert Rutter. 1986. "Dropping Out: How Much Do Schools Contribute to the Problem?" *Teacher College Record.* Vol. 87, Spring: 374-392.

Wilensky, Rona. 1988. *Case Study of Fall River Massachusetts Aiming for Equity and Excellence.* Education Commission of the States. Denver, Colorado: April.

SECTION III: SCHOOLS OF CHOICE

INTRODUCTION

Although the term 'choice' has been part of the language of vouchers and magnets since the inception of the current public discussion, 'schools of choice' is increasingly coming to be understood to mean choosing from among **public** schools, either the schools within a single district or from among schools in a wider geographic area. In the case of Minnesota, the geographic area is the entire state. In fact, the primary distinction between a voucher system and schools of choice is that a voucher system would include private as well as public schools; schools of choice would be only public. In addition, in a voucher system, a parent would receive a "chit" to be redeemed at a selected school; in a public choice system funds would go directly to schools.

However, the theme of this volume is that one cannot fully understand the current school choice proposals and the many arguments they engender without understanding the unfolding of the concept through vouchers and magnets, as well as a particular form of magnet —the alternative school.

A pervasive use of the concept of choice dates to the very beginning of the ongoing debate as it emerged over the Alum Rock project and the early proposals from Friedman for unregulated vouchers and Coons and Sugarman in the Initiative for Family Choice in the early 1980s in California. Although there are various perspectives on whether and why private schools should or should not be included in a school choice program, the basic dividing line among supporters of choice is between those who do and do not support this inclusion. And a large group of opponents to public school choice offer as their primary reason for opposition that it would be "letting the camel's nose into the tent" —private schools would soon be taking public money. And this gets into First Amendment questions that this author will consider at a later point.

Under most circumstances, most public educators oppose voucher support of private schools. However, when such support comes clothed as a literacy voucher for the underprivileged to use in an urban private (usually Catholic) school because the local public school is not doing its job, such as in Milwaukee, this unilateral opposition becomes somewhat diluted.

Magnets complicate the school choice picture even further. With vouchers, individuals receive them and thus improving education results from individual initiative. Magnets have been a systemic, but generally not system-wide, proposal for improvement, involving large groups of people, but not the whole system nor everyone. Schools of choice, by their very nature, are designed to impact on all educational providers and consumers in a specified geographic area, thus avoiding shortcomings of both vouchers and magnets. However, some of the ongoing opposition to schools of choice is the result of residue objections to vouchers and magnets.

HISTORICAL BACKGROUND

As suggested above, it is difficult to separate the historical development of the concept of schools of choice from that of vouchers and magnets. Clearly if everyone gets a voucher, not just a select few, then a universal choice system exists. This is what Milton Friedman visualized in the early 1970s, though his proposal was labeled a voucher proposal. This, too, was what Christopher Jencks and his associates had in mind when they designed the Alum Rock experiment. But, again, we called it a voucher system. So, too, with John Coons and Stephen Sugarman as their ideas evolved throughout the 1980s. Therefore, many who were opposed to vouchers, especially for private schools, and most especially when they were used to avoid court-ordered desegregation, transferred that opposition to school choice.

Just as the use of vouchers appeared as a means for white families to avoid desegregated (and the prospect of integrated) schools, magnets were seen as a means to accomplish the goals of desegregation. As research increasingly gave evidence of the success of magnets, the concept of providing choice for all grew stronger. School districts such as Cambridge, Massachusetts; District 4, New York; and Montclair, New Jersey, all developed district-wide magnet programs, i.e., complete choice systems. In 1988, after several years of legislation which expanded students' choices, the state of Minnesota passed an omnibus education bill which established a state-wide choice system, to be phased in over the next four years.

Another important feature of the conceptual development of school choice was that of the alternative school movement during the 1960s and 70s. Initially, "alternatives' were provided for those students who seemed unable to make it in the "standard" system in order to prevent them from dropping out. Thus there was a choice for them between the "one best system" and the alternative school. But those students were seen to be in the minority. Once the idea is accepted that there is no "one best system" but a wide variety of acceptable teaching and learning styles and that all students should have a choice of the learning environment most appropriate for them, there is no longer a need for "alternatives." Thus there would be a complete choice system.

VARIOUS PERSPECTIVES

Political Parties

Interestingly, both political parties have endorsed school choice. However, this means very different things to each. To the Republican party, as defined by presidents Reagan and Bush, choice came to mean providing some students the opportunity to use money raised through taxes to select a private school, i.e., a form of vouchers. It cannot be denied, however, that many times the "those" for whom they wanted to provide these opportunities were disadvantaged students, as in the Milwaukee plan or the well-publicized concept of literacy vouchers.

The Democratic party's position on school choice is somewhat more complicated. Although the majority of liberals in the education establishment —especially higher education— have voiced opposition to aid to non-public schools, prominent Democratic politicians, such as Daniel Patrick Moynihan, have supported tuition tax credits. Generally speaking, the Democratic party currently, as represented by President Bill Clinton, supports current proposals for public schools of choice.

Teachers' Assocations.

The two major national teachers associations —the National Education Association and the American Federation of Teachers— have taken different positions on school choice. Though the more conservative of the two, the NEA has remained mostly negative on school choice. The AFT —in the voice of Al Shanker, its president— has gone from total negativism to grudging acceptance to near enthusiastic experimental interest. But this interest is only in public school choice. Many of Shanker's weekly columns in *The Sunday New York Times* over the last few years have taken great pains to discount Coleman's and others' claims that students in private schools have an academic advantage over those in public schools and the accompanying view that private schools should, therefore, be included in a choice plan.

<u>Arguments for Choice</u>

Support and opposition for providing choice in schooling comes from many sectors with a variety of justifications. The broadest and most general support is contained in the idea that it is simply a vital part of the democracy that parents should be able to choose the form their children's schooling will take. From this perspective, it is simply inconceivable that parents should be able to choose housing, nourishment, and religious training for their children, but not schools. A choice system from this perspective would, of course, include religious and other private schools.

A second political/economic reason for support of school choice lies in the equity argument. Affluent families currently have all of the choice they want through either choice of residence or private schools. Further, inasmuch as real estate taxes, in most cases, by and large determine the quality of schooling, inequity between the rich and the poor becomes exponentially doubled. The poor —who must use the local public schools— frequently have neither choice nor high quality schooling. Thus, this argument goes, if all parents were given vouchers worth the same amount (resulting in a complete choice system), equity would be doubly achieved in that all would have an equal chance to choose from among available schools and all would have the same amount to spend.

In addition to these systemic arguments for total choice, there is a basic philosophical rationale that many supporters would offer. Mary Anne Raywid, in her Phi Delta Kappa fastback, *The Case for Public Schools of Choice*, points out that

The three fundamental premises underlying the choice idea are that 1) there is no one best school for everyone, 2) it is necessary to provide diversity in school structure and programs in order to accommodate all students and to enable them to succeed, and 3) students will perform better and accomplish more in learning environments they have freely chosen than in those to which they are simply assigned.[1]

Arguments Against Choice

Opposition to school choice, though less wide-spread than support in the general community (as evidenced by several years of Gallup polls), is extremely vigorous in the academic community and, up to this point, has been very successful in preventing its widespread implementation. This is because predominantly those who hold this view —teacher associations, administrators, board members, and academics in higher education— have a great deal of influence over educational policymaking, which influence they believe would be greatly lessened in a choice system.

The broadest argument against choice is the claim that its advocates are using it as a substitute for engaging in the system-wide restructuring that will really make a difference in the quality of education for the poor. This argument gained credibility from the Reagan and Bush Administrations' position that school choice is one means of bringing about excellence in education without spending any additional taxpayer dollars. Opponents go on to argue that wherever choice has existed, it has primarily benefitted the well-to-do and knowledgeable, that the parents of those most in need of improved education are least likely to know how to navigate the system to get it. This argument is frequently offered by spokespersons for African-Americans who have had vast experience with the current education system in which choice is offered only to a limited few.

The argument takes a slightly different twist as opponents argue that many parents and guardians are not qualified to choose the schools their children will attend, either because they lack education themselves or they would choose schools for the "wrong" reasons, such as being close to home or having good athletic programs. Furthermore, the argument goes, a choice system might lead to a situation in which some schools actively recruit and accept only the best students, thus increasing segregation.

---

[1]Raywid, M. A. (1989). *The case for public schools of choice.* Bloomington: Phi Delta Kappa Educational Foundation, 9.

One of the major sources of opposition to school choice comes from those who believe if permitted within the public sector, it would be simply a foot in the door to aid private schools, especially religious schools, and that eventually private religious schools would be equal participants in a choice system. Although this topic will be taken up in much greater detail in the last chapter of this book, it is important to point out here that the 1981 study by James Coleman comparing public and Catholic High Schools added substantial fuel to this opposition. When it was shown that with the same types of clients in terms of socio-economic class, ethnicity, amount of parent education, and other relevant factors, students in Catholic high schools had slightly higher academic achievement than those in public schools at roughly half the cost, choice opponents increasingly mounted church/state arguments against including Catholic schools in any kind of choice system.

Overview of Articles

In the last decade hundreds of articles have been published on school choice, large numbers of them in favor if it. Thus it was difficult to select only a few for inclusion in this volume. However, as the purpose of this collection is to show the historical and philosophical development of the concept of choice, articles have been selected over that time period that represent this development.

This section begins with an article by Denis P. Doyle, "Our one-size-fits-all public schools derive from a 19th-century concept in need of updating," in which he describes the "factory model" that is the basis of our public school system. He maintains that operating on this basis forces educators to "work to the lowest common denominator" and explains that the purpose of school choice is to give clients who cannot send their children to private schools "a voice in transforming" the present system.

The next two article present a strong case for instituting school choice. *The Right to Choose: Public School Choice and the Future of American Education*, an Education Policy Paper prepared by the Center for Educational Innovation at the Manhattan Institute for Policy Research, presents a three-part analysis of the current crisis in American education. The Problem, described by Chester Finn, formerly Assistant Secretary for Research and Improvement at the U. S. Department of

Education, is the "depressing" state of American education in the wake of (then) six years of educational reform since a Nation At Risk. The Theory is a two-part overview of the implications of recent research findings on the educational choice movement and its rationale. In the final section, John Chubb discusses a Brookings study of 500 American public and private high schools; James Coleman argues for the necessity of including religious schools in any meaningful choice plan, focusing on the importance of community in making schools˙ successful.

In her 1984 article, "Synthesis of Research on Schools of Choice," Mary Anne Raywid uses the terms 'alternative schools' and 'schools of choice' interchangeably as, in fact, all alternative schools were those chosen by the individuals who ran and attended them. She reviews the then-current research on school choice, in particular a survey of 2,500 secondary alternative schools conducted by herself in 1982 and another survey of 1,019 magnet schools and programs conducted by Patricia Fleming and others in that same year. After reporting on the organizational structures and processes of various alternative programs, Raywid describes the positive impact that choice has on educational goals, instructional methods, curriculum, and —most importantly— individuals: staff, students, and parents.

The next four articles examine choice programs in the states of Massachusetts and Minnesota. After reviewing the flaws of magnet schools, Charles Glenn, in "Controlled Choice in Massachusetts Public Schools," discusses and responds to seven major criticisms of choice, then offers several proposals which will further expand the vision of teachers and opportunities for parents to provide the best possible schooling. In "The Essential Principles of Minnesota's School Improvement Strategy," Ted Kolderie focuses on the thirteen essential ideas involved in Minnesota's statewide choice plan "...because these are so different in such critical respects from the ideas and the issues earlier and elsewhere associated with proposals for family choice." Joe Nathan, in "School Choice Works in Minnesota," reinforces Kolderie's views with a response to many of the charges made about the implementation of choice in Minnesota, including those in the next article by Finch. Nathan further provides a description of many of the details of the Minnesota plan that make it work. In "The Claims for School Choice and Snake Oil Have a Lot in Common," Louis W. Finch, a superintendent of schools in Minnesota and a constant antagonist in the school choice movement there, challenges what he calls "the exaggerated claims of Minnesota's success in school choice." This article, of course was published soon after state-wide choice legislation was passed, long before there were any longitudinal data to assess the success of the program. Nathan's 1993 *Wall Street Journal* article provides such data.

The next four articles consider the questions of choice from the perspective of the consumers of education: parents and students. In his article, "Here's Why School Choice Will Boost Student Motivation —and Learning," Denis Doyle attempts to persuade school board members that "father and mother know best" when it comes to choosing schools. He invites them to consider the restructuring of school governance along the lines of a modern, high-tech firm in which highly qualified managers are set loose to do their jobs and the CEO (superintendent) and board oversee their accountability, emphasizing that choice is a crucial component in this scenario.

The pair of articles by Duvon G. Winborne and Margaret D. and Theodore Tannenbaum present contrasting perspectives on the question of choice in relationship to students. Winborne asks "Will School Choice Meet Students' Needs?" and presents principals' views on the answer to this question. On the basis of the answers to a survey of 116 principals in a large mid-western school district populated by more than 70% African-American students, Winborne concludes that because the opportunity for meaningful choice among urban students is so limited, "...improving education offerings for urban children must be achieved through innovative uses of available resources."

The Tannenbaums surveyed over two thousand students at the secondary level in twenty-five different school districts in the South Jersey area regarding their attitudes toward school choice and the reasons they would select particular schools and reported the results in "Secondary School Students' Attitudes Toward Schools of Choice and What Choices They Would Make." This was part of a larger study in which over four thousand individuals were surveyed; in addition to students, included were teachers, principals, board members, and parents. In general, parents and students were very positive about school choice; teachers, principals, and board members where much less so. In particular, the Tannenbaums report "that a substantial proportion of students say they would be happier, would select a school because of its high academic achievement, would get better grades, and would be less likely to drop out in a choice system."

Fege and Waterman in "Where PTA Stands on School Choice," offer six conditions that they believe "alternate programs" must meet and thirteen sets of questions that should be asked to determine if the conditions are being met. In acknowledging the tension between the ideal of a common education for all students and meeting individual and diverse needs of students, they emphasize that policy must be based on what effect any plan will have on all children.

No consideration of the conceptual development of a choice system would be complete without examining the impact on teachers. Heid and Leak, in "School Choice Plans and the Professionalization of Teaching," maintain that teachers' role in developing schools of choice will not only provide empowerment at both the policy and classroom levels for current teachers, but make the profession much more attractive to "potential teachers with a creative bent," thus strengthening the profession.

The next set of articles —five of them— address the question of how school choice should be implemented. The first three endorse limiting choice to the public arena. In "Public Choice, Yes; Vouchers, No!" Mary Anne Raywid, in addition to making the case for public school choice, maintains that vouchers are a means for financing schools not improving them and discusses extensively what is wrong with the economic/business analogy that vouchers suggest when applied to schooling, maintaining that "vouchers, by contrast [to public choice], might well undermine education and leave public schools less capable of effective performance than they are now..."

Evans Clinchy, in "Public School Choice: Absolutely Necessary but Not Wholly Sufficient," agrees that limiting "choice among public schools and public schools only," is a good thing and discusses what he sees to be the three major conditions for choice to succeed: diversity, autonomy, and equity.

David Tyack asks "Can We Build a System of Choice That Is Not Just a 'Sorting Machine' or a Market-Based 'Free-for-All?'" Arguing against vouchers because of their potential for "accelerating segregation by class and race," he then reviews the choices that must be made about choice if it is to be successful.

In "Who Should Own the Schools?" Charles Glenn makes a case for school choice when he answers this question by stating that what we need is "...a credible way of thinking about the issues of autonomy, accountability, choice, and community that goes beyond the simple antithesis between bureaucratic strangulation and the free-for-all of individual selfishness." In describing the three voices that must be heard in this discussion —the parents, the society, and the school— he suggests that there is no immediately evident reason to exclude private schools from participation in the resulting system.

John Coons, in "Principle and Prudence in the Design of Choice," goes a step further. After listing the seven effects that a parent-empowering choice system must have, he describes eight technical criteria such a system must meet to be valid. The first three are that it must include both public and private schools, private schools must be "...fiercely protected against further regulation beyond the minimum necessary to protect the poor," and public school districts should be deregulated so they can operate like private schools. Criteria four through seven focus on funding and equity for low-income students. The last speaks to the importance of a gradual phase-in of such a system.

This section concludes with "Improving Schools and Empowering Parents: Choice in American Education," by Nancy Paulu summarizes the responses of participants in a 1989 White House conference on education regarding school choice as a means to improve schools through restructuring based on choice and empower parents in such a way that academic outcomes will increase. She concludes by considering the important aspects of implementing and overseeing a choice program.

Our One-Size-Fits-All Public Schools Derive From a 19th-Century Concept in Need of Updating

Dennis P. Doyle

Of the major social institutions in the Western democracies, only three are characterized by compulsion: prisons, the military, and public schools. Hyperbole? Perhaps, but it makes a point. Only the most important social objectives justify state compulsion. In the case of prisons and military service, the reasons are obvious—though conscription, except in time of war, is a fading memory in most Western nations. Even the Soviet Union has announced plans to introduce a volunteer army.

What, then, of schools? On what basis do we justify compulsory attendance? To protect the young from themselves and from their families. This is a case with substantial merit, for in the modern world, to be uneducated is a curse. So most enlightened people agree that the state properly exercises its police powers in requiring that all children of certain ages attend school.

But compelling children to attend school is not the same as limiting the choice of a child who attends public school to the district in which he lives. Yet we do this, too. And until recently, most Americans simply took for granted the necessity of attending a neighborhood school. To understand how this system, so familiar that it still seems inevitable, came into being, we must step back in time.

The neighborhood public school traces its organizational and intellectual origins to the early schools of Puritan New England. It hardly needs pointing out, but education is a profoundly moral and normative enterprise. A society teaches what it thinks is important, and it teaches using methods it thinks appropriate.

In this context, then, it is not surprising that the schools of the mid and late 19th century revealed both implicit and explicit values and that they mirrored the larger society: an emerging nation moving from an untamed to a tamed land, a society rapidly industrializing and incorporating untold numbers of immigrants.

The school's response was to Americanize the immigrant and to modernize the American. The schools of the 19th and then the 20th century were very much in synchronization with their times. In addition to the nation-building ideology of the day, another powerful force was a work, and that was the first understanding of how to rationalize work. The Industrial Revolution, begun in England, was brought to fruition in the New World with the development of mass production.

The assembly line reached its apogee in the Scientific Management movement of the later 19th and early 20th centuries. Its most ardent and well-known spokesman was Frederick Taylor, stopwatch and clipboard in hand. Taylor would no doubt be surprised to learn that this greatest impact has been in the public sector—especially in the schools, where he has left a legacy that is with us to this day. Its most obvious and lasting impact was the effort to establish "teacher proof" schools, to do for schools what the assembly line had done for manufacturing and assembly: dumb down work.

How do you make schools "teacher proof"? Centralize decision making, establish work rules and schedules that are inflexible, and most important, establish a curriculum from which teachers cannot deviate. Every teacher, student, and school board member in the U.S. will recognize the residue of this system in today's schools. Indeed, only in the nation's finest schools might it be termed a residue, for in most schools the model still obtains.

"One best system" is what Stanford historian David Tyack called it in his book of that title. One best system in which all the nation's schools would be run as one: The curriculum would drive the schools. Administration, management, organization, rules of work, and behavior would look almost exactly like the modern factory. Indeed, the factory model is still apt: The taxpayers are the shareholders; the school board, the board of trustees; the superintendent, the C.E.O.; the deputy superintendent, the division manager; the principals, the foremen; the teachers, the workers on the assembly line.

The product is students, turned out with about the same attention to quality control the factory paid to its product. (It is noteworthy that this factory model—in modern guise—still describes the Japanese school. But as in all things Japanese, the quality control is breathtaking.)

What this means for the workers—teachers—is only too painfully obvious. Teaching is not a profession; it is blue-collar work. True, many teachers are professionals, but they are professionals in spite of the system of which they are a part.

What does this mean for managers and policy setters? They, too, must work to the lowest common denominator. They, too, must make policy and establish rules and regulations, procedures and precedents, thinking always of "worst-case" scenarios. But worst-case planing is a poor guide for educators. It forces decisions toward the mean. Of necessity, the school board member in this "one best system" must plan for every contingency, which, in the modern world, is not pestilence and plague so much as interest-group politics. The objective the board member worries about, then, is keeping everyone happy.

Obviously, this goal cannot be met, and it simply translates into a set of policies that occupy the middle ground, policies that make no one very happy but do not make the majority very unhappy either. It translates into schools that are mediocre at best, rigid institutions that do not well serve any of their client groups. Clients who have the resources—financial and intellectual—have options. The purpose of school choice is to give other clients—the ones who cannot send their children to private schools—a voice in transforming the one-size-fits-all public schools we've inherited from the 19th century.

THE RIGHT TO CHOOSE
Public School Choice and the Future of
American Education

THE PROBLEM: A Depressing Look at Education in America Today
Chester Finn Jr.

I'm part of a beleaguered minority group: professors of education who believe that kids actually ought to know something by the time they finish going to school. Accordingly, most of what I say here today is going to be fairly depressing, since the state of American education itself is fairly depressing. The problem starts with the education departments of this country's university campuses, which have long since been overtaken by very, very bad ideas. Bad ideas eventually give rise to bad practices. In education, bad practices eventually give rise to ignorant kids. Ignorant kids are what our educational system is producing today.

I want to talk first, however, about "successful" kids, the ones who persevere and graduate from high school. Of those kids, 70% eventually enroll in college; of those who enroll in college, 50% graduate. We have 27 million adult Americans walking around the streets of this country with bachelor's degrees in their pockets. Unfortunately, the average "successful" product of our schools doesn't know much and has very few skills. Here's some corroborating data from the National Assessment of Educational Progress, which is the closest thing we have to a barometer of educational outcomes in the United States. The figures I'm going to give you come from the eleventh grade in 1986. Bear in mind that these are the kids who stuck it out until they were in the eleventh grade, who didn't drop out, who probably graduated from high school the following year:

- Only 6% of them could handle reading at a level of difficulty that enabled them to handle original source material, serious essays, scientific material and traditional college-level textbooks.
- Only 7% of them could handle math problems of the kind that require the use of simple algebra.
- Only 20% could write a letter that satisfied modest requirements for adequacy.

As for history and literature, Diane Ravitch and I wrote a book called What Do Our 17-Year-Olds Know? based on a 1986 assessment of what eleventh-graders knew about American history and Western literature the first such assessment ever made in the United States. This test included such questions as: "In which century was the First World War?" The students did "well" on that one. Some 55% of them successfully placed World War I between 1900 and 1950. But when we asked them in which fifty-year span the Civil War occurred, only 33% could answer the question correctly. Some of them placed it before Columbus, some of them placed it after Eisenhower. Keep in mind, by the way, that 80% of these kids were studying U.S. history that year.

Yes, there are wonderful exceptions all through American education. It's a huge system, and there are exceptions to everything you can say about it. But on the average, even the "successful" products of our system know very little and are functioning at a disturbingly low level of intellectual skill. They then go to college and, if they're lucky, are given the secondary education that they should have acquired in high school but didn't. They graduate with a bachelor's degree in their pockets—but without a higher education.

Six years ago, the Secretary of Education told us in A Nation at Risk that we had a problem. Indeed we did. Since then, we've been working very hard. State after state has passed comprehensive educational reform legislation. "Education" governors have been giving it their all. Legislators and business leaders and newspaper editors and crusading professional educators have been giving it their all. We're spending more, we're trying harder, we're fussing endlessly. What of it? As of yet, there has been no demonstrable improvement in the actual outcomes of American education.

Why? And what can we do about it? I don't know why, not entirely. But let me give you a couple of notions as to why we're not doing better.

First, and to me most vexing, is that while everybody seems to agree that the nation as a whole is at risk, almost everybody has simultaneously concluded that their own kids and their own schools are doing just fine. The most recent international comparative assessment of education looked at 13-year-olds in about seven countries in math and science. Our kids, as we're growing accustomed to discovering, did the worst in the world on math. But one of the background questions on the assessment asked the kids: "Do you think you're good at math?" Guess which kids led the world in thinking they're good in math while trailing the world in being good at math?

Parents are no better. Every state in the country that uses standardized tests is reporting to its citizens that their kids are above average. Now if you're told by the superintendent of public education that your kids are fine, your schools are fine, your city is fine, your state is fine well after enough years of being told it, you're probably going to believe it. But it isn't true. It's self-confidence rooted in quicksand. It's a house of cards. We're deluding ourselves about the state of our educational system, and that's one important reason why we're not doing better. Everybody is assuming that somebody else should alter his behavior because it's somebody else who's got the problem.

Second —and let me use a manufacturing metaphor, even though most educators hate it when I talk this way— we've never bothered to figure out what it is that we want the product of our educational system to look like. We've never paused to describe the specifications for the product that we want this system of production to yield. We've fiddled with the system, we've changed the rules by which we operate our schools, we've altered the finance arrangements and the incentive arrangements. But we did all of this without ever asking: "What would we like our kids to come out of school knowing? Or being able to do?"

A third possible explanation is that we have ignored what I respectfully suggest to you is the first great finding of educational research —which also happens to be the first great finding of common sense about education. Kids tend to learn that which they study, and they tend to learn it in rough proportion to the amount of time that they spend studying it. We know that this maxim is true. But we haven't lived by it in our efforts at educational reform.

Look at the high school graduating class of 1987. These are the kids who entered college a year and a half ago, the same kids who entered high school the year that the excellence commission declared the United States to be a nation at risk. How many of them actually took the high-school courses that the excellence commission said ought to constitute the "new basics" of American education? In 1983, the commission defined the "new basics" for high school students as follows: four years of English, three years of math, three years of science, three years of social studies, two years of a foreign language and a half-year of computers. Four years later, only 13% of American high school students were actually exposed to those courses. Eighty-seven percent took something less. If you drop the foreign-language and computer requirements from the list, the results aren't much better: 70% still took something less than the remaining "basic" courses.

If you care about the distribution of equal opportunity in American society, by the way, you should know that black and Hispanic kids as a group took that "basic" menu of courses at a rate of about 22%, while Asian kids took it at the rate of about 54%. If you're interested in at least one partial explanation for why Asian kids are doing well in American education, that's it.

Fourth, our education profession, by and large, is pursuing the wrong goals. It's obsessed with whether your mind is functioning —not with whether you're learning anything. I'm making a distinction here between skills and knowledge, and suggesting to you that our educators in general are so transfixed by cognitive skill that they've concluded that as long as you're thinking, it doesn't really matter whether you know anything; as long as you're reading, it doesn't matter what you're reading; as long as you're able to analyze, it doesn't matter whether you possess knowledge worth analyzing.

This is an oversimplification, of course, but it's only a partial distortion of reality. If you doubt it, look at the reception of E. B. Hirsch, who suggested in his book Cultural Literacy that there really is a body of knowledge that everybody ought to possess by the time they come out of school, if only so that they will have the shared background necessary to allow them to communicate with one another. For his troubles, Hirsch has been denounced as a cultural imperialist, as a latter-day Gradgrind. Every bad thing that can possibly be said about an educator has been said about Hirsch. The education profession has persuaded itself that he's some sort of lunatic, that as long as kids are "thinking," they don't really have to know anything.

Finally, while the private sector is currently engaged in herculean efforts to improve the educational system, it has not had any effect whatsoever on the actual quality of education. Why? Because it has allowed educators to set the agenda—and because it has not applied to education the norms that it would apply to business. Such as: What is the product? Are there ways of reconfiguring the production system that might produce a better product? Are we making a profit? Are we getting any return on our investment? What is the bottom line?

Business people are accustomed to thinking that way —about their businesses. But they go native when they turn their attentions to education. They stop looking for a bottom line. They end up indulging, with some honorable exceptions, in what I call "Lady Bountiful" programs. They give resources to schools to provide some additional service, but they do not in any significant way alter the rules by which the school systems operate, and do not in any significant way exact demands on the school systems for a better product. The result is predictable. They feel good about themselves. They get terrific public relations. But the schools don't improve one iota except insofar as those few kids who happen to be touched by the additional services are marginally improved by them.

If you want to improve education in America, you've got to keep this fact firmly in mind: educators, like the people who run every other large enterprise in American society, are deeply "conservative" in the sense that they don't wish to alter their accustomed ways of doing things. They may be politically liberal, they may vote for Democrats, they may have left-wing notions about foreign policy, but when it comes to their own work, they do it the way they've always done it, and they'll never change their ways unless somebody either induces or forces them to do so.

Needless to say, all of this would be perfectly fine —if you were content with the overall performance of American education, if you believed that American education exists primarily to serve its employees. But I don't believe that. I think that the American educational system and its employees are means to an end. That end is kids who come out of school having learned something. While there are ways of bringing that end about, we haven't embarked upon very many of them. The educational reform movement, despite its best efforts, has not altered the rules by which the system is operating. Neither has the business community. And these rules are not adequately serving American society in 1989.

THE THEORY: The Rationale for Educational Choice
What Makes Schools Work?

John Chubb

I want to try to explain why someone who considers himself something of a liberal is a supporter of educational choice. Choice, after all, is an idea that's been championed by Ronald Reagan and William Bennett, and most recently by George Bush. As a result, many people seem to think that it's some sort of a right-wing conspiracy: something intended to make the poor worse off, make minorities worse off, and help out kids who come from well-to-do families that can figure out how to use the choice system to their benefit.

Well, that's not what choice is all about. In fact, I support educational choice because I think it's our best hope for improving America's schools in general and for improving America's urban schools. which are, of course, largely attended by poor children and minority children—in particular.

Over the last six years, as Chester Finn points out, there has been a tremendous amount of effort nationwide and in cities around the country directed toward trying to improve our nation's educational system. Spending on education per pupil has increased somewhere from 40% to 50% in real terms. Teacher salaries are up more than those of any other occupational group. Students are being required to take more tests and being held more accountable for their performance. Teachers are also being held more accountable. More testing of teachers and more elaborate evaluation systems for teachers are being imposed. Graduation requirements are being increased around the country. Homework requirements within districts are being stepped up.

It stands to reason that some educators are responding to calls for parental choice by saying: "Why do you want to upset the apple cart? We're already trying to improve the schools." Unfortunately, their efforts simply aren't working. Our dropout rates are still roughly 25% nationwide and close to 50% in large cities. Our test scores are still poor in comparison to the scores of countries around the world as well as in comparison to scores in this country just twenty years ago.

Yes, there's been a tremendous amount of concern about the quality of education in this country, and a tremendous effort to try to do something about it. But while some aspects of these efforts are, generally speaking, good ideas, they aren't very promising when considered as overall approaches to school reform. Our research suggests that educational choice is far more consistent with what we now know about how schools can be improved.

My conclusions about choice come in large part from a recent study of America's high schools based on a random sample of 500 public and private high schools nationwide. Within these schools, we obtained responses from roughly 20,000 teachers, principals and students. We asked them questions about such things as family background; life at home; life within the classroom; teacher activity; decision making within the school; school policies; relationship of the school to outside influences; and the activities of school boards, administrators and unions. The data provide a fairly comprehensive picture of what our schools are like and how they are run.

Let's get down to the results. What kind of schools promote achievement? What is the key to student achievement? That's how we're rating schools, by the way, and I don't apologize to anyone for rating schools in terms of student achievement. Other goals are important, but student achievement is crucial.

What, then, is the most important determinant of student achievement? It's the aptitude, or entering ability, of the student. That's bad news, because it's hard to control what students bring to school. But the good news is that when you take into account a whole range of factors that promote student achievement, the second most important influence on student achievement is the school itself In fact, the influence of the school itself, measured comprehensively, was about as important as the influence of the wealth and education and occupational status of the family — and more important than the influence of peers.

We all know, impressionistically, that some schools are good and some are bad. You wander around from one school to the next and you can tell when you're in a good school and when you're in a bad school. Reformers have always known this, but we've never been able to systematically figure out what it is that distinguishes a good school from a bad one—until now. Our survey revealed that teacher salaries were unrelated to school performance. Per-pupil expenditures were unrelated to school performance. Class size was unrelated to school performance. Graduation requirements were unrelated to school performance. Homework policies were unrelated to school performance. In other words, the kinds of things that reformers are trying to change, the things that state legislatures are working so vigorously on right now, are basically unrelated to how schools are doing.

Those qualities that do seem to make a difference are not things that school reformers can easily influence with policies. Even so, they are immediately perceptible to anyone who walks into a good school. Effective schools have clear, ambitious goals that are clear to everybody. They are focused on excellence. The teachers and the principal agree about what the school is trying to accomplish. School reformers and school researchers who have looked at effective schools have often said that successful schools seem to have a "mission." Everyone in an effective school is trying to accomplish something, whether it's excellence in math and science, the performing arts or sports. Everyone in an effective school is on the same wavelength.

We also found that the leadership within effective schools was stronger. The principals knew where they wanted to go. They wanted to take the schools somewhere and they knew how to get there. These principals were much more focused on education than management. We asked them why they decided to become principals. In the effective schools, they said things like: "I wanted to take control of the personnel of this school. I wanted to take control over school policy. I wanted to control things around here." In the ineffective schools, they were more likely to say: "I preferred administration to teaching." Now what kind of a leader is that? That's not a leader, that's a manager. And the bottom line was that in the successful schools we saw educational leaders, not administrators or managers, running the school.

Professionalism was much higher in the effective schools. Within their classrooms, teachers were given the freedom to operate more or less as they chose. They were treated with respect as if they had a body of knowledge and a set of skills that should be allowed to operate freely. Teachers in effective schools also got along with one another much better. They treated each other as equals, as colleagues. They cooperated with one another. They coordinated their teaching. They knew what was going on in each other's classes. They typically characterized their schools as "a big family."

Putting these three things together sense of mission, strong leadership, high sense of professionalism we concluded that the effective schools operated like a community. By contrast, the ineffective organizations behaved much more like a bureaucratic agency—the kind of place where rules and regulations, not trust and shared values, hold things together.

We found that effective schools made a big difference in student achievement. By our estimate, a student's involvement in an effective high school for four years, regardless of that student's aptitude, peer group influences or family influences, yielded one full year of achievement difference over what would have been accomplished in an ineffective high school.

What encouraged some schools to become effectively organized while others remained ineffectively organized? Not surprisingly, it turns out that it's somewhat easier to have an effectively organized school if you have bright, well-behaved kids from well-to-do families. It's easier to organize an effective school out in some fancy suburb.

Still, you can have an effective school organization with just about any group of kids, just about anywhere. We found that the real key to whether a school became effectively organized or ineffectively organized was the autonomy that the school enjoyed from external control by administrators: that is, bureaucrats, superintendents, unions and school boards. The more freedom that the school was granted to chart its own course, the more likely it was to become effectively organized; the more that the school was imposed upon by requirements from outside, the more likely that it would be fraught with internal conflict, that it would be ineffectively organized and would perform badly.

Why is that? Let me offer one simple example. Control over personnel is the most important quality that a school needs to have in order to be effectively organized. If a principal has control over hiring and firing, that principal is likely to hire and maintain in the school a staff of professionals whom he or she respects, who share his or her values, who agree on the mission of the school, who agree on curriculum, who agree on instructional methods, who are inclined to cooperate with one another. A principal with that kind of control is not likely to dictate to teachers.

Instead, that principal is likely, because of respect and trust, to delegate responsibility and to involve the teachers as a team.

On the other hand, if you have a principal who doesn't have control over who's teaching in the school, that principal is going to distrust teachers and the teachers are going to distrust one another. Conflict will thus be inherent, and the school is not going to perform effectively.

Under what conditions are schools granted this kind of autonomy? The bad news is that within the public sector, autonomy is more the exception than the rule. The only time you can be pretty sure that a public school is going to enjoy autonomy and is going to be able to organize effectively is when that school is out in the suburbs, when the kids are performing and when the parents are well-educated and actively involved. In those settings, administrators and school boards are more willing to delegate responsibility to the school and the school can operate as an autonomous organization.

Unfortunately, the schools that need the most help are the inner-city schools with kids and uneducated parents—and those schools, rather than having the autonomy and encouragement to organize effectively, are the ones that usually are the recipients of crackdowns and mandates and instructions about how to perform, that are most completely crippled rules governing personnel. The public schools that most need autonomy, in short, are the that are least likely to get it. That's bad news for school reform.

The good news is that we've learned something from looking at private schools that has helped us understand how autonomy can be provided within the public schools. While public schools receive autonomy only under exceptional circumstances, private schools receive autonomy under all conditions, whether they're in big cities, whether they're part of large religious systems, whether they're teaching poor kids, whether the parents are poorly educated or well-educated.

Why? The answer is simple: competition. Private schools, regardless of their objectives, must please parents. They are under competitive pressures to please parents. Because of those pressures, they are encouraged to delegate decision making down to the level where parents can be most effectively engaged, where the needs of parents can be understood, where a bond can be established between the school and the parent to ensure that the parent is happy enough to continue patronizing the school. Parents are least happy when decision making is vested far away in some central office, out of their reach. If decisions are being made in a distant place, in a way that parents can't influence, parents are going to be unhappy—and they're not going to patronize that school.

To sum up, if you're going to have an effectively organized school and one that can perform well, that school is going to need autonomy. The real issue in school reform, then, is how do you provide autonomy and still hold schools accountable? After all, you can't just turn over the keys of the school to the teacher and principals and be sure that they're going to be held accountable. The structure of the existing system makes that impossible. The incentives are missing. There's no mechanism to hold teachers and principals accountable. That's why you see this profusion of testing and accountability systems that often end up choking off the very autonomy school reformers are trying to provide.

The only empirically and logically compelling way in which autonomy and accountability can be maintained is to move to a different system of accountability. You need a system that holds schools accountable not from the top down, but through the market process, through the competitive process. You need a system that holds schools accountable by giving them autonomy and by observing how well the schools succeed in winning the support of parents and students. Schools that are successful in promoting achievement and attracting parents in organizing effectively will be patronized and will flourish. Those that fail will not be patronized and will suffer and have to be rebuilt.

That kind of accountability system emphasizes the wishes of parents and students much more than the wishes of politicians and bureaucrats. But there's every reason to believe that it's the kind of system that will best promote academic achievement. Under it, schools will have the incentive and the flexibility to organize effectively, to develop missions, to operate more professionally. Schools will also have the incentive and this is crucial—to develop bonds with parents and students, those mutually reinforcing relationships which are so essential to good education. And students will be matched with schools and programs that fit their needs and are most likely to motivate them to succeed.

Now there are many ways in which these systems can be operated: through open-enrollment mechanisms, through universal magnet systems, even through voucher programs. One way or another, though, unless we move to a system that emphasizes more choice and competition, it's likely that forums like this will be held year in and year out, from now until eternity, as we watch our public schools struggle to improve—and improve very little.

What Makes Religious Schools Different?

James Coleman

I'd like to talk about some research results about schools that have significant implications for school policy—by which I mean not only policies affecting schools, but policies that also affect families.

These results derive from a large study of sophomores and seniors in American schools, a study that made it possible for me to compare private and public schools. Private schools in the United States constitute about 10% of the total school population, and about two-thirds of that private school population attends Catholic schools. With those figures in mind, let me discuss what I call the puzzle of the effectiveness of Catholic schools. This puzzle has six pieces:

• Catholic high schools are more effective in bringing about growth in student achievement. This difference can be seen when you compare students enrolled in Catholic high schools to students enrolled not only in public schools, but also in independent private schools. This greater growth doesn't occur in all subject areas—it doesn't occur, for example, in science. But it does occur in mathematics and in verbal test scores.

• Catholic schools are more demanding in terms of the course work that they require of a student than are either public schools or independent private schools. Students in a Catholic school take more mathematics, more foreign languages, more classes in other academic subjects, than do comparable students in either a public or an independent school.

• Not only do students in general learn more in Catholic schools than in other schools, but students from disadvantaged backgrounds —minorities and children of parents who have little education are especially benefitted.

• Children from families that are deficient but not disadvantaged (that is, children whose parents have adequate income and education but are otherwise deficient in establishing good parent-child relationships) show somewhat lower achievement rates and considerably higher dropout rates in public and independent and private schools when compared to similar students from non-deficient families. Their performance relative to children from non-deficient families, however, is much better in Catholic schools.

• Dropout rates from Catholic schools are much lower than dropout rates from public and independent private high schools. The difference in dropout rates remains substantial when background differences, achievement scores and school experiences (that is, grades, absences and the disciplinary history of the student) are statistically controlled. They also remain great when religious affiliation is statistically controlled.

• Finally, there is some indication that the results I've described hold true not only for Catholic schools but also for other schools with a religious foundation and a religiously homogeneous student body. This indication is based only on a small number of schools, and it has only been examined for dropout rates, not for the other outcomes that I've described. It does, however, suggest a possible similarity for other outcomes as well.

It makes sense that schools which are academically more demanding, as is the average Catholic school when compared to either the average public or independent private school, will bring about higher achievement among the students who survive those demands. What is puzzling is the coexistence of these results with lower dropout rates and with the special benefits for students from disadvantaged or deficient families. Ordinarily, greater academic demands increase the performance of children who are already performing above average but do so at the cost of forcing out some students who are doing badly and increasing the gap between high- and low-performing students for those students who do remain. In Catholic schools, the reverse is true. Catholic schools make stronger academic demands and exact higher performance, yet their dropout rate is much lower and the gap between children of different backgrounds is diminished over time.

Perhaps a start towards an answer can be made by asking this question: how is it that religiously based schools are able to make stronger academic demands than other schools? After all, this was not always the case. Catholic schools were long regarded as academically inferior to both the public schools and the independent private schools. What has happened?

One thing that's happened since the '60s is a radical transformation of the internal structure of the family. Parents now have a greatly diminished capacity to determine their teenage child's high school curriculum and to impose requirements regarding schoolwork. This transformation is part of a larger "revolution" in which the authority of parents over some areas of their teenage child's activities has been overturned. The most proximate cause of this revolution was the baby boom of the late '40s, which gave more power to the young by increasing their numbers. In addition, there was an increasing loss of community among adults resulting from high rates of residential moves and a decline of urban neighborhoods. To this was added the growth of the youth-oriented commercial culture, which had as one of its goals the breaking of parental norms and constraints.

High schools confronted in the late '60s and early '70s with post-revolutionary students were not prepared for the change. Colleges confronted with post-revolutionary students in the '60s and '70s, in attempting to make themselves more accessible to minorities, reduced entrance requirements, in some cases almost to the vanishing point. High schools were freed by the reduction in college entrance requirements to offer courses that would pacify post-revolutionary students. As student choice proliferated and parents no longer in authority acquiesced, a new kind of public high school evolved, one commonly known as the "shopping-mall" high school. Foreign languages went into eclipse, while college preparatory mathematics, physics and chemistry went into a decline that was only somewhat less steep.

What does all of this have to do with the puzzle of Catholic schools as I have described it? Schools grounded in a religious community did not, as did public schools, lose their community. Although the revolution within the family occurred in Catholic families just as in non-Catholic ones, it was unable to transform the Catholic school into a shopping-mall high school. This was because of the social connections among parents, and between parents and school, in Catholic schools. These connections helped to provide parents with what might be called "social capital" to aid in resisting the revolution.

Now some of the conditions that shielded religiously grounded high schools from the effects of the youth revolution can also be found in independent private schools. One condition, however, is missing: most independent private schools are not surrounded by a community. The absence of the community means that parents lack the social capital that would support their authority against the youth revolution. Thus the independent private school stands somewhere between the public school and the religious school in the balance of power between students and parents.

The social capital available to parents of students in the religiously grounded school has a number of consequences. First, the curriculum for students planning to attend college remains an academic college preparatory curriculum. The demands are not relaxed. Second, the schools remain able to impose demands—and parents have the recourse to help them enforce these demands. As a result, students take more academic courses, do more homework and learn more than do public-school students who have been liberated by the revolution.

This explains one part of the puzzle: why students in the average Catholic school take more demanding courses than do comparable students in public schools. But it doesn't provide an answer to this question: why is the greater rigidity of Catholic schools not accompanied by higher dropout rates? Why do the higher levels of achievement in Catholic schools not produce a greater gap between advantaged and disadvantaged students?

The answer here also appears to lie in the existence of social capital provided by the religious community surrounding the school. In this case, however, the social capital is made available to the student rather than the parent. One of the differences between a school which has a religious foundation and a secular school is the institutional connection between the family and the school. That institutional connection can have a special importance for the student whose family is weak or broken. The social capital of the religious community surrounding the school can substitute for that which would ordinarily be provided by the family. It is especially valuable for children from disadvantaged or deficient families, those students who are typically at the highest risk of doing badly or dropping out.

Now what does all this indicate about the kind of high schools that will be viable in the future? I've suggested that today's public high schools are less viable than those of the past because of changes in the family, not because of changes in the school. I've also suggested that it is only in special circumstances of the sort that are found surrounding some religiously grounded schools that the viability of today's schools remains relatively intact.

There are two quite different paths that public schools might take to reestablish their viability. The first path would be to follow the pattern of religiously grounded schools in strengthening the family's authority and replenishing the social capital that's available to students and parents. The idea is to recreate the school community, and by the school community I don't mean the community within the school, but the community that relates the school to the families outside the school.

The second path, by contrast, abolishes completely the conception that the student is under parental authority and that the school is functioning under a grant of authority from the parents. Instead, it establishes the principle that the relevant relation is directly between the school and the student—that it is the student who is an autonomous person, who is solely responsible for his or her own education.

The existence of these two paths quite obviously implies the abandonment of the current practice of assignment of children to particular institutions. Some form of parental choice is essential if parents and youth are to sort themselves into whichever of the two paths they find more desirable or appropriate.

But choice is necessary for a second reason. Given that the school is a social institution, the school-student relation should have the form of a contract—either a contract between family or student and school or a social contract among families or among students. The conception of a child assigned by the state to a particular school is a conception that was viable when the school was an outgrowth of a homogeneous community. It's no longer viable for most schools—or most students.

The best of the schools taking the first path that I described will excel not merely by concentrating on the narrow task of "education" but by extending this task to include rebuilding the community that's fallen into disrepair, by recreating the social capital that's been lost. This isn't a simple task. It involves drawing parents into school-related activities—even at the danger of seriously complicating the school's fundamental task of teaching. It involves reconnecting parents with different children so that those parents can, as a community, establish the norms that constitute the necessary social capital to support their children's educational activities.

The best of the schools following the second path, the path of autonomous student responsibility, will inevitably be boarding schools. Workable examples of the second path exist within the public school system as well as outside it. (I have in mind, for instance, the two North Carolina Governor's Schools.) It's possible, however, for a school to follow both of these paths: to attempt to build up its parental community, to facilitate parents regaining authority over their teenage children, but at the same time to create the conditions within the school that encourage responsibility on the part of youth themselves. If there's one single policy change on the part of a public school system that will aid both of these paths, it's the institution of a system of explicit choice among schools, a change which gives principals, teachers, students and parents greater responsibility for building a well-functioning school.

Synthesis of Research on Schools of Choice
Mary Anne Raywid

Thousands of secondary-level alternative schools have been found to improve student attendance, attitude, and involvement. Their impact on achievement is less clear, but the available evidence is positive.

Among the educational innovations introduced during the 1960s, alternatives—or schools of choice—have proved one of the most durable and are increasingly finding support from research. This support may be one reason why schools of choice continue to proliferate.

When looking at the research on schools of choice, it is necessary to understand that it is multifaceted. This is because schools of choice are multifaceted: they are not a curricular or an instructional or an organizational proposal, but all of these in combination. Since both interest and explanations of success have focused as often on the organizational features of alternative schools as on their programs, this review includes both.

A recent survey located 2,500 secondary-level alternative schools, but the estimated national total is several times this number (Raywid, 1982). The survey omitted elementary school alternatives and there is reason to believe that large numbers of magnet schools at all levels were also omitted. Simultaneously, however, another survey identified 1,019 magnet schools and programs in the nation1 (Fleming and others, 1982). The magnet investigators concluded that one-third of our urban districts offer such programs and that they enroll up to 31 percent of each district's youngsters.

Perhaps a characterization of alternative schools is a good place to begin. We shall purposely sidestep a definition since definitional attempts have proved troublesome. What seems common to most is an emphasis on choice, on responsiveness, on broadly construed educational aims, and on alternatives as grassroots or "home grown" programs (Deal, 1975; Smith and others, 1976; Parrett, 1981). It may be impossible to establish definitional accord, but it is possible to identify a series of characteristics common to most alternatives, albeit not all:

1. The alternative constitutes a distinct and identifiable administrative unit,

with its own personnel and program. Moreover, substantial effort is likely to be addressed to creating a strong sense of affiliation with the unit.

2. Structures and processes generative of school climate are held important and receive considerable attention within the unit.

3. Students as well as staff enter the alternative as a matter of choice rather than assignment.

4. The alternative is designed to respond to particular needs, desires, or interests not otherwise met in local schools, resulting in a program that is distinctly different from that of other schools in the area.

5. The impetus to launching the alternative, as well as its design, comes from one or more of the groups to be most immediately affected by the program: teachers, students, and parents.

6. Alternative schools generally address a broader range of student development than just the cognitive or academic. Typically, the sort of person the learner is becoming is a matter of first concern.

Many view magnet schools simply as alternatives developed to the purpose of desegregation. So viewed, it seems clear that they are currently the largest subtype of schools of choice. And they also seem to differ from the parent group in some important ways. The 1982 magnet school survey (Fleming and others) found that these programs are designed to "promote desegregation; develop an image of a 'high quality' public education; provide unique (or alternative) curricula or educational structures; retain public school students and draw nonpublic school students." The survey also found that, unlike other types of alternatives, magnets are located almost exclusively in large school districts or urban centers. Like other alternatives, they may consist of separate schools or schools-within-schools.

Organizational Forms and Structures

Schools of choice differ as to organizational type, although most are small in relation to conventional schools. Over half have fewer than 100 students, and 69 percent enroll fewer than 200 (Raywid, 1982). Some alternatives occupy the entire school building in which they are housed, while other smaller programs enjoy a comparable separateness by being placed in storefronts or other small quarters. Some are schools-within-schools, usually assigned a limited contiguous set of rooms within the comprehensive high school. During the early 70s, a number of comprehensive high schools were transformed into sets of mini-schools, with Quincy High School in Illinois and Haaren High in New York being two of the better known. Individual schools-within-schools and mini-schools have both been successful, but their main challenge seems to lie in meeting two particular conditions of success: (1) enough separateness to sustain a distinct climate and ethos, and (2) enough autonomy so that staff can develop and implement their own vision of schooling (Raywid, 1982; Wehlage and others, 1982).

There are numerous types of alternatives in addition to magnets—learning centers, continuation schools, schools without walls, street academies—each identifiable in terms of a particular student target group or a particular type of program. Not since the mid-70s have alternatives been associated with any specific ideological tendencies. Many of the early public schools of choice tended toward the informality and unstructured quality of free or open schools; but as early as 1973, some California parents began to assert that schools of choice ought to include some that are more conservative than the usual, as well as those which are less so. Thus, alternatives came to run the ideological gamut in education, ranging from relatively free schools to fundamentalist types, with even a military academy or two.

Alternatives are found at all school levels, K-12, although there are probably more at the secondary than at the elementary level. The situation appears to be reversed with magnet schools, with 59 percent at the elementary level (Fleming and others, 1982) Elementary school alternatives, including magnets, are most likely to define themselves in terms of a particular pedagogical style, such as open, basics, or Montessori. High school magnets tend to define themselves according to curricular specialities, while most other high school level alternatives seem to focus more on climate-related features than on curriculum. For instance, in the recent alternatives survey, 63 percent of respondents indicated that their foremost point of departure from other schools lay in interpersonal relationships within the school, rather than in curricular distinctiveness (Raywid, 1982)

Internally, the more conservative alternatives have tended to depart very little in structural terms from conventional schools (Zusman and Guthrie, n.d.) And magnet schools have sometimes focused on modifying little but their curricular orientation (Fleming and others, 1982). Other alternatives, however, have pioneered some novel organizational forms and have attracted considerable research attention by virtue of that. Perhaps one of their greatest, though less commonly recognized, contributions was to institutionalize a means for introducing variety into school systems. In the language of David Tyack (1974), alternatives represent a clear departure from the "one best system" approach that undergirded public schooling throughout the century. They presuppose, that is, that there is no one best way of educating all youngsters; instead, different learner needs and parent preferences call for a variety of educations. Alternative schools came to represent the mechanism for introducing departures—the means of institutionalizing diversity within a system highly resistant to novelty and change (Metz, 1981; Warren, 1978). They were also recognized by some as a means whereby school systems could inform, as well as reform, themselves: the demand for a new alternative would serve as an important indicator of community needs and interests, as would underenrollment in an existing option.

At least some alternatives modeled arrangements that have been elaborated as school-based or site-based management and budgeting plans. Schools of choice provided early opportunities to see what happens when typical central district control patterns are relaxed and greater control reverts to the individual school level (Duke, 1976; Nirenberg, 1977; Rand, 1981). They have also facilitated study of novel social control arrangements (Metz, 1978; Swidler, 1979); of human interaction patterns in nonbureaucratic institutions (Argyris 1974; Wilson, 1976); and of the impacts of school structure on both program (Gracey, 1972), and behavior (Gitlin, 1981).

Organizational Processes

Schools of choice are noticeably different from conventional schools with respect to their feel and flavor. They elicit quite different responses and behavior from the human beings within them— and a considerable amount of organizational research has sought to explain that and identify its elements. A number of aspects of the way alternatives are put together and operate daily have been singled out as major contributors to their unique climates.

Many analysts have pointed to the importance of choice in this regard (deCharms, 1977; Fantini, 1973; Grant, 1981). It not only provides an initial advantage to the chooser, but it serves to heighten one's investment in what has been chosen (Erickson, 1982; Nault, 1975-76). The choice arrangement also has the advantage of yielding a group of human beings who are similar or united in some educationally significant way. They are agreed upon a particular type of educational mission or environment. Thus, collectively the chosen constitute a more coherent group than do the students, staff, and parents of a comprehensive high school deliberately planned to bring all preferences and persuasions under a common roof. The importance of this likemindedness and cohesion have been underscored recently in both the private school literature (Erickson, 1982; Grant, 1981) and in the effective schools research (Rutter, 1979; Schneider, 1982-83).

Analysts have often named smallness as a key ingredient of the type of environment alternatives provide. Where numbers are limited, it is possible to run schools in such ways that the presence of thousands simply renders out of the question. One of the consequences of smallness is, of course, that everyone knows everyone else—an important ingredient of the personalization discussed below. Another consequence is that the limited number of staff make bureaucratic controls, with their tiers of formal authority, unnecessary. Limited numbers also make bureaucracy's elaborate divisions of labor impossible, and as a result, the responsibilities and prerogatives of everyone within an alternative school are likely to be much broader than in a conventional school. This means that the roles of both staff and students differ notably in schools of choice, and tend to be more expanded and diffuse—for instance, with teachers sharing administrative and counseling functions, and students and administrators sharing in more typical teaching roles.

As this suggests, the social order of schools of choice differs considerably from that in other schools, and is typically maintained in quite different ways (Metz, 1978; Swidler, 1979). Staff as well as students share a sense of substantial autonomy. Teachers feel they exert considerable control over their own programs, and students feel much less like pawns than in other schools (deCharms, 1977; Gladstone and Levin, 1982). The experience of autonomy is important since feelings of control over one's own fate are associated with a sense of ownership and affiliation; with teacher satisfaction (Wehlage, 1982); and, in the case of students, with educational achievement (Coleman, 1966). But the reason for the autonomy feelings is not always apparent, since alternatives students sometimes report such feelings even though their teachers describe the program as highly structured!

A number of early alternative schools sought to function as participatory democracies, with students and staff reaching decisions together in town meetings (Miller, n.d.). There are probably fewer alternatives making just that sort of attempt today (Raywid, 1982), yet students in schools of choice nevertheless often reflect a strong sense of power. This may stem from several causes. First, alternatives, as smaller organizations have less need for restricting students and hence have fewer rules and regulations (Duke and Perry, 1978). And many tend to permit a considerable amount of freedom with respect to clothes, language, and personal style. Second, students do retain the considerable final power to opt out if they are sufficiently dissatisfied. This right alone tends to make for a community of civility and respectful interaction. Third, as is commonly reported by youngsters who have rejected conventional schools, alternatives differ most by virtue of their "caring" teachers. Where teachers are so perceived, and relationships are marked by trust, formal enfranchisement may appear less vital to having one's concerns taken into consideration.

As the above suggests, the climate and the culture or ethos of schools of choice differ considerably from that of other schools. As Erickson (1982) noted, it is the difference between Gesellschaft and Gemeinschaft—between a formally constituted group held together by regulations, and a genuine community bound by common, mutual sentiments and understandings.

These distinctive elements in the climate of schools of choice seem closely tied to the remarkable levels of satisfaction of both students and their parents. Student attitudes toward school are widely reported to change for the better in alternative schools (Barr and others, 1977; Doob, 1977; Duke and Muzio, 1978), and the attitudes of parents toward these schools is consistently reported as unusually positive (Fleming and others, 1982; Metz, 1981). What is more, post-graduation surveys of former students of the alternative school suggest that they continue to regard it very positively, as a place where they received help that has proved relevant and adequate to their post-high school pursuits (Nathan, 1981; Phillips, 1977).

Goals

Most schools of choice demonstrate concern with multiple sorts of development in their students, not solely with cognitive growth or intellectual achievement. Although conventional practice in public education narrows the school's focus quite sharply from 1st to 12th grade—with the elementary school's interest in "the whole child" giving way to the high school's concern primarily with the academic—alternative schools continue to acknowledge and actively foster various kinds of student growth over this entire period. Even in back-to-basics, or fundamentalist alternatives initiated for more intense concentration on the academic, there is much explicit concern with molding character; that is, with shaping values, pervasive dispositions, and other personal characteristics (Zusman and Guthrie, n.d.).

The broad concern with the sort of person each youngster is becoming yields several tendencies common to many schools of choice. One is a program consciously designed to abet social growth and such personal development as decision-making ability, moral maturity, and self-knowledge. The pursuit of such goals may be integrated with more traditional learning or stand as separate activities. Either way, such development tends to be viewed as an integral part of the school's mission.

A second consequence of the alternative school's developmental orientation is often a stronger preoccupation with realizing individual potential than with achievement in relation to group norms. This does not mean an indifference to standards; many alternative school students report working far harder in the alternative than ever before. It does mean, however, that these standards are not likely to be imposed or regulated by standardized tests.

A third tremendously important consequence of the developmental orientation of many schools of choice is the personalization it yields, Quite simply, systematic efforts to help someone grow require extensive knowledge of that individual. This requisite alone calls for a personalized education in the sense that students must become known as individual human beings to school staff. They cannot remain unidimensional consumers of instruction. Furthermore, activities then built on this knowledge yield the responsiveness to individuals that developmental purposes require. Thus it is no accident that teachers and students both find alternative schools uniquely successful at meeting student needs (Gregory and Smith, 1983). This personalization feature seems strongly associated with the appeal of schools of choice to students, and to parents and teachers as well. It may also be an important factor in the other forms of success achieved by these schools.

Instructional Methods

Alternative school staff report instructional methods to be one of their main points of departure from conventional school practice (Raywid, 1982) and several studies have established differences in this regard (Baker, 1976; Zahorik, 1980). There is also evidence, however, that instructional practices in alternative schools do not differ very extensively from the methods of other schools. Yet, interestingly, both teachers and students in alternatives think that they do (Parrett, 1981). What accounts for this discrepancy? One reason may be that despite the group instruction often found in schools of choice, they manage considerable flexibility and have devised ways to respond to student needs and interests that are unshared. Perhaps the most typical mechanism is independent study.

There is wide variety in the form of such study, and it is a major means of providing the adaptiveness to individuals that participants again and again attribute to alternative schools. Independent study arrangements enable individual students to pursue topics or projects in which only they may be interested, such as participating in an archeological dig, designing a computer program, or investigating the case for Atlantis.

Independent study arrangements also permit the pursuit of traditional content at levels more advanced than those at which others are working, and hence where numbers do not warrant offering a course. At the same time, independent study may be enabling other youngsters to pursue remedial work, often in the form of contracts specifying assignments that differ from student to student. Collectively, these diverse arrangements may constitute the major device for "individualizing" instruction in schools of choice (Raywid, 1982).

One of the most prominent forms of independent study in both magnet and other schools of choice is experiential learning (Fleming and others, 1982; Smith and others, 1976). Some involve students primarily in learning through direct observation; for instance, in learning about the judicial system's operation through sustained courtroom visits. Probably more have stressed participation, and assign youngsters to internships and other arrangements for learning about such things as municipal processes, or industries and careers, by actually participating in them. Still other alternatives feature service learning, enabling students to learn from the experience of providing a needed service to other human beings. Helping in hospitals and nursing homes, aiding peers and younger children in classrooms, lobbying, doing research for a lawmaker, or staffing crisis centers are frequent forms of experiential learning.

This sort of learning is widely recognized to possess very distinct advantages. James Coleman (1972) declared it is what youngsters need most, growing up in an "information-rich, action-poor" society. There is substantial evidence that experiential learning stimulates moral development, enhances self-esteem, expands the interest of adolescents in social problems and their inclinations toward community involvement, and increases a sense of social and personal responsibility (Conrad and Hedin, 1982; Hedin, 1983).

Recent studies are also providing increasingly conclusive demonstration of the efficacy of experiential learning in relation to traditional academic content. For example, a study comparing the gains of experiential and classroom learners in a high school biology course found the action learners scoring significantly higher (Agnew, 1982). Peer tutoring investigations yield the most extensive evidence in this regard, consistently finding that the experience of tutoring yields significant academic gains for the tutor. Moreover, consistent with the idea of experiential learning, the tutored—who, of course, are not involved in action learning or exploring new roles, but just in being taught by a different teacher—show more modest academic gains than do the tutors (Hedin, 1983). There is also evidence that experiential learning contributes to higher-level mental processes, including problem-solving ability and complexity of thought, as well as to the gain of specific content.

Curriculum

In magnet or specialty high schools, curricular distinctiveness is the school's most distinguishing feature. According to Fleming and others (1982), the arts are the most prevalent concentration, with humanities or social sciences coming second, and vocational or career orientations tying with intensified academic focus for third. At the elementary level, basic skills magnets predominate, with Montessori or individualized learning programs coming second, and arts third.

As noted earlier, schools identifying themselves as "alternatives" are less likely to be marked by a particular curricular focus than by other things—a pedagogical style or a particular school climate. Nevertheless, some curricular tendencies are identifiable. Since staff within alternative schools have considerable control of content (Raywid, 1982), they often develop their own curricula. There is also evidence that teachers in alternatives frequently prefer to organize content according to themes rather than to leave it separated by disciplines. Thus themes such as "Our Town," "The Good Life," or "Power" may serve as integrating concepts or articulating ideas drawing on content from a number of different disciplines. At the elementary level, for instance, one well-known alternative named The Zoo School uses animal and environmental themes in the presentation and pursuit of a full range of learnings.

Although the choosing or devising of curriculum is a wide-spread practice in alternative schools, there are several curricular programs or approaches that have been adopted and adapted by a number of alternatives. One is the Foxfire approach to teaching English and history (and sometimes other subjects) by combining experiential and classroom learning and simultaneously building a bridge between school and community. Using cultural journalism techniques, students learn history, or lore and legends, or skills, from community residents, and compile these in journals or magazines (Sitton, 1980). Another widely used curricular approach has been the Walkabout idea, sometimes known as Challenge Education, which organizes the curriculum around a specified set of challenges, the full meeting of which demonstrates one's readiness to graduate. This is a program aimed at providing a better transition from the dependency of adolescence to the independence and self-responsibility of adulthood Still another curricular emphasis has been that of the "Just Community" schools inspired by the moral development theory of Lawrence Kohlberg. Just Community alternatives emphasize reasoning related to moral situations, as well as student participation in decision making (Kuhmerker, 1981). As popular as these particular examples have been, however, and as often used for inspiration and a source of ideas, it appears that most schools of choice develop their own curricula.

The People in Alternatives and How They are Affected

Although 73 percent of 1982 survey respondents indicated that their districts associate alternatives with all kinds of students (Raywid), a large number of schools of choice have been established to deal with groups posing special problems. The early success of a number of alternatives probably made it inevitable that they would be embraced as solutions for the most educationally challenging groups (the turned-off, disruptive, underachieving, dropout-prone), as well as the means for resolving wider social problems (segregation, crime youth, unemployment). Thus, today there are large numbers of alternatives targeted for dealing with particular groups and problems, as well as others reflecting a representative cross-section of local youngsters. Programs targeted for disruptive youngsters, underachievers, dropouts, and other varieties of "at risk" youngsters have provided instances of impressive success. They appear particularly effective at improving student attitudes toward school and learning (Foley and McConnaughy, 1982; Mann and Gold, 1980), self-concept and self-esteem (Arnove and Strout, 1978), attendance (Foley and McConnaughy, 1982; Wehlage, 1982), and behavior (Berger, 1974; Duke and Perry, 1978; Wehlage, 1982). They also lead to greater academic accomplishment on the part of those students variously known as "marginal," "resistant," and simply "at risk" (Arnove and Strout, 1978; Foley and McConnaughy, 1982).

The evidence suggests that similar benefits accrue also to quite different kinds of students in alternatives not targeted for "special needs" groups. Average and above-average students also profit from schools of choice. However, fewer investigations and comparative studies have been undertaken in these kinds of schools of choice and indeed, almost all the evidence, regarding impacts comes from individual program evaluations. There have, however, been three careful analyses of multiple evaluations (Barr and others, 1977; Doob, 1977; Duke and Muzio, 1978), and based on these it seems clear that the attitudes of students toward themselves and toward school are markedly enhanced in the alternative setting. Attendance and school involvement increase, and dropout rates decline. Higher grade-point averages and test scores, and gains in math and reading levels are common, although academic impacts are less clear and consistent in these evaluations than are other sorts of outcomes. The academic evidence seems positive, even though it remains tentative and somewhat scant.

In contrast to aggregate studies of many schools—which average out and thus obscure dramatic accomplishment along with dismal failure—there is now at least one individual school study with a highly credible and extensive comparative base. It demonstrates remarkable academic success. It was done in Pennsylvania where a state-administered quality assessment program not only yields statewide percentile rankings, but also assesses achievement levels in relation to reasonable expectations for a particular school. In the spring of 1982, the Alternative Program in State College ranked at the 99th percentile for its students' performance in reading, writing, math, knowledge of law and government, and analytic thinking. The percentile fell to 90 on humanities and science, but returned to the 99 level with respect to student self-esteem, interest in school and learning, understanding of others, sense of societal responsibility, and appreciation of human accomplishment. In eight of these 11 measures of school quality, the Alternative Program scored above what the state deemed appropriate expectations.2

There is no way to know at this point how typical such success may someday be found to be. The evidence is already clear enough that not all alternative schools are successful—so schools of choice are not the elusive model guaranteeing success under any and all circumstances. But perhaps subsequent research will further clarify the requisites of success and identify the pitfalls to avoid.

Meanwhile, however, there is one more group that needs attention in our review of the effects of schools of choice: this is their teachers, for there is evidence of considerable impact of alternatives on those who work within them. A number of the findings already mentioned would predict that such schools are pleasant places to be: the absence of discipline problems and the trust of students augur less adolescent-adult conflict as the tussle between student and staff subcultures evaporates. Furthermore, the amount of autonomy teachers enjoy and the unusual control over their own programs would suggest distinct professional rewards. Such predictions are borne out. Alternative school teachers report unusually high levels of satisfaction (Gladstone and Levin, 1982; Nirenberg, 1977), which they attribute to increased collegiality, and to greater professional autonomy and personal agency in their work. Although many report working harder in the alternative than in their previous school, morale is clearly enhanced.

The benefits to the school of such teacher satisfaction are reported by one researcher to fulfill the organizational idealist's dream, wherein staff become sufficiently identified with the school to find personal fulfillment, or self-actualization, in doing its work (Nirenberg, 1977).

Conclusion

It would appear, then, that schools of choice offer heightened satisfactions to the several groups most immediately associated with them: staff, students, and parents. They also claim other advantages with respect to climate and productivity. Although not all such schools succeed, the number of positive instances brings real promise to the diversification and choice arrangement reviewed here. Challenges and reservation that have been expressed have not been reviewed, since these have not been subjected to systematic investigation and thus remain speculative. But commentators and observers have wondered whether the diversification would prove culturally divisive (Broudy, 1973), whether it would increase social class isolation (Arnove and Strout, 1978), whether it would yield "skimming and dumping" (removal of the most desirable students from neighborhood schools, and concentration of the least desirable in separate programs), and whether it would in consequence diminish the quality of non-choice schools (Fleming and others, 1982). Investigation of these questions is certainly needed, along with much more extensive study of the correlates of success in schools of choice. We need much more of that kind of evidence, which will help practitioners to decide just which features are vital for such schools and which can and should be omitted.

[1]Definitions are cloudy, so that whether magnets are a first cousin to alternative, or a variety of alternative, or vice versa—may depend on no more than

who happens to be speaking. Here, we shall view magnets as one type of alternative and we shall use "alternatives" and "schools of choice" synonymously. This makes for fairly broad and inclusive usage, but it does exclude the punitive programs that in the South are called alternatives.

2Unpublished study. For further information, contact Rick Lear, Director, Alternative Program, 411 S. Fraser Street, State College, PA 16801.

References

Agnew, J. C. "Better Education Through Application." *Synergist* (Winter 1982): 44-48.

Argyris, Chris. "Alternative Schools: A Behavioral Analysis." *Teachers College Record* (May 1974): 429-452.

Arnove, Robert, and Strout, Toby. *Alternative Schools for Disruptive Youth.* Prepared for the National Institute of Education, Grants P-7—0217 and P-77—0254 (September 1978).

Baker, Thomas. "An Investigation of Teachers and Students Perceptions of Instructional Practices in Selected Conventional and Alternative Public Schools." Unpublished dissertation, Indiana University, 1976.

Barr, Robert; Colston, Bruce; Parrett, William. "The Effectiveness of Alternative Public Schools: An Analysis of Six School Evaluations." *Viewpoint* (July 1977): 1-30.

Berger, Michael. Violence in the Schools. Bloomington, Ind.: *Phi Delta Kappan*, 1974.

Broudy, Harry. "Educational Alternatives—Why Not? Why Not" *Phi Delta Kappan* (March 1973): 438-440.

Center for New Schools, "Some Conclusions and Questions About Decision-Making in Alternative Secondary Schools." In *Alternative Schools.* Edited by T. Deal and R. Nolan. (Chicago: Nelson-Hall, 1978, pp. 301-306.

Coleman, James. *Equality of Educational Opportunity.* Washington: Government Printing Office, 1966.

Coleman, James S. "The Children Have Outgrown the Schools." *Psychology Today* (February 1972): 72-75.

Conrad, Dave, and Hedin, Diane. "National Assessment of Experiential Education: Summary and Implications." *Journal of Experiential Education* 4 (1982): 6-20.

Deal, Terrence. "An Organizational Explanation of the Failure of Alternative Secondary Schools." *Educational Researcher* (April 1975): 10-16.

deCharms, Richard. "Pawn or Origin? Enhancing Motivation in Disaffected Youth." *Educational Leadership* (March 1977): 444-448.

Doob, Heather. *Evaluations of Alternative Schools.* Arlington, Va: Educational Research Service. 1977.

Duke, Daniel Linden. "Challenge to Bureaucracy: The Contemporary Alternative School." *Journal of Educational Thought* (May 1976:34-48.

Duke, Daniel Linden, and Muzio, Irene. "How Effective Are Alternative Schools? A Review of Recent Evaluations and Reports." *Teachers College Record* (February 1978): 461-483.

Duke, Daniel Linden, and Perry, Cheryl. "Can Alternative Schools Succeed Where Benjamin Spock, Spiro Agnew, and B. F. Skinner Have Failed?"

Adolescence (Fall, 1978): 375-395;.

Erickson, Don. The British Columbia Story: Antecedents and *Consequences of Aid to Private Schools*. Los Angeles: Institute for the Study of Private Schools, 1982.

Fantini, Mario. *Public Schools of Choice*. New York: Simon and Schuster, 1973.

Fleming, Patricia; Blank, Rolf; and others. *Survey of Magnet Schools: Interim Report*. Washington James H. Lowry and Associates, September 1982.

Foley, Eileen M., and McConnaughy, Susan. *Towards School Improvement: Lessons from Alternative High Schools*. New York Public Education Association, 1982.

Gitlin, Andrew. "School Structure Affects Teachers." *Educational Horizons* (Summer 1981): 173-178.

Gladstone, F., and Levin, Malcolm. *Public Alternative School Teacher Study*. Toronto: Ontario Institute of Educational Studies, Mimeo, 1982.

Gracey, Harry L. Curriculum or Craftsmanship. *Elementary School Teachers in a Bureaucratic System*. Chicago: University of Chicago Press, 1972.

Grant, Gerald. "The Character of Education and the Education of Character" Daedalus (Summer 1981): 135, 149.

Gregory, Thomas, and Smith, Gerald. "Differences Between Alternative and Conventional Schools in Meeting Students' Needs." Paper presented to the American Educational Research Association, Montreal,April 11, 1983. Mimeo, 16 pp.

Hedin, Diane. "The Impact of Experiential Learning on Academic Learning: A Summary of the Theoretical Foundations and Review of Recent Research." Mimeo, n.d. (1983).

Kuhmerker, Lisa, ed. *Moral Education Forum* (Winter 1981) (Issue devoted largely to Just Community Schools).

Mann, David W., and Gold, Martin. *Alternative Schools for Disruptive Secondary Students: Testing a Theory of School Processes, Students' Responses, and Outcome Behaviors*. Institute for Social Research, University of Michigan, December 1980.

Metz, Mary H. *Classrooms and Corridors: The Crisis of Authority in Desegrated Secondary Schools*. Berkeley: University of California Press, 1978.

Metz, Mary H. "Magnet Schools in Their Organizational and Political Context." Paper presented at the American Sociological Association, Toronto, August 23-28, 1981.

Miller, Lynne. "Patterns of Decision Making in Public Alternative Schools." National Alternative Schools Program, University of Massachusetts, n.d. (1974).

Nathan, Joe. Attitudes Toward High School Education Held by Graduates of a Traditional and an Alternative Public School in St. Paul, Minnesota. Unpublished dissertation, University of Minnesota, 1981.

Nault, Richard. "School Affiliation and Student Commitments," *Administrator's Notebook*. Chicago Midwest Administration Center, University of Chicago, 1975-76.

Nault, Richard, and Uchitelle, Susan. "School Choice in the Public Sector: A Case Study of Parental Decision Making." Edited by Michael E. Manley-Cuimir. In *Family Choice in Schooling*. Lexington, Mass: D. C. Health, 1982, pp. 85-98.

Nirenberg, John. "A Comparison of the Management Systems of Traditional and Alternative Public High Schools." *Educational Administration Quarterly* (Winter 1977): 86-104.

Parrett, William. "Alternative Schools: What's Really Happening in the Classrooms." Paper presented to the American Educational Research Association, Los Angeles, April, 1981. Mimeo, 40 pp.

Phillips, Gary. Descriptive Study of the Impact of a High School Alternative Learning Environment on Post High School Lives by a Group of Resistant Learners. Unpublished dissertation, Ball State University, 1977.

Raywid, Mary Anne. *The Current Status of Schools of Choice in Public Secondary Education.* Hempstead, N.Y. Project on Alternatives in Education, Hofstra University, 1982.

Rutter, Michael, and others. *Fifteen Thousand Hours: Secondary Schools and Their Effects on Children.* Cambridge: Harvard University Press, 1979.

Schneider, Joseph. "Stop the Bandwagon, We Want to Get Off." *R & D Report* (Winter 1982-83): 7-11.

Sitton, Thad. "Bridging the School-Community Gap: The Lessons of Foxfire." Educational Leadership (December 1980): 248-250.

Smith, Vernon; Barr, Robert; and Burke, Daniel. Alternatives in Education. Bloomington, Ind.: Phi Delta Kappa, 1976.

A Study of Alternatives in American Education, Vol. Vll: Conclusions and Policy Implications. Santa Monica: The Rand Corporation, August 1981.

Swidler, Ann. *Organization Without Authority: Dilemmas of Social Control in Free Schools.* Cambridge: Harvard University Press, 1979

Tyack, David B. *The One Best System.* Cambridge: Harvard University Press,, 1974.

Warren, Constancia. "The Magnet School Boom: Implications for Desegregation." *Equal Opportunity Review*, ERIC Clearinghouse on Urban Education. Columbia: Teachers College, Spring 1978.

Wehlage, Gary, and others. *Effective Programs for the Marginal High School Student.* Madison: University of Wisconsin Center for Education Research, 1982.

Wilson, Stephen. "You Can Talk to Teachers: Student-Teacher Relations In an Alternative High School." *Teachers College Record* (September l976): 77-100.

Zahorik, John. "Teaching Practices and Beliefs in Elementary Specialty Schools." *Elementary School Journal* (January 1980): 145-57.

Zusman, Ami, and Guthrie, James W. "Back to Basics: The 'New' Tradition in Public High Schools?" Berkeley: University of California, Mimeo, n.d.

Highlights from Research on Schools of Choice

- For all types of students, from the neediest to the most outstanding, alternatives seem to produce significant growth and achievement: cognitive, social, and affective.
- Both attendance and student behavior improve in schools of choice.
- Alternative schools prove highly attractive to those who are associated with them—staff, students, and parents. In various ways, all three groups show unusual satisfaction and approval rates.
- The success of alternative schools is variously attributed to the benefits of smallness, choice, climates, and degree of staff autonomy.
- Alternatives manage to "personalize" the school environment and to make it a genuine community of individuals.
- The two instructional modes most distinctive of alternative schools are independent study and experiential learning.
- Alternatives have institutionalized diversity. They exist in varying types and appear to be a well-established component of school districts across the country.

Controlled Choice in
Massachusetts Public Schools

Charles L. Glenn

The debate over school choice—the hottest item on the American education-reform agenda—has unfortunately generated more heat than light. Endorsed by presidents Reagan and Bush, by the nation's governors, and by many business leaders, school choice is strongly resisted by the National Education Association, by many civil rights leaders, and by most public educators. Supporters and opponents alike spin abstract scenarios in which choice will either solve the ills of American education or send it into a rapid decline. They would do better to consider the actual results of systems of parental choice that already function in other nations—and in ten Massachusetts cities.

The great majority of American schoolchildren are assigned to particular public schools on the basis of where their parents can afford to live. What choice of schools exists (and there is actually a great deal) is largely exercised by middle-class parents in choosing a neighborhood or suburban community. Otherwise, educational choice tends to exist only for children with handicaps or learning disabilities. While educators readily acknowledge that not every school will meet the distinctive needs of these pupils, somehow they generally consider it illegitimate to take educational considerations into account in deciding which school will be best for other children. Similarly, while teachers and principals constantly lament parents' failure to support the work of the schools, the same professionals often resist proposals that parents be allowed to select a school that they can support wholeheartedly.

Opponents of parental choice of schools have primarily argued that it will produce new inequities in educational opportunity, "winners and losers." The more sophisticated parents and the more academically able students will take advantage of school choice by leaving their urban neighborhood schools, the argument typically goes with the inevitable result that those left behind will be victims of educational neglect.

This argument is factually wrong in two ways: the present system of residence-based assignments has by no means made winners of urban and minority children, and there is ample evidence that parental choice need not lead to winners and losers, as we will see when we look at the evidence from Massachusetts.

Nonetheless, the argument is morally correct in this sense: if parental choice is to gain general acceptance, it must be shown to improve the quality of education available to all students. In arguing for the benefits of choice, it is not enough to point to the successes of some urban magnet schools—if this success comes at the expense of other schools and the pupils who must attend them.

While some supporters of choice accept inequitable outcomes with a certain complacency, choice plans that have been successfully implemented seek to protect equal access and, when relevant, to further desegregation.

The most consistent of these approaches is "controlled choice," whereby attendance areas for individual schools are abolished and all public school pupils are enrolled on the basis of choice. The public schools attended by more than 145,000 Massachusetts students now operate under this system. Unlike "winner-take-all, devil-take-the-hindmost" strategies of competition among schools, the Massachusetts system of controlled choice seeks to provide comparable benefits to all pupils. It also aims to increase the effective participation of low-income and minority children—and their parents—in the educational process, while stimulating every school (not just a few magnet schools) to become more effective. The usual opponents of controlled choice have been joined by more libertarian critics; the latter argue that any controls established in the name of equity fatally damage the very principle of the free market, give the misleading impression that parents have real options, and prevent fundamental school improvements.

A careful examination of the actual functioning and results of controlled choice in Massachusetts should lay these concerns to rest. The Massachusetts experience demonstrates that placing restrictions on choice to promote integration does not deprive it of its liberating power. It should also reassure those who see choice as a menacing elevation of private over public concerns. Letting parents choose is a policy that demonstrably works when well designed; it harms neither individual interests nor the common weal.

The flaws of magnet schools

Contemporary experiments with choice grew out of the creation of magnet schools that were launched to attract white students to inner-city schools. Suddenly, educational quality and innovation (at least in the magnet schools) became essential if school systems—and elected officials—were to avoid the controversy associated with mandatory desegregation. In the process, the belief that a single formula for schooling was best for every student received a blow

from which it shows no signs of recovering.

Massachusetts, which in 1965 had been the first state to adopt legislation calling for racial balance in its schools, repealed some of its enforcement provisions in 1974, substituting a program to encourage the development of magnet schools to promote desegregation. Funded initially at $2 million, the annual appropriation quickly grew to over $5 million, together with 90 percent of the cost of new facilities—nearly $500 million has been approved so far—and millions more in transportation necessary to operate magnet schools.

But despite the considerable success of magnet schools, it began to be clear that they had negative side effects. While expanding parents' opportunity to choose, magnet schools also increase the number of disappointed applicants and thus of children assigned involuntarily. Typically the schools have several times as many applicants as they can accept, so that hopes are raised only to be disappointed. Since magnet schools, limited in their capacity, cannot provide choice for all, parents have been placed in the position of having to wait all night to register their children for scarce magnet-school seats. In Springfield, Massachusetts, only 37 percent of magnet-school applicants could be accommodated this

year, while Worcester could accept only 600 of 1,700 applicants to a new citywide magnet school.

By definition intended to be more attractive than other schools, and often given additional resources and a freedom to be distinctive that other schools do not enjoy, magnets drain energetic and motivated staff and parents as well as funding from non-magnet schools. In many communities, though not in Massachusetts, magnet schools are also allowed to screen and select among applicants: thus they leave other schools with the more troublesome and less academically able students.

In addition, since the focus has been upon achieving a racially integrated enrollment at the individual magnet school rather than in the system as a whole, the effect may be to make other schools even more segregated. The federal magnet-school assistance program continues to operate under policies that force school systems "intentionally [to] maintain 100 percent minority schools in order to keep up white enrollment in their federally funded magnets," according to one recent Education Week article. In Chicago and other large cities that have relied primarily upon magnet schools to meet their desegregation obligations, many schools remain completely segregated.

How controlled choice works

In recent years, out of concern for the growing gap between magnet schools and other schools, Massachusetts cities have been encouraged to go beyond simply providing magnet schools by implementing system-wide controlled choice.

Controlled choice works like this: automatic assignment of pupils to schools on the basis of where they live is abolished, and the parents of children new to the school system or moving to the next level of schooling receive information and (if they wish) counseling about all options before indicating preferences. Then assignments are made, satisfying these preferences so far as is consistent with available capacities and local policies and requirements. For example, pupils living within a specified distance of a school may be given preferential access to the available seats, thus disadvantaging (though not excluding absolutely) those who live at a distance. Similarly, race- or gender-balance criteria may be applied. Such policy decisions vary from plan to plan. Though it would he incorrect to suggest that controlled choice must necessarily be linked to desegregation, it does constitute a powerful means of achieving desegregation when that is required.

Controlled choice is intended to accomplish four objectives:

(1) To give all pupils in a community (or in a geographical section of a larger city) equal access to every public school, regardless of where their families can afford to live;

(2) to involve all parents (not just the most sophisticated) in making informed decisions about where their children will go to school;

(3) to create pressure for the improvement, over time, of every school through

the elimination of guaranteed enrollment on the basis of residence; and

(4) where necessary, to achieve racial desegregation of every school with as few mandatory assignments as possible.

Ten Massachusetts cities, including Boston, Cambridge, and Chelsea, are implementing assignment plans based upon universal controlled choice. These ten school systems enroll over 145,000 pupils, 18 percent of Massachusetts's public school population. Six other Massachusetts cities, enrolling more than 60,000 students, have chosen to retain assignment plans driven by geography as well as by parental choice, and to seek to achieve desegregation by shifting programs from one school to another and by developing magnet schools. Choice is a major factor in school assignments in these communities as well, with up to a third of the newly enrolling elementary pupils in non-neighborhood schools. Thus over 200,000 students altogether (25 percent of the state's public school enrollment) attend schools in communities that are actively encouraging parental choice.

Controlled choice removes all enrollment guarantees for schools, while providing support for program development; thus initially unpopular schools will have a chance to transform themselves. The great unanswered question, as we will see below, is whether real sanctions will be imposed upon the staff of schools that continue to fail to attract applicants.

Criticisms of choice

Most comments on choice from advocates of educational equity have been negative, centering largely on the conviction that choice inevitably hurts poor and minority children and their families. It is possible to distinguish at least seven criticisms of parental choice:

(1) Choice is often among schools that can select or track students.

(2) Choice is usually among schools that, while formally equivalent, in fact differ in quality.

(3) Parents (at least poor parents) don't really want to choose a school for their children or, alternatively, are incapable of doing so in the best interest of their children.

(4) Choice is illusory, because many parents are disappointed as a result of desegregation requirements and other restrictions.

(5) School officials, eager to create the appearance that choice is satisfactory to those affected by it, mislead parents about the options available to them.

(6) Choice will lead to all sorts of weird and divisive options, as fanatics of every stripe and/or unscrupulous entrepreneurs take advantage of choice to peddle their wares.

(7) Choice will to the contrary not lead to true diversity, because school staff lack the imagination and professionalism to create real alternatives.

In short, critics of choice have predicted the onset of all sorts of disasters. Fortunately, however, after ten years in which choice has become the primary basis for school attendance in a growing number of Massachusetts cities, there is no sign that any disasters are occurring.

The first charge—that choice involving selective schools leads to inequity—has been advanced by the Chicago-based advocacy organization Designs for Change. The group's 1989 study, *The New Improved Sorting Machine: Concerning School Choice*, looks at a number of practices in secondary education, including "high school admission, within-school tracking and grouping, and practices employed in promotion from grade to grade." Data are drawn from New York City, Chicago, Philadelphia, and Boston.

Virtually all of the evidence showing that choice leads to inequities is based upon Boston's three selective examination schools, which long predate the introduction of school choice. Boston Latin School, as the authors note, "has continued for 350 years as the premier selective admissions high school within the Boston Public Schools."

Now it is certainly possible to argue that Boston operates a two-tiered system of education, and that poor and minority students suffer disadvantages as a result. It is also possible to argue that these highly selective schools represent a lifeline for hundreds of poor but ambitious students each year, offering them an opportunity that no comprehensive urban high school would provide. Furthermore, one can support the continued existence of these options (which enroll one-fourth of the secondary students in the system), while urging that their student selection and support practices be improved. As the state official with primary responsibility for such issues, I have taken all three positions.

But the argument about whether there should be selective secondary schools in a large system is not an argument about parental choice of schools at all; parents do not "choose" Boston Latin School for their children, any more than they choose a German Gymnasium. An invitation is extended, based upon academic achievement and a standardized test, and few decline such a privilege.

The problem in Boston is that until recently most parents have believed that the examination schools provide virtually the only desirable options among public secondary schools. Those whose children are not admitted are strongly inclined, if they have the resources, to quit the system; they tend to define other high schools more by what they are not than by what they are and can offer. The solution surely, is not to eliminate the examination-school alternative through reinstituting comprehensive high schools, but to assure that all schools and programs are clearly focused, demanding, and distinctive.

As Boston's comprehensive plan for secondary education evolves, each school will develop and offer a clear educational focus, because it will have to appeal to parents to secure an enrollment. The solution to the problems caused by "choice" among Boston high schools is more real choice, not less.

Hobson's choice?

Some critics claim that there are few desirable schools in most cities, so that few if any of the options would be worth choosing. My own experience over twenty years with children in eight different Boston public schools suggests that the charge is unfair, though certainly there are schools to which I would never want to send one of my children. Because controlled choice makes it possible for children of middle-class parents to be assigned to any school in the system, it creates pressure on the inferior schools, which must either become acceptable or go out of business.

This pressure is, in fact, one of the primary benefits resulting from the institution of universal choice. We are certainly wrong to continue to operate schools that well-informed parents would not want their children to attend even if the parents whose children actually attend them do not know enough to protest.

The existence of these deplorable schools is not an argument against choice, though; after all, children have been assigned to them involuntarily all along. In addition, critics of choice are wrong to assume that the initial condition of too few acceptable options will continue indefinitely. Instead, a well-designed system of choice ensures that schools go through changes that make them more attractive.

As an example of how school selections change, analysis of first-place preferences in Boston for sixth-grade enrollment in 1989 (the first year of controlled choice in Boston) and 1990 shows that the number of relatively popular schools doubled in only the second year of controlled choice. The strong lead of a few schools was reduced as others "tried harder." On the other hand, the least popular schools attracted even fewer applicants. Three schools were closed. Others are on the danger list; if they are not strengthened after an honest effort, they will be closed and perhaps reopened "under new management."

Realistically, the goal of a choice plan cannot be to assign each student to his or her first-choice school, but controlled choice will not function as it should unless every student can be assigned to an acceptable school. This can happen only over time, as the natural pressure of choice combines with outside support to strengthen the weaker schools or—if they cannot be strengthened—to change staff or close them down. Boston's controlled-choice plan provides explicitly for a three-year period during which schools that attract fewer applicants will be helped to change their programs and images—or else.

Children attend schools that are of uneven quality; that is an unfortunate fact, and it always has been. The blame does not lie with parents' choices but with neglect and complacency on the part of educators and public officials. The power of parental choice is that schools cannot remain seriously inadequate, so long as parents are given accurate information and honest counseling.

Dumb parents, foolish choices?

Schools will not improve, of course, if the third criticism of choice—that poor parents are uninterested in or incapable of choosing good schools for their children—proves accurate.

The first half of this charge can be dismissed out of hand; state-funded parent surveys conducted in Massachusetts cities implementing school choice consistently show ten- or twenty-to-one support for school choice. As for the second half, critics like Abigail Thernstrom, writing in these pages, have argued that "academic excellence is seldom what parents chiefly value in a school. A convenient location, a particular social atmosphere, good sports facilities: these are the sorts of considerations that govern." Perhaps it would be appropriate to respond: So what!

Academic excellence is not the only aspect of education that matters. Parents (including professional educators) may care as much or more about inculcating character, creativity, and social skills. We can demand that schools—and students—be adequate, that they meet proficiency standards, but whether to seek excellence is surely a personal decision. In fact, surveys of parents and their actual choices show clearly that they do care about the quality of schooling, however they may define it. Parents may not have clear understanding of the specific theme of a school, or know how it rates on test scores, but they respond to their perceptions of quality.

Location is important; other things being equal, parents will generally choose a school near home. If they think that a more distant school is better, however, most parents will prefer it. The assumption that parents want only neighborhood schools receives little support from the pattern of school applications in cities implementing choice. This is true even when race is at issue. Among seven middle schools in Boston's East Zone, 26 percent of white pupils entering sixth grade chose the Gavin School in largely White South Boston, but 39 percent chose the McCormack School in largely black Columbia Point.

The schools selected by minority parents follow the same pattern. In Boston's North Zone, for example, 31 percent of black applicants chose the Barnes School in East Boston, an area in which few black families live, while only 10 percent chose the Dearborn School, in a part of the city populated mostly by minorities. As a parent counselor in Boston wrote me recently, "The first question asked by most students and parents [when we make suggestions] is, 'Is it a good school?' Location does make a difference to many but it is only occasionally that a convenient location is requested, but mostly a 'safe' location, and considering what is going on in Boston, we expect this to be a prominent concern."

But do parents always make wise choices? Of course not. But parents' occasional failures should not preclude their choosing schools; despite their errors, no one suggests that parents be forbidden to decide how much television their children will watch or what kinds of food they will eat. After all, if it is wrong for parents to choose schools that would harm their children, it also is wrong to assign children to those schools involuntarily. Public policy should assure that there are no truly bad choices, through some form of public licensing and oversight; it should not, however, substitute the judgment of an official for that of a parent, simply because parents do not take into account every nuance of school quality. It is not as though educators themselves agree about the characteristics of good schools.

If, as Thernstrom argues, there are "drugged parents who won't and probably can't make informed choices for their children," that is all the more reason to create systems of universal choice that create pressure to improve all schools, not just to offer magnet schools that convince middle-class parents to keep their children in the school system. After all, how do the children of negligent parents benefit when their neighborhoods alone determine which schools they attend?

The risk that a few parents will make ill-informed choices or fail to choose altogether should not carry much weight. While society is not always successful in protecting the children of neglectful parents, the adequacy of schooling is comparatively easy to oversee. Perhaps we should be more concerned about the millions of children who suffer today through assignment to inadequate schools that are located in their neighborhoods.

Desegregation and other restrictions

Some believe that constraints imposed by the need to desegregate, along with other restrictions, will make for dissatisfied parents; constricted choice, they argue, is really no choice at all. To cite Thernstrom again: "[E]ven a cursory look at existing 'controlled choice' programs shows that controls for purposes of racial balance seriously compromise choice."

Given desegregation mandates, one could reply, the question is not whether choice is compromised, but whether any other method of allocating students can provide parents with as much choice. An inevitable cost of partial freedom is to render any remaining constraint galling. So long as children are assigned to schools involuntarily on the sole basis of where they live, of course, the issue of disappointment does not arise; it is unavoidable, though, when parents are allowed to indicate other preferences and when no school is guaranteed a captive clientele.

The entry-level Boston grades assigned under controlled choice last year and this year are more desegregated than was the case before, and the great majority of these pupils were assigned to schools that their parents had indicated were acceptable: 74 percent of incoming sixth graders were assigned to their first-choice schools, and another 10 percent to their second choices, only 13 percent were assigned to schools not selected by their parents. Only 15 percent of first graders and 9 percent of ninth graders were assigned to unrequested schools.

Some Boston pupils, it is true, were assigned involuntarily. A closer look at the figures reveals, however, that desegregation was not primarily responsible. Of Boston's fifteen high schools, seven did not attract enough applicants of any racial/ethnic category to fill their available places in the ninth grade voluntarily. Some mandatory assignments were necessary, because hundreds remained without school places—even though the capacity of the more popular schools had been increased to accommodate as many students as possible. Desegregation considerations did not "compromise choice"; instead, space limitations dictated the unfortunate denial of choice to some, regardless of their race, creed, or color.

In only one Boston high school out of fifteen did desegregation requirements lead to freshmen of one racial/ethnic category being assigned involuntarily, while those of another race or ethnicity who had made it their first choice were denied admission.

The fact that students in particular racial or ethnic categories must be assigned involuntarily because of an insufficient supply of places in acceptable schools is deplorable. It should be kept in mind, however, that Boston, like other school systems, has always assigned students to these least-popular schools. Choice has not changed that reality; it has simply increased public awareness of the problem, thereby creating pressure both to improve or close those schools and also to allow other entrants into the educational marketplace.

Even if desegregation were not a concern (as it must be in Boston, due to its past history of deliberate segregation), it is difficult to conceive of circumstances under which all pupils could be assigned to their parents' first choices, unless enrollment declines and budget surpluses lead to ample slack capacity in the more popular schools. For a variety of reasons, some schools will always attract more applicants than they can accommodate; this is also a problem in Great Britain, where desegregation is not a factor.

A wise assignment policy will use every bit of space in the schools that parents want, while leaving the less popular schools under-enrolled. Over several years the more attractive options are replicated and the less attractive are improved, closed, or converted.

Controlled choice functions perfectly well to assure fairness and to create pressure for every school to improve in a community in which desegregation is not at issue, like Fall River, Massachusetts. Controls are still needed, though: there must be some fair basis for deciding who will be admitted to a school with too many applicants and who—pending creation of new space or new options will be assigned involuntarily.

The danger of false counsel

A fifth criticism of controlled choice is that officials may mislead parents about the options available, in order to create the appearance that choice is generally satisfactory to those affected by it. "Many will be 'counseled' to list as their top 'choices' schools that they would never freely select," complains Thernstrom. She quotes a report in which I criticized "the failure or inability of the parent information staff to counsel parents away from choices which they should have known could not be honored." "In other words," Thernstrom continues, "if the parent information staff does its job properly, families will list only those schools in which there is room for children of their race. If the families comply, the state comes out ahead, since it can report that a large percentage of parents get one of their desired schools."

This charge is based upon a common misunderstanding of the implementation of parental choice. Just as high school guidance counselors commonly recommend that students apply to more than one college and include some less-competitive selections, to assure that they get in somewhere, so information-center staff encourage parents to distribute their preferences sensibly among schools that they find acceptable.

The process of making assignments does not discourage parents from selecting a popular school as their first choice. Here's how it works. The applications of students eligible to apply for ninth grade, for example, are assigned random numbers, and each application is dealt with in turn. Those with the lowest numbers are assured of assignment to their first-choice schools. If an applicant's first-choice school has been filled, the assignment program checks whether space is available in the second-choice school, and so on through the options indicated. There is thus no advantage to not selecting a popular school as a first or second choice, since that will not affect a student's chances of getting into a third-choice school: each applicant is dealt with in turn until the attempt has been made to assign the student in question, based upon all of the preferences that he or she indicated on the application.

Perhaps one student in five does not receive an assignment in the first round; none receives an involuntary assignment. An applicant with a high random number who has selected only the more popular schools may receive no assignment in the first round (generally in April). The parents are contacted and encouraged to make a new selection of schools, since their original choices are no longer available. Parents may ask to be placed on the waiting list for one or two of the original choices, but they are also counseled about schools that still have space available. During the summer months, the parent information centers are able to issue assignments on the spot to parents who select a school with space. If a parent does not eventually select a school with open slots, the student will be assigned to the school nearest where he or she lives that does have room.

My criticism of the parent information effort last year in Boston was that counselors did not know which schools had no space available; thus many parents wasted their efforts by requesting schools that were already full. For example, more than half of those requesting sixth-grade seats applied to four schools (out of twenty-two) that were already virtually full.

After all, the whole point of offering a second chance to apply is to get parents to take a closer look at schools that might not be familiar to them—and perhaps to discover some unexpected merits. There is no special virtue in disappointing more parents than strictly necessary.

Intolerance and fanaticism

Another common charge is that school choice will be exploited by fanatics and/or unscrupulous entrepreneurs, who will run schools that are divisive or educationally unsound. Although this is not a problem that could arise with controlled choice among existing public schools as it now functions in Massachusetts, the charge is brought so often that a response seems necessary.

Perhaps the best way to answer this speculation—advanced even by such otherwise sensible and open-minded educational leaders as Albert Shanker of the American Federation of Teachers and California schools superintendent Bill Honig—is to point to the history of parental choice in the United States and other nations.

The charge that educational diversity will lead to social divisiveness, as children are nurtured by fanatical teachers determined to instill intolerance and hatred, has been made repeatedly over the last two centuries in Western Europe and in the United States. Horace Mann saw a threat in the peaceful Shakers; Catholic schools have been accused in many nations of being the advance guard of papal tyranny; Dutch elites feared that Protestant parents' desire for sectarian schools would destroy the common school by which, they thought, the nation was knit together. More recently, many on the left—even those who are otherwise sympathetic to the social and cultural aspirations of immigrants—have been made uneasy by the request of Moslem parents in Western Europe for public support of Islamic schools comparable to that received by Christian and Jewish schools.

The argument that it is somehow dangerous to allow differences among schools that correspond to the desires of parents is often advanced by critics of school choice. It is too rarely challenged, though; there is no evidence that Catholic, Protestant, or Jewish schools have produced graduates who are more intolerant, fanatical, or undemocratic than the graduates of public schools. The Netherlands is a tolerant society, though 70 percent of its children attend non-government schools; the choice of publicly funded denominational schools in Australia, Britain, Canada, France. Germany, and other democracies has been a source of political peace rather than conflict.

Nor does immigration raise the stakes of educational monopoly, as some claim. Despite the mythology that surrounds the public schools on the Lower East Side of

Manhattan and in other ports of entry, there is no evidence that the children of immigrant families who chose religiously based non-government schools turned out to be less desirable Americans.

But would unscrupulous entrepreneurs take advantage of choice policies to create cut-rate, profit-making operations providing an inadequate education (but glitzy enough to attract the unsophisticated)? Surely this danger can be averted through accreditation and inspection, either by government or by semipublic associations. It is not as though the present restriction of public funding to government-operated schools has resulted in uniformly acceptable quality. Other nations have certainly shown that high educational standards can be maintained in schools not operated by the government.

The Massachusetts experience with choice among public schools suggests another important guarantee against truly awful schools: a system of parent information and counseling with a special mission of reaching poor and language-minority parents with accurate and user-friendly information. No system of school choice that fails to inform and counsel parents, especially those who do not respond to the printed word, deserves to be called fair. Genuine equal access to information and the skills to use it are essential to the empowerment of poor and language-minority parents and their children through education.

Beyond controlled choice

Finally, critics of school choice argue that it will not lead to real diversity in education because school staffs lack the imagination and professionalism to create true alternatives. This is probably the hardest charge to answer.

Although we have not always done enough, even in highly centralized school systems, to assure that every pupil has the opportunity to acquire a common body of knowledge and skills, it remains important to encourage the staff of each school to develop its distinctive character in response to the staff's educational vision and the desires of parents. This will not be achieved through adopting the latest fad or imitating what another school has done successfully; it requires thoughtful hard work over months and years.

Creating a few magnet schools is not so difficult. Every school system has some teachers and a principal or two who are eager to try out new ideas and create a school that reflects their strongly-held views about what works. But to expect the staff of every school to become clear about a shared mission is to ask staff members to change habits shaped by their training and careers in bureaucratically organized school systems.

Parental choice, like school-based management and restructuring, depends upon changing the culture of each school. As Eastern European economists have pointed out recently, we have plenty of experience in going from free markets to controlled markets, but very little in going the opposite way, It is hard to persuade those who staff schools to behave boldly and innovatively, so long as they continue to function within a centrally-governed hierarchical structure—especially if the rewards available to them are not tied to entrepreneurial risk-taking.

In the final analysis. controlled choice as implemented in Massachusetts may simply not go far enough to shake up the culture of mediocrity and the low expectations that dominate so many schools. To be sure, Massachusetts schools are getting better. becoming more purposeful and responsive as a result of parental choice. But the pace of change may be too slow to benefit thousands of children whose education has been neglected. And the education system's resistance to change may reassert itself: ways may be found to accommodate the pressures of parental choice, resulting in the failure of yet another reform initiative.

A number of possibilities that would increase the momentum of choice-driven reform deserve consideration:

(1) Groups of teachers could be permitted to open smaller, less formally organized schools that would operate within the public system free of the usual constraints—provided that enough parents want what they offer. This "charter school" idea has been proposed by Albert Shanker and implemented in East Harlem. Such schools could significantly expand parental options, but the limitation is that most teachers are not motivated to invest great amounts of uncompensated time and energy in creating new educational alternatives.

(2) Pupils could be permitted, as in Minnesota, to cross school-system boundaries and attend schools operated by other public systems. While this may significantly benefit some students, it does not affect the quality of the schools that are rejected, and it presumes that nearby systems provide schools that are markedly different and

better. If they are, they may run out of space

(3) Pupils could be permitted to attend existing private schools with their tuition paid by public funds, as in the current Milwaukee voucher experiment. This increases parental options, but it does not represent a strategy to expand the overall supply of desirable educational alternatives. Also, the exclusion of religious schools from participation in the Milwaukee program (in order to avoid First Amendment difficulties) raises troubling issues of equal treatment of belief and unbelief. A group of minority parents in Kansas City has gone one worthwhile step further; the parents have petitioned to modify orders in a desegregation case, hoping to receive public funding to enable their children to attend nonpublic schools, including explicitly religious schools.

(4) New educational options could be "franchised," as Ted Kolderie has recently suggested. Kolderie proposes that other providers of schooling be permitted to compete directly with public school systems; applicant groups would have to be chartered by a public body, which might be composed of educators, parents, social-service professionals, and representatives of private groups in the learning business. The Netherlands has had great success with educational alternatives that have been chartered in this way.

It seems likely that we will be exploring and testing such proposals intensively over the next years, as we see the limitations of choice within present constraints as a means of achieving fundamental reform. Any of these reforms could fit within the framework already created in communities that have adopted controlled choice. While parent information centers in Massachusetts provide information only about options within a single school district, the system could easily be adapted to offer options in other districts or among nonpublic schools.

In conclusion, then, controlled choice as practiced in Massachusetts will not solve all of the defects of American education. But we have found it to be a powerful way to expand the options available to children from poor families, and to put pressure on urban schools to become both more effective and more responsive. The next stage in the development of choice must be to find ways to expand options, in response to the demands of parents and the vision of teachers.

The Essential Principles of
Minnesota's School Improvement Strategy

Ted Kolderie

There is growing interest in Minnesota's strategy for causing its schools to improve. The interest is not in the effort to mandate higher standards, tougher tests, merit pay, etc. Minnesota has conspicuously not gone that route. Nor is it in the programs that enable schools to try out ideas for improvement: mastery learning, computer technology, effective school, etc. Most other states do those demonstrations.

Rather, the interest is in Minnesota's use of incentives; created by shift from "assignment" to "choice" as the basis for matching child with school. People elsewhere are curious about the origins of this strategy, about the rationale for it, and about the mechanics of it. They want to understand how it succeeded, politically, and how educators are reacting.

This brief article cannot answer all those questions. It will focus on what is most important, which means on the essential ideas involved, because these are so different in such critical respects from the ideas and the issues earlier and elsewhere associated with proposals for family choice.

1. Choice is instrumental. Choice is seen in Minnesota not as an end in itself but as a means to better education. It is not asserted primarily as a right of the family. It has been developed by the state as the mechanism by which it can cause its schools to improve.

2. Choice is the best instrument to cause improvement. Education needs to improve, and can improve. Improvement is an issue for the state, because education is the responsibility of the state. But the state does not run the schools. The schools are run by local districts. So the state has a problem: How does it cause improvement in an institution owned and operated by somebody else?

Appeals to altruism may be effective. So may additional financing. So may experiments that demonstrate improvements. The risk is that they will not. The current system operated by most states assures the schools, after all, that their students will arrive and their money will come in any event. What if, despite the state's exhortation, the system does not improve? Worse: What if some schools improve and others do not? What does the state do then? The state cannot make schools improve. Mandates establish minimums. A state may close the schools that are not adequate. But no state will close all schools that are not excellent. And no state can force a school to be excellent.

What the state must and can do is to create the dynamics that will cause the schools themselves to move toward excellence. The state can increase the opportunities for schools to change and to improve. At the same time it can increase the opportunities for students to move from schools that do not improve to schools that do.

Nobody has to do anything. But there are beginning to be consequences for improving and for standing pat. Districts' enrollment is being linked to the success of their efforts to change and to improve.

3. Choice exists now. The question is: Who gets it? Children have to go to school. But if they are not well served in one school they can choose another. And not only a private school. Families can choose their public school, by moving their residence. So choice exists. But it depends on family resources. A means-test has been applied: the more money you have, the more choice you have. This is inequitable. People who depend on having education paid for publicly should have a comparable opportunity to find the education that meets their needs. No case exists for denying this opportunity where the choice is among public schools.

4. In Minnesota "choice" does not mean "vouchers." The policy discussion in Minnesota now uses the term "voucher" only to refer to the proposal to use public funds to pay for children attending private school. That proposal continues to be made in bills submitted to the Legislature by the private schools. Periodically, the bill receives a hearing, but does not move out of committee.

5. Minnesota is opening up choice within the public system. Various state laws create opportunities for students to enroll in other public school districts. The only partial exception was the Post-Secondary Options Act in 1985, which makes available to 11th and 12th graders the courses of Minnesota colleges and universities.

6. It is not "open enrollment." As used in the Minnesota discussion "choice" means that a district can no longer refuse to release a student who wishes to attend a school elsewhere. This does not make is possible for the student to enroll in whatever school she wishes. The laws continue to permit districts to decide whether or not they will admit non-resident students.

7. Districts may not be selective in whom they admit. If a district does decide to admit nonresident students, it may not pick and choose, as a private school is permitted to do. It must either accept all who apply or, if the number of applications exceeds the number of spaces available, it must give all who apply an equal chance of being admitted.

8. Choice is controlled for racial balance.

The laws consistently provide that no district operating under a desegregation order either of a court or of the state board of education will have its racial balance impaired by the operation of a program of student choice. Districts may refuse to release and may decline to admit students where compliance would be impaired.

9. Choice is evolutionary, not revolutionary. Governor Rudy Perpich proposed in 1985 that all students have the opportunity to choose, but that choice be expanded in stages. In 1985 the Legislature enacted the post secondary option. In 1987 it extended choice to students age 12 or beyond who are at the other end of the curve—in some measurable way "not doing well." It gave them the option to start again, either in some special alternative program or simply in regular school somewhere else.

In 1987, too, the Legislature adopted a standard plan for inter-district choice, in which districts at the moment may or may not participate. Bythe fall of 1987 about 30 percent of the school districts—representing, however, almost half of the total student enrollment—had come in to this voluntary program of choice.

10. The responsibility for transportation is shared. A student wishing to transfer is responsible for getting to the border of the district s/he wishes to attend. Once there, s/he will be picked up by the school-transportation system of that district just as if s/he were a resident. Some help is available for needy students.

11. When the student moves, the money moves. The Legislature has used a variety of mechanisms to provide the attending district with the revenue for a student who transfers in. It may ultimately standardize on having the Pupil Unit move: That is, on treating a student simply as if s/he were in fact a resident pupil in the district s/he is attending. All but a handful of school districts are "on the formula," so in almost every district the state would cover in full the per-pupil cost.

12. Intra-district programs also exist, but are separate. The state deals with districts, not with schools, so its program opens up choice between and among districts. Choice among schools is a question for districts. A good many have for some years given their residents some choice among schools.

The two programs are increasingly linked. A student applying to a nonresident district usually has in mind attending a particular school. A district admitting non-residents also feels considerable pressure to give its resident students their choice of school.

13. Choice is for the kids who do not move. Opponents attack programs of choice by asking, 'What about the kids who are left behind? — assuming that the students who benefit are the students who move. Not so. The Minnesota discussion is explicit about this: Choice is instrumental. Relatively few students will move. Hopefully they will find a program better suited to their needs. That is important. But the purpose of making it possible for students to move is to induce districts and schools to improve education for the great majority of the students who choose not to move. (See #2.)

Is this working? It is too soon to know: Second-order effects take time to appear. The fullest evaluation so far has been on the Post-Secondary Option, which has been in effect the longest. Results there are quite encouraging.

In the 1988 session of the Minnesota Legislature, the education aid division of the Education Committee in the Senate amended its omnibus education bill to make choice available generally, beginning with the 1989-90 school year. All students, in all grades and in all communities, would have the opportunity to apply to any district under the policies described above. The concept of the "home" district having to give its permission would simply disappear. Most surprising, to most observers, has been the absence of opposition to, or controversy about, the amendment. The question will have been resolved in House/Senate conference by the time the session ends in early April.

The change in public opinion on the question of inter-district enrollment may have been important in this. From the spring of 1985 to the spring of 1987, the response shifted from 30 percent in favor and 66 percent opposed, to 56 percent in favor and 39 percent opposed. The second poll was taken before the surprisingly large number of districts voluntarily came into the program, in the summer of 1987.

School Choice Works in Minnesota
Joe Nathan

MINNEAPOLIS — Will President Clinton follow through on his support for public school and chartered public school choice? His proposed package to Congress announced yesterday, contained modest support for these ideas, permitting states to spend money on them. But the president's central role in education is to speak directly to the public. There is plenty of good news he could share about public school choice and charter schools, despite the intense effort by the education establishment to discredit choice in general, and Minnesota's programs in particular.

First, parent, teacher and legislative interest is growing. National and statewide polls find that more than 60% of the parents want the power to select among various public schools. The 1989 Arkansas Legislature followed then-Gov. Clinton's recommendations to adopt cross-district public school choice. Other state legislatures have expanded families' school choices in California, Colorado. Florida, Georgia, Idaho, Iowa, Massachusetts, Minnesota, New Mexico,Ohio, Utah, Washington and Wisconsin. Many laws are based on Minnesota's widely discussed, rarely understood programs.

A 1992 statewide poll conducted by major education groups found that 76% of Minnesotans endorsed our public school choice laws. More than 10,000 high school dropouts have returned to school because of the state's programs. But choice opponents have promoted five major myths. Mr. Clinton should help refute them.

More Options

• *Myth One: Minnesota's school choice plans haven't had much impact.* A recently released study of 126 Minnesota school principals concluded that choice "stimulated improvements to school curricula promoted greater parent and teacher involvement in planning and decision-making and increased ethnic diversity of schools." More than 150 new magnet schools and "schools within schools" have been created in the past five years. Minneapolis and St. Paul more than doubled their options over the past seven years, often attracting suburban as well as inner city youngsters.

Choice also helped produce several of the nation's first rural magnet schools, such as the Cyrus math-science magnet elementary school, which is run by a committee of teachers. Redbook recently named it one of the nation's 51 best public elementary schools. Teachers established other new schools in Delavan, Miltona, Randall, Nerstrand, Blackduck, Fairmount, Morris and Virginia. These rural schools along with recently developed suburban and inner-city options, give several hundred thousand students true choices within their own districts.

A recent report on school choice by the Carnegie Foundation for the Advancement of Teaching insisted that less than 4% of Minnesotans are using the state's choice program. Carnegie ignored "within district" choice programs, which have exploded over the past five years.

Minnesota's Post-Secondary Options law allows public-school 11th- and 12th-graders to attend universities, with tax funds following the students. More than 50,000 students have used this law since it began in 1985. Critics predicted that most high-schoolers would be lost at college. But at many post-secondary institutions, such as the University of Minnesota, high school students have earned a higher grade-point average than the freshman class.

What about the wider impact? The state's high schools responded by doubling the number of Advanced Placement courses offered since the program started. Post-Secondary Options also helped convince 46 high schools to work with the University of Minnesota to offer joint courses granting both college and high school credit. Carnegie said that there was little growth In Advanced Placement. But it compared changes in the past three years, not since the Post-Secondary program began in 1985.

• *Myth Two: Choice plans help rich students more than poor ones.* More than 10,000 young Minnesotans used the state's Second Chance cross-district choice laws to re-enter school after dropping out.

Youngsters from low-income families and minority groups are well represented in these programs. There's been a dramatic increase in aspiration levels among Second Chance students. The percentage of these students who reported that they planned to graduate and continue their formal education more than doubled after they transferred to another public school. Among teenagers using Second

Chance to attend private nonsectarian, nonexclusive schools, such as the (Minneapolis) Urban League's Street Academy, the percentages increased to 41% from 6%. This experience shows that private, nonsectarian schools can play a valuable role in the education to inner-city children.

• *Myth Three: Parents don't choose the schools for "good reasons."* Several carefully done studies show Minnesota parents' primary reason for choosing a school in another district is "academics." Those studies have been ignored. Critics say that too many parents prefer "convenience." Should public schools be inconvenient?

The Carnegie Report, for example. doesn't explain that before Minnesota's then-Gov. Rudy Perpich proposed open enrollment, one suburban district required youngsters to go 14 miles to the nearest school in their district, rather than walk one to two blocks to the nearest school just across district lines.

• *Myth Four: Choice is being presented as a panacea.* Not in Minnesota, or the 13 other states in which it was adopted, with bipartisan support. Mr. Clinton knew it was no panacea when he proposed it.

So do growing numbers of teachers. In a 1988 survey conducted by Minnesota's largest teacher union, more than 60% of its members supported cross-district public school choice. Choice expands opportunities for teachers to act like entrepreneurs. It is central to the "teachers as professionals" movement, even if unions often do not recognize that fact.

Award winning educator Deborah Meier has noted that "[public school] choice was the prerequisite" for her work in East Harlem—"schools with a focus, with staffs brought together around common ideas, free to shape a whole set of school parameters in accord with those ideas." Many terrific teachers recognize there's no one best kind of school for all students.

The best choice plans are accompanied by efforts to equalize funding among districts: help educators create new programs so that there are choices, not just choice; help parents make thoughtful decisions: prohibit school admissions tests: and provide transportation.

Minnesotans understand what many business groups have forgotten: that school choice and site management go together. Businesses grow by giving their employees more decision-making power. But employees know customers have options. If families don't have choices, how effective will site-management be? How effective would it be in your company. if employees had guaranteed customers?

• *Myth Five: Chartered public schools offer little to reform programs.* Both Mr. Clinton and Education Secretary Richard Riley have endorsed charter schools, which enable certified teachers to create new schools of choice with accountability for student results, rather than for following thousands of rules. Chartered public schools may not use admissions tests. Minnesota passed a limited version of chartered schools in 1991. California, Georgia and New Mexico are also experimenting with the idea.

A Powerful Tool

More than 25 groups of Minnesota educators in urban, suburban and rural areas tried starting such schools in just the first year of the law's operation. Most have been frustrated by the law's provision that a local school board must approve the charter. This is like allowing the New York Times to decide whether The Wall Street Journal can be sold in Manhattan.

Choice is a powerful tool, like electricity, which must be handled carefully. Some choice programs, including some public school plans, create more problems than they solve. Minnesota's plan isn't right for every state,

Mr. Clinton should repeat his frequently voiced presidential campaign recommendation that every state should provide options for families and educators. He could help Americans understand what Chris Wilcox, one of Minnesota's earliest school choice participants, told the nation's governors three years ago: "Choice not only gave me a chance to personalize my education, but it also gave me the confidence that I can make something of myself and control my destiny."

The Claims For School Choice and Snake Oil Have a Lot in Common

Lewis W. Finch

Allowing parents and students to select the school system of their choice—and forcing public schools into the competitive marketplace—seems as American as apple pie and Grandma's house at Christmas. Unfortunately, as I look at the open-enrollment program that allows a student here in Minnesota to choose any school statewide, I am reminded of the snake-oil salesman who plays on the great American passion for quick, cheap remedies to complex ailments.

Choice is a populist notion that's not entirely without merit. But unrestricted choice, as adopted here in Minnesota, bears more political than educational value. At best, choice offers little promise for school improvement. At worst, unrestricted choice could dash all hope for equal education opportunity for many students.

If your state is considering this latest reform movement, I urge you to scrutinize carefully the exaggerated claims of Minnesota's success in school choice. Virtually no valid evidence exists to support claims of higher test scores and lower dropout rates (nor do such claims mention that, long before choice, Minnesota historically has been a leader in keeping students in school through graduation). Fewer than 500 students actually have participated in the open-enrollment program so far.

Great claims have been made for a more limited version of choice, known as the postsecondary options program. In this program, Minnesota high school students may take college-level courses for high school credit. But the claims of success have largely been restricted to anecdotes about students who said they otherwise would not have been able to go to college. No in-depth analysis has been undertaken to determine the impact of postsecondary options.

Consider the claims made in support of choice—and the reality, as I see it, behind those claims.

Advocates of choice wax ecstatic about forcing public schools into the highly competitive dog-eat-dog, open market. (Never mind that the open market, as we know it, is fraught with insider trading, glitzy and often false or misleading advertising, government bailouts, and frequent bankruptcies.) Under the Minnesota plan, each school must vie for students to survive. In essence, choice becomes educational Darwinism—survival of the fittest. And because most states base public school funding on numbers of students, maintaining a high "body count" becomes imperative to survival.

The means of survival in such a system is marketing. One ardent proponent declared, "We want you to sell schools like business sells toothpaste." But I ask you: Do we really want public schools to emulate the corporate world in selling programs and services? A slick propaganda campaign such as the outrageous claims of "Joe Isuzu" about Isuzu cars and trucks—reveals little about the quality of product or service.

Imagine such an advertising campaign for a public school: It might attract customers, but it offers questionable assurance that students will learn to read and write. Worse, scarce revenue—which could and should be used to improve instruction—will go instead to pay for high-priced testimonials, flashy advertising campaigns, and high-powered Madison Avenue consultants.

Blueprint for disaster

Advocates claim choice will give parents and students access to excellence in education. Unfortunately, our experience in Minnesota over the past couple of years with a limited version of open enrollment (under which school systems could choose to participate) suggests the quality of education has little if any bearing on the school a parent or student chooses.

What factors do influence a family's choice? In the Minnesota experience geographic location (especially location of day-care providers) and parental convenience most often determine school selection. One central Minnesota school system, after raising graduation standards, found students were opting to leave and enroll in nearby school systems with lower graduation standards. This year, here in the Anoka-Hennepin schools (K-12; enr.: 33,500), we have processed several hundred applications for transfers, most of them in-district transfers. Virtually all the requests were based on convenience and location, rather than on the quality of education in a given school.

And then come the other attractions—such as the lure of strong sports teams. The principal of a large suburban high school in the Minneapolis-St. Paul area recently reported to a legislative panel that of the numerous calls he'd received this past year from nondistrict residents regarding potential transfers, none was related to the quality of education. Rather, students were frankly interested in the school's hockey program, which purportedly shows a bright future.

The other side of the coin: Schools might be tempted to pursue and recruit certain types of students under a choice plan. Attracting the brightest and the best to a school fits the corporate image. A winning football team and a snappy marching band do wonders for public relations and are likely to lure customers. Schools will do their best to attract top scholars and talented hockey players.

But handicapped or other students at risk of failure will be less desirable commodities. The reason is simple: They often are unprofitable. The cost of providing these students appropriate services exceeds the revenue provided by the state. If the open market has anything to teach schools, it's this: Promoting unprofitable services is a blueprint for economic disaster. Who, then, will champion the cause of educating the handicapped? My prediction: No one will. In the worst case, the U.S. will end up with a stratified, elitist education system such as those found in many countries.

A war of attrition

Choice, say advocates, is a means of getting rid of bad schools. Proponents of choice readily declare their intent to bankrupt—educationally and financially—many public school systems, especially those with poor records of student achievement. Encouraging a sufficient number of students to leave, they hope, will destroy these school systems. "It's market forces as work," declared one highly placed Minnesota politician.

In my judgment, this approach is tantamount to a declaration of war—a war of attrition—on some public school systems serving thousands of students. Some students will become refugees in neighboring systems But those who, for their own reasons, are not able to move or commute will become casualties of this war. Ultimately, the state will have islands of educational excellence surrounded by vast wastelands of deprivation

As I see it, Minnesota is using choice as a strategy to force a more effective and efficient (and long overdue) restructuring of the state's public elementary and secondary schools. It's consolidation, but it's described with a more generally acceptable term. The motive might be right, but the method is unconscionable. Certain politicians champion this strategy for restructuring simply because they lack the political courage and integrity to take more direct, positive action.

Advocates argue that to remain competitive and not lose students, schools will upgrade their education programs. The harsh reality is that some schools will be less able to compete. Under Minnesota's plan, state aid goes with the student to the receiving school system. The sending system, meanwhile, becomes less "efficient ." It's unable to reduce its costs proportionate to the loss—that is, it must keep a classroom open and running, a teacher in front of the class, and lights and heat on, regardless of the number of students in the room. Because it must spend proportionately more money on overhead, the school system has a diminished capacity to upgrade its education programs. It finds itself in the classic catch-22—a no-win situation.

Minnesota's postsecondary options program—which has been in place for several years—offers a case in point. The program purportedly provides high school students access to courses of greater academic rigor which, by implication, are not available in their home high schools. A preponderance of evidence would suggest that few participants actually have chosen postsecondary courses to improve the quality or rigor of their education. For many students, the program offers a chance for free college credit. For some, attending college classes offers more freedom—rules for attendance are often lax, students can smoke, and they have more unstructured time than if they attended their high school. Although college credit and increased freedom might be defensible reasons for a postsecondary options program, they hardly guarantee an improved quality of education, as has been claimed.

The private option

Another thinly veiled, ulterior motive of many choice advocates is eventually to include private and parochial schools among the options available to parents. These people cite a failure of public schools to perform adequately—though they seldom acknowledge that few private schools operate under the stifling mandates imposed on public schools. These mandates might be laudable, but they also are expensive, time consuming, and often unfunded. Public schools have no choice but to fulfill them. Nor do the private-school advocates point out that public schools have a mission to educate all students. Unlike private schools, public schools cannot pick and choose their clientele.

My prediction: After parents become accustomed to choice—and when they become dissatisfied with public schools—choice advocates will advance public funding for private schools as a remedy.

The die is cast

No matter what you hear from choice advocates, all is not rosy in Minnesota now that we have choice. To date, presentations featuring Minnesota's version of choice have been carefully staged and orchestrated by those who support choice. They avoid the dark side of choice, while basing their claims of success on contrived data.

What you don't hear when proponents of choice tout the idea is a story such as the following, from Mountain Iron-Buhl, a consolidated school district located in the northern part of the state, on the famous Iron Range. It's an example of what the future holds for those who opt for choice.

Owing to a split in the community—centering on the school board's decision to close one of the two senior high schools—a group of parents enrolled their children in a neighboring school system. The parents' move was not intended to improve the quality of the children's education. Rather, it was an act of defiance and retaliation, in which children were made pawns in a political chess game.

This case, I believe, foreshadows the future. If disgruntled parents can economically and educationally cripple a school system on the basis of political motives—such as the community controversy growing out of a school closing—wait until the first AIDS patient shows up to be served in our open-enrollment schools of choice.

Recently, a program titled "Gavel" was aired on Minnesota public television. The program identifies social issues and places them on trial before a judge and a six-member citizen jury. The issue of open enrollment was "tried" in this court, complete with testimony and cross-examinations by attorneys representing both sides of the issue. The decision of the jury—and of viewers who telephoned in their reactions—was that open enrollment should not be legislated in Minnesota. The finding of this jury might not be greatly significant, but it reflects the attitude of a great number of citizens who objectively consider the merits of Minnesota's open-enrollment program.

Tragically, Minnesota offers citizens choice in lieu of adequate, equitable funding of public schools. While proponents claim choice is making Minnesota the brainpower state of the U.S., class sizes are increasing; the number of underserved, at-risk students is rising; the disparity in revenue sources among school systems is getting wider; and several school systems are flirting with statutory operating debt (a step away from bankruptcy). Some school systems are initiating litigation against the state, contending that the state's failure to provide access to equal revenue is unconstitutional.

Teachers, school administrators, and school board members in Minnesota asked for help. The governor and a majority of legislators gave us choice—the great placebo. Some parents are happy because now they can send their children to a neighboring school system if they wish. Supporters of private education are elated at the possibility of private schools eventually being included in the choice plan. And free-market enthusiasts see their fondest dreams being realized. But choice offers Minnesotans little or nothing to improve the quality of education.

Choice probably will not bring about the demise of public education—but only because some professionals and parents refuse to be fooled by the glitz. They will persevere in the mission of serving and educating all students.

The die is cast in Minnesota. I hope we will avoid some of the pitfalls I foresee. But for any state considering choice based on the Minnesota plan, be advised: It could spell disaster.

Here's Why School Choice
Will Boost Student Motivation—and Learning

Denis P Doyle

The increasing demand for the right to select a public school can be partly understood by looking at our schools' historical development). But it also is part of a larger set of social processes and changes in the recent past. Society is not static. It has changed over the past few decades in ways that schools have not and in ways few educators appear to have noticed. The changes themselves are no doubt due in large part to the success of the U.S. public school.

With an unparalleled percentage of Americans completing high school and hitherto unimagined number going on to higher education, we enjoy an extraordinarily well-educated citizenry. And a well-educated citizenry is prepared to choose the schools their children will attend. The idea is hardly novel in the private sector; there parents have been selecting among schools from time immemorial.

What is different about choice in the public sector is the capacity of parents to choose among public schools. The rationale? Sy Fliegel, former associate superintendent of District 4 in New York City's Spanish Harlem, puts it this way "I have a simple philosophy: What's good enough for rich children is good enough for poor children."

The issue in school choice is the oldest idea in education motivation: A school that is chosen is a school in which children, parents, and teachers are collaborators, accomplices if you will. Each has a set of expectations about the other. Schools can expect students to meet their standards because the students are there voluntarily. So, too, parents and students can expect schools they choose to meet their obligations to their students.

It is clear that the most powerful explanatory variable in student performance is the student's own willingness to work. Native ability is clearly important; demanding schools are as well. But neither alone suffices. The "silver bullet" in student learning is student effort. And student effort cannot be ordered up by fiat or edict—it can arise only from the student himself. If the example were athletics, no one would question this assertion: A gifted but lazy athlete accomplishes nothing; without student motivation even the best coaching is an empty exercise. Mastery occurs when these three threads—ability, teaching, and motivation—are woven together. Coaches, fans, and players know it. Honest educators know it, too.

What, then, accounts for the indifference and even hostility so many school board members and administrators feel about choice systems? If they are convinced that this is the best of all possible worlds, that schooling should go on as it has—business as usual—they have every reason to be anxious.

I can think of three possible explanations for such a point of view: The first and most compelling, is the view that public schools are democratic institutions and that democracy somehow demands uniformity; the second is the belief that the school board and its chosen administration know more about good or appropriate education than parents and children. The third—and this is the least attractive—is moss-backed reaction, a refusal to entertain change and a determination to hew to the status quo at all costs. This point I leave to your imagination but the first two are serious, and their resolution speaks directly to the question of choice.

One best system?

Is there some interior logic to our democratic processes that requires democratically controlled social institutions to be all the same? No such interior logic is evident in publicly supported health care or higher education. Medicare recipients are free to seek medical services—with public funds—at hospitals and doctors of their choice. Higher education students may use Pell Grants and Guaranteed Student Loans at either public or private institutions, and they may select from within these two broad categories.

There is, then, neither empirical nor a priori reason to believe that democratic processes require uniformity. But just as there is no requirement that schools be made uniform, there is no requirement that it not be done. And just as democratic processes might lead to successes, so, too, they might lead to mistakes. The notion that there can be "one best system" of public education is such a mistake.

It is a mistake because it misconceives the nature of the educational undertaking—and this introduces that second possible belief I mentioned. Do school board members and their administration know something mere mortals do not? Do they have such refined powers of discernment and judgment that they are better able to decide what should be done than the man on the street? Are they privy to specialized knowledge? And if so, it is proper to exercise that knowledge by requiring certain kinds of conformity?

Put bluntly, who knows more about the child's welfare—the board member and the bureaucrat or the parent? Who has the child's interest most at heart, and who is best situated to act in the child's behalf?

In a democratic system to oppose choice on the basis of superior knowledge or better judgment is to lean on a slender need. If parents can vote for a board member and make that choice, are they not to be trusted in the more immediate choice of their children's school?

In addition to these rather arcane arguments, those who oppose school choice voice more prosaic and mundane arguments against it. The most obvious, if not the most important, is the stock-in-trade of obstructionists everywhere: administrative convenience. But what an argument, what a claim in this postindustrial, knowledge-based society. We can, as a society, administer anything we set our minds to. The notion that choice schemes might complicate the lives of schedulers is, if anything, an argument on behalf of choice. If schools are to be run for the convenience of the managers, what has become of schooling?

Administrators are meant to administer, just as managers are meant to manage; they are, after all, public servants. They are meant to arrange things to meet the needs and satisfy the interests of their students, not themselves. The administrative convenience argument conjures up the old chestnut about the librarian who observes that the library would run much more smoothly if people would just stop borrowing books.

But if this argument is specious, is there not a more important case to be made about "terminal disruption" about school closings? A recent series about choice in Education Week captured the flavor of board and administrator anxiety in a story about a school system in which "too few" children chose to enroll. From the standpoint of educators, this is a disaster. "Planning," they say, "is impossible." (But whose planning is important?) From the standpoint of the consumers—the students and their families—it is simply the recognition that the only holding power the school system exercised was through compulsion.

The most important insight of the great economic historian Joseph Schumpeter was that the greatest power of capitalism was "creative destruction," the capacity to bring appropriate and dysfunctional organizational forms to an end. No other form of government or of social organization is able to do this swiftly; indeed, few can do it at all. That is why centrally planned economies descend into downward spirals of hopeless inefficiency. As inefficient parts of the economy become apparent, instead of being reformed, more sources are poured into them. We can see this principle at work in some of our second and third-rate schools.

Vandalism, disrespect, low academic achievement and demoralization have no constituency, yet these conditions exist in abundance in many of our inner-city schools. They exist in spite of strong sentiments against them, and when such problems surface, the typical response is to spend more money on the same building with "more of the same" remedies. No wonder the remedies fail.

An exercise in imagination

Let me turn from the negative aspects of our present education system and briefly describe the benefits of a choice system to board members and their senior administrators. To do so will require what the social scientists call a thought experiment.

Imagine a school system in which each school is a magnet school and each family must choose the school its children will attend. And imagine a school system in which each magnet school has equal resources (that is, equal resources for similarly situated children and more money for special education and disadvantaged youngsters). As well, imagine a system in which the logic of school-site management has been faithfully combined with magnet schools and choice—each building is a cost center, and each building makes its own decisions about the allocation of its income.

Imagine, too, magnet schools in which principals, working in concert with the faculty make the important administrative and organizational decisions about the school, including such straightforward things as the janitor's schedule and responsibilities. Finally, imagine a school system in which each school gives teachers the pedagogical freedom to exercise their professional judgment about what should be taught and how it should be taught.

In this scenario, we are presented with a collection of schools that are virtually autonomous: From an administrative and instructional standpoint they look very much like private schools. In such a setting, what is the role of the school board, the superintendent, and the central office administrators? Roles responsibilities, and professional satisfactions would change—and change dramatically.

First, administrators would no longer sit astride a management pyramid; such an approach to management might have worked in factories and in schools run like factories, but it has no place in a choice system just as it has no place in the modern high-tech firm. Indeed, if there is a proper organizational analogue to the school, it is just such a firm. Staffed by highly trained professionals, producing goods and services that are the product of applied human intelligence, these firms are lightly administered organizations that rely on the full participation of its employees to move forward effectively.

It is not too much to observe that no firm could succeed in the modern world if it were organized like the typical, large-city school system. The reason is simple: The modern firm is an organization that is more than the sum of its parts. And its chief executive officer is not an autocrat, a manager who barks orders and maintains rigid discipline. Today's successful C.E.O. is better thought of as a choreographer or conductor, someone who sets broad goals and directions, establishes incentives and rewards, finds the best people available, sets them loose, and then steps back. The successful C.E.O. keeps a light hand on the administrative reins knowing that reins are first and foremost a means of communication. To think of them as a lever to exact mechanical compliance is to think that a heavy hand works. It might in the short haul but it will not work over the long one.

A vote of confidence

The school board that endorses choice then, is giving its community and its teachers a vote of confidence. It is saying, "We believe in the competence and good judgment of our principals and teachers."
It also is saying, "We believe in the seriousness and soundness of our parents."

Equally important, the board is recognizing that no "one best system" exists. Different strokes. For some children, a Mortimer Adler "Paideia" school is appropriate; for others, Ted Sizer's "essential" school is best; and for others, a music and art school is best; and for others an emphasis on science and mathematics is most suitable. Private elementary and secondary schools vary enormously and for a reason: Different people—parents, teachers and students, not to mention board members—have different interests, capacities and talents.

Teachers who choose schools will be more professional; they will be stakeholders in the education enterprise. Not only will they work harder; they will work smarter. And as they work smarter, they will be more effective. Their sense of professional efficacy will increase—the single most important improvement to the life of teachers and their students.

Concurrently, schools of choice will improve both the attitudes and performance of students and their families. No longer unwilling or indifferent participants in compulsory education, they will now be accomplices. They will share the school's values. And if they do not, they should be counseled to leave, just as students who are miscast in a college or university should find one that is better suited to their talents, interests, and capacities.

Broad but shallow

Finally, school board members have a compelling reason to consider choice schemes seriously: One of the main reasons school board members frequently find themselves beleaguered is that they are called on to adjudicate some of the most fundamental issues in modern society.

Questions of drugs, sex, and teenage behavior generally are daunting in and of themselves; but schools also must sort out complex and divisive issues such as bilingual education and busing for racial balance. They must deal with conflicting curricular interests and demands to satisfy the wide-ranging interests of a diverse society, including such disparate issues as ethnic studies and the relative importance of vocational education. They must deal with the financial and pedagogical demands of special education, and they must contend with the competing demands of extracurricular activities, both on campus and off.

In attempting all this, it is no surprise that many schools have descended into what is so powerfully described by Arthur Powell, Eleanor Farrar, and David Cohen as "the shopping mall high school"—a cafeteria of offerings so broad, and so shallow, that they satisfy almost no one in their efforts to satisfy everyone. There is only one way to offer diversity and breadth that can and will work, and that is building by building, school by school. Choice.

Choice schools can hew to a core curriculum and meet the goals and objectives laid down by the school board at the same time as they define their own distinctive personality. Choice will permit school boards to meet their broad responsibilities to the communities they serve without involving themselves in the minutiae of day-to-day management and oversight. It will permit them to adjudicate bruising disputes about everything from pedagogy to dress codes, from intellectual values to extracurriculars, not by seeking—and finding—a lowest common denominator, but by permitting informed consumers to choose among responsible alternatives.

Indeed, the analogue to the modern public school board should be the board of trustees of the corporation, private or not-for-profit, which provide general overnight and policy guidance, hires a responsible and competent C.E.O., gives the C.E.O. ample running room, and then steps back. It is a form of service both more congenial to the board member and better suited to getting results from the corporate body for which the board is responsible.

Will School Choice Meet Students' Needs?   Principals' Views

Duvon G. Winborne

We can successfully teach all children if we seriously consider the applications of relevant knowledge in connection with effective schooling and school improvement procedures. In this regard, we have access to more knowledge than we use. (Wilson & Fergus, 1988, p. 64)

Urban schools appear so ineffective and weakened by uncertain resources that alternative schools seem like a viable solution for improvement. Despite these appearances, there are urban schools and programs that produce academic successes and provide a choice for families interested in a quality education for their children.

The focus of this article is a survey of urban school principals about desirable alternative education programs for low-achieving students. The basic assumption behind this study is that a school cannot succeed without effective leadership (Sizemore, 1985). This article also identifies schools and programs that have been effective enough to promote educational excellence in low-achieving students. What follows, however, is more than a description of successful approaches.

This article explores the nature of effective schools. It examines the principal's role in establishing models for educating children in urban settings. As such, a view is projected of elements that must come together to produce schools that will attract both high-achieving students and those whose educational experiences have led parents and teachers to seek alternative instructional strategies. In addition, several alternative school models are presented, with a discussion of their relative merits. Practical barriers are reviewed that prevent poor and ethnically diverse families from participating in alternative schools.

Data from a survey of urban principals describe planning procedures that principals feel are necessary for implementing educational alternatives within a public school system. These data also suggest alternative programs for meeting the academic and developmental needs of students whose characteristics mark them for academic failure in traditional programs. While some families are able to take advantage of various choices among alternative programs, there are many that do not. Therefore, educators must create more alternative programs to attract more students. Results from the survey described in this article should provide suggestions for developing such alternatives.

SCHOOL LEADERSHIP

The major components of successful schools are the same, regardless of their sociogeographic location. Moreover, the primary characteristics of effective schools are found with equal frequency in middle-class suburban schools, as well as schools located in poor urban neighborhoods (Fortenberry, 1986; Lezotte,1985; Wilson & Fergus,1988). Research on effective schools during the past two decades, led by Ronald Edmonds (1980), identified the following components of successful schools:

1. strong administrative leadership
2. a sense of mission
3. clear instructional focus
4. high expectations of students and staff
5. regular use of student achievement data for remediation
6. safe, orderly climate
7. parent/community involvement.

Strong school site leadership is the most important component in effective urban schools. The principal must be aware of the school's mission and private a plan of action that will accomplish that mission. In the absence of a clear mission, successful principals generally create less definitive mission statements (Beachum, 1985). A mission statement serves as more than an expression of purpose, it establishes a climate for academic success that reaches beyond the school into the community.

Principals in effective urban schools set expectations for students, teachers, staff, and parents. Schools with outstanding achievement profiles have strong parent involvement and input from community groups (Mortimore & Sammons, 1987; Pink & Wallace, 1984; Steadman, 1985; Valverde, 1988). Such involvement does not occur without the influence of the principal. In urban schools, academic success is based on the ability of the principal to promote a comfortable climate that encourages parents to feel "connected" with the school. For example, opportunities must exist for parents to visit schools at convenient times of the day and on occasions other than regular school hours. Community organizations that work with students and their families for noneducational purposes must also be invited to develop cooperative activities in the schools.

Curriculum and instructional issues should also be a major concern of the building administrator. Central to successful instruction in a school is the high level of expectation held by all staff involved with the pedagogical process (Morgan, 1979). Teachers must believe their students can achieve and therefore must work toward that end. Achievement test data are used by teachers to improve student instruction in successful schools. This constant use of data contrasts sharply with the more traditional process, whereby test scores are used at year's end to summarize school activities (Beachum,1985). Effective urban schools are ones that provide teachers with achievement test data for monitoring student progress.

Raising teachers' expectations of their students can be difficult in schools populated with students who exhibit low academic achievement (Committee for Economic Development, 1987). Low student academic achievement is often correlated with poverty, and teachers working with these students arc often inclined toward apathy. Therefore, principals in poor neighborhoods must be capable of creating an atmosphere in which achievement expectations are high and teachers transmit these expectations to students.

The racial and ethnic diversity found in urban schools places considerable strain on selecting a curriculum that meets the needs of all students. For example, meeting the curriculum needs of African-American, Hispanic, and other ethnically diverse groups requires adjustments in instruction and course content. The need for curriculum refinements is also necessary when students come from homes where English is not the primary language (Conteras, 1988; Garcia, 1988). However, it is not immediately obvious that change in the curriculum is necessary in promoting higher academic achievement. High achievement levels are more likely to occur when the course content and materials are culturally relevant and relate to the ethnicity of students (Moody & Moody, 1988; Rashid, 1989). Successful principals are aware of these needs and urge teachers to be sensitive to the cultural needs of students.

SCHOOL CHOICE

Arguably, public education in the United States has been unsuccessful in addressing the needs of urban students (Wilensky & Kline, 1989). Those scholars in the forefront of the school reform movement have offered varying strategies for improving public education. Plans for providing educational options (choice plans) in large urban districts have been beneficial as well as detrimental to quality instruction for children. Attention is given in the following sections to choice plans at major urban schools and practical issues associated with these plans.

MAGNET SCHOOLS

Magnet schools are frequently seen as a viable option to urban schools. As an educational alternative, magnet schools offer parents the option of a particular theme school or program for their children. Magnet schools appear most often in urban areas, attracting students on the basis of program content and curriculum. These schools draw children from across the racial and ethnic spectrum and may produce voluntary desegregation of schools (Winborne, in press).

Research suggests that magnet schools have provided the only academically elite schools in urban school districts (Raywid, 1982, 1983). At the secondary level, these schools feature special content areas, while magnet elementary schools are usually distinguished by their overall academic orientation. Elementary magnet schools have been used predominantly as schools with back-to-basics teaching strategies. These elementary schools tend to stress more rigorous academic procedures and structures than traditional elementary schools.

With few exceptions, magnet schools at the secondary level focus on particular curriculum content areas. Secondary magnet schools frequently specialize in math and science, the humanities, or the visual and performing arts. Others may emphasize preparation for particular careers, such as technology or computer programming, or organize themselves along such broad occupational lines as health science or aviation.

Magnet schools generally provide elite opportunities at few schools at the expense of other district schools (Rossell, 1987). In short, they create a dual system of public education—the elite magnet schools and the mediocre regular schools. This situation exists in Boston, where the magnets are educational options within a mandatory reassignment desegregation plan. Because the alternative to the magnet school is a less desirable regular school, a dual system is created.

Undoubtedly, no choice plan will escape criticism; however, those associated with school desegregation should escape such pitfalls (Harris, 1984; Hess,1984). An effective choice plan for magnet schools should have a high degree of desegregation both in schools of choice and in schools from which students are drawn. There should be a fair distribution of benefits and costs for all schools in the district, and enrollment should be stable over a number of years. Quality education must be available to students in nonmagnet schools.

Most families are limited in their educational options (Boykin, 1979, 1984; Cureton, 1978; Rashid, 1989). As leaders, principals have a responsibility to develop alternative programs within their schools. The principal's role is particularly critical in large urban school districts where poverty abounds and multiple cultures exist (Levin, 1972). These challenges are further compounded by language barriers involving non-English-speaking students (Ortiz, 1988). Essentially, many students are academically "at-risk" due to a poor fit between their needs and the available resources (Wehlage, 1988; Winborne, in press). Thus, there is a need for many choice programs within public schools to serve the needs of all the students, because enrollment in any school is a choice.

THE STUDY

Planning and implementing alternative urban schools requires enlightened leadership and support by the community. In a large midwestern school district, principals were surveyed to determine the educational and developmental needs of students who were likely to perform poorly in school. The school district represented by these principals was populated by a majority of (more than 70%) African-American students.

STUDY PROCEDURES

All 118 principals employed in the school system were invited to workshop designed for planning innovative programs to augment existing programs. The goal of the study was to develop intervention programs improve the academic performance of their students.

As part of the data collection process, principals were placed into groups to explore concepts and issues regarding program development. Included in each group of principals were also persons from human service agencies, private foundations, and universities. Following group activities, principals were instructed to convene meetings with teachers in their respective schools to get their perceptions and opinions about the needs of low-achieving students.

A 37-item questionnaire was administered to the principals, following group discussions and building-level meetings with teachers. The instrument was designed to obtain information from principals about student intervention strategies, staff development needs, and resource needs; open-ended responses were solicited to identify issues not covered by the instrument. Items related to school resources were separated into three categories: personnel, material, and community involvement.

Principals were instructed that their responses should be based on the needs of academically at-risk students. Confidentiality and anonymity of data were guaranteed. Principals were given 1 week to complete and return the instrument. Of the original sample, only 2 of 118 principals failed to return a completed questionnaire.

The two-dimensional structure of instrument items sought to rate the importance of the program activities on a 5-point scale. Higher scores on the rating scale indicated a perception of greater importance and lower scores indicated little or no importance.

FINDINGS

A total of 116 principals responded to the survey, or 98% of all principals employed in the school district. On average, principals had 10.5 years of teaching experience and 8.2 years of administrative experience. The average number of years served as a principal was 5.7.

The average student enrollment was 400 for elementary schools, 390 for middle schools and 990 for high schools. Average staff size of the schools was 24 teachers, two administrators, and one counselor. There were nearly 20 volunteers working, on average, in each building.

Data reflect a need for student intervention and staff-development for schools serving low-achieving urban students. There were no statistically significant differences in the importance of the items surveyed, as viewed by principals. However, the ordering of the mean scores may be of interest to educators. Importance ratings of needs, as viewed by principals, ranged from 1 to 5.

Programs for disruptive students received the highest mean score as an intervention strategy, followed by a need for personal and social counseling and a need for teachers who are sensitive to at-risk students, with respective mean scores of 4.86, 4.69, and 4.65. With regards to staff development needs, classroom management techniques received the highest mean score, followed by alternative teaching strategies, and self-concept development in the classroom, with respective mean scores of 4.71, 4.69, and 4.47.

As for additional personnel resources, principals showed the highest need for the school counselor, followed by the school psychologist, and the school social worker, with their respective mean scores of 4.87, 4.73, and 4.70. Principals felt that they also needed additional rewards for students to influence their enrollment in academic incentive programs, followed by science equipment and computers for instruction, with respective mean scores of 4.71, 4.49, and 4.33. Relative to community involvement, principals felt that parents should be involved in more school activities. Also, there was a need for more collegiality among teachers and a need for students to feel an ownership in their school. The need for more collegiality among teachers received the highest mean score, followed by a need for greater student identification with their school, and more parental involvement in school activities, with respective mean scores of 4.70, 4.67, and 4.65.

Data were factor analyzed to identify clusters of responses that reflected major conceptual areas for developing educational alternatives for low achievers. The analysis sought to group items into clusters that would reflect major intervention areas, as viewed by principals. Reliability coefficients were generated for each factor to determine the internal consistency of combined items. Five factors were found: academic transition and enhancement, counseling and affective intervention, specialized intervention in content areas, alternative structure in content areas, and intervention for social needs. Thus the 37-item instrument was reduced to five major areas.

Principals indicated a general need for programs on academic transition and enhancement. Items loading on this factor produced an eigenvalue of 9.45 and a corresponding reliability coefficient of .84. Counseling and affective interventions was a second factor identified, with an eigenvalue of 3.29 and a corresponding realizability coefficient of .87. Specialized intervention in content areas produced an eigenvalue of 2.02 and realizability coefficient of .90. The remaining two factors were alternative structure in content areas and intervention for social needs. The respective eigenvalues were 1.84 and 1.42, with identical reliability coefficients of .80.

DISCUSSION AND CONCLUSIONS

The basic assumption underlying this article is that principals must establish a climate for educational excellence in their schools. While school choice is an option and may be necessary to improve urban schools, it is erroneous to believe that all families will be capable of taking advantage of such choices. Many educational options are not available to poor families, and serious discussions of school choice should avoid the misleading proposition of relating quality education to choice options.

Another question is: Can private urban community schools be viewed as a viable choice for poor urban families? The answer to this question is not clear. A few community schools of a private nature have been effective within urban communities; most of them were established by non-White and poor families disillusioned by public schools (Ratteray, 1983). These community schools are often designed to meet the developmental needs of African-American, Hispanic-American, Asian-American, and Native American children, emphasizing basic skills and multicultural education (Ogbu, 1988, Rashid, 1989).

The fact that public schools often fail to meet the needs of students is well established (Hahn & Danzberger, 1987; Monaco, 1987). Therefore, private community schools in some circumstances may be a solution for academic problems commonly experienced by non-White urban students. Funding for private schools may come from a combination of sources: tuition, donations from philanthropic organizations, and Chapter I compensatory government programs. But government funding of private schools is not legal (Coons & Sugarman, 1971; Friedman, 1973; Singleton, 1977). The exercise of school choice through government support of private schools has been viewed by some as supportive of educational reform and desegregation (Ratteray, 1983; Sowell, 1977).

It seems useful to focus on effective alternative approaches within existing public schools. Clearly, economic constraints on families and school districts will limit the number of alternatives available to urban children. This reality fosters the notion that solutions for improving education offerings for urban children must be achieved through innovative uses of available resources. Principals can make a difference in this regard. The curriculum can be modified to fit more precisely the needs of at-risk students.

New programs must be established to help at-risk students develop in a comprehensive and more holistic fashion. An interesting outcome of the survey was that urban principals thought at-risk students needed affective and social programs as much as cognitive-based programs. More specifically, data suggested that principals saw a need for programs and resources devoted equally to the emotional aspects of children. This finding suggests that much of the focus on school reform may be inappropriate.

Rather than focusing on new instructional strategies, it may be just as important to make children "feel good" about themselves and learning. This suggestion does not discount the need for stronger academic programs. These data suggest, however, that those involved with at-risk students feel a great need for balancing these programs to meet students' psychosocial and cognitive needs.

School choice, then, is within the purview of public schools. That is, schools must establish programs that will work for the children they serve. Magnet schools may help, but opportunities for educational excellence reside in every public school. As noted, knowledge on how to improve schools for at-risk students is available, and each principal must apply this information to meet the educational needs of his or her students. This study of principals recommends that urban schools need additional resources, but not necessarily different programs, to better educate their students.

REFERENCES

Beachum, L P. (1985). *Effective urban schools: Building student pride*. NASSP Bulletin, 69, 105-107.

Boykin, A W. (1979). Psychological/behavioral verve: Some theoretical explorations and behavioral manifestations. In A. W. Boykin, A. J. Franklin, & J. F. Yates (Eds.), *Black psychology and the research process: Keeping the baby, but throwing out the bathwater* (pp. 85-103). New York: Russell Sage.

Boykin, A. W. (1984). Reading achievement and the social-cultural frame of reference of African-American children. *Journal of Negro Education*, 53,

464-473.

Coons, J., & Sugarman, S. (1971). *Family choice in education: A model state system for vouchers.* Berkeley, CA: Institute of Governmental Studies.

Comer, J. P., Haynes, N. M., & Hamilton-Lee, M. (1988). School power: A model for improving Black student achievement. *Urban League Review, 11,* 187-200.

Committee for Economic Development. (1987). *Children in need: Investment strategies for the educationally disadvantaged.* New York: Author.

Contreras, A. R (1988). Use of educational reform to create effective schools. *Education and Urban Society,* 20, 399-413.

Cureton, G. O. (1978). Using a Black learning style. *Reading Teacher, 31,* 751-756.

Edmonds, R. (1980). *Search for effective schools.* Washington, DC: Horace Mann Learning Center. (ERIC Document Reproduction Service No. ED 212 689)

Fortenberry, R N. (1986). *Implementation of the effective school model in an urban district.* Illinois School Research and Development, 22(2), 60-70.

Friedman, M. (1973. September 23). *The voucher idea.* New York Times Magazine, p. 22-23.

Garcia, E. E. (1988). Attributes of effective schools for language minority students. *Education and Urban Society,* 20, 387-398.

Hahn, A., & Danzberger, J. (1987). *Dropouts in America: Enough is known for action.* Washington, DC: Institute for Educational Leadership.

Harris, I. M. (1984). The inequities of Milwaukee's plan. *Integrated Education,* 1(6), 173-177.

Hess, G. A., Jr. (1984). Renegotiating a multicultural society: Participation in desegregation planning in Chicago. *Journal of Negro Education,* 53(2), 132-146.

Levin, H. (1972). *The costs to the nation of an inadequate education.* Washington, DC: Report to the Select Committee on Equal Educational Opportunity of the United States Senate.

Lezotte, L. (1985, April). Effective schools. Paper presented at Conference on Effective Schools, New Orleans, LA.

Monaco, F. A. (1987). *Here's the data: At-risk OVT programs.* Pittsburgh, PA:

Pittsburgh Public Schools.

Moody, C. D., Sr., & Moody, C. D. (1988). Elements of effective Black schools. *Urban League Review*, 11(2), 177-186.

Morgan, E.P. (1979). Effective teaching in the urban high school. *Urban Education*, 14, 161-181.

Mortimore, P., & Sammons, P. (1987). New evidence on effective elementary schools. *Educational Leadership*, 45(1), 4-8.

Ogbu, J. U. (1988). Class stratification, racial stratification, and schooling. In L. Weis (Ed.), *Class, race, and gender* (pp. 163-182). Albany, NY: State University of New York Press.

Ortiz, F. 1. (1988). Hispanic-American children's experiences in classrooms: A comparison between Hispanic and non-Hispanic children. In L. Weis (Ed.), *Class, race, and gender* (pp.63-86). Albany, NY: State University of New York Press.

Pink, W. T., & Wallace, D. K. (1984). Creating effective urban elementary schools: A case study of the implementation of planned change. *Urban Education*, 19, 273-315.

Rashid,H.M.(1989). Variations in teacher behavior and teacher expectations: Implications for urban education. Paper presented at the Annual Conference of the Cleveland State University Urban Educational Research Center, Cleveland, OH.

Ratteray, J. D. (1983). *Alternative educational options for minorities and the poor. An interim project report*. Washington, DC: National Center for Neighborhood Enterprise.

Raywid, M. A. (1982). *The current status of schools of choice in public secondary education*. Hempstead, NY: Project on Alternatives in Education.

Raywid,M.A.(1983). Schools of choice: Their current nature and prospects. *Phi Delta Kappan*, 64, 684-688.

Rossell, C. H. (1987). The Buffalo controlled choice plan. *Urban Education*, 22, 328-354.

Singleton, R. (1977). California: The Self-Determination in Education Act, 1968. *In Parents, teachers, and children: Prospects for choice in American education* (pp. 77-83). San Francisco: Institute for Contemporary Studies.

Sizemore, B. (1985). Pitfalls and promises of effective schools research. *Journal of Negro Education*, 54, 269-288.

Sowell, T. (1977). Choice in education and parental responsibility. *In Parents, teachers, and children: Prospects for choice in American education*. San Francisco: Institute for Contemporary Studies.

Steadman, L. C. (1985). A new look at the effective schools literature. *Urban Education*, 20, 295-326.

Valverde, L. A. (1988). Principals creating better schools in minority communities. *Education and Urban Society*, 20, 319-326.

Wehlage, G. (1988). *School reforms for at-risk students*. Madison, WI: National Center on Effective Secondary Schools.

Wilensky, R., & Kline III, D. M. (1989). School reform and community renewal. *Equity and Choice*, 5(2), 13-18.

Wilson, C. D., & Fergus, E. O. (1988). Combining effective schools and school improvement research traditions for achieving equity-based education. *Equity & Excellence*, 24(1), 54-65.

Winborne, D. G. (in press). Perspectives on children "at-risk": Cultural considerations and alternative educational approaches. In J. Harris & C. Heid (Eds.), *Readings on the state of education in pluralistic America*. Bloomington: Indiana University.

Secondary School Students' Attitudes Toward Schools of Choice and What Choices They Would Make

Margaret D. Tannenbaum
Theodore Tannenbaum

Introduction

The issue of giving parents the right to choose the schools their children attend has waxed and waned since the early sixties when Milton Friedman (1962) first included it in his social proposals. From 1971 to 1976 the federal government funded a voucher experiment in Alum Rock, California, run by the Center for the Study of Public Policy at Harvard, directed by Christopher Jencks and based, to a large extent on a proposal put forth by him and Judith Areen (1971). Although there were many positive results from this experiment, political and financial complexities and the short duration of the experiment prevented development of any definitive conclusions (Cohen & Farrar, 1977).

Since Alum Rock there have been two major obstacles to the implementation of such a system: the constitutional question of aid to non-public schools and strong political opposition on the part of those currently in control of schools. In recent years the first obstacle has been eliminated by re-defining the issue of choice to exclude non-public schools (Raywid, 1988). The question of choice among public schools has now emerged as a major issue, with Minnesota achieving full state-wide implementation of such a system in 1990-91, a substantial number of states considering some form of a choice plan, Milwaukee implementing choice for low income families, and Presidents Bush and Clinton each endorsing a form of school choice. Phi Delta Kappan and the Association for Supervision and Curriculum Development have in recent years both published monographs examining this issue. Although there is a fair amount of evidence that choice systems bring positive benefits to all involved (Raywid, 1989), there is still strong opposition by professional educators and local school boards.

For a number of years the annual Gallup Poll of the Public's Attitudes Toward the Public Schools has asked respondents their views toward vouchers or schools of choice. What polls have not done is to ask those who would be most directly affected by this proposed change in the structure of schooling what their views toward it are. The present study undertook to do just that and surveyed students in public and private schools in grades 7 through 12 in Southern New Jersey regarding their attitudes toward choosing their schools and the reasons why they would choose particular schools. The underlying assumption of this study is that if families were given the right to choose the schools their children attend, by the time these students reached the secondary level, their preferences would have a major impact on what schools were chosen.

Methods and Data Source

This study is the largest of its kind, with a total of over 4,000 usable responses from 28 school districts, and has surveyed all of the populations that would be directly affected by a choice system. This particular section of the study focuses on the analysis of the 2027 student responses, almost half of the total. Its purpose was threefold:

1. To analyze the attitudes of students towards schools of choice;

2. To examine the implications for school reform and restructuring based on student preferences;

3. To examine whether or not student engagement with schools would be increased in a choice system and if academic achievement would thereby be improved.

A pilot study was conducted in the Spring of 1989 surveying the attitudes toward schools of choice of teachers, administrators, board members, parents, and secondary students. A total of 342 responses were collected by graduate students (most of whom are teachers or administrators) as part of the research requirements for the course Foundations of Educational Policymaking. As a result of this pilot, questionnaires were revised and these same populations in the seven southern counties of New Jersey were surveyed during the 1989-90 school year. Mailings were sent to all of the district superintendents of public school systems and to directors of all private schools listed in a directory provided by the State Office of Education. A total of 35 schools or districts responded to this mailing and over 6,000 surveys were sent out. As a result of both the New Jersey budget crunch and faulty estimates of the amount of available time, 7 schools or districts were not able to complete the study. Twenty-eight schools or districts returned completed questionnaires for one or more populations, including the major metropolitan area of Atlantic City. The method of distribution was through superintendents' offices, where the number of requested surveys were sent. It is not known how parents were selected for participation in the survey. Generally speaking all teachers, administrators, and board members were asked to complete questionnaires. In smaller schools and districts all students were given surveys. In larger districts a sample of students was selected, on a basis determined by the local administration. A total of 4302 usable responses were returned from the following constituencies: teachers - 1058; administrators - 110; board members - 48; parents - 1059; students - 2027.

The questionnaires contained 6-8 items about demographics and 3-4 items about regard for present school systems, and 17-20 items about attitudes toward schools of choice. Both a univariate and bivariate analysis was conducted. At the top of the questionnaire was the following introduction:

> Recently Governor Kean proposed instituting a system of "Schools of Choice" in New Jersey. There are three possible ways to implement such a system: (1) Intradistrict schools of choice would permit parents to select a school for their child from any public schools in their district of residence; (2) Interdistrict schools of choice would permit selection from any public schools in the state; (3) Vouchers would permit parents to select from any public or private school. We are interested in learning your feelings about schools of choice and would greatly appreciate your taking a few minutes to answer the following questions.

A five-point Likert scale was used and a Strongly Agree or Agree response was considered to favor schools of choice while a Disagree or Strongly Disagree response was seen as not favoring schools of choice. For two of the statements, number 6 and 10, the orientations were reversed.

Results

Of the students responding, 53% were female and 47% male; 35% were urban, 41% suburban, 23% rural; 34% were in 7th or 8th grade, 19% in 9th grade, 15% in 10th grade, 11% in 11th grade, 21% in 12th grade; 54% described themselves as usually getting A's or B's, 38% said they usually get C's, 9% said they usually receive D's or F's; by program 53% were college prep, 17% business, 16% vocational, 14% general.

Another more subjective set of questions was asked. In terms of their feelings for the schools they presently intend, 54% say they like them, 21% say they dislike them, and 25% say they are uncertain. Asked about the likelihood of dropping out of school, 91% say they are unlikely, 4% say they are likely, and 5% say they are uncertain. Finally, and most interestingly, only 7% of students believe their schools are doing an excellent job, while 25% believe they are doing a very good job, 56% average, 9% poor, and 3% very poor. To say this another way, two thirds of the students responding to the questionnaire believe their schools are doing an average or less job. This in itself sets the context for the analysis of the questions that follows and the implications for school restructuring based on students' choices.

This discussion will examine the attitudes of students toward schools of choice, especially focusing on the reasons students say they would choose particular schools, then analyze the data on the basis of age, sex, level, grades, program, and geographic location.

Table 1

A substantial proportion of students (70%) believe families should have the right to choose the schools their children will attend and 40% say they would attend different schools than the ones they presently attend. This is interesting in comparison to responses from parents. Far more parents (84%) than students believe they should have the right to choose schools for their children, while far fewer (21%) say they would choose a different school for their child(ren) than presently attended. One explanation for this latter difference could be that parents of children at both the elementary and secondary levels are answering the questionnaire. The percent of parents of secondary students who would choose a different school (32%) approaches the answers of the secondary students. There appears to be a great amount of dissatisfaction among secondary students with the schools they currently attend.

Of those students who would choose a different school in a choice system, 19% say they would select a private school; of these, approximately 84% say it would be one with a religious orientation. Among parents, 27% of those who currently send their children to public schools would send them to private schools, while 19% of private school parents would send their children to public schools in a choice system. This, of course, assumes a choice plan which includes private schools —generally described as a voucher system. If per-capita costs in public and private schools remained pretty much as they currently are, this would be a net positive gain in the school financing scene.

One area of particular interest is the impact that respondents, both students and parents, believe a choice program would have on discipline problems. Nearly a third of students (29%) and 40% of parents (48% of private school parents) believe there would be fewer discipline problems if students could choose the schools they attend. There is no way of knowing from this study whether these respondents are those who are having discipline problems or those who are not.

Although there is a fairly even distribution of students who say they would choose a school because of its thematic orientation (math/science - 44%, English/humanities - 44%, theater/fine arts/music - 49%), a far lower percentage (31%) would choose a vocational school. The two major reasons students give for selecting schools are high standards of academic achievement (75%) and athletics/sports (60%). Note that these are not mutually exclusive choices. Although 51% of students would choose a school because of its neighborhood and 32% would be influenced by their friends' choices, only 17% say they would choose a school because it was easy. At the same time, 41% of students believe they would get better grades if they could choose their school and 65% say they would be happier. Once again, it would seem that these student self-predictions, even if they were to come true by only half, would substantially improve school climate and increase students' involvements in school activities.

Table 2

Those factors which show no clear pattern in predicting students' positive or negative attitudes toward school choice are geographic location, grade level, and grades students receive. Urban and rural students show a slightly more positive attitude toward being able to choose their schools than do suburban students. This is to be expected in that suburban schools are generally more likely to provide the facilities and programs that students see as leading to success and the students in these schools would be less likely to see a need to be able to choose their schools.

Although grade level does not predict support for the choice concept, there are some interesting patterns that emerge in terms of what choices students would make by grade level. Seniors are far more likely to choose a school because of its high standards of academic achievement (86%) than are junior high students (71%), freshman (71%), sophomores (71%), or juniors (75%). In addition, seniors are more likely to choose a school because it has an English/Humanities orientation (53% compared to 44%, 39%, 35%, 46% respectively) and equally likely with junior high students to choose a school for its math/science orientation (45% compared to 42% for freshman, 43% for sophomores, and 39% for juniors). By contrast, junior high students are most likely to pick a school for its theater/music/fine arts orientation (62% compared to 40% of freshman and sophomores, 45% for juniors, and 42% for seniors), its athletic/sports orientation (67% compared to 55% for freshman and sophomores, 54% for juniors, and 58% for seniors) or a vocational school (45% compared to 24% for freshman, 26% for sophomores, and 20% for juniors and seniors). It is significant to note that nearly half of the junior high students, nearly an equal percentage of males and females (30% and 33%) say they would choose a vocational school and this is more than twice the percentage of juniors and seniors who say they would. In light of the current figures for college attendance and graduation, it might be that the preferences of junior high students are more compatible with the real world.

Although a higher percentage of students who receive A's and B's (72%) than those who receive D's and F's (62%) believe parents should have the right to choose the schools their children attend, students with lower grades are otherwise more positive in their expectations about choice. Not only would more of the students with lower grades (46%) choose a different school than they presently attend than would students with higher grades (38%), more believe there would be fewer discipline problems (40%, 26%) and believe they would get better grades (50%, 38%). At the same time, there is little variation among students by the grades they get regarding whether or not they would be happier in a school they chose (63%, 68%, 64%).

As might be expected, grades do have a correlation with what type of schools students would select. Those with higher grades are more likely to pick schools because they are in a good neighborhood, have high standards of academic achievement, and with math/science or English/humanities orientation. Those with lower grades are more likely to pick schools because they heard they were easy or pick a vocational school or a private school.

Closely related to grades students receive are the areas of liking or dislike for school and likelihood of dropping out of school. Students who dislike their present schools are more likely than those who like their present schools to believe that families should have the right to choose the schools their children attend (73%, 69%), to choose a different school (66%, 26%), to believe there would be fewer discipline problems (40%, 25%), to be willing to spend time commuting (44%, 33%), to choose a school because it was in a good neighborhood (55%, 50%), to choose a school because it was easy (23%, 14%), to believe they would get better grades (56%, 35%), to expect to be happier (77%, 59%), to select a private school (21%, 18%), and to want their schools to participate if a choice system were enacted (53%, 46%). Although several of these differences are fairly small (right to choose, good neighborhood, private school), four are significant and demand serious consideration in the discussion of student performance: those who would choose a different school, who believe there would be fewer discipline problems, who believe they would get better grades, who would be happier. Increasing students' happiness with their educational setting as a result of their selecting these settings would surely lead to the outcomes these students predict: better grades and fewer discipline problems —two of the major goals of school reform.

This pattern essentially repeats itself in regard to students who say they are likely to drop out of school in comparison to those who say they are unlikely to drop out. Although students who say they are unlikely to drop out of school are more likely to believe parents should have the right to choose the schools their children attend than are those who say they are likely to drop out of school (71%, 59%), in every other area, those who say they are likely to drop out of school are more supportive of choice than are those who say they are unlikely to drop out. They are more likely to choose a different school (48%, 39%), believe there would be fewer discipline problems (39%, 28%), would be more willing to travel up to an hour (46%, 35%), believe they would get better grades (49%, 40%), and would be happier (71%, 65%).

Interestingly, when it comes to the types of schools students would choose, their liking or dislike for school has little predictive value, with one exception. Those who dislike school are more likely to say they would choose a school that has a theater/fine arts/music orientation than are those who say they like school (57%, 47%). By contrast, students who say they are likely to drop out of school are more likely than those who say they are not to be influenced in their choices by their friends' choices (37%, 31%), to choose a vocational school (43%, 30%), to choose a school because it was easy (28%, 16%), and to choose a private school (37%, 17%) or one with a religious orientation (24%, 16%). Again, as might be expected, students who say they are unlikely to drop out of school are more likely than those who say they are likely to drop out of school to choose a school because it is in a good neighborhood (52%, 39%), has high standards of academic achievement (77%, 51%), or has an athletic/sports orientation (61%, 48%). With the exception of the private and religious school choices, none of these patterns are surprising.

Those students who believe their schools are doing a poor job are clearly more supportive of schools of choice than those who believe their schools are doing an excellent or good job. They are more likely to say they would choose a different school (61%, 27%), believe there would be fewer discipline problems (42%, 26%), be willing to spend time commuting (49%, 34%), to predict they would get better grades (60%, 35%), and to believe they would be happier (79%, 60%). They also say they would be more likely to choose an easy school (26%, 14%). None of these are surprising responses, but, again, this summary raises major questions about the general impact that providing choice would have on those students who believe their present schools are doing a poor job —a total of 12% of all students surveyed.

Without exception, those students who believe families have the right to choose schools are more positive toward schools of choice than those who do not believe this. There appears to be no correlation between this belief and the types of schools students say they would choose. An interesting point, however, in this category is that even among those students who do not believe parents should have the right to choose the schools their children attend, 63% believe they would be happier if they could choose. Only 16% of students disagree with the statement that families should have the right to choose the schools their children will attend, but it would be interesting to interview even this small population to find out what their reasons might be. Interview follow-up was not a part of this study.

With only one exception (get better grades) female students are slightly more supportive of schools of choice than male students, although the differences are minimal. In the area of reasons for selecting schools, females are more likely to choose a school because it is in a good neighborhood, because it has high academic standards, has an English/humanities of theater/fine arts/music orientation, or is a vocational school. Males are more likely to be influenced by what schools their friends choose, select a school with a math/science or athletic/sports orientation, and select a school because they heard it was easy. None of these differences are great, however, and the only one that is even slightly surprising is females' slightly higher selection of vocational schools.

Educational Significance of Study

Inasmuch as there is significant research evidence (Raywid, 1989) indicating that schools of choice have positive outcomes for students, parents, and teachers, it is important to ask why there has not been widespread implementation of them. This survey attempts to sample all populations that would be involved in or affected by the adoption of schools of choice in order to determine which populations with what characteristics view schools of choice positively or negatively. In general, parents and students —the consumers/clients— are overwhelmingly supportive of schools of choice; teachers, administrators, and board members —the producers/providers— are much less in favor of a choice system.

The focus of the current discussion is on those who would be most affected by the implementation of a choice system —students. On four of the five questions that ascertain overall attitudes toward schools of choice 40% or more of students see positive outcomes and fewer than 25% disagree. A substantial proportion of students say they would be happier, would select a school because of its high academic achievement, would get better grades, and would be less likely to drop out in a choice system. This should cause those school reformers who are focusing on student outcomes as a measure of school success to give serious consideration to choice programs as a means of raising students' positive feelings toward their schools and, thus, the likelihood of their becoming more involved and more successful in their studies. A growing focus in educational research is on the question of student engagement in schools in order to bring about more positive attitudes and, thus, higher academic achievement and greater ongoing success. This study strongly suggests that many of the factors that increase student engagement in schooling activities could be maximized in a choice system.

This issue must be addressed within the theoretical framework of what it means to educate citizens in a democracy and the extent to which those being educated have the right to choose the forms that education will take. This becomes an even more compelling issue when large portions of those being schooled receive inferior education because of their residence or social class. Examining the implementation of choice in schooling addresses the possibility of restructuring for school improvement along the lines of increased equity and higher achievement for those for whom the present system is failing —large number of students in major urban areas and others for whom social class has contributed to undermining the quality of education they receive because of the predominant means of funding schools through individual and community property wealth.

Bibliography

Areen, J. & Jencks, C. (1971). Education vouchers: A proposal for diversity and choice. *Teachers College Record*, 72 (3), 327-335.

Cohen, D.K. & Farrar, E. (1977). Power to the parents?— The story of education vouchers. *Public Interest*, Summer, 72-97.

Friedman, M. (1962). *Capitalism and freedom.* Chicago: University of Chicago Press.

Raywid, M.A. (1988). Public choice, yes; Vouchers, no! *Phi Delta Kappan*, 69 (10), 762-770.

Raywid, M.A. (1989). *The case for public schools of choice.* Bloomington, Ind.: Phi Delta Kappa Educational Foundation.

WHERE PTA STANDS ON...
Parental Choice

Arnold Fege
Millie Waterman

Many states and school leaders responded to recent calls for higher educational standards by universally mandating changes for all students. At the same time, however, there was a cry for more school options or "parental choices" to accommodate varying student interests. Currently there is tension between "the ideal of a common education shared by all students as an essential goal we all must follow" as claimed by Marvin Lazerman, author of An Education of Value, and that of providing a "deliberate selection of programs among alternates" to meet diverse student needs as articulated by David Seely, author of Education Through Partnership.

The National PTA Board of Directors recently adopted a position paper entitled "Guidelines on Parental Choice—An Educational Issue," which responds to various reform proposals that call for alternate programs and schools. The guidelines state that any plans for alternate programs should ensure that the following conditions are met:

- the community sustains a viable public school system;
- parents have the opportunity for involvement in their children's schools;
- appropriate and free transportation be provided for students to ensure equity;
- specialized schools provide for a fair and equitable selection process;
- standards governing school curricula, personnel and student performance provide access to equal opportunities; and
- adequate and objective information be made available to parents so that they can make informed decisions.

PTA's Position Paper

A condensed version of the National PTA's position paper follows.

The National PTA has historically been an advocate for all children and seeks to improve all schools. Any change in structure or funding should be measured by its effect on all children. Proposals differ from one community or state to the next; some offer options that include private and parochial schools; some permit crossing school system boundaries into adjoining systems in the state; some expand on already existing "alternative schools." Distinctions are not always clear because some are based on concerns about educational achievement and others a response to differing philosophies and values of the parents.

PTA goals, as listed above, should govern any consideration of proposed parental choice plans. This can best be done by seeking the answers to these questions:

1. What type of "choice" program is being considered? Does the proposal give parents full "choice" to any district in the region or state? Does it offer "choice" as open enrollment within the school district only? Are there options that allow "choice" in the district of residence or where the parents work? Does the "choice" plan include only accredited secondary schools?

2. How will access to schools be determined in a system of "choice?"

How will the problem of geographically isolated students/schools be addressed? Is admission based on testing or on a lottery? Is there a policy governing a waiting list? How will the issues of size of class, programs, school and district be addressed?

3. How does the plan promote equal educational opportunities for all children?

4. How will funding sustain the local schools from which some children transfer but where other parents "choose" to keep their children? Will their needs be met? Will local aid follow a child who "chooses" a school outside district attendance boundaries? If not, how will a receiving district absorb the costs of these children's education? Does the plan provide for the higher costs of transfer students who are in a program for the handicapped or disadvantaged?

5. What is the impact of such a proposal on the demographics of a community? On schools not currently under a desegregation plan that might become "minority" schools if a substantial number of "majority" students leave? Are local desegregation or integration plans protected under this proposal?

6. Will free transportation be offered so that "choice" is a reality even to a poor family who may not have other transportation options? Where will funds come from?

7. Will a changed system of school assignment meet the special needs of

children and not just the philosophical differences or views of their parents? For example, how will special education children's programs be effected? Are parents aware that current federal law limits special services to disadvantaged children to those attending schools designated as "entitlement schools" only, and if an entitlement-eligible child transfers to a noneligible public school, even in the same district, the money cannot follow the child?

8. What will be the administrative tasks new proposals will impose on both teaching staffs and administrators? What additional paperwork or regulations will be required?

9. How will the school system deal with the fears and concerns that such plans may skim the best students and teachers for selective schools? Will the plan provide an unequal allocation of resources, leaving schools that are not heavily selected with even greater problems and more limited resources to meet these problems?

10. How will the effectiveness of the "choice" plan be evaluated in assessing the ability to improve the educational progress of children? Is there a plan for a pilot before any districtwide change takes place? Will there be an ongoing evaluation process? Will the results of the evaluation be made public?

1 1. Under a plan of parental "choice," how will the public be informed in a way that is both fair and complete? Will each school "sell itself" or will the descriptions be done by the central district? If it is done by the individual schools, who will monitor "truth in marketing" and who will assure that unwritten selection rules will not be used by the individual schools? Will the public information materials be in languages that the parents can understand? What efforts will be made to reach parents who are themselves poorly educated or highly mobile?

12. How will the plan for "choice" deal with athletic recruiting at the high school level, and affect schools unable to compete athletically if their student pools are reduced?

13. How will such a change affect parental involvement? What evidence is there that a sense of ownership in a "choice" plan increases involvement or that physical distance and transportation problems do not decrease parental involvement?

The concept or "parental choice" in selecting the schools that children attend has gained considerable attention in discussions about educational reforms. When considering proposed changes in education, we should scrutinize them by posing the above questions. A crucial question for the PTA is not whether an individual parent is satisfied by a proposal, but what effect the plan will have on all children. Any suggested proposal must meet that test.

School Choice Plans
and the
Professionalization of Teaching

Camilla A. Heid
Lawrence E. Leak

The public debate surrounding the strengths and deficiencies of public education in the United States has rekindled discussion about educational choice options for parents and students. Although much of the discussion has centered on providing options for parents to consider when sending their children off to public schools, there are also options for teachers to capitalization market opportunities that will surface as traditional educational delivery mechanisms begin to change.

One legacy of the "Reagan revolution" was the privatization and deregulation of goods and services that have traditionally been thought of as public sector responsibilities. Even though educators saw few examples of the privatization of goods and services, the Republican administration favored educational vouchers and tuition tax credits promoted through the concept of school choice. Education at the precollegiate level is the responsibility of state governments, and the desire to have an institutionalized method of fostering an educated and informed public can be traced back to the establishment of our nation. However, the educational reform movements that dominated public debate in the past decade have served to underscore public dissatisfaction with our present public education system (Lieberman, 1989). This dissatisfaction has prompted national policymakers to embrace educational choice as the only acceptable method for improving education (Paulu, 1989).

Following the Reagan administration's lead, President Bush has characterized school choice as perhaps the single most promising initiative derived from the first wave of the educational reform movement. The current Secretary of Education, Lauro Cavazos, asserts that school choice can improve education in a variety of ways, including bringing about needed structural changes, recognizing student diversity, fostering competition and accountability, improving educational outcomes, and increasing parental involvement in the educational process (Paulu, 1989). Bush also followed Reagan's lead in using the choice movement as a way to promote state funding of private schools and to reduce busing for racial integration.

The notion of empowering parents to become active partners in reform efforts designed to hold school leaders accountable for the education of our nation's youth has taken hold and promises to challenge the traditional policies that govern public education. As parents seek direct involvement in the educational process, school leaders are hard pressed to defend educational policies that fail to promote excellence and diversity.

Increasingly vocal in their expectations of quality educational outcomes for their children, parents have demanded change, and many school leaders across the country have created or restructured instructional programs to meet the specialized needs of students. St. Paul (Minnesota), District 4 in East Harlem (New York), Cambridge (Massachusetts), and Eugene (Oregon) are just a few examples of school systems providing innovative options for students (Paulu, 1989). Many of these reform efforts established programs in which parents and students are free to choose among schools that house educational programs that appeal to various needs. Uniform pedagogy, lockstep instructional delivery structures, and "one best way" policy implementation processes, desired by school leaders as the basic operational mechanism for serving the needs of students, are no longer acceptable for all students.

If school choice options take place in school systems across the country, challenging opportunities may exist for the teaching profession. With parents seeking to gain a more responsive public education system, the teaching profession too must step forward to seek more direct involvement in the governance of their schools. The purpose of this article is to analyze the development of school choice plans by teachers and to examine the impact of this process on the professionalization of teachers.

TEACHER PARTICIPATION IN SCHOOL CHOICE

Anne Lewis (1989) outlines six types of public school choice plans, as described by the Education Commission of the States. These plans include interdistrict, postsecondary, second chance, controlled choice, magnet, and teacher initiated schools. Interdistrict and postsecondary plans give families the right to choose among existing public schools regardless of attendance zones. Second chance plans provide options to traditional schooling for at-risk youth through innovative intervention strategies. Families select the school their child attends, but equity is the focus of controlled choice plans. Magnet schools offer additional resources within the framework of school improvement and family choice. Schools that are restructured with direct faculty involvement describe teacher initiated plans.

Recent results from a Gallup-Phi Delta Kappa poll confirm that members of the teaching profession are concerned about their lack of involvement in formulating policies that have an impact on the operation of schools (Elam, 1989). Likewise data from the Metropolitan Life-Lou Harris (1989) survey reveal that teachers would like to strengthen their working relationship with school principals by forming school leadership committees comprised of teachers, administrators, and students. This strategy for participative management would enable teachers to become viable partners in the governance and decision-making structures within their schools.

One teacher initiated restructuring effort currently receiving international attention is the Key School in Indianapolis, Indiana. Using the principle of multiple talents of children, the Key School was developed by eight teachers who wanted to improve the educational outcomes of their students. The common vision shared by the staff, their ownership of the school program, and their commitment to quality education for all students are the main strengths of this school of choice (Olson, 1988).

Teacher initiated choice plans appear to be growing in momentum, as demonstrated by the formation of the Teacher Network Group in 1987, with support from the Ford Foundation, Rockefeller Foundation, and the National Science Foundation. The projects in this network value teachers' views on educational philosophy, curriculum, and pedagogy; they are bound together by a common theme that teachers play a significant and active role in any successful educational reform initiative (Lewis, 1989).

True partnerships between teachers and school-based administrators, where key decisions that affect the well-being of the school are discussed openly, would begin a process that dignifies the profession of teaching within the organizational structure of schools. Members of the teaching profession must be careful not to retreat from any participative management overtures because to do so would simply maintain the relationships that currently exist between teachers and principals and further perpetuate the "us versus them" mind set that exists in many schools across the country.

As proponents of teacher empowerment position themselves in the debate regarding school choice, professional educators will have opportunities to redefine the governance role teachers play in schools. Currently, teachers have little involvement in matters that serve to shape the very essence of how schools operate as an organizational entity. In most schools, teachers work in isolation, doing what they do best—the art of teaching—in the secluded environment of their classrooms; and principals spend very little time engaging teachers in meaningful discussions of school governance.

Because school choice is a dominant topic in the education reform debate, principals have come to realize that substantive discussions about school choice cannot occur without actively involving teachers. In reality, programmatic and instructional choices cannot be made readily available to parents and students without conceptualizing and implementing strategies designed to restructure schools. Choice programs require principals and teachers to transcend the traditional organizational roles, relationships, and regulations in addressing changes in schooling.

CAN TEACHERS DEVELOP A MARKET NICHE?

The current mechanism used to deliver public school education services is virtually unchanged over the past decades. Still, teachers have demonstrated that innovative educational practices can foster parental and student interest, thereby improving educational outcomes. For the most part, teachers develop and maintain operational control over structure, goals, and content in their classrooms. Waiting lists for students appear to be the rule rather than the exception for schools operating under the limited number of choice plans in operation.

In order to successfully implement a school choice plan, teachers must be involved. In the case of teacher initiated plans, teachers must develop a shared vision of their "market niche." The niche must include their philosophy, curriculum, and pedagogy and should contain clearly defined educational outcomes in order to gain support from administrators and parents.

For example, District 4 in East Harlem is the site of a 15-year experiment with school choice options. This school district was well known for extensive use of drugs, high dropout rates, and the lowest reading and math scores in New York City. Currently, 50 thematic schools in the district attract students from more affluent residential areas outside the district. Teachers participate in hiring of new faculty members, scheduling courses, and developing new instructional programs. "Signs of the program's success are everywhere: teacher morale is high, visitors report that hallways are orderly, vandalism and truancy are down significantly, and test scores have risen dramatically" (Paulu, 1989, pp. 4-5).

Most choice plans involve some degree of restructuring, but restructuring efforts that leave the basic school organization intact will only create the illusion of change. The organizational components of most schools are so strongly interrelated that any attempt to alter one aspect of the organization should trigger changes elsewhere (Chubb & Moe, 1987). In addition, any choice plan that depends on client interest involves a certain degree of risk. Teachers, therefore, should be knowledgeable of these risks and plan appropriately in order to avoid frustration and the cost associated with failure.

Teachers who work in schools are subordinate to local school boards, which create policies that govern educational practices. However, school systems must allow sufficient policy flexibility for school-based personnel to design and implement choice plans. The degree of flexibility must be clearly defined, so that educators know their roles and organizational boundaries. All rules cannot be eliminated in restructuring schools for choice. The local school system could establish general criteria for a school to be accredited, such as nondiscriminatory admission policies and minimal accreditation standards that relate to course offerings and graduation requirements. Most of the decisions concerning curriculum, staffing, instruction, discipline, and other school-related factors would be made by the teachers and principal in response to their clients, the parents and students who support the school (Chubb & Moe, 1989).

Obviously, with choice plans some schools will attract more students than others. In order to ensure that significant inequities do not occur, the concept of controlled choice, where equity is the focus, must be seriously considered.

Choice does not guarantee students or funds. Enrollments and financial support are available when students and their parents select to use particular schools. Schools that exercise control over staffing, curriculum, instruction, and discipline in ways that are unacceptable to parents and students will find themselves struggling for survival. Ideally, such schools would be closed and the staff would be in search of new employment. In reality, most school systems have negotiated union agreements and tenure policies which would force the reassignment of teachers from the closed schools to schools that are successful in terms of their choice plans. We cannot create and organize a new public education system; the restructuring and choice options must be implemented within the existing system (Chubb & Moe, 1989).

PROFESSIONALIZATION OF TEACHING THROUGH CHOICE

The centrality of the teacher in defining choice plans is emerging as a key factor in decisions that affect teaching and learning. Teacher participation in decision making promotes ownership and a sense of collegiality and enhances the profession (Owens, 1987). This, in turn, yields curricular innovations that can lead to improved student achievement. Participative decision making changes the way parents, students, teachers, and administrators interact with one another, resulting in a coherent and integrated response to organizational concerns. Organizational conflicts that "further fragment operations and diffuse energy" often are a result of ineffective implementation of participative decision-making practices (Timar, 1989, p. 274). Coherent and integrated responses to organizational concerns are not likely to develop without including teachers in the decision-making process.

Teacher initiated choice plans will obviously involve a redefinition of the role and responsibilities of teachers. Currently, the teacher's role is limited to instructing and supervising students. The redefined role should empower teachers to create and implement strategies that assist students in achieving a higher level of thinking skills and to improve learning outcomes. The redefined role of the teacher allows for more personalization or "more responsiveness to the strengths, weaknesses and desires of individual teachers" (Raywid, 1989, p. 21). This new role for teachers will not naturally emerge. Funds and will be required to provide effective staff development to enhance this new role.

A critical concern about professionalization centers around how administrators, school boards, and teacher unions engage in the discourse about teacher initiated choice plans. These groups often have little motivation to participate in discussions about teacher initiated choice plans because sharing power and control are issues that cloud these deliberations.

While teacher unions currently have not hindered choice efforts, the two major unions took different views on the issue. The American Federation of Teachers viewed school choice as a possible advancement toward teacher professionalism, while the National Education Association moved from initial opposition to lukewarm support and encouragement of local school choice efforts (McDonnell & Pascal, 1988). Although it is possible for choice plans to be initiated by administrators and school board members, ultimate success of the choice plan is dependent on the degree of support by teachers.

Any choice plan involving decentralization should expand the school leadership base through teacher empowerment. Teacher empowerment does not imply principals will loose their positions and power, but the concept reinforces the idea that people in an organization have various strengths and all can be leaders in one way or another (Brandt, 1989; Maeroff, 1988). Teacher empowerment means that teachers are viewed as valued members of the school's decision-making process with a major stake in a school's success.

Choice can alter the conditions under which teachers work. Poor working conditions, in the past, have included "administrative subservience, lack of control of the resources needed to teach effectively, loneliness, lack of recognition for excellence in teaching and lack of support" (Murnane, 1986, p. 172). As teacher empowerment increases, teachers will move from the individual autonomy of their classroom to a group of professionals who work collaboratively to expand their control over the quality of education. Professionalism fosters a proactive rather than a reactive approach to problems. Teachers will develop a sense of belonging, and the isolation that teachers often experience in the profession can be alleviated as the group gains security, knowledge, and experience.

Finally, the work environment of the current school structure lacks some of the key elements for professional work. Some elements frequently mentioned include

> access to frequent collegial interaction about complex problems of practice, access to the knowledge required lo enhance professional development, differential rewards for people who develop knowledge and skill at a significantly higher level than their colleagues and access to the basic resources necessary to good performance. (Elmore, 1988, p. 1)

The concept of choice would make public school teaching more attractive to creative people currently employed in public schools and to potential teachers with a creative bent (Clinchy, 1989). Teachers in schools of choice usually have the authority to vary instruction as the situation dictates. They work collaboratively and not in isolation. Their work is more defined by personal strengths and interests than divisions of labor. Schools of choice reward teachers with working conditions that teachers find more enjoyable and more conducive to successful instruction (Raywid, 1989). Talented college graduates who find it attractive to have control over the professional structure of their jobs would likely be drawn to schools of choice. School implementing choice for teachers are often able to eliminate sources of teacher dissatisfaction. Instead of a routinized environment, choice promotes invention and creation within the environment. To teach in a school of choice provides the opportunity to create and maintain a distinctive program through collaborative efforts, and it results in more autonomy for teachers within the school and within each classroom (Raywid, 1989). As recruiting and retaining professional talent is becoming increasingly difficult for school systems, the benefits of public school choice may serve as a vehicle for attracting new teachers to the profession.

CONCLUSION

Public school choice is perceived differently by educators and noneducators. It is viewed as a mechanism for school improvement, a vehicle to promote state aid to private schools, a means to reduce busing for racial integration, and a way to eliminate sources of dissatisfaction for teachers through the creation of a school developed by teachers. Public school choice is not a panacea and cannot solve all the problems in America's schools. It involves risks and requires time, changing roles and responsibilities, and flexibility in policies and regulations.

However, there are benefits to public school choice for teachers. As the market incentives expand, teachers will witness talented young college graduates attracted to the profession by the autonomy in the workplace, control over working conditions, and the professionalization of teaching. Teachers are more likely to enjoy their work and make the commitment to effective teaching when they have shaped the environment in which they work and have been actively involved in the development of school programs. Educators' expectations for school achievement, attendance, and attainment should increase when teachers, parents, and students select their schools (Elmore, 1987). The greatest benefit is that school choice may provide parents and teachers with the power to decide how best to educate children.

References

Brandt, R. (1989). On teacher empowerment: A conversation with Ann Lieberman. *Educational Leadership*, 46, 23-26.

Chubb, J. E., & Moe, T. M. (1987). No school is an island: Politics, markets, and education. In W. L. Boyd & C. T. Kerchner (Eds.), *The politics of excellence and choice: 1987 yearbook of the Politics of Education Association* (pp. 131-141). New York: Falmer.

Chubb, J. E., & Moe, T. M. (1989). *Report to the people of Connecticut: Educational choice*. Norwalk, CT: Yankee Institute for Public Policy Studies.

Clinchy, E. (1989). Public school choice: Absolutely necessary but not wholly sufficient. *Phi Delta Kappan, 71*, 289-294.

Education Commission of the States. (1989). *A state policy-makers guide to public school choice*. Denver, CO: Author.

Elam, S. M. (1989). The second Gallup/Phi Delta Kappa poll of teachers' attitudes towards the public schools. *Phi Delta Kappan, 70*, 785-798.

Elmore, R. F. (1987). Choice in public education, In W. L. Boyd & C. T. Kerchner (Eds.), *The politics of excellence and choice: 1987 yearbook of the Politics of Education Association* (pp. 79-98). New York: Falmer.

Lieberman, M. (1989). *Privatization and educational choice*. New York: St. Martin's.

Lewis, A. (1989). *Restructuring America's schools. Arlington, VA: American Association of School Administrators*.

Maeroff, G. l. (1988). A blueprint for empowering teachers. *Phi Delta Kappan*, 69,

472-477.

McDonnell, L., & Pascal, A. (1988). *Teacher unions and educational reform.* Santa Monica, CA: RAND.

Metropolitan Life Insurance Company. (1989). *The American teacher survey 1989.* New York: Author.

Murnane, R. J. (1986). Family choice in public education: The roles of students, teachers, and system designers. *Teachers College Record, 88,* 265-275.

Olson, L. (1988, January 27). Children flourish here. *Education Week,* pp. 1, 18-19.

Owens, R. G. (1987). *Organizational behavior in education.* Englewood Cliffs, NJ: Prentice Hall.

Paulu, N. (1989). *Improving schools and empowering parents: Choice in American education* (A report based on a White House workshop on choice in education). Washington, DC: U.S. Government Printing Office.

Raywid, M. A. (1989). The mounting case for schools of choice. In J. Nathan (Ed.), *Public schools by choice: Expanding opportunities for parents students and teachers* (pp. 13-40). St. Paul, MN: Institute for Learning and Teaching.

Timar, T. (1989). The politics of restructuring. *Phi Delta Kappan, 71,* 265-275.

Public Choice, Yes; Vouchers, No!

Mary Anne Raywid

In the minds of some, choice proposals are all of a piece, and there is little difference between public schools of choice and vouchers. For others, public schools of choice are just one step on the road to vouchers: where we find the one, we will soon find the other. Certainly there are those who espouse both public schools of choice and vouchers—President Reagan and Secretary of Education William Bennent being two prominent examples. But there are good reasons for separating the two types of choice rather sharply, and for advocating one while rejecting the other. Public choice may be the best possible solution for what ails U.S. education; vouchers could exacerbate our problems.

Brief definitions of the two terms, as I use them here, may be helpful to readers. By vouchers I mean an arrangement whereby individuals are in effect handed the funds (typically in the form of a chit) to purchase the schooling of their choice outside the public sector.[1] I define public choice as the deliberate differentiation of public schools, permitting students and their families to select the type of school each youngster will attend.[2]

Although I have been an advocate of public choice for more than a decade, I remain an opponent of vouchers. My opposition springs from my conviction that most youngsters in the U.S. will continue to rely on the public schools. Thus we need to improve these schools and to insure their continued good health. There is reason to believe that choice among public schools would be an excellent way to accomplish such purposes. Vouchers, by contrast, might well undermine education and leave public schools less capable of effective performance than they are now, by reducing—below levels of critical mass—enrollments (of middle-class students, in particular) school funding, and the willingness of an aging population to view education as a public good deserving of support.

I intend to elaborate on both of these stands: for public choice and against vouchers. Let me begin with vouchers.

VOUCHERS

Rather than run through the full list of objections that opponents have raised, I will focus on the handful of concerns that I happen to find most worrisome. The first of these is the tenuous position of public education today. Nationally, our hopes for refashioning education are high at the moment; if disillusionment follows, it could prove disastrous. Some business leaders have already concluded that the public schools will fail to deliver on the hopes raised by the excellence movement.[3] Simultaneously, many educators are seriously questioning whether the public schools can survive. Under the circumstances, we ought to be doing everything possible to shore up the public schools—which certainly would not include stimulating and facilitating the flow of students and resources our of those schools.

Building public appreciation of the importance of education to our national well-being is, perhaps, an equally fundamental challenge over the long run. Whether schooling ought to be seen primarily as a private benefit or as a public good that benefits the community at large has long been debated. There are abundant reasons to consider it both. But unless the understanding of education as a public good can be confirmed and maintained, a society in which fewer than one-third of the households have school-aged youngsters[4] is not likely to be highly supportive of the schools— especially when many youngsters attending those schools seem resistant to and ungrateful for the opportunity. Thus a sense of education as a public good seems crucial to the continued survival of public education.

I fear, though, that vouchers would have the opposite effect. To assign parents full and unfettered responsibility for choosing their children's education in an open market is to telegraph the message that the matter is solely their affair and not the community's concern.[5] Under most circumstances, a community could endorse that approach only if it felt that it had little stake in and would realize little value from the education of the young. Thus I fear that vouchers would bring in their wake a further downplaying of education on the public agenda and a further waning of public commitment to the enterprise. The nation would be much weaker and poorer for that.

A third important concern is that, in the cities, vouchers would quickly solidify a two-tiered educational system consisting of nonpublic schools and pauper schools. That development would impoverish us all, because it would represent an abandonment of efforts to improve education for disadvantaged youngsters, who are already a majority in most U.S. cities. A two-tiered system would prove injurious to those youngsters who need high quality education the most, if they are to escape poverty: inner-city minorities. The families of such youngsters may have few political, financial, or knowledge resources with which to force improvement in the schools (which have never really served them very well). A two-tiered system would be injurious to the more fortunate members of society as well. By constituting a step backward in the march toward opportunity, such a system would undermine the nation's long-term stability.

Minority demands related to schooling have shifted discernibly in recent years, due to a growing realization that access to desegregated schools is not enough to insure admission to the societal mainstream. What is essential is access to schools that work—to high-quality education.[6] For a large and growing number of minority youngsters, however, such hopes could become increasingly remote under a two-tiered system of schools. The experience with vouchers in France seems to confirm the likelihood of such an effect; private schools in that nation are reportedly attracting the affluent, and public schools are serving the poor.[7]

In the U.S., the evidence from which to project the degree to which access to private schools might help the disadvantaged is mixed. On the one hand, innercity youngsters have sometimes fared better in private and parochial schools than have their counterparts in public schools.[8] On the other hand, those proprietary schools that serve essentially the same group of students, grown older, have a fairly negative record.[9] their history suggests that only a highly regulated and closely monitored voucher arrangement could protect disadvantaged students from the ills of the marketplace.

This leads directly to another concern I have about vouchers: the unlikelihood of a voucher trial or experiment. As a number of analysts have noted, the political and social realities of contemporary life would make a decision to use vouchers extremely difficult to reverse. To implement a new approach affecting so many people would require institutionalization of that approach on a substantial scale, quickly generating large numbers of constituents and stakeholders who would begin to function as interest groups and coalitions. This could make reversal of the policy instituting vouchers virtually impossible, thus escalating the risk of experimentation.

A MISGUIDED ANALOGY

I want to argue now a different sort of case against vouchers. It seems to me that the voucher idea becomes fundamentally wrong-headed when applied to education and schools. I cringe at advocates' assurances that competition will improve the schools and force the bad ones out of business. Those individuals often seem to know so little about schools and classrooms, how they work, and what they require to succeed. Yet such lack of knowledge is not too surprising. Vouchers are actually a plan for financing schools, not for improving them. Advocates have argued that the change in method of financing will yield school improvement—but as a byproduct of competition in the marketplace, not of any particular plan for school improvement.

The voucher proposal, then, suggests that we cure the ills of the schools by borrowing and applying some concepts from economics (the study of the production and distribution of goods and services) and from business (our major form of economic organization). Since education appears to be a service, it seems plausible to seek enlightenment on how best to produce and distribute it from economists and business specialists. This thinking is flawed, however. The fundamental elements of the U.S. economy are a buyer, a seller, the good or service to be exchanged, and a marketplace in which the transaction occurs. In the case of the public schools, who is the buyer: the family or the society? Is schooling primarily an exchange of goods (e.g., plane geometry, the alphabet, Shakespeare), or is schooling a service industry? If the latter what kind of service? Custodial? Developmental? Something else?

As these questions suggest, there are major strains in the analogy right from the start. Not surprisingly, serious distortions result. For example, if education is a good or a service sold in the marketplace, what does that make students? Are they customers? Surely not, to few people assume that a 6-year-old—or even a 16-year-old—is ready for the "consumer sovereignty" that economists associate with buyers. Moreover, public school students are not buyers in the sense of paying from their own pockets for the ministrations they receive. For that same reason (and others), their parents are not the school's customers, either. Nor are parents the school's patrons in any economic sense.

Well, then, are the students clients —a relationship created by the purchase of certain other professional services? Not exactly. The client of a doctor, a lawyer, or an architect has entitlements and prerogatives that the very circumstances of school attendance would deny. As these examples suggest, roles from the economic metaphor don't seem to fit relationships in education, in part because of differences between buyers and students in their levels of maturity and in their capacities to assess and to finance. But there is another, equally important reason for the misfit: to place the student in the role of buyer is to obscure society's interest and stake in the transaction. Society has no real stake in whether an individual buys a Toyota or a Buick. What sort of education a youngster obtains can matter a great deal to the rest of us, however.

Is the fact that the economic metaphor fits education so poorly of any real consequence? Does thinking about education in this fashion change the way in which the schools operate? I suspect that it does. The economic analogy has major ramifications for school practice that its rejection would rule out.

For instance, the economic/business analogy seems to have shaped and propelled the drive for accountability in education during the last decade. Since there are no profits to serve as indicators of whether or not schools are doing a good job, test scores have been assigned that function instead. The insistence on quantitative measures of effectiveness has reduced educational outcomes to testable products and deemphasized the role of the school in other areas, such as preparing young people for civic participation, encouraging their personal development, and helping them master higher-level intellectual skills. It has also left little room for the "process" goals that are important to parents: the kinds and qualities of school experiences that they simply want their youngsters to undergo, quite apart from specific expectations regarding outcomes. All these features of the present push for accountability in education are, I suspect, very much tied to the widespread welcoming of economic solutions for educational problems. Reject the analogy—deny the applicability of the marketplace to schooling and the comparability of business to education—and these practices would have to be replaced.

From the perspective of many advocates, perhaps the central value of vouchers is the competition they would introduce. Some see competition per se as a good thing; others prize competition primarily for its alleged instrumental benefits. Specifically, the spur of competition is expected to improve schools (as they seek to attract customers) and to put the poorest schools and teachers out of business (as they fail to obtain a large enough clientele). Thus competition is expected to improve school quality.

But here again, the economic analogy is questionable. Competition quite understandably operates in the matter of which suit or which mayonnaise or which car to buy. But does it operate in the decision on whether to buy a car or a truck? Or a truck instead of an appendectomy? Of course, in one sense it does: if resources are limited and one purchase precludes another, then we can say that any two items are "competing" against each other. But the most important differences between a car and a truck—or a truck and an operation are not qualitative differences at all. The purchase of one or another is a matter of need. Thus one might quite plausibly settle for a second-rate truck in preference to a first-rate car, by virtue of one's needs. But if that is the case, where does competition fit in—and where is its widely touted stimulus to improvement?

Or, to take a different example, religious denominations—churches can be said to be "competing" against one another, in that virtually no individual affiliates with more than one of them simultaneously. A person is rarely a Methodist and a Presbyterian. Does this mean that one chooses one's affiliation on the basis of differences in quality between the two denominations? Or does the decision rest more heavily on some other factor, such as the denomination's particular doctrines, the match between the denomination's spiritual orientation and one's own, or other features that make one feel at home? Does the existence of more than one denomination spur each on to higher quality?

The two examples I have offered—the choice between a car and a truck and the choice between two religious affiliations—are not accidental. They represent, I think, the two major choices involved in selecting among schools. In other words, it makes sense to choose a school primarily in terms of need or primarily in terms of values and orientation.

One youngster, for instance, may need a program that provides a high level of activity and that emphasizes experiential learning. Another child may need the stimulation and the freedom of choice afforded by a variety of learning centers in an open classroom. A third youngster may need the structure and security of individual learning packets. Systems that afford educational options generally try to respond to such differences in learning style. They enable parents and students to find the kinds of activity structures that respond to such diverse needs. Thus, when given a choice, it is not uncommon for parents to select a different school for one child than for another.

For other families, the general orientation of a school looms larger. For them, choosing a school is not unlike choosing a worldview. Here again, the choice of a school has less to do with school quality than with how closely the school's philosophy and values accord with the family's view of life and of child rearing.

Where, then, does competition enter in? I suspect that it may play a much less important part in the choice of a school than is often supposed. Competition is a real and important feature of school selection if—and only if—we assume that the primary differences among schools are differences in their quality. If the only important difference between one school and another is that one is better and one is worse, then it makes sense to construe school selection of a competitive situation. But if we assume that schools differ in kind, then school selection seems a somewhat different matter, not readily explained by competition.

It is sometimes said that, in systems providing choice, schools do compete with one another and this competition accounts for the improvement that is often associated with choice. Certainly the improvement takes place. But it is not at all clear that competition explains it. In fact, many features and processes that have nothing whatsoever to do with competition, have been offered as explanations, e.g., the increased control that teachers have over instruction in schools of choice—the greater amount of teacher interaction and professional collaboration that take place in such schools; the stronger sense of affiliation that students, teachers, and parents have with schools of choice.[10] Research findings to date suggest that these factors play a larger role than competition in school improvement.

Choice brings other changes, as well. It creates a different kind of relationship between the home and the school, for example. It causes teachers to examine and reflect on their own practice more often, and it enhances their interest in exploring new solutions to old challenges. But to attribute such effects as these to competition is to embrace an "ether" theory, much as those scientists did who for centuries explained a variety of natural mysteries in terms of a ubiquitous gas. Similarly, our culture sometimes seems to view competition as an all-pervasive force that penetrates and controls all collective behavior. Yet the evidence suggests that schoolpeople deliberately mute and downplay the competitive aspects of a system of choice.[11] And additional lines of evidence substantiate the fact that educators are not likely to be highly competitive.[12] Thus the vision of principals and teachers hustling to outmaneuver the competition appears more fanciful than likely.

In sum, as all of this is intended to suggest, vouchers represent the application of economists concepts and solutions to the problems of education. Vouchers seek school improvement via deregulation and privatization. They would make schools more like businesses and cast educations and their families in the role of customers. But the analogy that likens schooling to business breaks down under close scrutiny. In fact, schooling may be a unique kind of endeavor that makes any root metaphor troublesome and the wholesale transfer of features from other enterprises dangerous.

A number of educational philosophies have foundered by likening the process of education to such other processes as "gardening," "taming," and "manufacturing." In the 1960s some observers urged that the schools become participatory democracies; they called for collective decision making, the principle of one person/one vote, and the right of the majority to determine the overall direction of the enterprise (in terms of goals as well as activities). A number of people were very uncomfortable with this line of reasoning—including. perhaps, some of those who are now espousing an economic analogy instead.

Schooling seems to be a unique enterprise, at least in some important respect. Schools are not marketplaces, nor are they governments. They are neither concerned primarily with the production and distribution of goods and services nor with regulating the interactions of citizens and organizations Schools require solutions tailored to their own needs, not devised to respond to the needs of some other undertaking.

THE CASE FOR PUBLIC CHOICE

If vouchers pose such problems for public education, why do pubic schools of choice seem such a good idea? The answer is twofold. First, choice looks to be perhaps the best solution to a number of the most pressing problems now facing public education. Second, it seems quite possible to have choice in the public sector without taking on the difficulties that vouchers would introduce.

Here again, I will confine my case to just a few crucial considerations rather than the full array. These considerations have to do with youngsters' needs, adult preferences, and the governance of public institutions.

First it seems clear that the wider the range of youngsters to be accommodated in the schools, the harder it is to deal effectively with them under a narrowly specified range of circumstances. Only 11% of the age group were attending high school at the turn of the century; in those days school officials could count on dealing with a fairly elite group of youngsters whose parents chose to have them in school and saw to it that they conformed to the schools expectations. Even when the high school population expanded sufficiently after World War II to yield diplomas for half of the age group, self-selection still limited the range of differences in such important factors as family background, level of aspiration, and socioeconomic status—factors closely tied to educational achievement. Today, to our credit, we are dissatisfied that 27% of American young people fail to complete high school. Viewed from another perspective, however, many of the youngsters attending high school today are simply not going to function well in the same kind of institutions that worked for smaller. more select populations whose home conditions and parents attitudes more fully supported the mission of the schools.

Today's schools serve youngsters whose backgrounds, interests, hopes, and talents vary widely. Not all of them will thrive under the single set of conditions we have laid down for our schools. To succeed, they will need different kinds of school environments, different kinds of instructional approaches, and differently packaged content. I do not mean to suggest that we now have two types of students instead of one, creating the need for two types of schools and programs. There are many types of students, creating the need for a wide variety of school programs and arrangements, if we are serious about responding to the needs of every youngster.

Clearly, we must call a halt to our century-long march toward standardization. We must forget such fruitless battles as whether or not to begin all reading instruction with phonics and seek instead to match our teaching strategies to particular students—starting some youngsters with phonics and others with drastically different approaches. The evidence supporting such a strategy is extensive, varied, and certainly not new; we know for a fact that different youngsters learn in different ways and according to different patterns. When we persist in imposing a single instructional approach on all children, we succeed with some students and systematically handicap others. There is no reason (beyond our own perversity) to continue to assume that some single, "right" approach exists that will suit every student.

Much the same thing can be said of school environments. Some youngsters thrive in large, comprehensive high schools that permit motivated students to pursue advanced knowledge under the supervision of highly specialized teachers. Other youngsters perform better in more personalized and supportive surroundings. Only by closing our eyes to human diversity can we continue to impose on all students a single, standardized school climate.

If choice enables differentiated schools to deal better with human diversity, it also enables them to motivate students more effectively. The excellence movement has largely ignored motivation proceeding instead as though educational achievement were simply a matter of backing up the right demands with sufficient insistence. Teachers who have given up on making schools work under prevailing conditions have also abandoned their efforts to motivate students. Recent studies offer all sorts of evidence—including truancy and dropout rates, classroom "treaties" that require minimal work, even direct student testimony—regarding the disengagement of students from schoolwork. But just as clearly, learner interest is absolutely essential, if the schools are to attain the excellence to which the nation seems so dedicated. Enabling students to select from among an array of schools—featuring different themes and emphases, different learning environments, and different instructional approaches—could go a long way toward restoring motivation among students of all ability levels.

Such an arrangement could also enable teachers (and thus schools) to function more effectively, since choice often fosters other features that collectively enhance educational quality. For example, choice yields a student body whose members are alike in some educationally important way—perhaps a shared interest, a common learning style, or a preference for a certain type of school climate. When choice is extended to teachers, it yields a faculty with a common philosophy of education and shared values. The outcome is a widely shared ethos, which makes group cohesion and a stronger sense of humiliation with the school more likely for all.

Choice and diversity almost automatically place greater instructional autonomy at the school level, and—in some schools, at least—this autonomy is distributed among the staff. The teachers in such schools enjoy a greater sense of professionalism, while, at the same time, a shared ethos sustains commonality and prevents fragmentation. Instructional autonomy requires teachers to collaborate more extensively, and this professional interaction improves their performance and increases their job satisfaction. The record suggests that these and a number of other ways, school differentiation and choice are likely to improve school quality.[13]

For several reasons, differentiation and choice are also likely to increase parental satisfaction with the schools. Clearly, parents held a range of views on how best to educate children. Parents at the extremes favor practices that most other people would judge misguided. But within such extremes, a wide spectrum of perfectly legitimate viewpoints exists on how best to educate children. (A similarly wide spectrum of viewpoints exist among educators of course.)

Consider, for example, the contrast between those parents (and educators) who see education in analytic, "divide up the skills and conquer each" terms and those who see education more holistically. The first group wants children to master distinct sets of knowledge and skills (phonics, the alphabet, the multiplication tables, spelling, grammar, vocabulary). The second group prefers having youngsters work on broad topics that draw on and integrate the desired learnings. There are children who learn best in each of these ways—and thus evidence to support both points of view. Given our growing understanding of the importance of a positive bond between home and school, why not enable parents and students to choose between these two approaches (and among other approaches, as well)?

Absolutely nothing prevents us from diversifying our schools to make them respond much more closely to the legitimate but varied views of adults regarding education. Indeed, there are important reasons for doing so. First, as I have already noted, diversifying schools would make them more effective. The feature of choice improves the performance of both teachers and students. Second, parents want the right to choose the public schools their children attend. In the 1986 Gallup Poll of the Public's Attitudes Toward the Public Schools, 68% of parents favored having that right (even though a large number of them were quite satisfied with their children's current schools).[14] Third, there are reasons why parents ought to be empowered to make such choices.

THE NEED TO RETHINK SCHOOL GOVERNANCE

The power that schools hold over youngsters is considerable, and their capacity to inflict long-term harm is substantial. If an institution with a policy requiring compulsory attendance is to avoid tyranny, surely those who attend that institution must retain the right to go elsewhere. But such a right does not currently exist. In most locales, the opportunity to go elsewhere is available only to families affluent enough to move to a different neighborhood or to pay tuition for a private school. To insure everyone the privilege of going elsewhere would require a change in school governance policies.

Such a change is sorely needed because, over the years, the balance of power between family and school has tilted sharply in favor of the school. Parents have no say today regarding which schools their children will attend which teachers will teach them, what content they will study, when and how they will study it, what values will be emphasized and enforced, which educational goals will be paramount, and which goals will receive short shrift. The fundamental commitment of Americans to a division and balance of powers calls for the restoration of some kind and some degree of parental authority.

Our political system relies on checks and balances to prevent tyranny including the kind of tyranny that public institutions can exert over their constituents. It also counts on the overlapping powers of the several interested parties to prevent instances of harm or injury. The application to schools of the principle of checks and balances has meant that the various levels of government (federal, state, and local) divide the authority for education, while the various parties to the enterprise (educators, school boards, parents, and students) divide the power. When conditions change to the point that such power sharing no longer exists and one party dominates the rest (or one of the parties is rendered impotent), the system's protections are no longer functioning. Many observers feel that this is what has happened to school governance.

We recognize in principle that, within most institutions, changing conditions call for periodic adjustments in order to keep the necessary protections working. Yet we have made no move in years to adjust school governance, despite major shifts in the balance of power that would seem to strongly recommend such action. Formal school governance arrangements today remain essentially as they were at the turn of the century.

Meanwhile, strong forces have shifted control of the schools further and further from parents and from those directly responsible for educating their children. As control has become increasingly centralized and increasingly inaccessible, many parents have come to see themselves as essentially powerless—caught between the school bureaucracy, professional education organizations, and, of late, state officials. At the same time, and partly because of these shifts in control, schools have become less responsive to individuals and more likely to perceive them as interferences than as citizens who are voicing appropriate questions, suggestions, and expectations.

The protests about school governance grow. They come not only from parents, but—increasingly—from other sources as well. Several of the recent national reports on school reform insist that structural arrangements (especially the machinery of governance) must be changed.[15] In fact, demands of this kind are about to become the major focus of the reform movement, in the view of some analysts.[16] School boards are clearly in trouble, since some reforms involve state takeovers of districts, while others shift power in the opposite direction, assigning extensive site-management prerogatives to individual schools. Vouchers would involve a different kind of change, shifting decision-making power from the public policy arena to the marketplace.

As dissimilar as these three proposals for structural change appear to be, they are similar in one important respect. Each of them would lodge most of the control of education in just one of the parties to the enterprise: the state, the individual school, or the parent. Each proposal is a kind of "reform by reversal," since its goal is to shift the preponderance of power from one set of hands to another, rather than to reapportion control more appropriately among all the parties involved. Unfortunately, such a remedy would begin immediately to generate new problems—and hence, the need for a remedy for the remedy. It would do so because it ignores the fundamental notion of checks and balances, an idea perhaps more important to the democratic operation of institutions today than in earlier centuries, because technology and social organization now concentrate power so narrowly.

Placing a preponderance of control in the hands of just one of the parties involved in the enterprise of education would introduce another and even more fundamental problem, as well. It would resolve by elimination those "tensions" that define a democratic system. The tensions are generated by the not-entirely-compatible values and goals to which this nation is committed. Political struggles often spotlight the potential conflict between, for example, majority rule and our national commitment to protect the rights of the minority. A major virtue of a democratic system is that it continually maintains and balances both majority rule and minority rights both individual interests and collective interests, both the values of the local community and those of the larger society, both the exercise of expertise and the accountability of experts to the public at large. By largely concentrating the control of schools in just one set of hands, we jeopardize the necessary balances between conflicting values, however. In the absence of authority divided by checks and balances, situations in which several values must be served simultaneously can easily result in the affirmation of one value and the discarding of the others—in the conversion of democracy's "tensions" (when multiple values must be served) into either/or choices.

The recommendation that we diversify public schools and allow parents to choose the schools their children will attend is quite a different kind of proposal for structural change. It would not simply shift the preponderance of control from one interested party to another. Rather, this proposal is congruent with the principle of dividing rights and prerogatives among the several parties involved in education and with the principle of distributing authority for education among the several levels of government that have a direct stake in that enterprise. It gives families a more influential voice in determining the kind of education their children will have; at the same time, it leaves to educators and school boards the decisions on what kinds of schools will constitute the options in a given community.

This would mean a different (but no less necessary and important) role for school boards. Instead of trying to hammer out a "one best way" for all schools in the district to operate, school boards would have to concern themselves with the range and diversity of the options provided by their districts. They would have to think much more carefully about which aspects of education should be standardized and which need not be. In some locales, school boards would undoubtedly have to explore the appropriate limits of pluralism, insofar as educational practice is concerned.[17]

As the foregoing suggests, school decision makers must take a variety of interests into account. Allowing parents to choose their children's schools might encourage school boards to address far more fully and more adequately the "tensions" that a democratic educational system must keep in balance. School boards could not content themselves with framing majority-sanctioned decisions; they would need simultaneously to be concerned much more actively with the interests of various minorities. School boards could not limit themselves simply to insuring that all children are exposed to common educational experience, they would need to allow for differences and encourage initiative and innovation. In sum, the governance chance that I have proposed here might impel school boards to renew their focus on such fundamental concerns.

It seems likely that some of the current interest in public schools of choice stems from their potential for changing school governance arrangements in a direction congruent with our fundamental assumptions and commitments regarding power and authority. Moreover, public schools of choice would require an alteration in school governance structures significantly more modest than other proposals now being discussed—such as further enlargement of the state role, school-site management, or vouchers—would entail. Finally, public schools of choice would cause school programs and practices to more fully reflect the multiple concerns to which democratic education must respond.

As I suggested earlier, however, the benefits of turning public schools into schools of choice go beyond improving school governance. Choice also makes sense in strictly educational terms, because it enhances the efficacy of teachers, the accomplishments of learners, the satisfaction of parents, and the confidence of the public in its schools.

1. Many arrangements and permutations now exist whereby public funds underwrite educational services, but most advocates of vouchers insist that funds be handled in exactly the manner I have described—rather than, for example having funds allotted to private schools and paid directly by some public agency. This point is important because the rationale for vouchers focuses on such features as

competition, consumer sovereignty, and the discipline of the marketplace. Obviously, a different arrangement for distributing funds would diminish, if not eliminate such features.

2. These brief definitions omit the fine distinctions—between regulated, unregulated, compensatory and second-chance vouchers, on the one hand, and between magnet schools alternative schools open enrollment, and options systems, on the other. For more information on the nature and varieties of vouchers, see Christopher Jencks et al., *Education Vouchers: A Report on Financing Elementary Education by Grants to Parents* (Cambridge, Mass.: Center for the Study of Public Policy, 1970). For more information on the various kinds of public schools of choice, see Mary Anne Raywid, "Family Choice Arrangements in Public Schools A Review of the Literature," *Review of Educational Research*, Winter 1985, pp. 435-67.

3. This finding comes from a July 1986 Louis Harris poll, conducted for the Carnegie Forum on Education and the Economy. See Educational Excellence Network, November 1986, p. 77.

4. The most recent U. S. Census figure (for 1983) is 30%.

5. Inviting parents to select from among publicly provided options is quite another matter, as I will demonstrate later.

6. See, for example, Derrick Bell, ed., *Shades of Brown: New Perspectives on School Desegregation* (New York Teachers College Press, 1980).

7. Frances C. Fowler, "The French Experience with Public Aid to Private Schools," *Phi Delta Kappan*, January 1987, p. 358.

8. See, for example, James Coleman, Thomas Hoffer, and Sally Kilgore, *High School Achievement* (New York Basic Books, 1982); Valerie Lee, "Catholic School Minority Students Have 'Reading Proficiency Advantage,'" *Momentum*, September 1986, pp. 20-24; and Diana T Slaughter and Barbara L. Schneider, *Newcomers: Blacks in Private Schools*, final report to the National Institute of Education, February 1986.

9. See, for example, *Many Proprietary Schools Do Not Comply with Department of Education's Pell Grant Program Requirements* (Washington D.C.: U.S. General Accounting Office, 1984); and *Staff Study on the Tuition Assistance Program for Registered Business Schools* (Albany Office of the New York State Comptroller, 8 July 1986).

10. See, for example, Mary Anne Raywid, "Success Dynamics of Public Schools of Choice," in *Content, Character, and Choice in Schooling: Public Policy and Research Implications* (Washington, D. C.: National Council on Educational Research, 1986), pp. 101-8.

11. See, for example, Francesca Galluccio-Steele, *Choice and Consequences: A Case Study of Open Enrollment in the Acton, Massachusetts, Public Schools* (Doctoral dissertation, Harvard University, 1986).

12. Susan Moore Johnson and Niall C. W. Nelson, "Teaching Reform in an Active Voice," *Phi Delta Kappan*, April 1987, pp. 591-98.

13. Rolf Blank et al., *Survey of Magnet Schools—Final Report: Analyzing a Model for Quality Integrated Education* (Washington, D.C.: James H. Lowry & Associates, 1983); and Mary Anne Raywid, "Synthesis of Research on Schools of Choice," *Educational Leadership*, April 1984, pp. 70-78.

14. Alec M. Gallup, "The 18th Annual Gallup Poll of the Public's Attitudes Toward the Public Schools," *Phi Delta Kappan*, September 1986, pp. 56-57.

15. See, for example, *Carnegie Task Force on Teaching as Profession, A*

Nation Prepared: Teachers for the 21st Century (New York Carnegie Forum on Education and the Economy, 1986); *Barriers to Excellence: Our Children at Risk* (Boston: National Coalition of Advocates for Students, 1985); and *Time for Results: The Governors' 1991 Report on Education* (Washington, D. C. National Governors' Association, 1986).

16. See, for example, Chris Pipho, "Restructuring the Schools: States Take on the Challenge," *Education Week*, 26 November 1986, p. 19; and Thomas A Shannon, "Second Wave of Reform Outlined by Terrel Bell," School Board News, 11 June 1986, p. 3.

17. Adherence to the principle of checks and balances would surely call for placing some limits on a school board's power to deny choice. There is no reason why such limits cannot be set; the California legislature, for example, has proposed that school boards be required to establish educational alternatives upon petition by a specified number of parents (AB 1425 introduced on 4 March 1987).

Public School Choice: Absolutely Necessary but Not Wholly Sufficient

Evans Clinchy

Twenty years ago it was a wild and crazy idea. Today, public school choice is rapidly becoming the latest tidal wave in an ocean of public school reform. School districts across the country are instituting choice in a variety of intradistrict forms, ranging from a few magnet schools to entire school systems. Moreover, such states as Minnesota have instituted laws permitting interdistrict choice—allowing students and parents to choose to attend schools in other school districts and to take courses in public colleges and universities for dual credit.

George Bush, seeking to become the "Education President," has declared public school choice to be "a national necessity." He appears poised to make choice the educational centerpiece of his Administration and thus the school reform of the 1990s.

For those of us who began to wonder seriously about the possibilities of choice two decades ago, the burgeoning success of this idea is heartwarming. Especially pleasing is the fact that the movement now appears limited to choice among public schools and public schools only. Apparently we have managed—at least for the moment—to put to rest vouchers, tuition tax credits, and other forms of nonpublic school choice that would harm the national effort to improve public education. While all this success may warm our hearts, it is just a bit frightening to some of us.

Why frightening? First, we see many states and school systems riding the tidal wave of choice with little thought and virtually no planning. Choice instituted in a hasty, ill-conceived fashion can easily turn out to be—and in all too many cases is turning out to be—no choice at all: a charade and even a hoax, a pseudoinnovation that produces no significant change in the old authoritarian school system that adopts a choice plan. A new plan may seem to present genuine alternatives when in fact it is offering only a few minor variations on the theme of the standard, traditional school.

Second, we are frightened because we see a danger that choice may be oversold as a magical solution to all the problems that afflict our public schools—a possibility for which those of us who have enthusiastically (and perhaps indiscriminately) promoted choice for so long are no doubt partly responsible. If this happens and choice does not produce the expected magical cures, then the resulting disappointment could turn everyone against the whole idea.

WHY CHOICE IS NECESSARY

Worried though some of us may be, I do not know of a single one of us who would question the basic notion that empowering parents to specify and then to choose the different kinds of public schooling that they want for their children is absolutely necessary if our public schools are to improve. Nor would we restrict empowerment to parents. Professional practitioners, our teachers and principals, must also be empowered to specify and then to put into practice the various kinds of schooling that they believe are best for their students.

Above and beyond these obvious virtues, both parental choice and professional choice, when properly conceived and executed, are necessary because thy turn our traditional authoritarian system of public education upside down. And this shakeup is genuine change, real reform, true restructuring.

Our traditional system, the one that is gradually changing into something quite different, has attempted at every turn to hold parents, students, and professional educators hostage. It has taken for granted that it has both the right and the duty to tell its clients where and when to go to school; what the educational philosophy, the curriculum, and the organization of that school will be; who can and cannot teach there; whether the children are succeeding or failing in that school; and whether those children can graduate from that school and go on to the next level of schooling designated by the system.

That same system has told its teachers and principals where they can and cannot work, what they will teach and how they will teach it, how the school will be organized and operated, how the students will be judged and graded, how the professionals themselves will be evaluated, and how they will be rewarded financially.

Choice is changing all of that. At least choice has the potential to change all of that if it is properly understood, carefully thought through, and implemented in gradual stages, with no stage begun until the previous stage is successfully in place.[1]

THE REQUIREMENTS OF CHOICE

A considerable measure of care in implementing choice plans is necessary because choice clearly implies and requires but in no way automatically guarantees two profound alterations in the way the present system operates.

First, choice requires that we abandon our cherished notion that there can be a single, all-inclusive definition of "educational excellence": a single, standardized approach to schooling; a single, canonized, culturally literate curriculum; and a single way of organizing and operating a school that is suitable for all students and serves all students equally well. Quite the opposite. We need genuine diversity in our approaches to schooling, creating different kinds of schools to serve our diverse student population and to accommodate the range of parental and professional beliefs about what public education should be and do.

As Howard Gardner, a professor of developmental psychology at Harvard University, has put it:

> The single most important contribution education can make to a child's development is to help him toward a field where his talents best suit him, where he will be satisfied and competent.
> We've completely lost sight of that. Instead, we subject everyone to an education where, if you succeed, you will be best suited to be a college professor. And we evaluate everyone according to whether they meet that narrow standard of success.
> We should spend less time ranking children and more time helping them to identify their natural competencies and gifts and cultivate those. There are hundreds of ways to succeed and many, many different abilities that will help you get there.[2]

"Genuine" diversity means just that: a range of educational options that extends from preschool through high school and that encompasses everything from a very traditional "back-to-basics approach, through such modest departures from the norms as "continuous progress" or "individually guided" education, to such truly radical types of schooling as Montessori, "open," or even "microsociety" schools. We also need more schools that specialize in particular aspects of the intellectual and artistic worlds, schools that offer interested students a chance to develop their talents in the fine and performing arts, in science and technology, or in the humanities.

As Mary Anne Raywid, one of the pioneers in the field of public school choice, has aptly put it:

> Clearly, we must call a halt to our century-long march toward standardization. We must forget such fruitless battles as whether or not to begin all reading instruction with phonics and seek instead to match our teaching strategies to particular students—starting some youngsters with phonics and others with drastically different approaches. The evidence supporting such a strategy is extensive, varied, and certainly not new; we know for a fact that different youngsters learn in different ways and according to different patterns. When we persist in imposing a single instructional approach on all children, we succeed with some students and systematically handicap others. There is no reason (beyond our own perversity) to continue to assume that some single "right" approach exists that will suit ever student.[3]

Seymour Fliegel, another of the champions of choice and formerly deputy superintendent in Community School District No. 4 in East Harlem, has described how that district has actively sought to provide the kind of diversity Raywid advocates:

> The aim here has been to create a system that—instead of trying to fit student into some standardized school—has a school to fit every student in this district. No one gets left out; no one gets lost. Every kid is important; every kid can learn if you put him or her in the right environment. But since kids have this huge range of different needs, different interests, and different ways of learning, we've got to have a wide diversity of schools. Which is what, after 13 years at it, we've just about got.[4]

This truly diverse range of approaches to schooling is precisely what many of the school systems riding the crest of the wave of choice are not providing. All too often, the local school board and the central administrators of a school system will make a great show of instituting a choice plan, either for purposes of peaceful desegregation or because parents and professionals are demanding it. In many cases, however, the decisions as to what choices the school system will offer are made by the school board and (still more likely) the central administration. With a few notable exceptions, neither parents nor teachers and principals have been involved in making these decisions.

In only a few cases (e. g., Indianapolis and three districts in Massachusetts—Worcester, Lowell, and Fall River) have parents been asked to describe the different kinds of schooling that they want for their children. In these school systems, all parents of children in the public elementary and junior high schools were given a list of choices and asked to select the ones they believed would provide their children with the educational excellence that all parents seek.

In Worcester, Lowell, and Fall River, the range of options contained in the parent surveys was determined not by the central administration but by citywide parent councils representing the parents of every school in the city. And in Fliegel's East Harlem district, the "alternative concept" schools were created by teachers who were encouraged to step forward and describe to the district administrators the different kinds of schools that they had always dreamed of working in. The district helped the teachers to establish their dream schools and helped the parents and students to choose among them.

But active participation by clients and practitioners in the decision-making process is not the norm. Moreover, even when parents are asked what they want, the school systems do not necessarily go on to create the schools that parents request. In Lowell, for example, the two schools most desired by parents were a K-8 school for the fine and performing arts and a K-8 microsociety school.[5] These options were provided in the form of brand-new schools that draw students from all over the city (which is often the only solution to the problem of creating truly diverse and unusual schools). In Worcester, on the other hand, parents have asked for a Montessori school, an open or developmental school, and a microsociety school. However,these options have not been created.

A second—and also rarely successful—approach to the creation of diversity in the public schools is for the school system simply to allow each existing school to devise its own "distinctive" or "magnet" program. Since the parents and students in such existing schools are there because they happen to live in the school's attendance area, and since the teachers are there for the most part because they happened to be at the top of a list when a vacancy occurred in that particular school, there is little reason to hope that such a motley assortment of people (none of them there by real choice) could ever agree on anything but a minor variation on the traditional school As one parent in Boston recently put it, "If you give me a choice of five or 10 or 20 schools that are all just about the same and if they're all mediocre and not what I want anyway, what kind of a choice is that?"

Indeed, the power of parental and professional choice is (or should be) precisely the fact that there can be a genuinely diverse range of schools that parents and teachers want, because no one is forced to be in a school that they do not want to be in. Everyone in a true school of choice has freely chosen that school. The staff and the students are there because they all agree on the educational approach they want, including the educational philosophy of the school, what its curriculum should be, and how it should be organized and run.

Given this situation, everyone in the school shares a sense of the school's mission. Parents, students, teachers, and administrators can buckle down to the task of making the school a truly excellent example of its particular approach to public education. In schools that do not have such a shared mission, conflicts and disagreements almost inevitably produce unhappiness, low morale, apathy, and —finally— the mediocrity we all deplore. In short, choice without genuine diversity is no choice at all.

THE NEED FOR AUTONOMY

The second great alteration in our traditional way of organizing a school system that is clearly required - but not guaranteed by choice is the bestowal of autonomy on individual schools. Once a system of truly diverse schools has been created, each one of them should be given the power to determine its educational philosophy, its curriculum, and its organization and governance structure; to choose its teaching and administrative staff; and to set its own spending priorities.

This powerful idea (often called "school-based" or "school-site" management) is currently being espoused by many educational thinkers, most notably Albert Shanker, president of the American Federation of Teachers; Joe Nathan and Ted Kolderie of the Hubert H. Humphrey Institute of Public Affairs at the University of Minnesota; members of the Task Force on Teaching as a Profession of the Carnegie Forum on Education and the Economy (in that group's 1986 report, A Nation Prepared: Teachers for the 21st Century); and members of the National Governors' Association (in their 1986 report, Time for Results: The Governors' 1991 Report).

Even in terms of such a simplistic measure of success as student achievement, the empowerment of individual schools appears to have yielded some remarkable results. Using data from a national study of 1,000 public and private high schools,

John Chubb and Terry Moe of the Brookings Institution came to several provocative conclusions.6 One was that the most recent wave of school reform—the one that has emphasized mandates handed down from state governments and central offices of school systems—has produced and will continue to produce little or no real improvement in student performance. These mandates imposed from on high have called for stricter "academic standards," more homework, more testing, greater uniformity and standardization of curriculum and teaching methods, and increased control over what schools and teachers do.

When all their data were analyzed and such factors as student aptitude, minority/majority mix, family income, and money spent on the schools were controlled, the researchers concluded that the most crucial element of those schools in which student achievement was high was the effectiveness of the school's organization, defined as the school's freedom from higher-level administrative control. Given such freedom, the staff members and parents can create "a common school purpose" or "a shared view of education." The researchers concluded that, "all other things being equal, attendance at an effectively organized [high] school for four years is worth at least a full year of additional achievement over attendance at an ineffectively organized school."7

THE THIRD NECESSITY

True diversity and genuine autonomy may be necessary for the achievement of both choice and educational excellence. However, neither of these good things should be instituted without an overriding concern for the third great necessity: educational equity for all students, especially poor and minority students and women.

Thus all forms of choice, be they within a district or between districts, must be carefully controlled to make sure that every parent and every child has an equal chance to benefit from the advantages that choice confers. How this goal can be achieved within school districts is exemplified in the Massachusetts districts of Cambridge, Lowell, and Fall River districts in which every school is a magnet school or school of choice.

In each of these school systems, equity is provided through policies that guarantee equal access to (and thus the legal desegregation of) every school for all students. Each school has quotas of minority representation that are roughly comparable to the minority/majority mix of the public school population as a whole, and each school seeks to maintain about a 50/50 balance between males and females. Thus spaces are reserved in all schools for poor and minority students and for females. No school has academic or behaviorally selective admissions criteria; all schools are open to all students by parental choice within these equity guidelines.

Such controls do mean that choice cannot be absolute or totally unfettered. Constraints imposed by concerns about equity will mean that parents will not always get their first choice of school. However, if this situation occurs frequently, it probably means that the district either has failed to survey parents to find out how many of them want which kinds of schools or has failed to provide an adequate number of the schools parents do want.

Charles Glenn, executive director of the Office of Educational Equity for the Massachusetts Department of Education and one of the prime movers behind the push for choice and equity, has discussed the relationship between the two objectives:

> It has become clear that choice can do much to promote equity. It does so by creating conditions which encourage schools to become more effective, it does so by allowing schools to specialize and thus to meet the needs of some students very well rather than all students at a level of minimum adequacy, and it does so by increasing the influence of parents over the education of their children in a way which is largely conflict free.[8]

Thus we should pursue choice by all means—but never choice that benefits primarily the already advantaged segments of our society and leaves poor and minority parents and students right where they have always been behind society's eight ball.

THE ROLE OF CENTRAL ADMINISTRATION

Do the revolutionary changes described above render central administrators and local school boards irrelevant and unnecessary? Quite the contrary. Indeed while the role of the central administration is turned upside down, its importance is diminished not one whit.

As Rhoda Schneider, then acting commissioner of the Massachusetts State Department of Education, explained in 1986:

We have high expectations for all students and we're convinced that the best education occurs when those nearest the student make the key decisions about how they will learn. That is why over recent years, we have developed an extensive program of support for diversity among urban schools, providing parent choice on the basis of different approaches to education...

Our commitment in Massachusetts has been to make schools different in focus but equal in quality and to give all parents the opportunity and the information to make significant choices for their children....

In this process the role of central administration [and of the local school board] has been to orchestrate diversity, to insure that the common educational goals of the school system are met, even if in many different ways, and that no student is neglected in the process.[9]

"To orchestrate diversity," a lovely phrase, eloquently expresses the crucial set of tasks that local school boards and central administrators are now called on to perform. First, they need to set the common educational goals for all schools and all students (but not the ways in which those goals will be met); second they need to make sure that parents, older students, teachers, and principals all have played a role in making the decisions about the creation of a full range of diverse schools and can now freely choose the schools they want; third they need to guarantee that poor and minority students and their parents are fully empowered to take advantage of everything that diversity and choice can offer them.

A NEW FRAMEWORK

It is tempting to believe that if we introduce diversity, choice, autonomy for individual schools, and strict equity controls, thereby turning the old system upside down, we will have done enough to insure that our local school systems will be able to provide genuine educational excellence. Would that it were so. As good and necessary as all these changes are, public school choice and its associated restructurings provide only a framework within which our chances of solving many seemingly intractable problems are improved.

This new framework for instance should make public schooling much more attractive to the creative people already working in our public school systems and to all such people who might be thinking about teaching as a career. As Mary Romer-Coleman, assistant director of alternative concept schools in New York's Community School District No. 4, has noted:

> [The fact that] we are able to treat teachers as adult professionals and
> give them a chance to do what they've always believed should be done...
> has helped prevent teacher burnout and kept many of the best teachers in our
> schools.
> I was a teacher here in District No. 4, and let me tell you I would have
> been long gone if I hadn't had a chance to work in the kind of school I
> believed in. And this is true, I think, for most of the teachers in the
> alternative concept schools...[10]

Choice does not guarantee that this increased satisfaction will come about nor
does it in any way guarantee that the deadwood in our systems (whether teachers,
principals or central administrators) will be quickly and easily replaced—or that the
people taking their places will necessarily be convinced that the new school system
required by diversity and choice should be immediately instituted.

Indeed, in all too many instances the policy of diversity and controlled choice
has been installed as a citywide desegregation measure only to languish as the
entrenched bureaucracy dreams up all sorts of ingenious reasons why it should not
and will not work, why surveys of parents and teachers should not be conducted,
why decision-making authority should not be transferred downward from the
central bureaucracy to the individual school.

Even in Buffalo, New York, where we find one of the leading and most
successful examples of what choice can do for a large urban school system, things
do not change that rapidly. The attitudes of a handful of Buffalo schoolpeople have
been forcefully characterized by Florence Baugh, a member and former president of
the Buffalo Board of Education and a leader of the black community in that city:

> Let me tell you what I think about you educators... I'm talking about
> most educators, including many right here in Buffalo. I think you are the
> most staid, dyed-in-the-wool, dull, the most resistant-to-change people on
> earth. You know, we have procedures, ways things are done in the school
> system which have been done since Day One. I'll talk to some of our people
> about doing something differently, and I'll get the response, "But that's the
> way we've always done it." It doesn't matter whether it has any merit. It
> doesn't matter if there's anything happening as a result of doing it this way
> other than protecting the way it's always been done.
> I give this lecture to superintendents all the time. The schools are for
> children, not for the convenience of you staff folk. We could do all sorts of
> wonderful things in our school systems if only you educators weren't so
> inflexible.[11]

THE ULTIMATE NECESSITY

Now it is true that a new system of public schooling based on diversity, choice, and empowerment for individual schools does not by itself cost a great deal more than the traditional system, since it is essentially a new and better way of spending the money we are currently spending. There will be extra costs involved in reorganizing the existing system, in creating the new schools that will be required to achieve true diversity, and in creating the parent information and support systems that we need. There are also some additional costs for transporting students. Even if these associated costs are minimal, that doesn't mean we can get a world-class system of public schools on the cheap.

While the new educational framework provided by diversity and choice may dramatically improve the public satisfaction with its public schools and thus may make taxpayers more willing to invest in public education, there are simply too many other necessities that diversity and choice do not guarantee to provide. These include adequate salaries for teachers, better working conditions in schools (including adequate supplies, equipment, materials, and support services), and decent school facilities. We also need to provide vastly increased funding for our crumbling urban school systems and for all the additional educational, health, and social services that poor and minority children in those systems require if they are to break the cycle of poverty and disadvantage and to escape from the underclass.

It is becoming clear that we need early childhood education for all children and that we need to make radical changes in the education of teachers and administration. Although diversity and choice do constitute an almost automatic, built-in system of educational research and development, we need a much more elaborate, better-organized, and better-funded system of support for genuine innovation and experimentation.

Just as this partial list guarantees that we will have to spend a great deal more money on our public schools than we do now—at least twice as much. In these days of federal, state, and local budget deficits and consequent cutting of education budgets, such a statement may strike many readers as outlandish. If so, then I submit that those people have their heads (and their pocketbooks) in the educational sand. Throughout our history, this country has nickel-and-dimed public education and yet expected it to perform miracles. We have paid for a modest, utilitarian Model T and expected it to outperform a luxurious Dusenberg.

We still spend more of our gross national product (6.4% in 1988) on weapons and defense than on our entire system of public education from preschool through college and university (4.5% in 1988). Surely these figures should be reversed. Just a single stealth bomber will cost at least half a billion dollars (not counting the inevitable cost overruns and the costs of fixing all the things that turn out not to work). That's more than the federal government currently puts into the creation of magnet schools ($413 million). A fleet of 100 such bombers would cost us at least $50 billion over the next decade or so, which is the minimum amount of money that should be added to the federal education budget every year in that same period.

What we need is a more civilized set of national priorities that could lead to a wiser and more humane (or kinder, gentler) American society. There is nothing stopping this country from having a superb system of public education—if we really want it. Do we?

1.For a detailed description of how school systems can implement diversity and choice in a carefully staged fashion, see Evans Clinchy, *Planning for Schools of Choice: Achieving Equity and Excellence*, 4 vols. (Andover, Mass.: New England Center for Equity Assistance, The Network, 1989). See also Joe Nathan, ed., *Public Schools by Choice: Expanding Opportunities for Parents, Students, and Teachers* (Bloomington, Ind.: Meyer-Stone, 1989).

2.Howard Gardner, quoted in Daniel Goleman, "Rethinking the Value of Intelligence Tests," *New York Times Education Life Supplement*, 9 November 1986, p. 23.

3.Mary Anne Raywid, "Public Choice, Yes; Vouchers, No!," *Phi Delta Kappan*, June 1987, p. 766.

4.Seymour Fliegel, quoted in Evans Clinchy, "An Educational Renaissance in East Harlem," unpublished paper, Institute for Responsive Education, Boston 1987.

5.For a description of the microsociety school in Lowell, see George Richmond, "The Future School: Is Lowell Pointing Us Toward a Revolution in Education?," *Phi Delta Kappan*, November 1989, pp. 232-36.

6. John E. Chubb and Terry M. Moe, *What price Democracy? Politics, Markets, and American Schools* (Washington, D.C.: Brookings Institution, 1988).

7.Ibid.

8.Charles Glenn, "Looking Back, Looking Ahead," in *Equity Choice and Effective Urban Education*, (Quincy, Mass.: Massachusetts State Department of Education, April 1985).

9.Rhoda Schneider, keynote address at the Conference on Diversity and Choice, Worcester, Mass., 5 May 1986.

10.Mary Romer-Coleman, quoted in Clinchy, "An Educational Renaissance...."

11.Florence Baugh, quoted in Evans Clinchy, "Choice, Stability, and excellence: Parent and Professional Choice in Buffalo's Magnet Schools," *Equity and Choice*, Spring 1986, p. 106.

Can We Build a System of Choice That Is Not Just a "Sorting Machine" or a Market-Based "Free-for-All"?

David Tyack

Parents and students thronged the auditorium of Martin Luther King, Jr. High School on the Upper West Side of Manhattan during New York's October High School Fair. Recruiters from thirty-six public high schools set up booths where they displayed their wares and dispensed calendars, cupcakes, and banners. People from specialized magnet schools advertised their programs. Families flocked around the booth of Stuyvesant High School at the center of the stage, learning about its admission test and excellence in mathematics and science. Seward Park High School, one of the traditional neighborhood institutions required to admit everyone who came to the door, had its station at the end of the auditorium. Amid the competition for New York's students, Seward Park had few obvious resources and faced disdain for its location on the Lower East Side. "Look at this," muttered Seward Park English teacher, Jessica Siegel, when she looked about the hall. "Every kind of huckster thing." Here were the trappings of choice, observes Samuel G. Freedman, but underneath was "a system in which certain schools are engineered for success and others, like Seward Park, for failure."

Not just at the "High School Fair" but also in national policy talk about education, choice has become a word to conjure with. An extraordinary range of reformers rally around the magical concept, united by opposition to the public school "monolith" but agreeing on little else: President George Bush, Black activists, state governors both Democratic and Republican, business leaders, union leaders, libertarians, liberals, and conservatives. But for every person who sees choice as prologue to a pedagogical nirvana of efficiency or equity, there seems to be an opponent who sees it as a pathway to disaster for the public schools.

Suitably elastic, the word choice now refers to several practices: an open marketplace of schools in which parents, assisted by public vouchers (or scholarships), can choose either public or private schools for their children; a chance to select specialized schools within public school systems (often called magnet schools); open enrollment within districts and even states, a policy permitting students to attend schools other than the ones in their neighborhoods;

and permutations of these and other choice plans.

During the last generation, many reformers have advocated alternative schools—or "schools of choice"—within public education . They have argued that there is no one best school and that giving parents, teachers, and students the opportunity to create distinctive institutions will lead to greater parental commitment, more creative instruction for teachers, and more engaged learning for students. In recent years, however, two other rationales have dominated policy talk about educational choice. The first is that increased choice within public education—usually in the form of magnet schools in cities—provides a method of racial desegregation that is less controversial than busing and less likely to produce White flight from urban public schools. As a form of "controlled choice," such plans are compatible with earlier efforts to differentiate public schools and to make them more socially integrated and equitable.

The second rationale, by contrast, poses a radical challenge to traditional educational ideology and practice. It asserts that public education has become a "monopoly" that is wasteful, overregulated, unresponsive to captive clients, and shockingly inefficient. What is needed is competition between schools, both public and private, an open market in instruction in which parents can choose how to educate their children. When Americans shift from a monopoly to a market economy in education, ineffective schools will wither from lack of patronage and the number of effective schools will expand. As parents and students exercise choice, competition will winnow out the weak and reward the successful schools. As a result, test scores will rise, and the United States may once again become competitive economically.

Choice, advocates of an open marketplace say, is as American as cherry/apple/blueberry pie (take your pick). Consumer sovereignty and the market have ruled in other domains. What is surprising is not that citizens want choice of schooling but that they have so long endured the public school monolith. Merely tinkering with a failed system will not do; fundamentally changing the funding and governance of schools is the pathway to effective reform. The answer is not more regulation but radical deregulation that empowers the family. The poor will benefit even more than the prosperous from such a system of choice, for they have lacked the resources to take advantage of existing educational alternatives such as private schools or public education in affluent suburbs.

Critics of the marketplace model of choice take issue at almost every point in the argument. Education, they say, is a common good, like the air one breathes, not simply a consumer good. The way in which the next generation is educated affects everyone ultimately, and for that reason Americans have wanted democratic governance of public education. All people, not just parents, should have a say about how to educate the young. This debate has been a traditional arena for negotiating differences and finding common ground. If the "effectiveness" of schools becomes narrowed to a competition between schools to produce good test scores and all else is regarded (in the revealing word borrowed from economists) as "externalities," a catastrophic constriction of purpose in education will occur. Treating schools simply as the product of marketplace forces subverts an essential democratic institution.

Choices about "Choice"

In much of our current discourse, as Charles Glenn has written elsewhere, "choice seems to be considered a matter of 'all or nothing,' reduced to the stark choice between social engineering and a free-for-all." There are many choices to be made about "choice" and no one correct answer.

One form of choice, however, seems to me extraordinarily risky, especially in its effects on the poor and those who face racial discrimination. This version of choice treats schools as an open marketplace in which parents select either private or public schools for their children at public expense, paying tuition by a voucher. Competition for a scarce resource—fine schools—between families that start out highly unequal in information, influence, and resources seems hardly likely to benefit the have-nots, although it might be attractive to the haves. Only a new and complex set of bureaucratic institutions and regulations could prevent a rapidly accelerating segregation by class and race under such a system.

Studies of magnet schools within urban public school systems cast light on this question. They have shown that when schools of choice serve a minority of the students, such magnets often become "sorting machines" that attract educationally activist middle-class parents who gain places for their children in the most favored schools. Meanwhile, the children most at risk tend to remain behind in the neighborhood schools. A choice plan that throws open the market to all kinds of schools, private as well as public, would be almost certain to compound that problem.

In theory, providing vouchers might generate thousands of new and effective schools in the ghettos where they are most needed. But is this likely to happen? Have doctors as private service providers rushed to create model health care for the poor in exchange for Medicaid vouchers? Did the deregulation of mental health care and privatization of professional and social services help those most in need? So splintered are public and private services for the families who need them, today, many reformers want to coordinate social and health services through public education. What would happen to such a safety net for families at risk if schooling became an open market place?

And finally, an economic model of open competition endangers the traditional political functions of the common school. All Americans, not simply parents, have a stake in the education of the next generation. What happens to democratic process and collective debate, including the voices of nonparents, when parents control the system as autonomous consumers? What happens to common purposes when the goal is individual satisfaction, to children with special needs when many schools are not required to deal with them, and to balanced academic standards when schooling is deregulated?

I would limit choice plans, then, to public schools. What are the problems in public education to which some forms of "choice" might be remedies? Advocates of public schools of - choice make several arguments. Prosperous parents already have educational alternatives within public education because they can choose to live in a good public school district. Low-income parents do not have such an opportunity, and that is a problem. Families differ in the values they want taught to their children, and for such reasons of conscience and culture some groups have felt themselves duty-bound to create nonpublic schools. Choice between schools that honor different ethical outlooks might respond to this problem of conscientious objection by attending more to parents' values. Teachers, parents, and pupils also favor different approaches to pedagogy. If they could choose schools that express their educational philosophies, their commitment to its mission would create better climates for learning. Public schools have failed to serve the children most in need, despite decades of attempted reforms; a jolt to the system in the form of parental choice is needed to bring about change.

People already have many ways of expressing both collective and individual choice within the public system. Collective choices arise through the election of public officials on school boards to represent the public interest, mediate conflicts, and seek common purposes. Individual choices within the system, in part, take the form of selection among a wide range of programs and courses. Both school board and the elective system have serious inadequacies; both need reform. Conflicting mandates to school boards from different levels of governance have led to confusion of purpose and organizational deadlock. The movement to "restructure" school governance stems in part from a widespread perception that systems have become too large and bureaucratized for school boards adequately to express the collective choices of citizens. Many elective courses offered to students constitute the educational equivalent of junk food.

In some respects, public education is too heterogeneous. Districts and individual schools differ enormously in resources, the advantages or pathologies of their neighborhoods, the social backgrounds and needs of their students, and the quality of instruction. "Geography is destiny for millions of American children," writes Glenn; "where they live affects profoundly the kind of education they will receive and what they will learn about life in our society."

In other respects, schools may be too much alike in medium and message. They tend toward similar pedagogy and a standardized curriculum set by textbook and test writers rather than toward a creative adaptation of curriculum to students by teachers. And the attempt to avoid conflict over social values, to teach only a minimal common moral denominator, has often led, observes Glenn, to a situation of "the bland leading the bland."

In the past, groups that dissented from the moral or religious teaching of the public school took collective action to create alternative nonpublic schools. Under a system of public schools of choice, like-minded parents and public educators could together create schools of choice within public education that seek to honor different ideals of character. This would be a tricky undertaking: such "moral magnet" schools should not violate the separation of church and state or inhibit the formation of basic democratic values. But already such public schools exist in embryo. "Fundamental" schools, for example, stress strict discipline, deference to adults, mastery of the "basics," and proper dress. Certain features of such a "fundamental" school resemble Christian day schools, and Afrocentric academies in public systems have points in common with the day schools of the Black Muslims. "Free" schools, by contrast, stress the creativity, informal communication, and individualistic standards of behavior and achievement that other parents would favor.

There are many other kinds of experiments in public schools that have moved toward greater differentiation of schools and more parental choice. For over a generation, school districts have generated "alternative" schools ranging from progressive to traditional that have provided safety valves for discontented parents and students. New York City's specialized high schools—elective academic high schools like the Bronx High School of Science and institutions that prepare students for distinctive careers, for example—have been in place for many decades. As I have said, however, when only a minority of district schools are "special," they tend to "cream"—to attract the more motivated students, even when there are some controls for racial balance. The regular neighborhood schools lose some of their most apt pupils in this system of triage in which, as Freedman said, "certain schools are engineered for success and others, like Seward Park, for failure."

An alternate approach, which corrects some of these problems, is a system of "controlled choice" now being tried as a desegregation strategy in cities like Cambridge, Massachusetts, and Milwaukee, Wisconsin. Essentially, this seeks to magnetize the whole system, to give all parents a choice of schools while controlling for racial balance. This strategy goes well beyond freedom of choice or open enrollment plans because it is less passive: it requires all schools to be agents in differentiating education—to develop their own charters or missions—and requires all parents to select schools for their children. Essentially, this approach seeks to subvert "geography as destiny" in the assignment of pupils. Instead, it seeks to give all students, majority and minority, "proportional access to all schools and programs of choice." It differs from systems that have a few magnet schools in that it seeks to upgrade all schools within the district and targets poor schools for special assistance or, in dire cases, elimination.

There are many obstacles in implementing "controlled choice," just as in any novel and comprehensive educational reform. Surveys reveal that a majority of school board presidents, superintendents, and principals oppose public school choice. Planning distinctive and effective schools requires scarce resources: school staffs and parents need autonomy, time, and talent to design programs. If parents are to make informed choices, districts must have aggressive outreach programs that give clear and honest information. The plan for processing choices needs to be fair, and schools must find equitable ways to deal with parents who fail to secure their choices (in Milwaukee in 1977, out of 108,000 choice requests, 95 percent of first choices were granted by the district; most of the rest of the students were assigned to neighborhood schools).

There are promising examples of how parental choice and decentralization of collective decision making by parents, teachers, and administrators can improve the education of the dispossessed. Community School District Four in New York City's Spanish Harlem was near the bottom of the city in academic performance in the early 1970s and ranked eighth in welfare families among the twenty-six poorest districts of New York. Seymour Fliegel writes that the leaders of District Four "chose to take risks and be innovative, in part because it had nowhere to go but up." Believing that good schools are organic, created from within by educators with a distinct vision, they started building alternative schools one by one, beginning with a school for "acting out" students, one in performing arts, and Central Park East (CPE), which attracted innovative teachers and applicants from the district and across the city under the leadership of Deborah W. Meier. As time passed, other teachers and principals designed alternative schools, many of them small and occupying only a part of a school building (CPE and Meier sought to distinguish between a "school" and a "building," freeing the way for smaller communities of teachers and students).

The results of the reforms were striking. Before the creation of alternative schools, Fliegel notes, "only one child in six in District Four was reading at or above grade level; after the introduction of parental choice, more than three in five are doing so." The district climbed to the middle range of performance among the city's districts in mathematics and reading, and the number of junior high graduates admitted to selective high schools rose from 10 to more than 250. In addition to these improvements in quality, the alternative schools offered greater pedagogical diversity as teachers, given much greater freedom, developed innovative programs at the same time that they stressed democratic forms of decision making. "While public education may be useful as an industrial policy," Meier declared, "it is essential to healthy public life in a democracy."

District Four offers one example of how greater choice for parents and autonomy for teachers can reinvigorate inner-city schools. It is a delusion, however, to think that an open market will solve the problems of American schooling. If employed within the democratic structure and purposes of public education, choice can be one tool among many to expand opportunities for those, like the people of East Harlem, who have been denied a fair chance.

Who Should
Own the Schools?

Charles L. Glenn

A primary theme of recent education reform proposals has been the need to secure the autonomy of schools—that is, of the teachers and others working together to educate a group of children for whom they share responsibility—as professional organizations. The case has been made strongly by Albert Shanker of the American Federation of Teachers, by the Carnegie Forum on Education and the Economy, by the National Governors' Association, and by countless others that real educational reform will become possible only when the staff of a school are given scope to define how they will organize and carry out their work.

It is time, the reformers say, that we begin to think of schools as institutions with their own inherent reality, not as mere emanations of the state or local franchises of an educational bureaucracy. School autonomy is the necessary complement to parent choice policies, and some believe that neither will ultimately be effective without the other.

This point is by no means as obvious as it may seem. Educational policy has often been debated as though schools were passive vessels waiting to be filled with purpose and content by government decision makers, even though actual experience suggests that in most instances these folks have little positive effect on what schools do. Most schools are shaped in essential respects by other influences: vaguely defined professional norms, textbook publishers, and the tendency of teachers to teach as they were taught. American education, as political scientists say, is a "loosely coupled system."

Government—and parents—do influence schools, but that influence tends, unfortunately, to consist more of imposing limits than of shaping education in a positive way. School people learn to behave cautiously, teaching and disciplining defensively, out of a fear that something they do or say will incur the disapproval of a well-connected parent or someone above them in the system, state, or federal bureaucracy.

As a long-time state education official and also the parent of seven children, I can bear witness that school people seldom looked to me in either of my capacities for ideas about how they should do their work. Unfortunately, this isolation from outside influences does not often translate into real autonomy, into purposeful, bold measures to assure that children learn to their full potential.

It is legitimate and indeed necessary to protect schools on the one hand from being smothered to death by governmental regulation and agenda setting, and on the other from being nibbled to death by the conflicting demands of parents. They must be given a chance to become effective, mission-driven organizations, free to do the best job they can in the best way they know how. But they must do so within a framework of clear accountability to individual parents and society at large. The great majority of schools are dependent for their pupils on parents and government (through compulsory attendance laws), and most are entirely dependent for their funding on government or parents, although not, in the United States, on both.

Not unnaturally, with these resources come strings. Those who entrust children to schools and who provide the funding essential to their existence also impose expectations.

The 1991-92 state legislative sessions saw many initiatives to extend parent choice of schools and even to allow nongovernment schools to offer their services to parents on equal terms with schools operated by government, whether in the weak (and predictably ineffectual) form of school-based management within an unchanged institutional structure or in the bolder proposals for "charter schools" functioning as independent public schools and for education vouchers. We can expect more such efforts in 1992-93.

As states consider legislation to expand parent choice and school autonomy, a continually recurring problem is how the expectations of society should be defined and imposed. A less visible but equally important problem is how parents can be helped to clarify their own expectations and to function as effective "consumers" of education on behalf of their children.

Nor is this interest in new forms of school autonomy and parental choice, and their implication for systems of accountability, limited to American reformers. The policy under which state schools in England can "opt out" of the control of their local education authority and become grant-maintained schools funded by the central government, with extensive control of budgeting and decision making, and the proposal, in Russia's draft education statute, that every school become autonomous under its own statute, seek to move equally sclerotic systems in the same direction. In both cases, the move toward autonomy and choice is linked to new national standards for outcomes.

In the debates that have accompanied these political struggles, opponents of school choice have charged that the weakening of direct government control will allow irresponsible and undesirable education hustlers to take advantage of the naiveté of parents, and some advocates of nongovernment schooling fear that any change in the present arms-length relationship with government will result in fatal infringements on educational freedom. Some have suggested that a market in schooling should be allowed to operate without any government intervention at all.

If present education policy leans too far toward defining the interests of society (commonly identified with the agenda of government institutions) as paramount, the enthusiasts for radical privatization lean too far in the direction of recognizing only individual interests. What the process of thinking about educational reform has needed has been a credible way of thinking about the issues of autonomy, accountability, choice, and community that goes beyond the simple antithesis between bureaucratic strangulation and the free-for-all of individual selfishness.

David Osborne and Ted Gaebler have provided such an alternative perspective in their recent book Reinventing Government (1992); indeed, for once it is fair to apply the overworked label of a "new paradigm" to their discussion of a radically limited but crucial role for government and a greatly expanded but socially accountable role for other institutions.

Osborne and Gaebler point out that we are not limited to the alternatives of government provision of services and their privatization into a marketplace in which common social goals have no place. They remind us of the existence of "organizations that are privately owned and controlled, but that exist to meet public or social needs, not to accumulate private wealth . . . we call this group of institutions the 'third sector.' "

> The public sector tends to be better, for instance, at policy management, regulation, ensuring equity, preventing discrimination or exploitation, ensuring continuity and stability of services, and ensuring social cohesion.... The third sector tends to be best at performing tasks that generate little or no profit, demand compassion and commitment to

individuals, require extensive trust on the part of customers or clients, need hands-on, personal attention . . . and involve the enforcement of moral codes and individual responsibility for behavior. (Osborne and Gaebler 1992, 44-46)

They are careful to distance themselves from "conservative calls to 'leave it to the market,' " stressing that "structuring the market to achieve a public purpose is in fact the opposite of leaving matters to the 'free market'—it is a form of intervention in the market" (p. 283).

Government is more effective, they argue, if it concentrates on doing what it does well, rather than seeking to provide services through the creation of unwieldy structures that cannot respond flexibly to changing needs. This does not mean that government should abdicate its responsibility (as some market enthusiasts urge) to intervene actively in the interest, for example, of poor and minority children.

Governments that focus on steering actively shape their communities, states, and nations. They make more policy decisions. They put more social and economic institutions into motion. Some even do more regulating. Rather than hiring more public employees, they make sure other institutions are delivering services and meeting the community's needs. (p. 32)

Osborne and Gaebler do not provide a single answer to our question, "Who should own the schools?" Their discussion of education suggests, indeed, that there should be many "owners," many providers of education, within a framework of accountability and equity established by government as its essential, although limited, role. "Third sector" organizations like the community center, the YWCA, or a local church or temple would be appropriate providers of "public" education, from their perspective. So, presumably, would a group of teachers or a group of parents.

In the Netherlands, where about 70 percent of the schools are not operated by government, the Protestant schools do not "belong" to the churches but to associations of parents. There is a group of schools around Barcelona that are parent owned under an interesting arrangement: each family must purchase a "share" costing roughly a thousand dollars when the first child enrolls, and this amount is returned in full when the last child completes the school. Each school is literally owned by the current parents, in a self-perpetuating system that also provides a fund of capital in addition to the tuition flow.

Clearly there is a need for a great deal of experimentation along these lines, if American schools are to become autonomous within a framework of accountability to parents and to society. It is helpful to think of schools as needing to hear and to respond, in a coherent way, to three sets of interests or "voices," those of parents, of society, and of the school team itself.

Although there is considerable overlap in the concerns of these three parties, it is possible to make a rough working distinction among the voices that should avoid confusion. Parents, society as a whole, and the team of each school should each have the lead role in answering the basic questions about schooling: why, what, and how.

The Voice of Parents

Poor parents, perhaps more than others, need to be given opportunities to make important decisions about the well-being of their children; it is the responsibility of policymakers to assure, so far as that is possible, that there are no educationally bad choices.

Research that we have carried out for the U.S. Department of Education shows that urban parents of all racial/ethnic groups are keenly interested in making school choices for their children and use a variety of means of obtaining information and reaching conclusions about which schools would best meet their needs (Glenn and McLaughlin forthcoming).

Parents and teenagers have a particular concern with the why of schooling, with the sort of life that a particular school prepares its students to live. They should be enabled to make decisions among schools on the basis of each school's vocational character in the broadest sense and also on the basis of each school's philosophy of education and guiding principles, including its worldview or religious character.

Making such decisions is possible for parents only to the extent that schools are explicit about their guiding principles. It is to be feared that the unclarity of many schools in this important respect reflects the fact that no sustained discussion has occurred among the faculty about the purposes of their work.

In this respect, the intense efforts under way in many Dutch schools to define clearly their distinctive identities should be seen as a rational response to an increasingly competitive (because of declining enrollments) environment. Because the Netherlands (with Belgium) has the most fully developed system of parent choice of schools in the world, we may reasonably expect to see a similar concern emerge in other countries.

The Voice of Society

Although the family —parents and children— is the primary source of differentiation in what is demanded of schools, society has an interest in assuring that the education include some common elements that are considered essential. The family's primary concern is with the why of education; that of society should be with what is learned at each stage of formal schooling.

Much of what needs to be learned is relatively easy to measure, because it consists of skills of literacy, numeracy, and problem solving, together with information about our nation and the natural and political worlds. The recent emphasis on establishing national standards in key areas is an encouraging sign that clarity is beginning to emerge from what has been the chaos of American education. Along with standards, of course, it will be important to identify several alternative means of determining whether individual students have reached them and whether individual schools have met their obligation to reach these benchmarks.

Some measurable competence in these cognitive domains does not exhaust what society can legitimately ask of the education of each of its future citizens, because qualities of what we can best call "civic virtue" are also essential, although far more difficult to measure. We must not forget Aristotle's concern, echoed by generations of American leaders and political thinkers, for schooling that will "produce a certain character in the citizens, namely to make them virtuous, and capable of performing noble actions."

In the past, this concern has often taken the form of attempts to establish a state monopoly of schooling or, if alternatives were tolerated, to assure that they would be available only to the relatively prosperous. The fact that the education policy in the United States, almost uniquely among contemporary democracies, denies funding to nonstate schools has to do, above all, with a conviction that the common school is the essential point of unity in a highly diverse nation.

It has become clear through experience and recent research that schools operated by religious organizations and other groups can be at least as successful as state schools in developing civic virtue. What is unclear is whether public policy can and should include qualities of civic virtue among the what of schooling that are demanded of every school in the name of society and, if we were to do so, how that accomplishment would be measured. It is tempting—and perhaps necessary—to simply leave the definition of these goals and the measurement of their attainment up to the good judgment of parents and to the sense of responsibility of educators, but a good case can be made that society's interest in education should not be limited to outcomes that lack moral weight.

On one aspect of the shaping of civic virtue I continue the unfashionable view that we should, as a society, encourage the racial integration of schools and provide incentives for schools to make extra efforts necessary to accomplish such integration successfully in the face of residential segregation and an unfavorable racial climate. An important distinction exists, however, between racial discrimination and deliberate segregation, which should continue to be forbidden by law and administrative action, and racial integration, which should be accomplished by voluntary means, as we have done in Massachusetts.

The Voice of the School

If families are concerned with the why of education, and society as a whole with what is learned, it is up to the community of educators that we call schools to concern themselves with how learning and the shared life of the school will be organized.

Only through the ongoing collaboration of those working in the school can sound decisions be made about how the instructional program will be structured and its parts articulated. Only through thoughtful engagement with the school's objectives can sound strategies be developed to keep track of pupil progress and to determine how teaching should be modified to make it more effective. Only in the individual school can standards be set and enforced for behavior and effort. These essential aspects of meeting the mission of the school must be worked through by those engaged in its day-to-day life.

It has grown fashionable to say that these aspects of the work of the school must be sheltered from interference from outside officials, whether of the school system, the state, or the federal government. Unfortunately, experience to date with school-based management suggests that it is easier to tell school people to make decisions than it is to abandon the habit of second-guessing those decisions at higher levels or so constraining them that they lose much of their purpose. For this reason, more radical reform is needed, reform that dismantles the structures within which most publicly funded schools operate. Over the next several years, we can expect to see considerable ingenuity employed in developing new organizational forms for schooling that are able to satisfy the legitimate demands of parents and of society for accountability while maintaining a sufficient level of independence for each to function coherently according to its own dynamic and vision.

References

Glenn, C. L., and K. McLaughlin. Forthcoming. *How parent information for school choice works in six Massachusetts cities.* Boston: Boston University, Center on Families, Communities, Schools and Children's Learning.

Osborne, D., and T. Gaebler. 1992. *Reinventing government.* Reading, MA: Addison-Wesley.

Principle and Prudence in the Design of Choice
John E. Coons

Many of the mechanisms adopted and proposed in recent years for educational choice have seemed to me ill conceived. At the editors' request, I will say a few words about the issue of proper design.

No design works unless it gets you where you want to go, and obviously not all who promote choice seek the same outcome. Some reformers hold the reduction of the tax burden as the primary objective. Others wish to expand the private sector; conversely, many public educators wish to limit choice to state schools with the aim of diminishing the private sector. And more than a few enthusiasts seem willing to sign off on any instrument that bears the name choice; I am not always certain where the latter suppose they are headed.

Because we must first decide where reform should take us, I should specify the particular objectives that carry weight for me. Few of these are transcendental; I have no private picture of the ideal world or the perfect graduate. Broadly speaking, above some very minimum standard set by the state, I prefer to trust parents and families to set the ideals for their own children, and whatever mechanism we adopt should facilitate that. This much is banal, and perhaps no choice supporter disagrees. Beyond this, however, I do have my own slant on the particular values at stake, and a few paragraphs will suffice to describe them. In the process, I will sometimes use the word we to implicate Stephen Sugarman, my collaborator for twenty-seven years. The two of us have just completed a little book on the mechanisms of state-supported scholarships or vouchers. It seems to me that the principles of design that undergird scholarships for children to attend public or private schools are the same that describe proper techniques for choice plans of other types. Because the book was prepared pro bono and without royalties, I can without shame report that it is entitled Scholarships for Children and it is published by the Institute for Governmental Studies at the University of California at Berkeley. We hope legislators will find it useful.

Systems that empower parents through state scholarships ought to seek the following effects: (a) enhancement of family dignity and responsibility; (b) reduction of social resentment, generally; (c) amelioration of the injustice created by the traditional design of tax-supported education; (d) practical hope for voluntary class and racial integration; (e) enhancement of teacher welfare and professionalism; (f) assembling of a larger political constituency for education; and (g) more "efficient" schools (more learning per tax dollar).

Any system that aims for these seven ends must meet eight technical criteria. *First*, it must include private and public schools on the same basis. There will be no authentic reform so long as exclusive "public school choice" is taken seriously as a policy option. The current proposals to that end that are floated in virtually every state are cosmetic only and consciously designed to be so. Here is the one area where the free-market economists have long been correct. Until jobs are threatened by a potential exodus to private schools, the government sector will remain stagnant. *Second*, private schools should be fiercely protected against further regulation beyond the minimum necessary to protect the poor (see below). The aim overall is deregulation, not more of the same.

Hence, *third*, public school authorities (districts, etc.) should themselves be empowered to operate exactly like private schools except for the federal constitutional limitations regarding religion. Districts should have authority to create new schools in the form of nonprofit public corporations that can be given every imaginable form of mission and management. They should be designed like their private counterparts to prosper or perish by their ability to attract customers carrying state scholarships. A "public scholarship school" that fails should be subject to the same bankruptcy process that governs producers of services in the private sector. The employees of unsuccessful firms would have to seek new jobs. Persons unsuccessful at teaching would enter other professions. By the way, public schools of choice will remain indispensable in the new system, simply because there are parents who will choose them.

There are several technical criteria necessary to protect children who are likely to be excluded by some popular providers. We use income as a proxy for this group. Therefore, *fourth*, every school—public or private—to redeem scholarships should be required to set aside a modest percentage of new places for low-income children (if so many apply). There are many ways to protect the admission rights of children of the poor; we have aired and debated a dozen of them over the last twenty-five years. Of all these, the set-aside is by far the most appealing to the public as a whole, and it is most likely to succeed in its aim of securing opportunity for all. We add, *fifth,* that if participating schools charge tuition over and above the amount of the scholarship, they must apportion this charge to the family's capacity to pay. Many private schools do this now. If this rule were not included, popular schools would have the incentive to control the number of low-income families by price. *Sixth,* the poor must receive a reasonable transportation allowance.

Seventh, and very important, the scholarship must be large, and the amount must vary according to grade and other circumstances. On average, for each type of child it must approach in magnitude the dollars spent in the traditional public schools for a child of similar circumstance. Otherwise, there will be too little incentive to form new schools, and no competitive pressure will be put on the public schools presently warehousing the poor in the inner city.

Eighth, both prudence and politics require a gradual phase-in of any system that will affect the entire state system. Over a quarter century, we and others have suggested many feasible devices for this purpose.

These are the eight essential components. There are other features that I would consider optional. For example, I used to argue that an elaborate state information system would be necessary to assist the unsophisticated parent. I am now less certain, having become more impressed with the potential role of private welfare agencies and churches as informers of educational consumers. Likewise, although I still support testing for informational purposes, I do so largely in the hope that in the future tests will become more focused on school effects than on the natural endowment of students.

It should also be said that the scholarship should come from the state and should be uniform statewide for all children in similar circumstances. There are complexities here caused by the irrationalities of the existing school finance structure. The goal, however, is clear, and it would be a welcome bonus, if choice should drive us at last to realize the "equity" half of this journal's mission.

So much for the necessary and useful machinery. I should now add parenthetically that some of these requirements can be relaxed where the state is providing the scholarship *only* to the poor or *only* to some other target group such as dropouts or students who are at risk. Where eligibility is limited to a disadvantaged group, at least the scholarship is doing no *harm*, even if participating schools take only a sprinkling of these children. It is in the design of more comprehensive systems that all eight criteria come into play.

With these in mind, it is possible systematically to evaluate the various mechanisms that have appeared in reform proposals over the last decade or so. Applying these criteria, Sugarman end I have found ourselves reluctant opponents of initiative drives in Michigan, the District of Columbia, and Oregon. All of these were well intended, but—at least for us—in each case they were flawed in ways that we could not accept. All three proposals were crushed at the ballot box. Considering the strong showing for choice in opinion surveys, one suspects that the design of these instruments have been wanting not only technically but in political terms. California may have the chance to prove us wrong. In November 1994, an initiative is likely to appear on the statewide ballot. It is an instrument slightly more sophisticated than the Oregon effort; unfortunately, it shares much of what Oregon's voters seemed, like ourselves, to find objectionable. I will conclude with a few remarks about this California effort.

This is a constitutional initiative. If passed by a majority, it will become the organic state law, beyond the reach of the legislature. It will offer every child a scholarship worth at least $2,700 (half the public expenditure). The scholarship may be spent in any private school or one of the newly formed public schools that will be designed to look essentially like private schools; the legislature is required within a year to provide a mechanism for public schools to reorganize, to redeem scholarships and, essentially, to be run by their teachers without the burden of the old Education Code. These public scholarship schools would live or die on their ability to attract customers.

Every scholarship-redeeming school would be free to admit or exclude applicants as it wished within the limits of existing law. Private schools would be elaborately protected against new regulation by the legislature whether they took scholarships or not. Participating schools would be required to test their children, and the school's performance on these tests would be public; the individual child's performance, however, would be available only to his or her parent. No limit would be imposed on the charging of additional tuition.

There are, of course, other parts to what is a long, and I fear, clumsy vehicle, but I have said enough to allow its evaluation. I should start by conceding a personal stake. Sugarman and I spent considerable time and resources in 1991 trying to assure the right design for the initiative. Until almost the very end, the draft satisfied all eight of the criteria. At the last moment, for reasons we do not fully understand, the entire instrument was rewritten in the form I have just described. The most important changes were these: (a) The scholarship was cut from 85 percent of public spending per child to the smaller guarantee of 50 percent ($2,700); (b) the admissions set-aside for the poor was eliminated; (c) schools redeeming scholarships will be permitted to charge what they please irrespective of family capacity to pay; (d) no allowance for transport is guaranteed; (e) no adjustment for differing needs is guaranteed. Having consistently insisted on these protective features, at this point we felt constrained to withdraw from the process.

The initiative—known as the Parent's Choice in Education Amendment (PCEA)—will do considerable good. It will allow perhaps 25,000 children from low-income families to take up places in inner-city private schools, mostly denominational. It is possible that some unused Catholic schools in the cities will be reopened. In addition, there will be an unpredictable number of new schools in the cities—the kind of schools that can be founded on $2,700 plus whatever extra dollars poor families can afford to pay.

In my judgment, there will be relatively few new schools in the inner city. The amount of the scholarship is sufficient to meet the marginal costs of some of the existing private providers, but it is not easy to start on $2,700. At most, one in ten poor children will receive the advantage of choice. The rest will presumably remain in public schools in Los Angeles, Oakland, or San Francisco, and those schools will feel very little threat from the exodus of what will be but a fragment of their population. The educartel is reassured that, however it performs its function, the increasing school-age population of low-income families in California will continue to provide the bodies to fill the seats and protect the jobs.

The suburbs will be a different story. In Berkeley, for example, a third of the parents already pay private tuition to elude the public schools. The addition of

$2,700 to whatever else the middle class can afford would be an invitation to the formation of many new private providers of high quality. In itself, this would be a good thing. The students in these schools would benefit directly, and the community would benefit from the unprecedented pressure that would be put on the public schools in these areas to improve their performance. It is also likely that the suburban private schools would begin to offer more financial aid to "deserving" children from disadvantaged homes. Further, many of the religious schools would waive the deserving criterion and assist poor families whose children don't happen to be clever. Who could complain of this shower of blessings?

Maybe nobody. If choice is the particular camel you want in your tent, here is its nose and a bit more. Supporters make exactly that pragmatic argument. They say this initiative will break the log jam, demonstrate the blessings of choice, and, in due course, move us to a new comprehensive system of choice which will meet all eight of the criteria I have suggested. I hope so.

But I am not working for the PCEA, and I may or may not vote for it. The camel of choice would be welcome in my tent, but I'm not convinced that this initiative will get him all the way in—ever. My doubt is partly political, and here is the precise question: Does this peculiar mechanism have the political promise in the near future to get the camel in so that all the children of the city may be served? My deepest fear is that choice in this current proposal will be sufficient to reform suburban schools and—in the process—will satisfy the middle class. The worst tactic may be to start by serving those who are already the best off in a bad system. We are unclear whether this would be the beginning or end of choice. The politics of the next decade are simply too uncertain.

In addition—and quite apart from these problematic political notions—there is no justification for relegating impoverished inner-city families to the alternative of cheap private schools and ineffectual public schools. If we are content today to spend $7,000 per student on the poor in Los Angeles schools that don't work, we ought to be ready to spend that much in schools—public and private—that do work. I would rejoice for the suburban child whose lot is improved by the PCEA, but I hesitate to leave a million disadvantaged California children in the same old schools with the cheery prediction that their liberation will soon follow.—

IMPROVING SCHOOLS AND EMPOWERING PARENTS: CHOICE IN AMERICAN EDUCATION
Benefits of Choice
Nancy Paulu

Participants at the White House Workshop on Choice in Education agree that choice programs can benefit children in innumerable ways. But they warn that these benefits are most likely to materialize when the programs are intelligently planned, implemented, and monitored. "We should extend parent choice, but we need to do it with care and with integrity," explained Charles Glenn, Jr., executive director of the Office of Educational Equity in the Massachusetts Department of Education.

When educators and policymakers proceed with these thoughts in mind, programs of choice can improve schools and empower parents.

Improving Schools

In a speech delivered in May 1989 to the Education Press Association, Secretary Cavazos deplored the Nation's three deficits—its budget deficit, trade deficit, and education deficit. The first two cannot be resolved without addressing the third, he said, which is reflected in many ways: by the Nation's 27 million illiterate adults, its declining or static SAT and ACT scores, and its 28 percent high school dropout rate.

These and other discouraging statistics can best be reversed by making basic organizational changes in public education, he said, concluding that "I consider choice the cornerstone to restructuring elementary and secondary education in this country."

Workshop participants discussed five ways in which choice can improve our schools. Restructuring was the first of them.

1. Choice can bring basic structural change to our schools.

Scholars and others studying American education have noted what Secretary Cavazos describes as "a remarkable national uniformity in the methods and organization of our schools." Although we have begun to see more diversity, most American schools remain controlled by politicians and administrators in a central office. Educators in individual schools still have little say in key decisions.

This has profound and unfortunate consequences for American education, according to John Chubb, a senior fellow at the Brookings Institution and a workshop participant. In a study of American high schools, Chubb and his associates found that good schools have more autonomy and possess the power to influence their own educational policy. He writes:

Those organizational qualities that we consider to be essential ingredients of an effective school—such things as academically focused objectives, pedagogically strong principals, relatively autonomous teachers, and collegial staff relations—do not flourish without the willingness of superintendents, school boards, and other outside authorities to delegate meaningful control over school policy, personnel, and practice to the school itself.[1]

School administrators are reluctant to allow school autonomy because, Chubb explains, this might "threaten the security of political representatives and education administrators whose positions are tied to the existing system and who now hold the reins of school reform."

Schools will not improve until the balance of power shifts, Chubb concludes—and programs of choice provide the best avenue to making this happen. Schools of choice diverge from the organization of most conventional schools in several ways, he says. The roles of their staff members and administrators are generally less delineated and more flexible; teams of people in schools of choice make decisions on everything from budgets to curriculum. Teachers in schools of choice assume more power over their professional lives, which contributes to their reporting higher levels of job satisfaction and having better attendance records. Other researchers report that giving teachers more autonomy improves their relationships with students and provides teachers with more leeway to tailor their instruction to individual circumstances.

Chubb reported in his high school study that all things being equal, students in schools that are extensively controlled by politicians and administrators in a central office learned about one year less academically during high school than those in schools with more autonomy to make decisions that affect them.

Schools of choice. in short, help to create organizations in which educators, parents, and students cooperate with one another and become more involved in their schools. And this encourages them to invest more of themselves. Former East Harlem administrator Sy Fliegel explained to program participants:

[I]t's an old capitalist idea that people just treat what they own much better than things that they don't own. So, in our schools, you see very little graffiti, even though they're old buildings .... There's a respect. In our schools, you can walk through a junior high school and bulletin boards will not be touched.

2. Schools of choice recognize individuality.

Americans celebrate many traditions, personalities, hopes, and strengths. Yet historically, American schools have been based on the premise that there is "one best way" to educate students. Educators are now coming to recognize that youngsters require different settings. Wisconsin's Governor Thompson told workshop participants:

The concept of parental choice recognizes that children are not all the same. They have individual talents and specialized needs. [In schools of choice] children would no longer be assigned to schools as if they were all the same. Schools could design curricula to meet specialized needs.

Minnesota's Governor Perpich explained the advantages of matching student to school:

There are many students in the Nation . . . who simply need a change of scenery, a community of people that better suits their needs. When students find their niche, and when they find a school in which they feel at home, the evidence is showing that they thrive.

Stacy Condon from Minnesota is one such student. The Minnesota governor reported:

She was a very bright student who was frustrated with her teachers and the learning atmosphere in her school. Two years ago, she was ranked in the lower third of her class and had announced to her parents that she was quitting school at the age of 16 to become a drummer in a rock band. But her mother read the ad about our Postsecondary Options Program and encouraged her to try it . . . Last June . . . Stacy Condon simultaneously graduated from high school and completed her first year of college with a full 45 credits and a high B average.

Programs of choice recognize differences not only among students, but also among teachers and educators. They, too, work best in atmospheres that suit them. Joe Nathan, a senior fellow at Minnesota's Hubert Humphrey Institute of Public Affairs and the editor of Public Schools by Choice,[2] noted at the workshop:

[T]here is no one best school that is going to meet the needs of all kids, regardless of how terrific it is, or that is going to do well for all teachers.... My wife is a public school teacher. She hates the idea of working with junior high school kids. She loves working with severely and profoundly handicapped children. She wouldn't like a Montessori program. I like working in an open school. There are other teachers who hate those kinds of programs.

3. Choice fosters competition and accountability.

Many educators believe students benefit from competition because it fosters educational excellence. The National Governors' Association wrote in its 1986 report, Time for Results:

If we first implement choice, true choice among public schools, we unlock the values of competition in the marketplace. Schools that compete for students, teachers, and dollars will, by virtue of the environment, make those changes that will allow them to succeed. Schools will, in fact, set the pace, forcing governors and other policymakers to keep up.

These sentiments were expressed at the workshop by Jackie Ducote, executive vice president of the Louisiana Association of Business and Industry:

I believe that competition can be the catalyst to make our system of public education in the United States second to none, and that choice can be the glue to make sure that it stays that way.

Fourteen-year-old Andre Lawrence from New York City told workshop participants how he believes competition ultimately benefits students. "I was very happy to decide which school I wanted to attend," he explained. "It was like shopping, buying a pair of shoes, shopping around until you found something you like."

While some critics fear that choice will strand poor youngsters in disadvantaged schools, workshop participants argue just the opposite. They say that requiring schools to compete for students encourages those providing substandard education to be more accountable for their educational programs. Ultimately this may force educators either to make needed improvements or risk folding. District 4 in New York has closed schools with declining enrollments. But this need not be the end result; changing a principal or moving teachers in or out may be all that's needed to revive an ineffective school.

Workshop participants agreed that competition does not have to be ruthless. Denis Doyle, a senior research fellow at the Hudson Institute in Washington, D.C., and an authority on education policy, explained:

> [T]here is in the popular mind a vision of cutthroat competition, of profit-taking buccaneers swashbuckling across the State, people who are . . . merciless, kind of Atlas Shrugged/Ayn Rand types. Well, there certainly is that type of competition, but there is competition which is closer to home . . . and that is the competition which emphasized the supremacy of the consumer; consumer sovereignty, and that, in fact, is what competition is all about.

4. Choice can improve educational outcomes.

"Family background, economic status, [and] residence all matter a great deal in determining whether a youngster will succeed in school," writes Mary Anne Raywid, a professor at Hofstra University who has spent more than a decade studying schools of choice. "But," she continues, "it is possible that the particular school attended and whether he or she is there by choice matter even more."[3]

Critics contend that we lack solid research to confirm the educational accomplishments of schools of choice. Raywid, as well as many at the workshop, disagree. Many studies provide statistics showing that the academic achievement and behavior of students enrolled in schools of choice improve. Unfortunately many of these studies do not compare schools of choice with conventional schools, which makes it hard to separate out choice from other variables that could contribute to school success. Within such limits, however, one can find impressive correlational evidence of the success of individual programs and schools of choice.[4] Some of this evidence is described below.

• In East Harlem, where almost 60 percent of the students fall below the poverty line, less than 15 percent of students read at grade level in 1972, and the district ranked last in reading among New York City's 32 districts. Then East Harlem introduced choice. Today, 64 percent of its students read at or above grade level, and in recent years, the district's ranking has ranged from 20th to 16th in reading. And on State tests administered in 1988, 84 percent of East Harlem's 8th graders were judged competent writers.[5] Secretary Cavazos noted another long-term benefit for the district's children:

[M]ore important than ranking is how District 4 alumni have fared in entering the city's specialized high schools, which are highly competitive and are regarded as the gateway to career opportunities. In 1973, only 10 District 4 students were accepted; last year the count was 250.

• Studies of magnet schools in New York State, Los Angeles, California, and Montgomery County, Maryland, all found that students' reading and math scores on average were above district and/or national averages.[6] Montclair, New Jersey, reports similar academic gains among students attending schools of choice.

• Students enrolled in Catholic schools outperform their public school counterparts, according to a study by James S. Coleman and his colleagues at the National Opinion Research Center and the University of Chicago. (The same conclusions appear to hold for other schools with a religious foundation and a religiously homogeneous student body.)

This study, initiated by the U.S. Department of Education, found that the Catholic school advantage is not due to their ability to select students; significantly, the study found that Catholic students do better than public school students when matched for race, socioeconomic status, and parental education. In a May 18, 1989, article in The Wall Street Journal summarizing his research, Coleman wrote:

[S]tudents from Catholic schools are more likely to attend college than are comparable students from either public schools or independent private schools, and more likely to continue in college without dropping out.

Coleman attributes the advantages to several interrelated factors: Catholic schools make higher academic demands of their students; they have shunned the phenomenon of "course proliferation"; and these schools have been shielded from the effects of the youth revolution, which has diminished the ability of many parents to determine their teenage children's high school curricula and to impose schoolwork requirements.

Coleman and his colleagues conclude that many attributes of Catholic schools—for example, school order and discipline and involved teachers—could also improve the performance of public school students.

• One study reports that vandalism and violence in schools of choice are lower than in conventional schools.[7] Other studies report that student behavior improves substantially in schools of choice[8] and that student suspension rates in New York State's magnet schools are below district averages.[9]

This last study also reports that student attendance rates were higher in 90 percent of New York's magnet schools than in nonmagnets. And in a national survey, Raywid found that attendance rates of particular students improved over their previous records in 81 percent of the alterative schools polled.[10]

5. Schools of choice can keep potential dropouts in school and draw back those who have already left.

Three years ago, Chris Wilcox from North Branch, Minnesota, was enrolled in a traditional high school, where he was failing four out of seven classes each trimester. He told workshop attendees, " When I should have been home studying or doing homework, I would be hunting, snowmobiling, chasing girls, or whatever. It just wasn't working for me."

Wilcox is now enrolled in an area learning center in Minnesota, which allows him to earn credits for working at a job operating heavy equipment during the day and to attend classes for academic credit at night. "Without the area learning center, I probably would not graduate," Wilcox said.

The realization that Minnesota needed to accommodate many students like Wilcox was behind the State's decision to approve the High School Graduation Incentives Program, which enables teenage and adult dropouts to return to school. Governor Perpich explained, "We began to publicize the program around the slogan that the students on the verge of dropping out don't need a lecture, they need an alternative." Within the first 6 months of the program, which began in 1987, 1,500 students had signed up.

Student choice programs can provide students like Wilcox with a setting that matches their learning styles and interests. Educators have long known that there is no one best school for every student, and that students are most apt to flourish when they are in an appropriate educational environment. Research suggests that this truth should be kept in mind in attempting to reduce the dropout rate.

Many studies have found that low achievers make remarkable gains when moved to a new and different school; their academic records, behavior, attendance, and attitude toward school all improve.[11] And a study of dropout patterns in Portland, Oregon, shows that the school a youngster attends has a bigger impact on whether a student drops out than his or her economic background or race.[12] This same analysis found that students attending schools of choice are less apt to drop out than those in other schools.

Empowering Parents

Throughout American history, the success of the Nation's schools has hinged in part on the close ties of parents, teachers, students, and local administrators. Together these four groups once made American public education the envy of the world. But today this relationship has broken down. As Secretary Cavazos lamented in his speech to the Education Press Association, we have "placed our trust in processes and institutions that [have] distanced parents and students from their educational systems."

Programs of choice can help draw parents back into the educational fold. "A free and productive society thrives on empowerment of the people," the Secretary said. "The American economy and our democracy are products of empowerment, and this approach can revitalize schools around the country."

Participants at the White House Workshop on Choice in Education recognize that allowing mothers and fathers to select schools for their children can be a crucial first step to returning American education to its rightful position of prominence. Those in attendance discussed several ways in which schools of choice empower parents.

6. Schools of choice increase parents' freedom.

Choice programs place, the decision of which school a child should attend where it rightly belongs—within the family. And in doing so, they allow the close relationship that once existed between parents and schools to be recreated. As President-elect Bush explained at the workshop, choice plans ". . . give parents back their voices—and their proper determining roles—in the makeup of children's education." Wisconsin Governor Thompson agreed:

> Parents should have a right to decide where their children should go to school. It's as simple as that. Parents are responsible for overseeing their children's education, and they, not State government, not school boards,

should decide what influences dominate the prime hours of their children's day.

Schools of choice have provided freedom for both parents and students who attended the workshop, including 14-year-old Andre Lawrence. Without the choice program, Andre would attend school near his home on the Lower East Side of Manhattan. But the program gives him the freedom to board a subway at 7 a.m. each morning to attend the Jose Feliciano School for the Performing Arts in East Harlem. He notes:

> Growing up and attending school on the Lower East Side would have been a challenge. I knew I didn't want to attend my zone junior high school because right across the street drugs were being sold, and I wanted to be out of the neighborhood, and also I wanted to meet new friends.

In order to increase the freedom of parents, however, programs of choice must provide more than cosmetic differences among schools. Sy Fliegel, formerly of East Harlem, notes:

> [C]hoice has no real meaning if you don't have quality and adversity to select from.... If I have seven blue ties, I don't think it's much different than having one blue tie.

Parents and students must be able to select programs providing different climates, activities, goals, and emphases. However, although schools of choice use different approaches, they must all provide a solid education. Otherwise, Fliegel cautions, "You may have a youngster who will travel for a half hour to go to a different lousy school. That doesn't make sense to me."

Freedom to choose a nonpublic school?

Today, much of the discussion about choice centers on public school choice. However, some proponents of choice believe that real freedom doesn't exist unless parents are allowed to select from nonpublic as well as public schools. At the workshop, this issue prompted lively debate.

Jackie Ducote from the Louisiana Association of Business and Industry argued that restricting choice to public schools hampers reform by failing to change the current bureaucratic structure. She said:

> I commend those who are working for public school choice.... My only fear is that it may not be any more successful than the reform efforts of the past because the people who have been in charge of the system in the past

are still in charge. By limiting the power of parents to choose only among government-operated schools, the bureaucracy will still be in charge, and the parents will still be at their mercy. To be successful, any education reform must have an external force operating that is free from the control of those who are in charge of the present system. That external force is competition.... The only way to get true competition is to empower parents to choose among all schools—government-operated, and nongovernment-operated.

Another workshop participant, John E. Coons, professor of law at Berkeley, argues that restricting choice to the public schools insults ordinary families. "If private education is good enough for the rich, why not for the poor?" Coons, the coauthor of Education by Choice and Private Wealth and Public Education, wrote.[13] Furthermore, he fears that "choice confined to public schools may prove largely cosmetic," since some elite public schools continue to exclude outsiders.

Those who wish to extend freedom of choice to parochial schools included Sister Elizabeth Avalos, a teacher at Mercy High School in San Francisco, which educates predominately minority students. Sister Avalos explained:

[C]hoice is not only choice for academic excellence or choice for a student being able to go to a school because they are at risk educationally . . . but choice is also for those parents who would like a religious education.

A senior at Mercy High School, Sophia Alvarez, agreed that choice should include parochial as well as public schools:

My experience in an all-girls, private Catholic school has been great, and I think other people should have an opportunity to attend these schools because they are excellent. They not only have high academic standards, but they incorporate moral values in them.

Other workshop participants, however, want choice restricted to public schools. A difficult issue facing choice programs is whether State revenue, which generally follows the student to the school of choice, can be used to allow families to choose among public, private, and parochial schools. Some participants cautioned that First Amendment and other legal concerns, as well political hurdles, may confront those trying to include private or parochial schools in choice programs. For example, the Minnesota Federation of Teachers (MFT challenged that State's program for allowing students to take nonsectarian courses at private as well as public colleges and universities. The U.S. District Court ruled that the MFT was not the proper party to raise this issue and dismissed the case. The district court's decision is now on appeal to the U.S. Court of Appeals for the Eighth Circuit.

It is too early to know how this challenge will be resolved, but it is worth noting that in Muellery. Allen, the U.S. Supreme Court upheld a Minnesota statute permitting tax deductions for public, private, and parochial school expenses.

Furthermore, political opposition has stalled efforts of many State officials to include nonpublic schools in choice plans. Wisconsin Governor Thompson's first choice proposal would have allowed low-income parents to send their children to any public, private, or parochial school in Milwaukee. It was staunchly opposed by those who argued that such a program would break up the Milwaukee Public Schools. Governor Thompson's new proposal backs off from universal parental choice. In response to a question at the workshop, Governor Thompson said:

> Why I did not include religious [schools] is that I want to Win ... I have learned in 22 years in State government that sometimes it's better to take half a loaf and build upon that than try the whole loaf and lose everything.

Several workshop participants argued that the quality of educational programs is a more important consideration than whether the school is public, private, or parochial. Joyce Duncan, who directs the East Harlem Career Academy, a liberal arts school of choice in District 4, said:

> The most important thing is to make sure that parents feel that the schools that they send their children to are doing a quality job.... I don't care whether it's a Catholic school, I don't care whether it's a private school, I don't care whether its a public school, as long as it works.

7. Choice plans increase parent satisfaction and involvement in the schools.

People are most inclined to invest themselves in causes and endeavors in which they are committed—ones in which they feel the pride of ownership. When geography instead of choice determines where one's child attends school, parents often fail to support the schools in ways that can help their youngster learn. They are less apt to attend parent-teacher conferences, to volunteer to chaperone field trips, or to contact the school if a problem arises.

Critics charge that schools of choice cannot rely for support on the natural constituency of parents that forms around neighborhood schools. But many workshop participants report otherwise. They say that parents of students in schools of choice are substantially more satisfied and involved than are parents who cannot choose a school. Often the contrast is dramatic.

Research offers several explanations. Donald Erickson, professor of education at the University of California at Los Angeles, speculates that parents who can chose become sensitized to special educational benefits that they might not otherwise notice. Moreover, he writes, "having made a choice, human beings do not like to be proven wrong and hence tend to demonstrate commitment by attempting to ensure that the choice turns out well." Furthermore, Erickson says, "Freedom to choose may generate a sense of power that itself enhances commitment."[14]

The Reverend Gregory Anton McCants, a former president of the East Harlem School Board and the father of three children, believes that schools of choice forced more parents in his community to take an interest in their children's education, and that this helped to boost the district's test scores. But still more important, McCants told conference participants the schools of choice:

> . . . provided my youngsters with a chance to enjoy education tailored not only to their needs, but also their interests. It's so nice when young people really want to get up and go to school. It's a wonderful feeling!

Students at the workshop were similarly enthusiastic. Alvarez explained her affection for Mercy High School in San Francisco:

> Although attending Mercy was only one of the many decisions I will make in my lifetime, I have no doubt in my mind that the education and values I have acquired at my high school will be a strong foundation for my future success in college and the rest of my life. Mercy not only fulfilled my expectations and those of my parents but it helped me to examine my life, learn about myself.

One reason so many parents report being satisfied with schools of choice is that they are allowed to contribute their advice and ideas. Educators in schools of choice are less apt to assume that they know what is best for students. In districts with some of the most successful schools of choice, parents have initiated the plans. For example, in Eugene, Oregon, parents proposed the new "family alternative school," which will open at the start of the 1989-90 school year. This school was set up to allow parents to be more intimately involved in school practices and policies. A family council does everything from govern the direction of curriculum to participate in the hiring of teachers (although their plans must be consistent with State law, school board policy, and the teachers' contract).

One workshop participant reported that parents who become more involved in their children's schools often become more educated themselves. Joyce Duncan, who directs the East Harlem Career Academy, said:

> In working in my particular school and within the district with parents, I have seen some transformations—not only in terms of what happens to students in schools of choice, but also what happens to parents. Parents are beginning to take the same skills that we've instilled in their [children], and to apply those skills to their own development.... I've witnessed parents in my school return to school, get their high school diploma, go on to college, get a college degree. Some have entered teaching, some have gone on to nursing, others have gone on to business.

8. Schools of choice can enhance educational opportunities, particularly for disadvantaged parents.

Programs of choice can empower all mothers and fathers. But the potential advantages are particularly dramatic for those who historically have been the most cut off from the schools parents of low-income youngsters and of whose who speak little if any English.

Critics charge that programs of choice run the risk of creating inequities among schools. They say that schools of choice can drain the most talented students from inner-city schools to more affluent ones, and that this can divert funds from schools most urgently needing them.

Workshop attendees felt otherwise, and so do most low-income Americans. Public opinion polls consistently show that poor Americans support schools of choice. A recent Gallup Poll found that blacks and residents of our largest cities are the most apt to favor them of any demographic group surveyed.

Governor Thompson echoed the sentiments of many workshop participants. He said:

> Parental choice will provide an equal starting line of opportunity for all of

our students, an elevator of opportunity for individuals from the inner city to have the same educational opportunities that your children and my children have.

Similarly, workshop participant Robert Woodson, Sr., president of the National Center for Neighborhood Enterprise, believes that schools of choice can help the disadvantaged to "overcome the plague of poverty, both in their minds and their own hearts, and also in the larger society."

Opponents also worry that schools of choice might destroy small rural districts lacking the resources to provide the range of classes available in larger, wealthy districts. However, Minnesota Governor Perpich reports no significant trend favoring either small or large districts, although wealthy districts in Minnesota have gained slightly more students than have poor ones.

Already, magnet schools offering a specialized curriculum have played a major role in rectifying educational inequities. During the past 20 years, magnet schools from Los Angeles to East Harlem have helped to achieve voluntary desegregation while simultaneously providing better educational possibilities for disadvantaged youngsters. Other research shows that school districts using choice to promote desegregation tend to achieve more long-lasting results while those relying on mandatory assignments suffer from more "white flight."[15]

Magnet schools and other programs of choice can also help to establish more heterogeneous schools. Governor Perpich explained that a good program of choice:

...adds to the cultural diversity of our schools and exposes students to peers from different backgrounds. If we recognize education is as much about social interaction and adaptability as it is about test tubes and textbooks, then this exposure better prepares our students for life in the melting pot of our society and for careers in our global economy.

Some participants warned however, that creating schools of choice does not automatically lead to more equitable schools. The gap between fortunate and less fortunate students may widen in a district with both magnet and nonmagnet schools. Charles Glenn, Jr., from the Office of Educational Equity in Massachusetts reported:

Nonmagnet schools, as in Boston, have no real incentive or invitation to be distinctive or to satisfy parents. Parents are simply assigned. Its like the U.S. Post Office. You just open the doors and let the kids come. That's why we in the Massachusetts Department of Education have been encouraging school systems to move toward making every school a school of choice. Cambridge, Lowell, Fall River, Lawrence have done so. Boston is working on doing that.

And a recent study by the Chicago-based group Designs for Change found that selective magnet schools in four urban districts serve far more middle class and high-achieving students than poor youngsters. But it must be kept in mind that many of these schools were designed primarily to prevent white flight; therefore it is not surprising that they fail to meet the needs of the disadvantaged. The report concludes:

> In these school systems, school choice has, by and large, become a new improved method of student sorting, in which schools pick and choose among students. In this sorting process, black and Hispanic students, low-income students, students with low achievement, students with absence and behavior problems, handicapped students, and limited-English-proficient students have very limited opportunities to participate in popular options high schools and programs.[16]

Overseeing choice programs

Workshop participants were of two minds as to whether schools of choice must be carefully regulated to improve educational opportunities for the disadvantaged. Joe Nathan from the Hubert Humphrey Institute of Public Affairs in Minnesota argued that it is insufficient to create the schools without also developing policies to assure that they work. He said, "[S]imply basing improvement strategies on competition ... will not solve all the problems, particularly for low- and moderate-income people."

He and other workshop participants urge districts to oversee carefully the following aspects of choice programs:

• **Parent information.** Opponents of schools of choice sometimes argue that disadvantaged parents are unable to make sound educational decisions on behalf of their children. Proponents disagree. Parent choice is most apt to succeed if all parents have sufficient information. But special efforts should be made to provide information to at-risk families, since they often have less experience with bureaucracies, may be intimidated by the schools, or may have limited English skills. "It's ironic that we have more information in this country right now about how to select among cars and refrigerators than we have about how to select among schools," Nathan wrote in an article on choice that elaborates on comments he made at the workshop.[17] Some school districts, including Cambridge, Massachusetts, consider their parent information centers to be key elements of their choice plans.

• **Student assignments.** Assignment policies must be fair, widely understood, and legally sound. Because desegregation must be considered in assigning students to schools, unlimited choice generally cannot be provided in metropolitan areas. Most educators advise against policies favoring those with a sophisticated knowledge of the school system, or with special influence. They also suggest that the schools avoid first-come, first-served policies, which can be chaotic and tend to favor the most informed and aggressive parents. And they advise that districts prohibit admissions on the basis of students' past academic achievement or behavior.

• **Transportation.** States and districts must give careful thought to this matter, since low-income parents are less able to transport their children to school at their own expense. "If transportation is not made available, opportunities for [low-income] youngsters will not truly expand," Nathan notes.[18] Most districts with choice programs pay to transport children to whatever school they select within their own district. However, in Minnesota and other States, students crossing district lines must make their own arrangements to get to the border of the district housing their new school, at which point the receiving school district provides transportation. Low-income parents receive some financial compensation from the State for transporting their children to the district boundary.

In contrast to Nathan, some policymakers and educators fear that too much regulation deprives low-income parents of the ability to make important decisions for themselves. At the workshop, Robert Woodson of the National Center for Neighborhood Enterprise said that society often assumes that low-income people are incapable of helping themselves. For this reason, professionals are paid to act on their behalf and to regulate their lives. Woodson argues, however, that the disadvantaged possess the skills and entrepreneurial talents to help themselves—and that this includes the ability to decide matters pertaining to the education of their children. He cited the many independent neighborhood schools that have been started by disaffected public school teachers and low-income parents. In many communities, these schools have enabled students once viewed as uneducable to succeed.

CONCLUSION

"Ten years from now, people will be surprised that there ever was vigorous debate about public school choice," Nathan predicated in a recent newspaper column.[19] "It will be an accepted right, like voting, equal pay for equal work, and nondiscriminatory housing."

Public acceptance for schools of choice is steadily growing. Although many view choice as critical to the improvement of American schools, skeptics still remain. William Bulger, president of the Massachusetts State Senate and moderator of a workshop panel, notes:

> It's my experience and my observation that every person favors choice. A hundred percent favor choice for themselves. The problem for people who want to institute and broaden and enhance choice Is that group of people who favor choice for themselves but oppose it for all the rest.

Opposition is the most pronounced among educators. 'There is a puzzling resistance among educators to the extension of parent choice," Glenn notes.[20] He attributes this partly to educators' fears that their jobs will be threatened, and to concerns that teachers and principals would be under new and overwhelming pressures.

Those who have created schools of choice warn that the task involves hard work and ample fortitude. Most of this work must be accomplished at the grassroots level. Secretary Cavazos told the audience:

> [I]t is you who will ultimately convince the Nation—school by school, district by district, State by State—that the principle of choice must play an important part in the solution to our formidable educational problems.

The White House Workshop on Choice in Education was designed to serve as a source of information to those just beginning this endeavor. Organizers of the workshop also hope the gathering will serve as a catalyst for change. Lamar Alexander, president of the University of Tennessee and former governor of Tennessee, explained:

The fact that so many people have come together . . . shows that this movement is kind of beyond all of us. It's bigger than all of us. It will keep on going after us, but perhaps we can do something to nourish it, and that's what we're all here for today.

The benefits of choice are too numerous to delay action. President-elect Bush emphasized:

The evidence is striking and abundant. Almost without exception, wherever choice has been attempted—Minnesota, East Harlem, San Francisco, Los Angeles, and a hundred other places in between—choice has worked.... Bad schools get better. Good ones get better still and entire school systems have been restored to public confidence by the implementation of these choice plans. Disaffected families have been brought from private schools back into public education. Any school reform that can boast such success deserves our attention, our emphases, and our effort.

Endnotes

1. Chubb, John E. (Winter 1988). "Why the Current Wave of School Reform Will Fail," in The Public Interest, No. 90, 28-49.
2. Nathan, Joe, Editor (1989). Public Schools by Choice: Expanding Opportunities for Parents, Students, and Teachers. St. Paul, Minnesota: The Institute for Learning.
3. Raywid, Mary Anne (1989). 'The Mounting Case for Schools of Choice," in Public Schools by Choice, 13.
4. Many of the studies mentioned in this report are cited in 'The Mounting Case for Schools of Choice" by Raywid. A special thanks to her for calling them to the attention of the U.S. Department of Education.
5. Information supplied by Deputy Superintendent Juana Dainis, Community School District 4, July 18, 1989, interview.
6. Magi Educational Services (January 1985). New York State Magnet School Research Study. Albany: State Education Department.
   Larson, John C., and Allen, Brenda A. (January 1988). A Microscope on Magnet Schools, 1983 to 1986. Volume 2: Pupil and Parent Outcomes. Rockville, Maryland: Montgomery County Public Schools.
   Los Angeles Unified School district (1985-86). Report on LAUSC Integration Programs, Publication No. 488.
   Los Angeles Unified School District (1986-87). Report on LAUSC Integration Programs, Publication No. 504.
   Los Angeles Unified School District (1987-88). Report on LAUSC Integration Programs, Publication No. 523.
7. Arnove, Robert F., and Strout, Toby (May 1980). "Alternative Schools for Disruptive Youth." Educational Forum, 452-471.
8. Perry, Cheryl L., and Duke, Daniel L. (1978). "Lessons to Be Learned about Discipline from Alternative High Schools." Journal of Research and Development in Education, 11(4), 78-90.
   Raywid, Mary Anne (1982). 'The Current Status of Schools of Choice in Public Secondary Education." Hempstead, New York: Project on Alternatives in Education, Hofstra University.
9. Magi.

10. Raywid, MaryAnne (1982). "Evaluation of the Alternative School." Unpublished manuscript, East Meadow, New York.

11. Foley, Eileen M., and McConnaughy, Susan B. (1982). Towards High School Improvement: Lessons from Alternative Schools. New York: Public Education Association.

12. Sexton, Porter (Summer 1985). "Trying to Make It Real Compared to What? Implications of High School Dropout Statistics." Journal of Educational Equity and Leadership, 5(2), 92-106.

13. Coons, John E. (January 2, 1989). "Don't Limit 'Choice' to Public Schools Only." Los Angeles Times. See also Coons, John E., and Sugarman, Stephen D. (1978). Education by Choice: The Case for Family Control. Berkeley and Los Angeles, California: University of California Press.

14. Erickson, Donald A. (1982). "Disturbing Evidence about the 'One Best System.'" The Public School Monopoly, edited by Robert B. Everhard. San Francisco: Pacific Institute for Public Policy Research and Cambridge: Ballinger, 393-422.

15. Rossell, Christine H. (March 1987). "The Carrot or the Stick in School Desegregation Policy?" ERIC ED279781. Rossell, Christine H., and Hawley, Willis D. (1983). The Consequences of School Desegregation. Philadelphia, Pennsylvania: Temple University Press.

16. Moore, Donald R, and Davenport, Suzanne (February 1989). "School Choice: The New Improved Sorting Machine." Remarks prepared for the National Invitational Conference on Public School Choice, sponsored by the Education Commission of the States. Minneapolis, Minnesota.

17. Nathan, Joe (June 1987). "Results and Future Prospects of State Efforts to Increase Choice Among Schools." Phi Delta Kappan, 67-73.

18. Ibid.

19. Nathan, Joe (April 5, 1989). Column in The Christian Science Monitor.

20. Glenn, Charles, Jr. (1989). "Parent Choice and American Values," in Public Schools by Choice. 41-54.

SECTION IV: A NEW FORM OF SCHOOLING

INTRODUCTION

A completely new conception of schooling is needed. Otherwise choice would surely result in all the dire outcomes predicted by its opponents. This new conception is based on several assumptions. First, children learn differently. Second, teachers teach differently. Third, parents have different needs and values. Fourth, if a successful teaching/learning community is going to be established, it is necessary for those with common interests, needs, values, learning styles, and teaching styles to be able to freely choose to join together in the educational enterprise. Fifth, if educational activities are freely chosen, commonly valued, and mutually supported among teachers, parents, and students, then we can expect that children will learn better than under any other circumstances. Sixth, the joint accountability entailed in a system in which all participants freely choose to be involved is far more likely to lead to overall system quality than is forced participation.

To what extent is the present system of schooling built on these assumptions? It is this author's contention that the terms that best describe the present system are monopoly, uniformity, inequity, and lack of accountability. A system such as we have in which the only "free" schooling is that provided by the state is one in which there is little incentive for those who provide the schooling to attempt to develop programs to meet the needs and interests of their educational clients. And, widespread uniformity in the structure and functioning of schools throughout this country does not lead —as one might expect— to uniformity of outcomes. Rather, the failure to meet individual needs of students and to base variations in spending on those needs results in overwhelming inequity in both opportunity and academic achievement. This situation is exacerbated by the fact that there is little incentive for educational professionals to work any harder than they do because it will have no impact —once they receive tenure— on whether they keep their jobs or make more or less income. This is not to say that the majority of tenured teachers in the present system are poor nor that those in a restructured system would automatically be outstanding. However, after decades of "tinkering" with pieces of the educational system, it is clear that the present conditions will not change until a new conception of schooling provides the basis for the restructuring of education based on a workable system of accountability.

What do these assumptions imply in terms of how to restructure schools? With a broad brush, let us paint a picture of what steps would need to be taken and what the resulting system would look like. First, we should establish that every schooling unit will be a magnet, i.e., each will have a curricular or structural theme. This means that the charge will be given to teachers to form themselves into groups to offer schooling collectively, organized around a common theme that they all value. Once this is accomplished, these offerings will then be made known to parents. Geography would no longer be the prevailing determiner of their choices, because they would now really have choices. What's more, if there were a large enough group of parents who wanted a school of a particular kind, certainly a group of teachers could be found who could provide such a program. Thus, the process is collaborative and all would be empowered: teachers to maximize their skills as professionals; parents to select what they believe is in the best interest of their children; and students —especially as they mature— to be provided with the opportunity to make important life choices.

Once such a system was actually implemented, two other major structural changes would be necessary for choice to realize its fullest potential. First, site-based management, in which teachers and parents have much more say than they do presently in how schools are run, is crucial for the system to succeed. Thus the school, not the district, would become the locus of control; districts (and school boards) might even disappear completely. Second, choice as described here would entail a form of collective professional accountability at the school level. If a group of teachers has the right to set the goals, design the program, and plan the delivery system, then it is inescapable that these same teachers should be responsible for the results.

Two major components are evident in the picture drawn above: choice and accountability. It is important to examine these in some detail to understand why they are both necessary to make schooling meet the demands of equity, diversity, and excellence.

CHOICE

It is a testimony to the sense of felt importance of universal schooling to homogenize the diverse American population in the nineteenth century, that those who worked to bring it about believed that it should be the responsibility of the state not only to mandate universal schooling, but to provide it. Although government leaders and union spokespersons believed tax-supported, non-sectarian, universal public schooling was crucial to the success of the democracy, neither rank-and-file labor nor the well-to-do concurred. And in both cases the objections were based in economic concerns. Parents who worked in factories believed they had a right to use their children to support family income through either factory labor or care of younger siblings. The wealthy saw no reason why their tax dollars should support schooling for the poor, as the poor did not value it anyway, they argued. So strong was the resistance to universal public schooling that the state found it necessary to pass laws not only requiring municipalities to provide schooling, but children to attend those schools. Thus, in 1852 Massachusetts was the first state to pass compulsory attendance laws. Child labor laws soon followed. In 1918 the last state, Mississippi, required school attendance by law.

At the same time, there were challenges to the right of the state to tax the general public to provide compulsory schooling. In 1874 the Supreme Court of Michigan ruled in the *Kalamazoo* decision that the state had a right to tax the general public to support secondary schools. Implied in the acceptance of this ruling was that a secondary education must meet the needs of all who might attend, not only those preparing for additional education in college. Nonetheless, in 1892 The Committee of Ten raised the question of just what should comprise a secondary education; the answer was almost a foregone conclusion that it should be college preparatory. By 1918 when the question was again raised, the answer in *The Seven Cardinal Principles* of Secondary Education was much broader than the 1892 answer; yet it was nowhere considered that a secondary education should provide schooling that would maximize the potential of each individual and be highly varied. The effort at that time was to eliminate variation and to standardize schooling as much as possible.

This hegemony of the state grew until *Pierce v Society of Sisters* in 1925 permitted compulsory schooling requirements to be met in private as well as public schools. Thus, in particular, Catholic schools grew, receiving a major impetus during the waves of late nineteenth and early twentieth century immigration from southern and eastern Europe and the subsequent nativism that resulted in persecution of Catholic school children in the increasingly Protestant-dominated public schools.

As the twentieth century progressed, the outrage that the state could take one's children for many hours a day, many months out of the year and inculcate them with state-endorsed values about life diminished. Those who dared to take issue were viewed as extremists, usually of the religious variety. The neighborhood school to which children were automatically assigned became an accepted phenomenon —at least in the North. It was not until *Brown*, the Civil Rights Act, and mandatory busing to achieve desegregation that people on a widespread basis began to question the state's right to assign children to attend particular schools, irrespective of the wishes of their parents. And both black and white parents questioned this right. But this questioning took the more frequent form of individual action rather than organized challenges to the system, and many inner-city parents moved to the suburbs or put their children in private schools —for other than religious reasons. In the South, of course, vouchers acquired their bad name through the attempts made by many states to use them to avoid mandatory integration.

During the same time period, the revolutionary sixties, the alternative school movement emerged. In this case, taking students out of regular public schools and placing them in alternative public schools was not generally the result of individual parent initiative, but a decision made by the school in an effort to prevent the students from dropping out. However, this, unlike "White Flight," was endorsed by the system and reached the status of a recognized movement. Thus, the focus in choice moved from individuals making schooling decisions within a larger system in which choice was negligible for most to a choiceless macrosystem in which there were microsystems of choice for identified (and sometimes stigmatized) groups of students who did not "fit the mold." This was a major opening of the door of the school monopoly to begin to consider whether all students should have the opportunity to select the environment in which they are schooled.

Despite these developments, a strong push for choice did not appear until the 1980s when several other social forces emerged to raise consciousness about parents' right to choose the schools their children attended. The increasing disparity between expenditures for students in the wealthiest and poorest districts, together with the growing costs of private schools, focused attention beyond individuals and small groups of students for whom "alternative" provisions should be made, to the structure of this system —a system that attempts to force everyone into state-run schools with state-developed curriculum. This was especially true in light of the fact that many of those schools, often in urban areas, provided an unquestionably poor quality of education in an environment of violence and fear.

On the face of it, having families choose the schools their children attend would just seem like "the right thing to do." If adults have the right to have children in the first place, have full control over their rearing for the first four or five years of their lives, and can determine what religion to indoctrinate them with, why should the state have the prerogative to rip away these rights when the children turn five years of age?

The answer, many educational policymakers will tell us, is that the rights of individuals must be balanced with the interests of the society. The institution of schooling is the primary means we have to prepare individuals to be law-abiding, productive members of the society and all must be given an equal chance to benefit from that institution. Thus, school attendance is mandatory and tax support of schools is legally required.

The question that must be raised, however, is: Given that we agree that the legal guardians of children should have no choice over *whether* to school their children, why should they not have the choice of what kinds of schools to place their children in? The answer most frequently given is that in far too many cases the choices that individuals would make to benefit themselves would harm society as a whole. More specifically, it is argued, an overwhelming proportion of white and/or middle class parents would always choose to educate their children in schools that exclude poor and/or black children. It is acknowledged that we are not currently providing an education for poor children equal to that received by the more affluent, but permitting parents to select the schools their children attend, this argument continues, would only exacerbate this problem. The schools with the least financial support and the most problems currently would become even further aggrieved by the departure of those students whose parents would choose to place them in better schools.

Another answer often given to this question is that a substantial number of parents are incapable of making the best educational choices for their children. On the one hand, it is argued, many don't care or don't have adequate education themselves to be knowledgeable enough to make "informed" decisions. On the other hand, it is maintained, schools would be chosen for the "wrong" reasons, like proximity to one's home or good athletic programs. Further, it is clear that given complete choice, many parents would send their children to religious schools and, it is claimed, that is clearly a violation of the separation of church and state.

Thus, any proposal for developing a robust system of school choice must minimally answer these objections. At the same time, it is also important to address the issue of the degree to which the present system manifests these problems already and the extent to which the present system manages to balance the rights of the individual against the needs of society.

Inequity

Little doubt exists that there is enormous inequity between the quality of schooling provided for the children of the affluent and the children of the poor in this country. This inequity manifests itself in three major ways.

(1). The affluent are able to choose the schools to which they send their children, the poor are not.

(2). The children of the affluent have a great deal more spent on them for education than the poor.

(3). The children of the affluent receive a higher quality of education than the poor.

Attempts to address these glaring inequities have been made at all levels of government since they were first officially acknowledged in the *Brown* decision.

From mandatory interdistrict busing to state-wide educational finance reform, success has not been realized. To this day the difference in annual per capita expenditure for public schooling can vary by as much as $10,000 from one district to another. This unquestionably impacts on the quality of education received. Parents of inner city poor children have no choice of where to send their children to school. Little we have done as a society has made a difference in these three forms of inequality. Although a few disadvantaged children have benefited through isolated short-term programs, it seems clear that these are not the answer to systemic inequality in schooling. This inequality is exacerbated by the refusal of the public school establishment to recognize the ways in which many religious private schools more clearly serve the "public" functions required of schools for our society than "public" schools do as a whole, e.g., urban Catholic schools.

Religious considerations

We know that if parents choose to send their children to religious schools, they will be provided with little or no tax support for the costs. What support they do receive has been hard won through court battles and is for peripherals such as text books and transportation or for special needs children —if the local district can provide the means to meet these needs. Considering the major role private, especially Catholic, schools have played in education in our society and the large number of parents who send their children to them, it is vital that any meaningful reconceptualization of schooling look at the legal relationship of government to religious schools.

Upon close examination, it is evident that it is a violation of both the Establishment and Free Exercise clauses of the First Amendment to tax the public to provide state-run schools. The First Amendment begins: "Congress shall make no laws respecting the establishment of religion or prohibiting the free exercise thereof." Consider first the Establishment Clause and the ways in which our present system of schooling violates it.

Establishment of Religion

Education, by *its very nature*, cannot be conducted as a value-free enterprise. The simplest definition of education —"the act or process of imparting knowledge"[1] — immediately raises the epistemological question of what will count as knowledge— that which is acquired through revelation or that which is gained by our experience and interaction with the world around us. The way in which one answers that question is determined by one's underlying metaphysical assumptions about the nature of reality —is it primarily physical or spiritual? As soon as one makes a decision about the nature of reality and which form of knowledge is of more worth and to be transmitted in the schools, one has made a decision about values (axiology).

When this set of metaphysical, epistemological, and axiological assumptions posits a supreme being, a reality that is primarily spiritual, knowledge that is gained mostly through revelation, and an authoritarian moral order, we usually call the resulting set of beliefs "religion." When this set of assumptions maintains that the only form of reality that exists is that which can be perceived by the senses, that knowledge is only that which can be verified empirically, morality is determined by nature, and "god" is in human beings, we call this set of beliefs "science." Such a distinction opens up the entire question of what counts as a religion.

Ordinary language usage of the term 'religion' invariably includes the concept of the supernatural and, usually, some form of worship. However, such usage has been challenged more than once by the courts. In 1987 in *Smith v Board of School Commissioners of Mobile County*,[2] the district court concluded that secular humanism was a religion. Although this decision was reversed by the Eleventh Circuit Court of Appeals, it is interesting that the court noted that if the First Amendment prohibited mere "inconsistency with the beliefs of a particular religion there would be very little that could be taught in the public schools." Such a statement calls attention to the near impossibility of carrying out the educational enterprise as a value-free activity that does not make some metaphysical assumptions. Though not so intended, the court's defense of their ruling helps to

---

[1]William Morris, Ed. *American Heritage Dictionary of the English Language,* (Boston: Houghton Mifflin), 1969.

[2] *Smith v Board of School Commissioners of Mobile County*, no. 87-7216 (11th Cir. September 26, 1987).

make the case that state-mandated curriculum can be seen as violating the Establishment clause.

Yet another ruling, this time by the U.S. Supreme Court in *U.S.v Seeger*[3], lends support to the argument that the concept of a religion does not have to include reference to the supernatural. Responding positively to the actions of a non-theistic conscientious objector to be exempt from military service, the Court ruled that religion is: "A sincere and meaningful belief which occupies in the life of the possessor a place parallel to that filled by the God of those admittedly qualifying for the exemption." This provides the basis for arguing that the set of metaphysical, epistemological, and axiological assumptions described above as "science" can equally be described as a "religion." Our present system of schooling validates this set of "religious" beliefs and repudiates the other. This is religious establishment. Furthermore, as any system of values must be grounded in basic (unprovable) underlying assumptions about the worth of human beings and their relationship to the universe, it is *impossible* not to have some form of establishment in government-provided schooling.

With the Supreme Court's removal of mandatory prayer and devotional Bible-reading from the schools, we went from Protestant establishment to an officially recognized one based on science and humanism. Our public school system reflects the assumptions that reality is physical, knowledge is determined empirically, and values are based on what is in the best interest of humankind. Thus, our official curricular creed omits a supreme being and spiritual existence, includes evolution and the scientific method, and exhorts Johnny not to steal his neighbor's pencil not because he will be punished by God for doing so, but because he would not want his neighbor to steal his. This does not deny that there are pockets of resistance in which prayer and Bible-reading as well as Christian holiday celebration go on. But these activities are not the official, legally recognized school practices

None of this is meant to be an argument for which set of beliefs is true or false, right or wrong, but to show that they are all *equally* derived from a set of assumptions. Nor is this an argument to change the set of assumptions on which we base our system of public schools. And, finally, it is not an attempt to have the public schools reflect a wide set of belief systems in their structure and educational

---

3 *U. S. v Seeger,* 326 F 2d 846 (2d Cir. 1964).

content. It is meant to argue that it is impossible to have the government providing *any form* of schooling and avoid religious establishment.

Free Exercise of Religion

The constitutional basis for the separation of religion and government includes not only the prohibition against the government's supporting a single religion but the First Amendment's promise that the government will not deny anyone the free exercise of his or her religion. Many religions mandate that children be educated by precept and example based on religious beliefs. As we have seen, it is not possible to have public schools incorporate those beliefs into their delivery systems and avoid establishment. What alternative is there? One possible alternative is schools set up by religious (or other) groups that educate in conformity with their religious beliefs. However, as long as parents are required to use their tax dollars to support government-run schools, most are extremely circumscribed in their freedom to exercise their religion by sending their children to religious schools, where they must pay tuition. In fact, the large majority are effectively prohibited from the free exercise of their religion. In the last decade, some parents have chosen to educate their children at home (in states that permit this), because they cannot afford the tuition in a "private," nonpublic school and they do not want to expose their children to the belief systems of "public" schools.

Surely the way out of this dilemma is for the government to provide the funds for schooling to be accomplished and to mandate that schooling be carried out (compulsory attendance laws), but to leave to the parents the actual selection of schools and the value system in which curriculum is developed and offered up.

Reconceptualization of public/private

At this point, this author would like to propose that we need to reconceptualize the distinctions between 'public' and 'private.' Historically there have been two major differences between public schools and private schools and a third that has evolved out of these two. The two major differences have been a) sources of funding and b) control over admission of students. Private schools have been funded through a combination of "private" (religious organizations, businesses, gifts, etc.) sources and tuition; public schools have been funded through taxes. Private schools have the right to deny admission to whomever they choose; public schools must accept all who apply. In theory, these have been the differences.

And, in theory, as a result, public schools were supposed to provide all who came through their doors an equal chance at a high quality of schooling.

It is not necessary to do any more here than to refer broadly to all the research that tells us this has not happened. Our system of using real estate taxes to fund "public" schools has effectively limited admission to "good" schools to those whose parents can afford an expensive piece of real estate. A very select group. At the same time, most Catholic and evangelical Christian schools, as well as some non-religious private schools, have tuitions so low that many parents who are not satisfied with their local public schools are able to afford them. Thus in these schools, those in low income groups can far more frequently have access to a high quality of education than they would in available public schools.

A third difference between public and private schools —derivative from the first two— has been the requirement to adhere to state regulations regarding curriculum, student policies, and staff qualifications. The original nineteenth century concept of the common public school that was funded through taxes and open to all included implicitly that it would be responsive to the public through its elected representatives who developed and enforced these regulations. In most states, private schools are not controlled in the same way by elected governance bodies. They can teach anything they consider appropriate, do not have to accept special needs students, and their teachers do not have to meet state certification standards.

In theory, this is all true, but again practice needs to be examined. First let's look at what the public schools have been like in these regards. Have these schools been responsive to those governance bodies that control them, those elected representatives of the people? Certainly not in such a way as to provide a uniformly high quality of education or there would not a growing number of parents taking their children out of them and placing them in private schools. We need to consider responsiveness in a different way. It seems clear that if parents are paying for education directly out of their pockets, they will demand a responsiveness from schools that is absent in most public, especially urban, schools. If a satisfactory quality of education is not being provided, these parents will take their children elsewhere. This is the kind of responsiveness we find in those schools currently labeled "private."

Furthermore, we need to examine the extent to which private schools do, in fact, demonstrate adherence to state regulations, even though they are not required to do so. Increasingly teachers in private schools are acquiring the same levels of education as those in public schools. In terms of students, as noted above, inner city Catholic schools often have a wider mix of students than suburban public schools. Further, if private schools are not serving as many students with special needs as public schools, it has more to do with inability to fund supplementary services as a result of the *Aquilar v Felton* decision (1985) than lack of desire. Finally, except for the lack of funds to provide up-to-date technological equipment, the curriculum in private religious schools differs little from that in public schools.

It would appear extremely difficult not only on legal but also educational grounds to support any system of choice which does not include private religious schools. In her PDK Fastback, Mary Anne Raywid offers the following:

> The last several years have added substantial evidence that it is, indeed, school climate differences that most clearly distinguish successful from less effective schools.
>
> Erickson and his colleagues (1982) are probably the only group to have undertaken comparison studies of the climates in private schools, regular or "mainstream" public schools, and public schools of choice. Although they found the climate in private schools superior, they found public schools of choice to have a clear advantage over other public schools with regard to climate. ...
>
> The superiority of private over public schools is now being argued on a variety of grounds in addition to climate. Claims are made that parochial schools in particular produce more and better learning, especially for disadvantaged youngsters (Coleman et al. 1981; Lee 1985). Some researchers now claim that the private school advantage is inherent and inevitable (Chubb 1987).[4]

Despite this straightforward summary of the literature regarding the educational advantage of private schools, Raywid[5] has argued elsewhere in favor of public schools of choice and against vouchers on the basis that vouchers are merely a means of financing schools, that the forces that drive consumers' choices in

---

[4]Raywid, M.A. *The Case For Public Schools of Choice,* (Bloomington: Phi Delta Kappa Educational Foundation), 1989, 14-15.

[5]Raywid, M.A. "Public Choice, Yes; Vouchers, No!" *Phi Delta Kappan,* Volume 68, No. 10 (June 1987).

education are not analogous to those in education itself, that the implementation of vouchers would destroy the already tenuous public school system, and that nothing of educational advantage is to be gained through a voucher system. This contention on Raywid's part appears to be in stark contradiction to the evidence she, herself, cites.

In sum, two of the three historic differences between public and private schools, in the majority of cases, now appear meaningless: composition of the student body (although control over admissions remains for private schools) and responsiveness to the public which results in a high quality of education for all students. If anything, religious schools have an edge over public schools, particularly if we exclude public schools of choice.

One might argue that the primary explanation for this "edge" is that, however poor and uneducated inner city parents who select private religious schools might be, the fact that they made such a selection makes all the difference in the world. The response to this can only be: Give all parents such an edge through providing them with a voucher. This then would be the basis for doing away with the remaining differences between public and private schools. All schools which participated in the voucher system would be required to accept the voucher in full payment of schooling costs. Thus, no school in the system would be charging tuition. Further, no schools would be able to refuse students admission for non-programmatic reasons and receive voucher monies. These aspects of a reconceptualized public school system will be discussed at greater length in the section on accountability.

The foregoing discussion answers only one of the three objections offered by opponents of school choice as to why parents should not be given the right to choose the schools their children attend —they might choose religious schools. The other two —that they do not care enough and/or have adequate knowledge to make these choices and that they would choose schools for the wrong reasons— must now be addressed.

Care and Knowledge of Parents

The argument that parents do not care enough and/or have adequate knowledge to choose their children's schools needs to be responded to at two levels. In the first place, it seems safe to assume that in the majority of cases, even among the poor, the parents care more about the welfare of their children than even the most well meaning social institution. Further, although undoubtedly mistakes are made, certainly parents —for the most part— know their children better than school personnel, especially in light of the fact that the children get new teachers every year. Parents are thereby better equipped to make decisions about the best environments in which to school their children than are teachers, principals, and counselors. Surely, in general, parents will care more about and know better if their children are happy than even the most caring counselor or teacher.

But interestingly, even this discussion suggests that as things presently are, school staff consciously review what is in the best interest of each student and make placement decisions on that basis. Of course, that is no where near the truth. Students are primarily assigned to the schools they attend on the basis of geography. The reasons why they are assigned to particular teachers are as varied as the principals who make those assignments. It could hardly be argued that these principals know the students well enough to select the teachers with whom they would have the best educational experiences. In fact, it is probable that the students who get the "best" assignments are typically those who have already had the "best" experiences, with the most outspoken parents who know how to work the system.

School and class assignments in our present system of schooling could not be otherwise. There is no way a school district's staff could find the resources to maximize the likelihood that every child is placed in the best possible schooling environment. The most we could hope for in a system where the primary basis of assignment is geography and beyond that the whim of principals, is that those students whose placements are truly detrimental to their growth will, when parents protest, be moved.

The second level of response to the argument of parents' inability to make appropriate schooling choices for their children is at the political level, as the charge is an attack on the very nature of the democracy. How can those same parents be judged capable of electing those officials who will be responsible for making the laws and policies that will govern the education provided for everyone's children if they are not capable of making individual choices for their own children?

Reasons for Choosing Schools

The claim that parents cannot be trusted to select their children's schools because they would make these selections for the wrong reasons must also be examined at two levels. The "wrong" reasons usually given are convenience and a good athletic program. As Joe Nathan (1993) has pointed out in this volume, the claim that convenience is a primary basis on which parents would select schools is based on a questionable study carried out in Minnesota. He further suggests that objection to this as a reason for selecting a school is hardly questionable anyway as we would not want to make inconvenience the evidence of effective schooling. If, in fact all schools are required to meet minimum standards, as described below, having a good athletic program will be as legitimate a reason for selecting that school as its having a good science program.

Again the response to this objection must be raised to the structural level. As it now stands, it is to be expected that convenience would be a major basis on which parents would select schools for their children because there is such little variation among schools that they have no reason to select one over the other. In a choice system in which all schools were magnets, undoubtedly convenience —location— would still form an important role in school choices, but not the primary role as finding a school to meet the needs of one's children would be a meaningful reality.

It must be emphasized, however, that for choice to work as a means of restructuring schooling as a whole in order to address systemic problems of inequality, it must be available to everyone, not just a select few. This has been the major problem in urban districts that have created magnets. Although those students who are accepted in the magnet schools are better off than they would have been in their neighborhood schools, *the system as a whole is no better and is probably worse.* A recent proposal being considered in California, Minnesota, and New Jersey is for charter schools, giving certified teachers "the opportunity to create new, distinctive schools with accountability for student results, rather than for following thousands of rules." Initially this would appear to be consistent with the goals of the choice movement. However, unless the movement for charter schools is seen as the beginning of the process of making all schools develop themselves around a theme from which all parents will then be able to choose, it will have the same limited effect on the system as magnets. In fact, charter schools could have a double whammy on the current system by drawing off not only the best students but also the best teachers.

In sum, the claim of improved academic and other school outcomes through a voucher system rests on several important assumptions. In the first place, if individuals *choose* to be part of a particular endeavor, rather than being arbitrarily (on the basis of geography) assigned to it, their willingness to participate fully and work hard are likely to be greatly enhanced —on the part of both students and parents. Secondly, in such a system, those choosing a particular school will have in common a defining characteristic or set of characteristics that will form the basis of community, described above by Raywid. It is this sense of community that creates the positive climate out of which higher academic achievement may be expected. Without a doubt, one of the strongest influences in forming a sense of community is religion. Why, then, should schools formed with religion as their "tie that binds" be excluded from their share in the taxpayer's money, *especially when the evidence indicates that they are more successful at a lower cost*?[6] Finally, if there is going to be system-wide improvement in both the quality of education and the satisfaction of clients —both students and parents— choice must be a system-wide reality, available to all parents.

ACCOUNTABILITY

A reconceptualization of schooling which ignores the traditional distinctions between public and private must focus on how schools are run and what their outcomes are rather than focus on who runs them and their value orientations. Two basic concepts would define the structure and implementation of such a system. One of these, *controlled choice*, has been described by Charles Glenn in the developing of magnets and choice in the Boston public schools. The other, *managed competition*, has been manifested over the last fifteen years in the growth of the Montclair School System.

Each of these concepts focuses on the opposite side of the producer/consumer continuum in education. The more familiar in this context —controlled choice— identifies the prerogatives of the consumer —the parents and students. Choice is

---

6Coleman, J.S., & Hoffer, T, & Kilgore, S. (1981). *Public and Private High Schools.* Washington, DC: National Center for Education Statistics.

provided, but it is "controlled" in the sense that parents are not free to choose a particular school for their child if that choice will have an increased segregative effect on the system as a whole.

By contrast, managed competition, which has been a proposal for solving the nation's health care problems, focuses on the responsibilities of those policymakers who are currently at the top of the educational bureacratic structure. Unfettered competition, as initially presented by Milton Friedman and recently elaborated on by Chubb and Moe[7], has been decried by some of even the strongest supporters of school choice. Allowing schools in a choice system to charge tuition and in no way restricting their right to select the students who would attend their schools would almost inevitably, it is argued, have a discriminatory effect on poor and minority students. In managed competition, neither of these would be permitted. All schools participating in such a system would have to accept the per-student stipend/voucher as full payment and the school would have to operate on the monies thus acquired. Further, as long as there was room, schools would have to accept all who applied except for specialized schools —only at the secondary level— which could establish certain performance-based entrance requirements. This means, for instance, that religious schools, if they wished to participate in this funding scheme, would have to accept students not of their religious faith. Many currently do anyway, especially inner-city Catholic schools. Does this mean these schools could not teach their religious beliefs? No. If parents choose for their children to attend religous schools not of their faith even though they know that religion is taught, no First Amendment rights are being violated. Only when attendance is compulsory in government-operated schools is the teaching of religion in those schools a form of establishment.

In addition to these restrictions on educational providers, managed competition would place with the level of government controlling the educational system the responsibility for maintaining balance in the system. It would be important to guarantee that information and incentives were in place to maximize the likelihood that both the needs and interests of educational clients were being served. For example, as explained by the then-superintendent of Montclair Public Schools,

---

[7]Chubb, J.E., & Moe, T.M. (1990)*Politics, Markets, and America's Schools*. Washington, DC: Brookings Institute.

Mary Lee Fitzgerald[8], once all of the schools in the system had become magnets, if one school languished an analysis of the reasons was made and action was taken. Such action could include changing principals, surveying exiting parents regarding problems, providing additional financial support for needed supplements to programs or better public relations, or —in extreme cases— phasing out the program/school. Such actions taken by education officials would be a form of managed competition that maintained a balance between a state of monopoly of education, such as we currently have, and a "survival of the fittest" type of competition that would further bifurcate the quality of education received by the rich and the poor.

From this writer's perspective, Chubb and Moe's proposal that every school would operate as a completely independent entity is unrealistic. Although accountability, as described more fully below, would be placed at the school level, it would still be necessary to have a more centralized educational agency to guarantee managed competition among participating schools. Inasmuch as one of the major reasons for proposing school choice is to ameliorate the current widespread inequality of educational opportunity and outcomes, it would seem clear that the responsibility for maintaining the system would have to be far more centralized than the district level. In fact, especially in states such as New Jersey —with over 600 separate school districts and an ongoing legislative quagmire over equalizing expenditure between the rich and the poor, the dissolution of individual school districts would seem to be crucial to the success of a choice system. From an historical and constitutional basis, the state is responsible for providing for the education of its citizens. Thus, a state educational choice agency, with regional sub-units no lower than the county level, would appear to be the most practical and efficient means for governing a choice system. These Regional (broader than current districts) Educational Agencies would be responsible for managing the competition among schools through the collection and distribution of information about schools, administering and surveilling of admission activities, redeeming of vouchers with the state government, providing counseling for choices, and redressing parent complaints.

---

[8]Interview, May 1990.

At the same time, responsibility for determining basic operating procedures of each individual school must be carried out through a school-based council, consisting of both teachers and parents. We now have few such models and certainly no widely accepted ones. Currently public schools are run by elected board members at the district level —with rarely any direct parent input in the formulation of policy. By contrast, private schools are generally governed by whatever board their sponsoring agency selects and parent input comes primarily through selection or rejection of the school. A system of governance which required teachers and parents to work cooperatively in the development of school policies would establish the basis for ongoing involvement on the part of parents in providing the best possible education for students.

Thus, the decades-old pendulum swing between centralization and decentralization of the governance of education can be resolved through having the best of both. On the one hand, the state would establish the standards and monitor their fulfillment. On the other, individual schools would have the liberty to design curriculum and methodology to meet these standards and would be held accountable for students' success.

Managed competition and controlled choice are complementary aspects of protecting the interests of both the individual and the society in the educational process. Having described the governance system for a restructured system of schooling, we turn now to questions of requirements for participating in the system and distribution of funds.

Requirements for participation

Schools participating in such a restructured system would have to meet three basic requirements.

1. Educational standards. Review of curriculum and student performance would need to be ongoing. However, student failure would be no more justification for removing funding than it is presently in public schools. Voucher supplements would be made on the basis of the difficulty of educating students and "rewards" could be given to those schools who succeed beyond expectations. This, then, would make variances in educational expenditure based on factors relating to educational need rather than wealth, as they presently are.

These standards would be validated on a national basis and average performance levels of students in the schools would become part of the information made available to the public. Having such standards is crucial to the success of a choice system. Opponents have argued that parents do not have the resources necessary to make appropriate schooling choices for their children. Disseminating information about the academic outcomes of schools will go a long way toward providing parents with what they need to make informed choices. This will not necessarily result in all parents trying to get their children into the schools with the highest academic achievement levels. Some parents, for example, may prefer a school with less academic emphasis, but a notable drama, fine arts, or athletic program. The point is that all schools would be expected to maintain minimum levels of academic achievement to continue to receive government funds and all parents would have the opportunity to select from among successful schools that represent their value orientations.

This raises the much-debated question of a national curriculum. Having national standards does not necessarily imply having a national curriculum. But having national standards is necessary to address opponents' concerns that an educational choice system meet the needs of society for an educated citizenry and not snooker parents. Having a system of school choice as described above is a near guarantee that we will not have a national curriculum. As schools will vary widely on the basis of both theme and methodolgy, what will count is that children will have verbal and numerical literacy, have an understanding of our basic social structures, can explain the workings of the natural world, and are prepared to be productive citizens. Whether they acquire these skills in a Montessori or back-to-basics school, a school of technology or drama, or one in which religion is a defining characteristic is immaterial. But a requirement to meet national standards will go a long way toward minimizing the inequity of educational outcomes based on race, region, and social class.

2. Non-discrimination standards. All schools receiving vouchers would be required to provide evidence that they do not discriminate in either faculty/staff hiring or the acceptance of students on the basis of irrelevant factors. In situations where there are more applicants for a school than there are spaces, a selection system by lottery would be implemented. This, however, should be seen as temporary until a group of teachers appear with a new school to meet the market

demand. This would be an important dimension of managed competition. Regional Education Agencies would be responsible for providing the information and public relations necessary to bring together interested parents and capable providers.

3. Reporting standards. All participating schools would be required to provide information regarding philosophy, theme, structure, classroom practices, student outcomes, faculty qualifications, and other relevant data for annual publication for distribution to both parents and governing agencies. Another role of the Regional Education Agency would be to guarantee that all parents receive this information and are actively involved in making a choice. Although this, like transportation, would be an added cost to the present system, it is doable. Just as presently no child can be admitted to school without having the required vaccinations, no child would be admitted without a parent or guardian's reviewing available school choices with an education agency official, who would provide the information about available schools described above and, when necessary counsel parents regarding the best choices for their children. This review process would be required again as the child leaves one school and anticipates entering another.

Thus school accountability would be based on these three criteria. How, exactly would they be implemented? In the first place, accountability would be school-based. In the last several decades several attempts have been made to develop a fair and practical form of educational accountability. Proposals for holding individual teachers accountable for student outcomes were doomed from the start because teachers, as individuals, have control over so few of the variables that affect student learning. Educational malpractice suits, which attempted to hold entire school systems accountable for students' failures have not succeeded in the courts because the process was viewed as too complicated to determine liability in the system. Giving individual schools the autonomy to determine philosophy, structure, curriculum, and staff provides them with the means to control educational processes in such a way that those who run the schools can be held collectively accountable for the educational outcomes of its students.

One of the questions that is perennially raised by educational researchers and teacher educators is why research does not inform practice in education. Why do American school teachers not read educational research and apply it in their classrooms? More specifically, why don't teachers read educational research journals the way doctors read medical research journals. The answer is that teachers are not accountable for achieving outcomes in their clients in the same way that doctors are. A system which held teachers accountable in this way could expect to see far greater familiarity on the part of teachers with educational research, classroom practices reflecting this knowledge, and student learning outcomes improving as a result. Furthermore, this would increase the respectability of teaching as a profession. Of course, this requires that there be a far greater emphasis than presently on research in the preservice preparation and ongoing inservice of teachers.

Accountability goes in two directions: to the governance system and to the parents. Historically public schools have been accountable only to the governance system and that has been shaky, at best. This accountability has been primarily regarding such things as holding school for the minimum number of days required by the state, maintaining appropriate physical facilities, offering required courses, and completing necessary reports. Never has the state or local government proposed withholding of funds if the schools did not meet the academic and other needs of students.

By contrast, private schools have been minimally accountable to the government but fully accountable to parents. If parents were not satisfied with the school's philosophy, curriculum, staff, or treatment of their children, they would withhold funds from the school by placing their children somewhere else. This is certainly a more robust form of accountability than that required of public schools. A system of school choice such as that described here would combine the best aspects of these two types of accountability to form a solid basis on which to provide parents with the widest range of choices while assuring them of the quality of educational outcomes.

Distribution of Funds

Vital to the success of this choice system is a fair and equitable means of funding. Currently, in most states, the amount of per capita expenditure for education is a direct function of individual and community wealth. This circumstance has been the basis of numerous court cases and legislation. California, Texas, New Jersey, and Kentucky have all attempted to remedy this problem. Most recently, Michigan has passed legislation abandoning the use of real estate taxes to fund schools[9], simultaneously citing the opportunity for developing a choice system. If the goal of equity is to be met, per capita expenditure will have to begin as equal, then vary on the basis of the needs of the students and the costs of their educational programs. For example, each parent would be given a voucher for $5500. Those with children with handicaps and/or identified risks would be given a supplement to the basic voucher. Schools with more expensive equipment needs to deliver their programs would be provided with funds for equipment purchases apart from per capita expenditure.

It is important that the annual costs of educating children be done through a system in which parents, rather than the schools, are given the money. In the first place, in the reconceptualized school system described above in which those schools currently considered non-public are included, this process would clearly avoid the church/state issue, as it would be individuals and not organizations receiving state money. This would be no different than presently with the GI Bill or supplemental income subsidies provided by the government. If an individual chooses to give a portion of the subsidy to a religious organization, there is no church/state issue involved. Similarly, a parent could choose to purchase educational services from a religious organization.

A second reason why it is important that vouchers go directly to parents is to heighten their awareness of the connection between the collection of their tax money and the expenditure of it for education. Undoubtedly, the current remoteness between these two activities contributes to the lack of parental involvement in the schools. If the very process requires that parents take the vouchers to the Regional Educational Agency, review the available schools for their children, and make a selection, there is a far greater likelihood that these same parents will become more involved in the schools their children attend.

---

[9]Harp, L. (1993, August 4). Michigan law bans property tax use to fund schools. *Education Week, 1, 35.*

CONCLUSION

In summary, choice and accountability must define a reconceptualization of public education. All parents must be empowered to choose the schools their children attend. For this to be a meaningful activity, all schools must organize themselves around a common theme and staff must choose to teach in those schools. This would provide true diversity in schooling to meet the wide and varied needs and interests of students. Each school must have the autonomy to determine how it would carry out its educational activities and be held accountable for meeting minimal requirements established by the state. Regional Educational Agencies would practice the managed competition necessary to maintain balance in the system and parents would be provided with controlled choice among a wide range of educational offerings. All schools, whether previously identified as public or private, which meet the educational, non-discrimination, and reporting standards described above would be eligible to participate in the system and receive government funds. Such a system would balance the needs of both individuals and society and would equalize not only opportunity to choose schooling, but also per-capita expenditures, and the quality of educational outcomes.

Bibliography

Addonizio, M. F., et al. (1991). *Financing school choice*. Elmhurst, IL: North Central Regional Educational Laboratory. (ERIC Document Reproduction Service ED No. 335 779)

Adler, M, Petch, A., & Tweedie, J. (1989). *Parental choice and educational policy*. Edinburgh, Scotland; University of Edinburgh Press.

Alexander, L. (1993, June). School choice in the year 2000. *Phi Delta Kappan*, 762-766.

Alkinn, M. C. (1983, April). *Magnet school programs evaluation: A new and more effective approach to school desegregation*. Paper resented at the annual meeting of the American Educational Research Association, Montreal.

Alves, M. J., & Willie, C. V. (1987). Controlled choice assignments: A new and more effective aproach to school desegregation. *The Urban Review, 19* (2), 67-88.

Anglin, L. W. (1979, May). Teacher roles and alternative school organization. *Educational Forum*, 438-452.

Archbald, D. A. (1991). School choice and changing authority: An analysis of the controversy over the Minnesota postsecondary enrollment options law. *Journal of Education Policy, 6* (1), 1-16.

Arnnove, R., & Strout, T. (1980, May). Alternative schools for disruptive youth. *Educational Forum*, 452-471.

Arons, S. (1971). Equity, option, and vouchers. *Teachers College Record, 72* (3), 337-363.

Arons, S. (1971, January). The joker in private school aid. *Saturday Review*.

Ascher, C. (1985, December) *Using magnet schools for desegregation: Some suggestions from the research*. (ERIC/CUE Trends and Issues Series Number 3). New York, NY: ERIC Clearinghouse on Urban Education, Teachers College, Columbia University.

Aten. M. (1989). Religion's public role in U. S. Society. *Religion and Public Education, 16* (1), 43-44.

Atkins, A. (1989). Choice: The hottest education issue. *Better Homes and Gardens, 67* (10), 18-21.

Bainbridge, W.L., & Sunder, S. (1990). School choice: The education issue of the 1990s. *School and College*, 21-23.

Barth, R. S. (1991, October). Restructuring schools: Some questions for teachers and principals. *Phi Delta Kappan*, 123-128.

Becker, B. B. (1986, 24 March). Give all parents a say in choosing schools. *Business Week*, 19.

Berube, M. R. (1971, January). The trouble with vouchers. *Commonweal*, 414-417.

Blank, R. K. (1984, December). The effects of magnet schools on the quality of education in urban school districts. *Phi Delta Kappan*.

Blank, R. K., Dentler, R. A., Baltzell, C. E., & Chabotar, K. (1983, September) Survey of magnet schools: Analyzing a model for quality integrated education. Report prepared for the U. S. Department of Education, Washington, DC: James H. Lowry and Associates.

Blatchford, L. (1993). What's a student got to do with school reform? *Contemporary Education, 64,* 91-93.

Boles, D. E. (1989). Religion and education at the end of a decade. *Religion and Public Education, 16* (1), 35-37.

Bortin, B. H. (1982) *Magnet school programs: Evaluation report, 1980-81.* (Milwaukee ESAA Title IV). Milwaukee, WI: Milwaukee Public Schools, Department of Educational Research and Program Assessment.

Boyd, W. L., & Kerchner, C. T., eds. (1987). *The politics of excellence and choice in education, 1987 yearbook of politics in education.* New York: Falmer.

Boyd, W. L., & Walberg, J. (1990). *Choice in education: Potential and problems.* Berkeley, CA: McCutchan Publishing Company.

Boyer, E. (1992). *School choice.* Princeton, NJ: Carnegie Foundation for the Advancement of Teaching.

Bradley, A. & Snider, W. (1989, June 21). Backlash against choice plans emerges among minorities. *Education Week, 7.*

Bridge, R. G., & Blackman, J. (1978). *A study of alternatives in American education. Volume IV: Family choice in schooling.* (Report No. R-2170/4 - NIE). Santa Monica, CA: The Rand Corporation. (ERIC Document Reproduction Service No. ED 206 058)

Broder, D. S. (1993, September 6). With more choices, the public schools in America are facing more challenges. *The Philadelphia Inquirer,* A 10.

Brodinsky, B. (1993). How 'new' will the 'new' Whittle American school be? *Phi Delta Kappan, 74,* 540-547.

Brown, F. (1991). School choice plans and the politics of decline. *Education and Urban Society, 23* (2), 115-118.

Brown, F. & Contreras, A. R. (1991). Deregulation and privatization of education. *Education and Urban Society, 23*(2), 144-158.

Brown, S. M. (1992). The choice for Jewish day schools. *Educational Horizons, 71* (1), 45-52.

Bryant, M. T. (1988). Parental choice — differences in schools, teachers afford wide range of possibilities. *NASSP Bulletin,* (72), 65-69.

Burns, L. T., & Howes, J. (1988, August). Handing control to schools: Site-based management sweeps the country. *The School Administrator,* 8-18.

Byron, W. J. (1987, 6 June). Needed: A new educational partnership between government and families. *America,* 460-469.

Cameron, D. (1992). Preserving the American dream: Toward a recommitment to public education in America. *Educational Horizons, 71* (1), 31-37.

Camuto, R. V.(1990). Public money and private lessons: An experiment in choice puts a city in the spotlight. *Religion and Public Education, 17* (3), 325-327.

Cappell, F. J. (1981). *A study of alternatives in Americn education. Volume VI: Student outcomes in Alum Rock.* (Report No. R-2170/6 - NIE). Santa Monica, CA: The Rand Corporation. (ERIC Document Reproduction Service No. ED 216 426)

Carrison, M. P. (1981, January). Do magnet schools really work? *Principal, 60* (3), 32-35.

Carter, D. G., & Sandler, J. P. (1991). Access, choice, quality, and integration. *Education and Urban Society, 23*(2), 175-184.

Casimer, M. M. (1982). *Family choice in shooling: Issues and dilemmas.* Lexington, Mass., Lexington Books.

Cavazos, L. F. (1989). Restructuring American education through choice. *Vital Speeches,55*(17), 17-20.

Chance, W. (1986). *The best of educators' reforming American's public schools in the 1980's.* Chicago: John D. and Catherine T. MacArthur Foundation.

Chubb, J. E. (1987, May 4). The dilemma of public school improvement. *Spoor Dialogues on Leadership.* Hanover, NH: Dartmouth College.

Chubb, J. E., & Moe T. M. (1990). *Politics, markets, and American schools.* Washington, DC: Brookings Institute.

Chubb, J. E., & Terry, M. (1985, November). *Politics, markets, and the organization of schools.* Stanford University: Institute for Research on Educational Finance and Governance.

Chubb, J. E., & Terry, M. (1986, Fall). No school is an island: *Politics, markets, and education.* Brookings Review.

Cistone, P. J. (1989). School-based management/shared decision making: Perestroika in educational governance. *Education and Urban Society, 21* (4), 363-365.

Cistone, P. J., & Fernandez, J. A., & Tornillo, Jr. P. L. (1989). School-based management/shared decision making in Dade County (Miami). *Education and Urban Society,* 21 (4), 393-402.

Citizens for Educational Freedom. (1990). Education vouchers give family power through choice. *Religion and Public Education, 17*(3), 316-319.

Claybaugh, G. K. (1992). "Choice" in schooling. *Educational Horizons, 71* (1), 8-10.

Claybaugh, G. K. (1992). School choice: Easy out, poor solution. *Educational Horizons, 71* (1), 2-3.

Clayton, A. S. (1970). Vital questions, minimal responses: Education vouchers. *Phi Delta Kappan, 52* (1), 53-54.

Clinchy, E. (1992). Choice and the transformation of schools: A superintendent's perspective. *Equity and Choice, IX* (2), 32-34.

Clinchy, E. (1992). Making diversity happen. *Equity and Choice, IX* (2), 22-27.

Clinchy, E., & Cody, E. A. (1978, December). If not public choice, then private escape. *Phi Delta Kappan,* 270-273.

Clune, W., & Witte, J., eds. (1990). *Choice and control in American education, Vol. I: The theory of choice and control in education.* New York: Falmer.

Coleman, J. S. (1985, April). Schools and the communities they serve. *Phi Delta Kappan,* 527-532.

Coleman, J. S., & Hoffer, T. (1987). *Public and private high schools: The impact of communities.* New York: Basic Books.

Coleman, J. S., & Hoffer, T., & Kilgore, S. (1981). *Public and private high schools.* Washington, DC: National Center for Education Statistics.

Comerford, J. P. (1980, May). Parent perceptions and pupil characteristics of a senior high magnet school program. *Integrated Education, 18* (5-5), 50-54.

Conley, S. C, (1989). Who's on first? School reform, teacher participation, and the decision-making process. *Education and Urban Society, 21* (4), 366-379.

Conley, S. C., Schmidle, T., & Shedd, J. B. (1988, Winter). Teacher participation in the management of school systems. *Teachers College Record,* 259-276.

Convey, J. J. (1986, April). Parental choice of Catholic schools as a function of religion, race and family income. Paper presented at the annual meeting of the American Educational Research Association, San Francisco, CA. (ERIC Document Reproduction Service No. ED 273 047)

Conway, G. E. (1992). School choice: A private school perspective. *Phi Delta Kappan, 73* (7), 561-563.

Cookson, Jr., P.W. (1991). Private schooling and equity: Dilemmas of choice. *Education and Urban Society, 23*(2), 185-199.

Coons, J. E. (1981). Shanker vouchers — is the genie out? *Phi Delta Kappan, 63* (4). 255.

Coons, J. E., & Love, R. (1979). Point/counterpoint: Would a statewide voucher system work? *Instructor, 88* (10), 10.

Coons, J. E., & Sugarman, S. (1978). *Education by choice: The case for family control.* Berkeley: University of California Press.

Cooper, B. S. (1989). Bottom-up authority in school organization: Implications for the school administrator. *Education and Urban Society, 21* (4), 380-392.

Corwin, R. G. & Dianda, M. R. (1993, September). What can we really expect from large-scale voucher programs? *Phi Delta Kappan,* 68-74.

Crain, R. L., et al. (1992). *The effectiveness of New York City's career magnet schools.* National Center for Research in Vocational Education.

Crow, G. M. (1992). The principals in schools of choice: Middle manager, entrepreneur, and symbol manager. *Urban Review, 24* (3), 165-174.

Dandy, C. (1992, Nov./Dec.). Give choice a chance. *School Leader,* 27-31.

Darling-Hammond, L.(1993, June). Reframing the school reform agenda, *Phi Delta Kappan,* 753-761.

Darling-Hammond, L. & Kirby, S. N. (1985, Dec.). *Tuition tax deductions and parent school choice: A case study of Minnesota.* (Report No. R-3294 NIE). Santa Monica, CA: Rand. (ERIC Document Reproduction Service No. ED 273 047)

David, J. (1991). What it takes to restructure education. *Educational Leadership, 48* (8), 11-15.

David, J. L. (1989). Synthesis of research on school-based management. *Educational Leadership 46* (8), 45-53.

Davies, D. (1992) Who should decide? *Equity and Choice, 8* (2), 60-61.

Davis, B. S. (1983, Winter). Education vouchers: Boom or blunder? *The Educational Forum.* 161-172.

DeDakis, J. H. (1987, 15 May). Should government help kids attend private schools? *Christianity Today,* 52-53.

Dentler, R. A. (1991). The national evidence on magnet schools. *Occasional Paper Series.* Los Alamitos, CA: Southwest Regional Laboratory for Educational Research and Development. (ERIC Document Reproduction Service ED No. 335 780)

Depa, M. (1986). *Educational vouchers: A educator's metamorphosis from skeptic to advocate.* Unpublished manuscript.

Diegmuller, K. (1993). The palatable choice. *Teacher Magazine, 13* (14), 23-25.

Doerflinger, R. (1985, November). Who are Catholics for a free choice? *America,* 312-317.

Doerr, E.(1986). Vouchers and vultures. *Humanist, 46,* 41.

Dorgan, M. (1980, August). Integration through magnet schools: Goals and limitations. *Integrated Education, 18* (1-4), 59-63.

Doyle, D., & Levine, M. (1983). *Magnet schools: Education policy studies occasional paper, 83* (4). Washington, DC: American Enterprise Institute.

Doyle, D. P., & Levine, M. (1984). Magnet schools: Choice and quality in public education. *Phi Delta Kappan, 65,* 265-270.

Duke, D. (1976, May). Challenge to bureaucracy: The contemporary alternative school. *Jouurnal of Educational Thought,* 34-48.

Duke, D., & Perry, C. (1978, Fall). Can alternative schools succeed where Benjamin Spock, Spiro Agnew, and B. F. Skinner Have Failed? *Adolescence,* 375-395.

Echols, F. (1990). Parental choice in Scotland. *Journal of Educational Policy, 5* (3), 207-222.

Elford, G. (1972, January 29). The voucher plan debate. *America,* 87-91.

Ellison, L. (1991). The many facets of school choice. *Educational Leadership, 48* (4), 37.

Elmore, R. F. (1988). *Choice in public education.* Santa Monica, CA: RAND Corporation.

Elmore, R. F. (1990/1991). No easy answers to the complex question of choice. *Educational Leadership, 48,* 17-18.

Erickson, D. A. (1986, February). *Research on private schools: The state of the art.* Manuscript. National Invitational Conference on Research on Private Education.

Everhart, R. B. (1982). *The public school monopoly.* San Francisco: Pacific Institute for Public Policy Research.

Fantini, M. (1971). Options for students, parents, and teachers: Public schools of choice. *Phi Delta Kappan, 52* (9), 541-543.

Fantini, M. D. (1971, March). Public schools of choice and the plurality of publics. *Educational Leadership,* 585-591.

Fege, A. F. (1992). Public education: Can we keep it? *Educational Leadership, 50* (3), 86-89.

Fine, M. (1993, Winter). A diary on privatization and on public possibilities. *Educational Theory,* 33-39.

Finn, C. E., Jr. (1987). Education that works: Make the schools compete. *Harvard Business Review, 65* (5), 63-68.

Fiske, E. B. (1988, 6 July). Parental choice in public school gains. *The New York Times,* 1-6.

Fizzell, R. L. (1987). Inside a school of choice. *Phi Delta Kappan, 68* (10), 758-761.

Fleming, D. S., Blank, R. K., Dentler, R. A., & Baltzell, D.C. (1982). *Survey of magnet schools. Interim report.* Chicago, IL: James H. Lowry and Associates.

Flygare, T. J. (1973, November). An abbreviated voucher primer. *Inequality in Education,* 53-56.

Flygare, T. J. (1977). Schools and the law: Finally, a partial victory for parochial schools. *Phi Delta Kappan, 58* (1), 51-53.

Fobert, R. J. (1971, May). The voucher plan: Is it worth the investment? *The School Administrator,* 2.

Foley, E. M., & McConnaughy, S. B. (1982). *Towards high school improvement: Lessons from alternative schools.* New York: Public Education Association.

Fowler, C. W.(1980). Must voucher plans kill public schools? *The American School Board Journal, 167* (1), 34-35.

Fullan, M. G., & Miles, M. B. (1992). Getting reform right: What works and what doesn't. *Phi Delta Kappan 73* (10). 744-752.

Garber, D. H. (1987). Tuition exemptions: an experiment in vouchers. *Journal of Education Finance, 13,* 167-173.

George, D. (1992). Is the market a solution for school problems? *Educational Horizons, 71* (1), 14-15.

George, G. R., & Farrell, W. C. (1990). School choice and African American students: A legislative view. *Journal of Negro Education, 59* (4), 521-525.

Gest, T. (1987, March 16). Is 'Humanism' a religion? *U. S. News and World Report,* 10-11.

Ginsburg, E. (1971). The economics of the voucher system. *Teachers College Record, 22* (3), 373-387.

Gitlin, A. (1981, Summer). School structure affects teachers' work. *Educational Horizons,* 173-178.

Glenn, C. (1985, Spring). The significance of choice for public education. *Equity and Choice,1*(3), 5-10.

Glenn, C. (1987). The new common school. *Phi Delta Kappan, 69* (4).

Glenn, C. L. (1989). Putting school choice in place. *Phi Delta Kappan, 71* (4), 295-300.

Glenn, C. L. (1992). Do parents get the schools they choose? *Equity and Choice, IX* (2), 47-49.

Graham, M. W. & Ruhl, M. (1990). Superintendents respond to school choice. *Religion and Public Education, 17*(3), 361-366.

Grant, G. (1981, Summer). The character of education and the education of character. *Daedalus,* 139-149.

Grant. G. (1982, March). The elements of a strong positive ethos. *NASSP Bulletin,* 84-90.

Grant, M. A. (1982). How to desegregate — and like it. *Phi Delta Kappan, 63* (8), 539.

Gratiot, M. H. (1980). Why parents choose nonpublic schools: Comparative attitudes and characteristics of public and private school consumers. *Dissertation Abstracts International,* 40 4825-A. (University Microfilms No. 8006315).

Greeley, A. M. (1982). *Catholic high schools and minority students.* New Brunswick, NJ: Transaction Books.

Gregory, T. B. (1985, Fall). Alternative schools as Cinderella: What the reform reports don't look at and don't say. *Changing Schools,* 2-4.

Gregory, T. B., & Smith, G. R. (1983, Spring). School climate findings. *Changing Schools,* 8.

Gregory, T. B., & Smith G. R. (1987). *High schools as communities: The small school reconsidered.* Bloomington, IN: Phi Delta Kappa Educational Foundation.

Grover, H. (1991). There's no magic elixir in school choice. *The School Administrator, 48* (1), 38 & 40.

Hamer, Jr., I. S., & Ampadu, M. (1982, April). Research and alternative schools: A critique of strategies for working with problem students. *Urban Education,* 3-12.

Hamilton, S. F. (1981, July). Alternative schools for the '80s: Lessons from the past. *Urban Education,* 131-48.

Harrington-Leuker, D. (1993). Public schools go private. *American School Board Journal,* 180, 35-39.

Harris III, J. J., Ford, D. Y., Wilson, P. I, & Sandidge, R. F. (1991). What should our public choose? The debate over school choice policy. *Education and Urban Society, 23*(2), 159-174.

Harris, K. H., & Longstreet, W. S. (1990, November/December). Alternative testing and the national agenda for control. *The Clearing House,* 90-93.

Havighurst, R. J. (1970). The unknown good: Education vouchers. *Phi Delta Kappan, 52* (1),52-53.

Heller, R. W. (1972, February). Education vouchers: Problems and issues. *Educational Leadership,* 424-429.

Henkoff, R. (1991). For states: Reform turns radical. *Fortune, 23* (7), 137-144.

Henley, M. (1987, December). Something is missing from the educational reform movement. *Phi Delta Kappan,* 284-285.

Hill, F. W. (1970).Voucher system — Bane or boon? *American School and University, 42* (11),16-17.

Hodgkinson, H. (1990). Danger sign: Vouchers masquerading as vouchers. *Religion and Public Education, 17*(3), 355-356.

Hollister, C. D. (1979, July). School bureaucracies as a response to parents' demands. *Urban Education,* 221-235.

Houston, P. D. (1993). School vouchers: The latest California joke. *Phi Delta Kappan, 75* (1), 61-64.

Hoyt, K. B. (1991). Administrators and teachers express their support, opposition to reform proposals. *NASSP Bulletin, 75* (534), 67-74.

Hunter, B. (1990). Are fad diets good for education? *Religion and Public Education, 17*(3), 320-322.

Hunter, E. (1989). The role of teachers in educational reform. *NASSP Bulletin 73* (518), 61-63.

Inger, M. (1991). *Improving urban education with magnet schools.* New York, NY: Teachers College, Columbia University. (ERIC Document Reproduction Service No. ED 340 813)

Insight - Private schools and vouchers. (1985, September 21). *America.* 128.

Ische, T. L. (1988, June). Minnesota's choice plan is 'dangerous experiment.' *Education Week, 7.*

James, T., & Levin, H. M., eds. (1988). *Comparing public and private schools. Volume 1: institutions and organizations.* New York: Falmer Press.

James, T., & Levin, H. M., eds. (1988). *Comparing public and private schools.Volume 2: school achievement.* New York: Falmer Press.

Jencks. C. (1968, November 3). Private schools for black children. *The New York Times Magazine.*

Jencks, C. (1970). Giving parents money for schooling: Education vouchers. *Phi Delta Kappan, 52* (1), 49-52.

Jenkins, E. (1973, November/December). The debate intensifies: Stand by for vouchers. *Compact,* 7-9.

Johnston, M., & Slotnik, J. (1985, February). Parent participation in the schools: Are the benefits worth the burdens? *Phi Delta Kappan,* 430-433.

Kapel, D. E., & Pink, W. T. (1978). The schoolboard: Participatory democracy revisited. *The Urban Review, 10* (1), 20-34.

Kellory, D. (1986). Learning the hard way there is a compelling case for separating school and state. *Barron's, 66,* 11.

Kemerer, F. R., Hairston, J. B., & Lauerman, K. (1992). Vouchers and private school autonomy. *Journal of Law & Education, 21,* 601-627.

Kirkpatrick, N. D. et al. (1991). Houston Independent School District magnet school program description 1990-91. Houston Independent School District, Department of Research and Evaluation. (ERIC Document Reproduction Service ED No. 338 767)

Kirp, D. (1972). Vouchers, reform, and elusive community. *Teachers College Record, 74,* 201-207.

Kolderie, T. (1992). Chartering diversity. *Equity and Choice, IX* (2), 28-31.

Komisar, B. P. (1992). Should we push the button? *Educational Horizons, 71* (1),18-22.

Kozol, J. (1992, November). I dislike the idea of choice and I want to tell you why. *Educational Leadership,* 90-92.

Krashinsky, M. (1986). Educational vouchers and economics: A rejoinder. *Teachers College Record, 58* (2), 163-167.

Krashinsky, M. (1986). Why educational vouchers may be bad economics. *Teachers College Record, 58* (2), 139-150.

Kratcoski, L. D. (1986). A voucher for the arts. *USA Today, 114,* 98.

Kretovics, J., Farber, K., & Armaline, W. (1991). Reform from the bottom up: Empowering teachers to transform. *Phi Delta Kapppan,* 73 (4), 295-299.

Lambert, M. D. & Lambert L. G. (1989, October). Parent choice works for us. *Educational Leadership,* 58-60.

Lamm, R. D. (1986). Can parents be partners? *Phi Delta Kappan, 86* (4), 211-213.

Larson, J. C. (1981). *Takoma Park magnet school evaluation: Part II, final report.* Rockville, MD: Montgomery County Public Schools.

Lausberg, C. H. (1990). Site-based management: Crisis or opportunity? *School Business Affairs, 56* (4), 10-14.

Lawton, S. B. (1986, Summer). A case study of choice in education: Separate schools in Ontario. *Journal of Education Finance,* 36-48.

Lee, D. R., & Sexton, R. L. (1988, September). The public school lobby vs. education vouchers. *USA Today,* 79-81.

Lerner, B. (1981). Vouchers for literacy: Second chance legislation. *Phi Delta Kappan, 63* (4), 252-255.

Leslie, C. (1988). Giving parents a choice. *Newsweek, 112* (12), 77-80.

Levin, J. M. (1973). Vouchers and social equity. *Change, 5* (8), 29-33.

Levin, J. M. (1973, Fall). Educational alternatives within the public school system. *Educational Horizons,* 26-31.

Levine, D. U., & Eubanks, E. E. (1980, January-August). Attracting nonminority students to magnet schools in minority neighborhoods. *Integrated Education, 18* (1-4), 52-58.

Levine, D. U., & Moore, C. C. (1976). Magnet schools in a big-city desegregation plan. *Phi Delta Kappan, 57* (8) 507-509.

Lewis, A. C. (1986). ED's 'pro-choice' plan: If at first you don't succeed... *Phi Delta Kappan, 67* (5), 331-332.

Lewis, F. C (1981). The year of the voucher. *Phi Delta Kappan, 63* (4), 256-257.

Lieberman, M.(1986). Privitization and public education. *Phi Delta Kappan, 67* (10), 731-734.

Lieberman, M.(1989). *Privatization and educational choice.* New York: St. Martin's Press.

Lieberman, M.(19 90). Informational conflicts of interest under public school choice. *Religion and Public Education, 17*(3), 381-386.

Lindquist, K. M., & Mauriel, J. J. (1989). School-based management: Doomed to failure? *Education and Urban Society, 21* (4), 403-416.

Lipsky, D. K. (1992). We need a third wave of education reform. *Social Policy, 22* (3), 43-45.

Lissitz, R. W. (1992). *Assessment of student performance and attitude: St. Louis metropolitan area court order desegregation effort. Report submitted Voluntary Interdistrict Coordinating Council.* (ERIC Document Reproduction Service No. ED 342 794)

Lomotey, K., & Swanson, A. D. (1989). Urban and rural schools research: Implications for school governance. *Education and Urban Society, 21* (4), 436-454.

Mackey, P. E. (1977). An untimely revolution: Vouchers. *NJ School Leader, 5* (6), 4-5,17.

Maddaus, J. (1988, November). *Parents' perceptions of the moral environment in choosing their children's elementary schools.* Paper presented at the annual meeting of the Association for Moral Education, Pittsburgh, PA. (ERIC Document Reproduction Service No. ED 321 873).

Maddaus, J. (1990). Parental choice of school: What parents think and do. *Review of Research in Education, 16,* 267-295.

Maddaus, J., & Maarochnik, D. (1992, Winter). Town tuitioning in Maine: Parental choice of secondary schools in rural communities. *Journal of Reseaarch in Rural Education, (1),*27-40.

Maddaus, J., & Mirochnik, D. (1991, April). *Parental choice options in Maine.* (Occasional Paper No. 11). Orono, ME: University of Main College of Education.

Maddaus, J., Mirochnik, D., & Marion, S. (1992, April). *School test scores as a factor in parental choice of school: Testing an assumption of 'America 2000' in Maine.* Paper presented at the annual meeting of the American Educational Research Association, San Francisco, CA.

Maddox, R. L. (1990). Educational choice and the First Amendment: A separationist perspective. *Religion and Public Education, 17* (3), 322-325.

Magi Educational Services. (1985, January). *New York State magnet school research study.* Albany: State Education Department.

Mandel, D. (1976). Schools on the market. *New York Times Educational Supplement, 3181,* 20-21.

Manley-Casimir, M. E. (1982). *Family choice in schooling.* Lexington, MA: Lexington Books.

Martin, M. (1991). Trading the known for the unknown: Warning signs in the debate over schools of choice. *Education and Urban Society, 23*(2), 119-143.

McCann, W., & Areen, J. (1971). Vouchers and the citizen —Some legal questions. *Teachers College Record, 72* (3), 389-404.

McDonnell, L., & Pascal, A. (1988). *Teacher unions and educational reform.* Santa Monica, CA: RAND.

McIntyre, R. G., Hughes, L. W., & Say, M. W. (1982). Houston's successful desegregation plan. *Phi Delta Kappan, 63* (8), 536-538.

McLaughlin, J. M. (1992). Schooling for profit: Capitalism's new frontier. *Educational Horizons, 71* (1), 23-30.

McLaughlin, K. W. (1992). The role of parent information centers in the school selection process. *Equity and Choice, IX* (2), 42-46.

McLaughlin, M. W., & Shields, P. (1987). Involving low income parents in the schools: A role for policy? *Phi Delta Kappan,* 157.

McMillan, C. B. (1977). Magnet education in Boston. *Phi Delta Kappan, 59* (3), 158-163.

McMillan, C. B. (1980). Magnet schools: An approach to voluntary desegregation. *Phi Delta Kappa.,* Bloomington, IN.

McNeil, L. M. (1987). Exit, voice and community: Magnet teachers' responses to standardization. *Educational Policy, 1* (1), 93-113.

Meier, D. (1986, January). In education, magnets attract controversy. *NEA Today,* 54-59.

Metz, M. H. (1986). *Different by design: The context and character of three magnet schools.* London: Routledge & Kegan Paul.

Metz, M. H. (1987). Teachers' pride in craft, school subcultures, and societal pressures. *Educational Policy, 1* (1), 115-132.

Metz, M. H. (1988, January). In education, magnets attract controversy, *NEA Today,* 54-60.

Mirga. T. (1986, February 5). Supreme Court ruling cheers voucher proponents. *Education Week,* 17.

Molnar, A. (1992, November). What are our choices? *Educational Leadership,* 84-85.

Moore, D. T. (1978). Alternative schools: A review. *Urban Diversity Series 53.* New York: Institue for Urban and Minority Education.

Moynihan, D. P. (1978). The case for tuition tax credits. *Phi Delta Kappan, 60* (4), 274-276.

Mueller, V. D. (1987). Choice: The parents' perspectives. *Phi Delta Kappan.*

Murname, R. (1986). Family choice in public education: The roles of students, teachers, and system designers. *Teachers College Record, 58* (2), 170-189.

Narus, B. (1992). Home rule, provincial school: Finding a better way to run public education. *New Jersey Reporter, 23* (5), 33-37.

Nathan, J. (1983). Shouldn't we give vouchers a try? *Learning, 12* (1), 74-79.

Nathan, J. (1983). The rhetoric and reality of expanding educational choices. *Phi Delta Kappan,* 476-480.

Nathan, J. (1987). Results and future prospects of state efforts to increase choice among schools. *Phi Delta Kappan,* 746-752.

Nathan, J. (1989). *Progress, problems, prospects of state educational choice plans.* Unpublished manuscript. Office of Planning, Budget, and Evaluation, U.S. Department of Education.

Nathan, J. (1989). Helping all children, empowering all educators: Another view of school choice. *Phi Delta Kappan, 71* (4), 304-307.

Nathan, J. (1993, January). President Clinton, school choice, and education reform in the 1990's. *Educational Excellence Network,* 22-27.

Nathan, J. (1990).School choice in Minnesota. *Religion and Public Education, 17*(3), 345-354.

National Board Association.(1970, October). Boardmen can't think of one good thing to say about vouchers. *American School Board Journal.*

Odden, A. (1992).School finance in the 1990s. *Phi Delta Kappan, 73* (6), 455-461.

Office for Civil Rights. (1989). *Promoting equal opportunity and quality education.* Washington, D.C.

Oliver, D. (1992). Making the choice: One parent's story. *Equity and Choice, IX* (2), 39.

Oliver, K. et al. (1991). *Key elements of selected educational choice programs: A telephone survey summary.* Northwest Regional Educational Lab.

Olsen, L. (1992, October 28).Claims for choice exceed evidence, Carnegie reports. *Education Week,* 1-12.

Olson, L. (1986, 16 April). Teachers' work environment not 'supportive,' poll confirms. *Education Week.,* 1, 43.

Olson. L. (1987, March 25). Louisiana businesses urge vouchers. *Education Week,* 7.

Olson, L. (1991). Milwaukee voucher plan found not to 'skim' cream. *Education Week, 7* (3),12.

Overland, S. F. (1972). Do vouchers deserve at least a sporting chance? *The American School Board Journal, 85* (9), 20-22.

O'Looney, J. (1993). Redesigning the work of education. *Phi Delta Kappan, 74* (5), 375-381.

O'Neill, J. (1993, February). Can national standards make a difference? *Educational Leadership,* 4-8.

Parental choice programs gain popularity. (1988, October). *Learning,* 6.

Pearson, J. (1989). Myths of choice: The governor's new clothes. *Phi Delta Kappan,70,* 821-823.

Penning, N. (1992). Saying 'no' to choice. *The School Administrator, 49* (4), 34-35.

Perelman, L. J. (1988, September). Restructuring the system is the solution. *Phi Delta Kappan,* 20-24.

Perry, D. L., & Duke, D. (1978). Lessons to be learned about discipline from alternative high schools. *Journal of Research and Development in Education, 11* (4),78-90.

Perry, W.E. & Tannenbaum, M. D. (1992). Parents, power, and the public schools. In L. Kaplan (Ed.). *Education and the family.* (pp.100-116). Boston: Allyn & Bacon.

Pickard, B. W., & Richards, D. M. (1976). Educational vouchers. *Canadian Adminstrator, 15* (4), 1-5.

Pipho, C. (1979). The voucher system: Will it divide American society? *Compact*, 13 (3), 26-27.

Pipho, C. (1985). Student choice: The return of the voucher. *Phi Delta Kappan, 66* (7), 461-462.

Pipho, C. (1989, February 1). Switching labels: From vouchers to choice. *Education Week*, 27.

Pipho, C. (1991). Stateline: Tents and push camels. *Phi Delta Kappan, 72* (7), 494-495.

Pipho, C. (1991).Stateline: The vouchers are coming! *Phi Delta Kappan, 73* (2), 102-103.

Pipho, C. (1992). Choice, vouchers, and privatization. *Phi Delta Kappan, 74* (5), 6-7.

Pitsch, M. (1990). Coalition assails private school vouchers as 'unwise public policy'. *Education Week, 10* (15).

Pochoda, E. (1985, 25 May). Everything's up-to-date in Minnesota. *The Nation*, 654-651.

Pollard, J. S. (1989). Thinking it through. *Insights on Educational Policy and Practice,* Number 8. Austin, TX: Southwest Educational Development Laboratory. (ERIC Document Retrieval Service No. ED 329 017)

Powell, A. G., & Farrar, E., & Cohen, D. (1985). *The shopping mall high school: Winners and losers in the educational marketplace.* Boston: Houghton Mifflin.

Premazon, J., & West., P. T. (1977). Requiem or rebirth? From voucher to magnet. *Clearing House, 51* (1), 38-40.

Puckett, J. L. (1983, Summer). Educational vouchers: Rhetoric and reality. *The Educational Forum.*

Purkey, St., & Smith, M. (1983). Effective schools: A review. *Elementary School Journal,* 83 (4).

Quie, A. H. (1987). More 'choice' is key to public school reform. *Education Week.,* 4(34).

Rand Corporation. (1978). *A study of alternatives in American education.* R-2170/1-NIE through R-2170/7-NIE. Santa Monica, CA.

Randall, R. E. (1993). What's after school choice? Private-practice teachers and charter schools. *The Education Digest, 58* (8), 38-41.

Raywid, M. A. (1981). The first decade of public school alternatives. *Phi Delta Kappan, 62* (8), 551-554.

Raywid, M. A. (1982). *The current status of schools of choice in public secondary education.* Hempstead, N. Y.: Center for the Study of Educational Alternatives, Hofstra University.

Raywid, M. A. (1983). Schools of choice: Their current nature and prospects. *Phi Delta Kappan, 64* (10). 684.

Raywid, M. A. (1985). Family choice arrangements in public schools. *Review of Educational Research 55* (4), 435-467.

Raywid, M. A. (1987). *Reflections on understanding, studying, and managing magnet schools.* Unpublished. U. S. Department of Education.

Raywid, M. A. (1987). Excellence and choice: Friends or foes? *The Urban Review, 19*(1): 35-47.

Raywid, M. A. (1989). The case for public schools of choice. *Phi Delta Kappa*, Bloomington, IN.

Raywid, M. A. (1990). Contrasting strategies for restructuring schools: Site-based management and choice. *Equity and Choice, 6* (2). 26-28.

Raywid, M. A. (1990/1991). Is there a case for choice? *Educational Leadership,* · *48,* 4-11.

Raywid, M. A. (1992). What kind of choice? Issues for system designers. *Equity and Choice, IX* (2), 6-10.

Riddle, W. (1986, Summer). Vouchers for the education of disadvantaged children. *Journal of Education Finance,* 9-35.

Rist, M. C. (1989, September). Should parents choose their child's school? *The Executive Educator,* 3-6.

Rosenbaum, J. E., & Presser, S. (1978). Voluntary racial integration in a magnet school. *School Review, 82* (2), 156-186.

Rossell, C. H. (1988). How effective are voluntary plans with magnet schools? *Educational Evaluation and Policy Analysis, 10* (4), 325-42.

Rozycki, E. G. (1992). 'Fat free' foods and schooling options: The pathologies of enthusiasm. *Educational Horizons, 71* (1), 37-44.

Rozycki, E. G. (1992). Opting out of public school: Eluding the bureaucracy. *Educational Horizons, 71* (1), 11-13.

Ruffin, D. C. (1986, September). Do vouchers equal choices for the poor? *Black Enterprise,* 25.

Russo, C. J. (1990). Religious groups and public schoool facilities: A passing or the emergence of a new trend? *Religion and Public Education, 17*(3), 357-360.

Ryan, F. (1992). The first to opt out: Historical snapshots of Catholic schooling in America. *Educational Horizons,71* (1), 53-64.

Salganik, L. H. (1981). The fall and rise of education vouchers. *Teachers College Record, 83* (2), 263-279.

Schools: Luxury of choice. (1988). *The Economist, 308* (7563), 20.

Scott, C. A. (1990). Education in the 21st century: A issue of equity and excellence. *Perspectives For Policymakers, 2* (2), 1-10.

Scovic, S. P. (1990). Let's stop thinking educational choice is the answer to restructured schools. *Religion and Public Education, 17*(3), 387-394.

Scovic, S. P. (1991). Let's stop thinking educational choice is the answer to restructured schools. *School Administrator, 48* (19), 16-17.

Shanker, A. (1989, January 22). Choice plan can bolster public schools: But it's no education cure-all. *New York Times,* 9.

Shanker, A. (1990). The end of the traditional model of schooling and a proposal for using incentives to restructure our public schools. *Phi Delta Kappan, 71,* 345-357.

Shanker, A. (1992, July 26). Confused about school choice?... *The New York Times,* E7.

Shanker, A. (1993, August 22). California vouchers.*The New York Times,* E7.

Shanker, A. (1993, August 8,). Students as consumers. *The New York Times,* E7.

Shanker, A. (1993, October 3). No profit, no loss. *The New York Times,* E7.

Shannon, T. (1986, April). Speak out — Finn's voucher plan invites disaster. *Instructor Magazine,* 18-19.

Shared goals found hallmark of exemplary private schools. (1984, December 5). *Education Week.*

Sickler, J. L. (1988, January). Teachers in charge: Empowering the professionals. *Phi Delta Kappan*, 354-356.

Simpson, M. (1992). The court and school choice. *NEA Today, 10* (6), 31.

Sinclair, R. L., & Ghory, W. J. (1987). *Reaching marginal students: A primary concern for school renewal.* Berkeley, CA: McCutchan.

Sizer, T. R. (1969). The case for a free market. *The Saturday Review, 52* (2), 34-43.

Sizer, T. R. (1984). *Horace's compromise: The dilemma of the American high school.* Boston: Houghton Mifflin.

Snider, W. (1987, 24 June). The call for choice: Competition in the educational marketplace. *Education Week*, 16-17.

Snider, W. (1988, May 18). School choice: New, more efficient 'sorting machine.' *Education Week*, 1, 8.

Snider, W. (1988, May 4). Minnesota backs nation's first 'choice' system. *Education Week*, 1,13.

Snider, W. (1989, 15 March). In nation's first open enrollment state, the action begins. *Education Week*, 18.

Spicer, M. W., & Hill, E. W. (1990, February). Evaluating parental choice in public education: Policy beyond the monopoly model. *American Journal of Education*, 97-112.

State legislators embrace charter schools over choice.(1993). *Education Daily, 26* (107), 1-3.

Stevens, M. (1985, Spring). Characteristics of alternative schools. *American Educational Research Journal*, 135-148.

Sugarman, S. D. (1977). Education reform at the margin: Two ideas. *Phi Delta Kappan, 59* (3), 154-157.

Tannenbaum, M. D. (1985). *An analysis of the 1971-1976 Alum Rock voucher demonstration experiment.* Unpublished manuscript.

Tannenbaum, M. D. (1990). *Perceptions and attitudes toward schools of choice of teachers, administrators, board members, parents, and secondary students.* A paper presented to the American Educational Research Association, Boston.

Tannenbaum, M. D. (1993). Opting out is not the issue: Taking down the walls is. *Educational Horizons, 71* (2), 67.

Tannenbaum, M.D. (1990). Vouchers and First Amendment Rights. *Religion and Public Education, 17*(3), 367-379.

Tannenbaum, M. D. & Tannenbaum, T. (1992). *Administrators' and board members' attitudes toward schools of choice: Implications for restructuring.* A paper presented to the American Educational Research Association, San Francisco.

Tannenbaum, M. D. & Tannenbaum, T. (1992). *Perceptions and attitudes toward schools of choice of teachers, administrators, board members, parents, and secondary students.* A paper presented to the American Educational Research Association, San Francisco.

Tannenbaum, M D. & Tannenbaum, T. (1993). Using school choice to increase parental involvement in schools. In F. Smit, W. van Esch, & H. J. Walberg (Eds.). *Parental involvement in education.* (pp. 23-32). Nijmegen, the Netherlands: Institute for Applied Social Sciences.

Thernstron, A.(1991, July). Hobson's choice. *The New Republic,* 13-15.

Thompson, S. (1992). On choosing change. *Equity and Choice, IX* (2), 35-38.

Time may be right for choices. (1990, December 25/January 1). Insight, 40-41.

Toch, T. (1991, 9 December). Investment in learning. *U. S. News and World Report,* 76-77.

Toch, T. (1991, July). Choices about school choice: How far should we go? *The American School Board Journal,* 18-20.

Toch, T., & Wright, A. (1993). Public schooling's opportunity gap: School reformers debate rigor and fairness. *U. S. News and World Report, 115* (5), 45.

Tucker, M. S., & Mandel, D. R. (1987, 7 October). A voucher plan for worker education. *Education Week,* 6-9.

Uchitelle, S. (1989). What it really takes to make school choice work. *Phi Delta Kappan, 71* (4), 301-303.

Wanat, C. L. (1991, December). Federal choice programs. *Congressional Digest,* 291.

Wangberg, E. G. (1987). Listening to teachers: The missing link in reform. *Clearing House, 61,* 76-80.

Warren, J. (1976, March). Alum Rock voucher project. *Educational Researcher,* 13-15.

West, E. G. (1981, Winter). Choice or monopoly in education. *Policy Review,* 103-117.

West, P. T. (1981). Big bucks and funny money. *The School Administrator,* 38, 14-15.

Westbrook, K. C. & Seay, B. M. (1992, April). *Obscuring problem definition: Changing metaphors, choice and educational policy.* A paper presented to the American Educational Research Association.

Wiggins, G. (1988, March). Ten 'radical' suggestions for school reform. *Education Week,* 3-6.

Wiggins, G. (1991). Standards, not standardization: Evoking quality student work. *Educational Leadership, 48,* 18-25.

Williams, M. F., Hancher, K. S., & Hutner, A. (1983, December). *Parents and school choice: A household survey.* Washington, DC: United States Department of Education. (ERIC Document Reproduction Service No. ED 240 739)

Willie, C. V. (1991). Controlled choice: An alternative desegregation plan for minorities who feel betrayed. *Education and Urban Society, 23*(2), 200-207.

Wingert, P., Houston, P., & Springen, K. (1988, November 19). Consumerism comes to the schoolyard. *Newsweek,* 77-81.

Wise, A. E., & Gendler, T. (1989). Rich schools, poor schools. *The College Board Review, 151,* 12-17, 36-37.

Wohlstetter, P. & Buffet, T. (1992). Decentralizing dollars under school-based management: Have policies changed? *Educational Policy, 6* (1),

Wortman, P. M., & Pierre, R. G. (1977). The educational voucher demonstration. A secondary analysis. *Education and Urban Society, 9* (4), 471-492.

Yanofsky, S. & Young, L. (1992). A parent school-choice plan for racial-ethnic balance. *The Education Digest, 54* (9), 11-15.

MELLEN STUDIES IN EDUCATION